DATE			

IN SYSTEM

Journeys to the Other Shore

MUSLIM AND WESTERN TRAVELERS IN SEARCH OF KNOWLEDGE

Roxanne L. Euben

PRINCETON UNIVERSITY PRESS

PRINCETON AND OXFORD

Library of Congress cataloging-in-Publication Data

Euben, Roxanne Leslie, 1966–
Journeys to the other shore : Muslim and Western travelers in search of knowledge /
Roxanne L. Euben.
p.   cm.   (Princeton studies in Muslim politics)
Includes bibliographical references and index.
ISBN-13: 978-0-691-12721-7 (hardcover : alk. paper)
ISBN-10: 0-691-12721-2 (hardcover : alk. paper)
1. Travel, Medieval. 2. Voyages and travels. 3. Travelers—Arab countries.
4. Travelers—Europe. 5. East and West. I. Title.
G89.E93   2006
910.4—dc22   2006017894

British Library Cataloging-in-Publication Data is available

This book has been composed in Palatino

Printed on acid-free paper. ∞

pup.princeton.edu

Printed in the United States of America

1   3   5   7   9   10   8   6   4   2

For Jonathan

———————————

He who does not travel will not know the value of men.

الي ما جال ما يعرف بحق الرجال.

Travel, you will see the meaning [of things].

جل ترى المعاني.

—Moroccan proverbs, Edward Westermarck,
Wit and Wisdom in Morocco (1930)

CONTENTS

ACKNOWLEDGMENTS

THE RESEARCH for this has taken me literally and figuratively through many epochs, regions, languages, literatures, and disciplines. In the process of crisscrossing these domains, I have incurred innumerable debts to scholars, colleagues, assistants, and librarians who have patiently and generously given of their time and expertise to critique a particular chapter, point out a relevant argument, track down an elusive hadith, or locate a rare nineteenth-century Arabic monograph. This book is thus in many ways a collaborative enterprise, although I bear full responsibility for the use (and misuse) of the resources, knowledge, and materials put at my disposal.

First and foremost, I wish to express my profound gratitude to Lawrie Balfour, J. Peter Euben, and Keith Topper for reading every word of this book at least once. The project has benefited immeasurably from their imagination, expertise, expansive intellect, and willingness to endlessly discuss travel by telephone, e-mail, and in walks around Chicago; Washington, D.C.; Boston; and Durham. I am also grateful to a variety of colleagues dispersed in academic institutions located everywhere from Massachusetts to Morocco whose engagement with various aspects of this project continually challenged me to think at once more broadly and deeply. In this connection, I want to thank Rachid Aadnani, Shahrough Akhavi, Dale Eickelman, Wael Hallaq, Nabil Matar, Louise Marlow, Pratap Mehta, Susan Miller, J. Donald Moon, Abderrahmane El Moudden, Anne Norton, James Petterson, Nancy Rosenblum, Jeremy Waldron, Stuart Warner, Muhammad Qasim Zaman, and my fellow fellows at the Radcliffe Institute for Advanced Study (2004–5). A special note of thanks is due to Carol Dougherty and Marilyn Sides, my dedicated and generous partners in an interdisciplinary research group on travel narratives sponsored by Wellesley's Multicultural Education and Research Initiative (MERI). Their expertise and humor were indispensable to this endeavor at its inception.

This book could not have been completed without the help of several research assistants I have been fortunate to work with, even briefly, at one time or another over the years. Their various investigative talents and linguistic skills, not to mention an electronic expertise far surpassing my own, have often made a daunting interdisciplinary project substantially more manageable. In this regard, I would like to thank Samia Adnan, Lamees al-Ashtal, Katherine Flaster, Rachel Isaacs, Hilary Jaffe, Mary (Kathy) Roche, Himmet Taskomur, Abdallah Salam, Tarek Shamma, and Rachael Ward, as well as Michael Fodor and Deborah Hayden in particular for assisting me with the French translations. In addition, I am grateful for the support of several fellowship programs under whose auspices I have conducted much of the research for and writing of this book at various stages: the American Council of Learned Societies, the Radcliffe Institute for Advanced Study at Harvard University, and the Mellon Foundation Mid-Career Enrichment grant program. I also want to thank my students at Wellesley College, particularly those in my comparative political theory classes: their enthusiasm for the subject and willingness to engage in heated debates about travel and translation greatly enlivened the early stages of research for this book. I am, moreover, very grateful for the generous financial, intellectual, personal, and institutional support provided by administrators and colleagues alike at Wellesley College. Last but most certainly not least, I am indebted to the diligent, efficient, and hardworking staff in the Interlibrary Loan office at Clapp Library at Wellesley College, who gamely and successfully delivered on an unending barrage of requests for even the rarest of Arabic materials.

This book is dedicated to Jonathan Perry who, despite his intense distrust of airplanes, is my fellow-traveler in all voyages of discovery, both literal and imaginative.

NOTE ON TRANSLITERATION AND SPELLING

As THIS BOOK is intended for readers with a variety of backgrounds and interests, I have opted to approach the complexity of Arabic transliteration with a nonspecialist in mind. Toward this end, unless they appear in titles or direct quotations, the only diacritics used here are ʿ to represent the letter *ayn* (as in, for example, *ʿilm*) and ʾ to represent *hamza* when it appears within a word (as in, for example, Qurʾan). For the sake of consistency and accessibility, in the renderings of common Arabic words and Muslim names, I have followed the conventions established by the *International Journal of Middle East Studies*.

Chapter 1

FRONTIERS: WALLS AND WINDOWS

SOME REFLECTIONS ON TRAVEL NARRATIVES

> Because many people of diverse nations and coun-
> tries delight and take pleasure, as I have done in
> times past, in seeing the world and the various
> things therein, and also because many want to know
> without traveling there, and others want to see, go,
> and travel, I have begun this little book.
> —Gilles Le Bouvier, *Le Livre de la Description*
> *des Pays* (1908)

IN A GLOBALIZED world grown smaller by progressively dizzying flows
of people, knowledge, and information, "travel" seems to have become
the image of the age. Porous borders, portable allegiances, virtual networks, and elastic identities now more than ever evoke the language
of mobility, contingency, fluidity, provisionality, and process rather
than that of stability, permanence, and fixity.[1] Scholars who traffic in
the lingo of deterritorialization and nomadism increasingly traverse
disciplines and regions, mining disparate experiences of displacement
such as tourism, diaspora, exile, cyberculture, and migration as "contact zones," sites that articulate the preconditions and implications of
cross-cultural encounters.[2]

In a geopolitical landscape scarred by colonialism and the workings
of global capital, however, such encounters often proceed under conditions of radical inequality between and within regions, cultures, nations, and transnational and subnational communities. The corrosive
consequences of such real and perceived disparities of power are evident in daily newspaper headlines around the world, demanding and
receiving attention if not redress. The events of September 11, 2001, the
U.S.-led war on terrorism, and growing opposition to it have galva-
nized interest in the haunting of contemporary politics by grievances
rooted in poorly understood historical narratives of marginalization
and persecution. Long a feature of political discourse within postcolonial societies, such grievances and narratives now press on European
and American political consciousness in unprecedented ways. What

Foucault aptly called research into "the history of the present" is no longer of interest only to scholarly specialists, for the imperatives of geopolitics have lent a new sense of urgency to attempts to bring these pasts into an often "presentist" social science.[3]

The recent emphasis on mobility and displacement as both features of and metaphors for an increasingly globalized world has thus been accompanied by detailed investigations of the historical relationship between travel and imperialism, mobility and domination. Within the last twenty years, there has been a virtual explosion of scholarship on "Western" travels to the "non-West" (I will turn to these terms in a moment): travel writing by Europeans in particular has come to be regarded as a window onto the production of knowledge and, more specifically, onto the mutually constitutive images of colonizer and colonized. These efforts are vital interventions into the operations of power, particularly in a postcolonial world in which such operations establish distinctions between center and periphery and constitute their relationship hierarchically. Yet paradoxically, attempts to deconstruct these mechanisms of domination have tended to reproduce this structure and organization. From hermeneutically informed ethnography that aims at the "comprehension of the self by the detour of the comprehension of the other" to investigations into the way colonial European travel writing "*produced* 'the rest of the world' for European readerships at particular points in Europe's expansionist trajectory," the West is continually reconstituted as epicenter.[4] Seeking to displace a hubristic self-image of the West as the beacon that "shows to the less developed the image of its own future," these analyses inadvertently reestablish Western primacy, now refigured from model to hegemon whose global reach has called forth new powers of the nether world it can no longer control let alone understand.[5]

What would it mean to invert the questions that reproduce the West as the epicenter of the world? Instead of only investigating how Western travel writing produces the "colonized other," what features of travel, politics, and knowledge past and present might be brought into view by shifting the theoretical perspective? How, for example, have travel and exploration by Muslims produced and transformed their own sense of self and other, of membership and to which communities? How do journeys by Muslims within and beyond the *Dar al-Islam* (Abode of Islam) as well as travels by Westerners serve to articulate and transfigure the parameters of home and a scale of the strange and estranging? If the Syrian poet Adonis is right that frontiers can be either walls or windows, where and when do such borders emerge for Muslim and Western travelers and who are the assorted Others that mark them?[6] What is the shared knowledge presupposed and reworked by way of practices of translation between familiar and unfamiliar, home and abroad? And what might such itineraries, exposures, and mediations suggest about the scope and scale of moral and political obligations among human beings enmeshed in a dialectic of localism and cosmopolitanism characteristic of membership in communities with fluid and fluctuating boundaries?

To even ask these questions in this way is to beg a series of others, perhaps most obviously what it could possibly mean in these shape-shifting times to invoke "the West," "non-West," and "Islam" as if they correspond to stable, fixed, and clear entities. Indeed, to conjure these categories without explanation would reinforce the very essentialism the present inquiry aims to destabilize. The worry about essentialism here is not mere academic cant. Words have power, and whether the opposition is between "the West and the Rest" or the "West and Islam," the presupposition of two uniform and identifiable entities whose boundaries are clearly demarcated from one another carves up the world in ways that erase fissures within each category and the mutual historical indebtedness between them, not to mention the extensive cross-pollination of the present.[7] Such Manicheanism presumes and reinforces a view of the world in which messy, multiple, and interpenetrating histories and identities are pressed into the service of binaries that distort rather than illuminate the political landscape. As this way of seeing the world gains steam, it becomes increasingly difficult to hear and see, for example, all the people and evidence that challenge, complicate, or contradict it. Under these circumstances, such manicheanism becomes a self-fulfilling prophecy, and the attention continually paid to this worldview, even if it is to detail the ways in which it both creates and deforms political life, becomes yet another expression of its scope and power.

In this context, it becomes politically and intellectually crucial to (again) recall that the West is not a civilization with homogeneous roots and clearly delineated historical and contemporary boundaries. As a geographical marker, it is virtually impossible to pinpoint exactly where the West begins and ends, and this is especially so now that peoples, information, and material goods traverse cultural and national borders at will, creating all kinds of transnational and subnational identities that shift and reconstitute themselves in unpredictable ways. Many suspect that what are defined as Western interests are really only the interests of the most powerful of the developed nations; thus while the West may once have been shorthand for Europe, it is now shorthand for the United States and its global reach.[8] The West is also an amalgamation of multiple traditions—the Greek, Roman, Judiac, and Christian to name a few—and has been perpetually influenced by and shaped in terms of other cultures and civilizations.[9] Indeed, crucial components of Western intellectual history may not be Western in any meaningful sense at all; as one scholar argues, "the real heirs of Roman civilization were not the chain-mailed knights of the rural West, but the sophisticated Byzantines of Constantinople and the cultivated Arab caliphate of Damascus, both of whom have preserved the Hellenized urban civilization of the antique Mediterranean long after it was destroyed in Europe."[10]

Moreover, the West is today made up of citizens who embrace radically diverse ethnic, religious, and racial identities. There are those who are American by birth who, by virtue of race or ethnicity or some other marker of difference, feel themselves at once in but not of the West, and scholars have come to designate certain situations *within* the West as colonial—for example, mining communities in central Appalachia.[11] Furthermore, while it is now obvious that colonialism has shaped the "Third World," more recently many scholars have pointed out the ways in which the West has been profoundly transformed by its colonial encounters as well.[12] Those who take the West as shorthand for a series of "values"—for example, democracy, liberalism, constitutionalism, freedom, the separation of church and state—rarely recognize the extent to which such values are defined in contradictory ways and are belied by the very diversity of practices within the West. Finally, such invocations capture as uniquely Western ideas and norms that appear elsewhere in other guises, or whose most powerful articulations emerge in confrontation with, not as an expression of, Euro-American power.[13] Indeed, "many of the standards exported by the West and its cultural industries themselves turn out to be of culturally mixed character if we examine their cultural lineages."[14]

Critical assessments of nearly every aspect and claim associated with the West have, of course, become commonplace. By contrast, such endless parsing is not commonly brought to bear on Islam, detailed knowledge of which largely remains the purview of specialists. Yet Islam is inescapably diverse, multiethnic, and defined as much by disagreement as consensus. The very term *Islam* in the singular obscures the fact that this is a religion embraced by more than a billion people in countries ranging from the United States to China. If Islam is defined as the religious practices of actual Muslims, one can only conclude, along with Aziz al-Azmeh, that there is no such thing as a single Islam, but rather many different Islams practiced by millions of different people in a stunning variety of places.[15] Positing multiple Islams may finesse but cannot solve the problem of essentialism, however. As Peter Mandaville points out, to "speak of 'Islams' is to be haunted by a sense of boundaries; it gives the impression that there is some point

where one Islam leaves off and another picks up," while simultaneously flying "in the face of the fact that the vast majority of Muslims,
despite a clear cognisance of their religion's diversity, see themselves
as adhering very firmly to a single Islam."[16]

Yet to speak of a singular Islam is almost invariably to speak of the
sacred texts (the Qur'an and hadith, the reports of the words and deeds
of the Prophet), an emphasis that has tended to privilege juridical
Islam and its gatekeepers at the expense of more heterodox, popular,
and mystical practices.[17] Moreover, despite the historical ebb and flow
of claims about an "authentic Islam" constituted by fixed and self-evident truths residing in the "original texts," scriptural Islam is multiply
indeterminate. As Khaled Abou El Fadl has argued, for example, while
the *Sharïa* (Islamic law) is presumed to be Divine and necessarily perfect, Islamic jurisprudence (*fiqh*) is by contrast a human and imperfect
endeavor, a fluid and fallible process that "ultimately justified the practice of juristic diversity and culture of juristic disputations."[18] Far from
conveying one single message clearly, Qur'anic verses have long confronted scholars with a wealth of indeterminacies that have, in turn,
generated a dizzying variety of interpretive strategies designed to finesse if not resolve instances of apparent Qur'anic contradiction. There
are entire disciplines and literatures devoted to distinguishing fabricated from authoritative reports of the Prophet's life, with much riding
on the outcome: hadith judged *sahih* (sound) may further illuminate
the meaning of revelation itself, particularly when unclear or contradictory. And there are four schools of Islamic Law just in Sunni Islam,
not to mention those of Shi'i Islam and even less well known branches.
To make matters more complicated, *Sharïa* is not really fixed even
within any single school (*madhhab*), in part because "law is a mirror of
society . . . [such that] the evolution of Islamic law reflected a degree
of pluralism and religious heterogeneity which was possibly more in-
grained than in any other contemporary society."[19]

As the current political climate attests, however, there is much more
at stake here than whether or not categories such as Islam and the West
are *accurate*, in the sense of corresponding, more or less precisely, to
actual geographic, political, historical, and/or normative borders in
the world. "Islam versus the West" is an entire system of representation embraced with equal intensity by many contemporary Islamists[20]
and American neoconservatives, both of whom apparently have the
will to remake the world in this image.[21] Moreover, the political purchase of such categories extend well beyond these narrow circles; there
are, after all, many people for whom "Islam versus the West" is not
only a powerful system of representation but for whom "Islamic" and
"Western" designate zero-sum identities to which they feel an intense

loyalty despite persistent disagreements about the precise *object* of such allegiance. Given what Muhammad Bamyeh characterizes as the heteroglossic properties of Islam enacted in a "unity imagined" rather than "disunity proclaimed," a singular Islam thus captures and organizes the subjectivities of millions who self-identify as Muslim (among other things), even or especially if such identities enact a reworking of Islamic norms and practices.[22] As Talal Asad points out:

> While narrative history does not have to be teleological, it does presuppose an identity ("India," say) that is the subject of that narrative. Even when that identity is analyzed into its heterogeneous parts (class, gender, regional divisions, etc.), what is done, surely, is to reveal its constitution, not to dissolve its unity. The unity is maintained by those who speak in its name, and more generally by all who adjust their existence to its (sometimes shifting) requirements.[23]

Importantly, such categories are secured not only by an individual's subjective identification but also by what Robert Gooding-Williams calls those third-person practices of classification—racial, ethnic, and religious—that establish the range of self-conceptualizations available to describe "our intended actions and prospective lives."[24] In other words, to identify oneself as "Muslim" at this moment in history is not just a matter of where and how one prays but also of, for example, security practices of racial and religious profiling at American and European airports, train stations, and seaports.

What this means is that those engaged directly or indirectly with the dilemmas of contemporary politics cannot simply dispense with such categories by reference to all that they miss, distort, or exclude. Instructive in this connection is Linda Zerilli's discussion of how it is that the category of "woman" persists as part of a "passionate system of reference" despite mounting challenges to its strategic utility and empirical validity—from feminist objections to the exclusions enacted by any attempt to define "woman" to scientific repudiations of sexual dimorphism.[25] Expressed in and reinforced by the daily linguistic practices of ordinary people, "Islam" and "the West" are similarly part of a system of representation that resists argumentation and counterevidence because, to quote Ludwig Wittgenstein, "what stands fast does so, not because it is intrinsically obvious or convincing; it is rather held fast by what lies around it."[26] It is not that those who "hold fast" have failed to think critically or rationally, then, but rather because such categories and identities are embedded in mythologies whose force derives from a deeply human desire to make sense of the world around us:

A mythology cannot be defeated in the sense that one wins over one's opponent through the rigor of logic or the force of the evidence; a mythology cannot be defeated through arguments that would *reveal* it as groundless belief. . . . A mythology *is* utterly groundless, hence stable. What characterizes a mythology is not so much its crude or naive character—mythologies can be extremely complex and sophisticated—but, rather, its capacity to elude our practices of verification and refutation. A mythology, as Jacques Bouveresse observes, is the force of an idea, a form of representations, a manner of speaking that provides a universally valid explanation of my world, convincing me "a priori because of the desire, and not the thought, that it should be able to account for every case."[27]

The point here is that in the everyday practice of ordinary lives such categories come to constitute a grammar that "is not a metaphysical given but a form of representation that sets limits to what it makes sense to say and that is held in place—I do not say justified—not through grand theories but small acts: daily, habitual practices of speaking, acting, and judging."[28] As part of what Wittgenstein describes as a passionate commitment to a system of reference, such grammar is "really a way of living, or of assessing one's life . . . it's passionately seizing hold of *this* interpretation," the relinquishment of which will not be achieved by the piling on of contradictory evidence but rather, as Zerilli puts it, "coming to see differently what has been there all along."[29]

As all politics entails the making of claims for this or that community which are "inevitably partial and thus exclusive," Zerilli suggests abandoning the rehearsal of feminist arguments against such claims in favor of attending to the multiple ordinary contexts in which words such as *woman* are used and acquire particular and variant meanings—and then are contested and challenged. By asking, for example, how travel and exploration by Muslims have produced and transformed their own sense of self and other, home, and frontier, I would similarly like to set aside the endless rehearsal of inaccuracies and exclusions erased by terms such as *Islam, non-West,* and *West.* I do so not because such arguments are unimportant but, on the contrary, because their very logic points to the next step: of moving beyond incantations about hybridity, fluidity, and translation to a substantive and textured inquiry into how particular imaginaries and identities are at once articulated and transfigured by way of jagged and unpredictable exchange with other practices and peoples.[30]

Shifting the focus from inevitably contested and infinitely contestable abstractions means resisting the temptation to wrap quotation marks around such terms as *the West* and *Islam* in an attempt to finesse the tension between categories that are clearly inadequate and their obvious political purchase.[31] It also means retaining these terms despite the fact that they are not parallel constructs, however construed; as the West is not a religion (although it can elicit religious devotion), a contrast of equivalents would juxtapose Islam and Christianity or contrast Islam with Judaism. Moreover, while Islam is a "discursive tradition" with a long and rich history,[32] the West is a category of relatively recent provenance through which history is increasingly organized (the ancient Greeks, for example, understood themselves as geographically west of the barbarians, but not Western in the contemporary sense).[33] Indeed, historians suggest that even the First Crusade, that supposedly paradigmatic moment in the "clash of civilizations," was read as such only after the fact.[34] Given all this, I deploy these terms in a very specific way, as instances of "master signifiers" along the lines suggested by Bobby Sayyid and Peter Mandaville in connection with Islam; here Islam as well as the West "does not refer to a specific set of beliefs or practices, but rather . . . functions as a totalising abstraction through which meaning and discourse can be organized."[35] Taken as master signifiers, then, the West and Islam capture what is imagined as continuous and unitary in dialectical relationship to those concrete articulations and enactments by which they are transformed and adapted in different contexts for plural purposes.

To return, then: travel narratives have been particularly suspect for the representational power they enact over those they survey, not to mention the Western imperial endeavors the travel genre is said to both express and facilitate.[36] Yet this does not exhaust all that travel narratives can reveal, particularly if the travelers and narratives are pluralized to incorporate precisely those perspectives and peoples silenced or eclipsed by the almost single-minded focus on Western journeys abroad.[37] Rather than adding to the ongoing anatomization of the past, present, and future of Euro-American peoples—our histories, our intellectual traditions, even our erasures of others' histories and intellectual traditions—in the chapters that follow, I seek to shift the theoretical perspective by bringing into view the ways in which travelers of all kinds, past and present and from many directions, produce knowledge about others and themselves comparatively. Doing so not only contributes to a more textured history of our present "complex, overlapping, disjunctive order," but also answers Sanjay Subrahmanyam's call to not only compare from within our boxes, but spend some time and effort to transcend them, not by comparison alone, but by seeking out the at times fragile threads that connected the globe, even as the globe came to be defined as such. This is not to deny voice to those who were somehow "fixed" by physical, social and cultural coordinates, who inhabited "localities" . . . and whom we might seek out with our intrepid analytical machetes. But if we ever get to "them" by means other than archaeology, the chances are that it is because they are already plugged into some network, some process of circulation.[38]

Toward this end, the following inquiry is concerned less with matters of historical and empirical accuracy and more with those representational practices that arrange human experience into narrative accounts, and in particular, what such practices disclose about the ways in which these travelers make sense of themselves and the worlds through which they move. As Mary Gergen argues, such practices are themselves embedded in

> traditions of storytelling, dramatic performance, literature and the like [that] have generated a range of culturally shared forms of emplotment, or narrative forms. When the individual attempts to understand him/herself, these culturally embedded forms furnish a repertoire of sense making devices. It is through embedding one's actions within one or more of these forms that one's actions take on meaning; they belong to a person with a certain past, heading in a certain direction, and with a future that will represent an extension of this past. Yet . . . narrative constructions are not the mere product of cultural history. The particular form that they acquire for any person is an outgrowth of the social relationships in which one is currently embedded. One's narratives typically include the positioning of others in relationship to self. . . . Likewise, others' self-narratives contain constructions of other individuals embedded in their mutual social surrounds. Thus, the narrative constructions within a community of interlocutors may be viewed as a communal achievement.[39]

As the narratives that follow often graphically detail jagged skirmishes among different subjectivities and modes of life, they are particularly illuminating windows onto the ways in which a whole range of categories, identities, and norms are articulated and transfigured. They not only disclose, for example, what Islam means to particular Muslim travelers at specific moments but also where, at what moments and under what circumstances this broad discursive construct (however distinctively articulated) dissolves or recedes in importance, supplanted by other, equally powerful constructs that emerge and combine to organize experience and produce knowledge through layered contrasts. More specifically, I will argue that these journeys and the ways they are given narrative shape illustrate how a sense of home and other is produced and transformed though shifting sets of nested polarities—Sunni and Shi'ite, West and East, male and female, white and nonwhite, Muslim and Christian, among others—that are plastic, contingent, and persistent. In contrast to those who take identity and membership as given by God, nature, lineage, or territorial locality, the continual traction and mutability of these polarities suggest that home and away, self and other, familiar and foreign are "not an instant property or possession" but rather emerge, transform, and recede in the course of the journey itself, much like the flow of a river nested between solid embankments.[40]

As I will suggest by argument and example throughout this book, there is more at stake in pluralizing the investigation of travel as a metaphor for and practice of the pursuit of knowledge than simple recognition that "non-Westerners travel too." This pluralization is, in fact, part of a wider effort to recuperate a more capacious understanding of political theory than one defined in terms of a parochial mapping of Western answers to fixed questions posed by a pantheon of (almost exclusively) Euro-American philosophers. This builds on my argument for comparative political theory advanced elsewhere, and in particular the claim that theorizing involves examining and making explicit the assumptions and commitments that underlie everyday actions, a practice on which no time, culture, or institution has a monopoly.[41] Inasmuch as such examination requires a measure of critical distance, theory so defined entails a kind of journey to a perspective that makes larger patterns and connections visible. What this means, then, is that theory is not only embedded in actual practices and experiences, but that theorizing is an inherently comparative enterprise, an often (but not inevitably) transformative mediation between what is unfamiliar and familiar and, by extension, between rootedness and critical distance. In this context, then, "travel" signals both a metaphor for and a practice of journeying, in Nietzsche's words, to "the other shore," to worlds less familiar, and in terms of which a traveler may well come to understand his or her own more deeply and fully.[42]

This argument and enterprise can be usefully illuminated by way of a contrast with Edward Said's "Traveling Theory," an essay that tracks how theories and ideas circulate, and in particular how they are adapted, transfigured, undone, reworked, and domesticated "from

person to person, from situation to situation, from one period to another."[43] As the particular journey that preoccupied Said was the "aca-
demicization" of theory as it moved from European contexts to the uni-
versities in the United States, the essay was, no doubt, intended to
simply "offer a metaphor for reading certain aspects of intellectual
life."[44] Yet its own peregrinations through subsequent academic scholarship has invested it with enormous methodological and political
weight, transforming "Traveling Theory" from a brief set of provocative reflections into an entire methodology and mode of inquiry. Setting aside such ex post facto freight, what is particularly instructive
here is how the present inquiry differs from Said's in the way it defines
and locates the practice of theory, a shift in focus that brings into view
aspects of the production of knowledge that "traveling theory," as either metaphor or method, cannot.

In Said's analysis, "theory" is largely used synonymously with
"ideas," both of which are opposed to a critical consciousness whose
job is to "provide resistances to theory, to open it up toward historical
reality, toward society, toward human needs and interests, to point up
those concrete instances drawn from everyday reality that lie outside
or just beyond the interpretive area necessarily designated in advance
and thereafter circumscribed by every theory."[45] For Said, the fact that
"every text and every reader is to some extent the product of a theoretical standpoint, however implicit or unconscious such a standpoint
may be" is part of what makes theory inevitably incomplete and neces-
sitates the oppositional services of the humanist critic.[46] By contrast, I
define theory as a practice of inquiry in which critical distance plays
an integral role, thereby shifting the emphasis from "theory" as a body
of ideas subject to domestication or in need of constant chastening to
"theorizing" as a reflective activity engaged in by ordinary people at
particular moments in time. In this way, the particular standpoint at
work in all theorizing represents not an inadequacy of the theoretical
enterprise but a critical component of it, along the lines suggested by
Sheldon Wolin's description of political theory as a practice of vision
inevitably dependent on where the viewer stands.[47]

The focus here is not on the circulation of ideas through concrete
contexts but rather on embodied travelers whose sense of self, knowledge, time, and space at once emerges and is transfigured by the doubled mediation between rootedness and distance, familiar and unfamiliar. Tracking subjectivities rather than theories places front and
center much that transpires between and below those moments when
ideas touch down in different scholarly settings. It suggests, for example, that what Said describes in the passive voice as the "distance traversed" by ideas is often rough terrain negotiated by ordinary people

whose identities are themselves the product of travel and the conduit by which meaning moves and changes from place to place.[48] But more important for my purposes, the circulation of big ideas through the work of extraordinary thinkers at epoch-making (or profession-establishing) junctures rarely brings alive what I want to call those theoretical moments that erupt erratically in ordinary lives, those less than grand encounters with what is strange and estranging that occasion the translating practices I am arguing are central to theory. Travel narratives that enact these mediations, moreover, enable generations of readers to witness vicariously those instances in which quite ordinary people willingly and unwillingly run up against the disorienting friction between what they think they know and what they do not yet know, and the openings and closures this sometimes explosive tension produces.

Such theoretical moments may or may not ultimately be systematized into a body of knowledge that rises to the level of what most would call theory, and there are examples of both in the chapters that follow. Yet I want to suggest that in themselves such moments are windows onto what Charles Taylor calls "social imaginaries," that is, the "ways people imagine their social existence, how they fit together with others, how things go on between them and their fellows, the expectations that are normally met, and the deeper normative notions and images that underlie these expectations."[49] Both factual and normative, a social imaginary may be informed by and in turn transform intellectual ideas about social reality, yet because of its "indefinite and unlimited nature," it exceeds those explicit doctrines and theories that largely remain "the possession of a small minority."[50] Understood in these terms, what I am referring to as theoretical moments are not only windows onto social imaginaries in flux but are also crucial instances of the "everyday cultural practice through which the work of imagination is transformed."[51] Whether the imagination transformed is that of the traveler or of the reader, then, such practices are more than quaint exercises in fantasy; they represent those rare moments by which people might not only come to "see differently what has been there all along" but also "conceive of themselves living differently."[52]

So understood, such "journeys" need not be across vast distances; indeed, depending upon where and how one lives, they might entail simply crossing the street. Moreover, as I will discuss in the concluding chapter, in some instances they may not even require physical movement. If L. P. Hartley is right that "the past is a foreign country," imaginative travel across history, for example, may well involve exposure to what is strange and estranging, a dislocation that can initiate awareness of and reflection on modes of life other than one's own.[53] Needless to say, not all journeys, imaginative or literal, by definition produce enlightenment. In fact, as becomes clear in the chapters that follow, the motivations for travel as well as its consequences are contingent and unpredictable, a complex and mercurial interaction of the personal, political, historical, and institutional at once suggestive of loose patterns and resistant to any attempt to "model" which journeys and conditions will produce or predict a critically reflective or tolerant "attitude."

Much as the field of political theory is itself organized around rich texts, this inquiry tends, somewhat unavoidably, to privilege those experiences that ultimately issue in written form (although several here originate in oral cultures or were first delivered orally). There is much about the phenomenon of human mobility not captured in writing, and many travelers past and present do not have the education, leisure, or institutional power to produce a written text of what often were and continue to be harrowing experiences of dislocation.[54] Nevertheless the capacity of written narratives to convey how people see and refashion the world through contrast provides an invaluable window onto the double mediations I am arguing are constitutive of comparative theorizing. This is precisely why the stakes of an investigation of travel narratives from all different directions exceed the matter of simple inclusion: just as the "add-women-and-stir" approach to accommodating questions of gender within political theory avoids interrogation of its constitutive assumptions, the following analyses raise questions about the relationship between how political theory is defined—as an institutionalized discipline, a canon of books, a set of interrogatives, a philosophical genre, or a practice of inquiry—and who may be recognized as theorizing, in what locales, and in which genres.[55]

The genre of Arabic literature known as the *rihla*, a book recounting travels, and particularly those undertaken in pursuit of knowledge (*talab al-ʿilm*), is an opportunity to explore just these questions. This is not because all Muslim travel is theory, or because all accounts of travel in pursuit of knowledge are by definition reflective or even interesting—wonder is, after all, the "beginning of wisdom [only] when it leads to further thought."[56] Rather, as theorizing is, in my view, inherently comparative, and as comparisons entail acts of translation that simultaneously make sense of and distort the unfamiliar, the *rihla* is an occasion to map complex connections among travel, theory, and knowledge rarely developed outside of the confines of Euro-American political thought. Such connections challenge the sequestering of *rihla fi talab al-ʿilm* (travel in search of knowledge) in fields guarded (sometimes jealously) by specialists of Arabic, Islam, and Middle Eastern history. At the same time, they challenge a definition of theory as a systematic body of knowledge produced by extraordinary thinkers in epochal moments. Finally and relatedly, they trouble the widespread assumption that political theory is and should be organized around particular Western texts whose canonical status both presupposes and secures the preeminence of the philosophical treatise as the genre most appropriate to the discipline.

Some scholars have recently begun to mine the *rihla* as a treasure trove of political, cultural, and historical knowledge. The following inquiry is intended to build on and complicate such studies, many of which suggest that Muslim travel narratives serve as a lens for regional and historical comparisons and as a vehicle for heightening consciousness of the extent and nature of the *umma* (Islamic community).[57] Divided by time and region, the *rihlas* I analyze refract the complex, permeable, and constantly shifting contours of membership and community within and beyond the *Dar al-Islam* across history. More specifically, these accounts span several centuries and so make possible a comparative analysis of such journeys in the precolonial and colonial periods, illustrating the ways in which Muslim travel has varied by region and by epoch, often transforming and codifying notions of Islamic heartland and frontier. Indeed, while many scholars of cross-cultural encounters tend to focus on how other people engage with the West, these *rihlas* foreground those journeys in pursuit of knowledge both in lands demarcated as Western and those within *Dar al-Islam*, loosely linked territory which, in its heyday, constituted a transhemispheric Afro-Eurasian civilization in almost continuous intercommunication by way of an extraordinary fluidity of people and knowledge across political, cultural, and linguistic boundaries.[58] The *rihla* thus provides an opportunity to see the ways in which critical reflection as well as narrowness of vision is borne of encounters with multiple Others, where otherness is defined not just against the West but also by regional, racial, ethnic, linguistic, sexual, and other differences somewhat closer to home.

In the following chapters, then, I investigate the connections among travel, theory, and knowledge in several representative texts of the *rihla* genre and in several texts regarded as central to Western political thought in which the association among travel, theory, and political wisdom is particularly salient. Each chapter is an attempt to enact as well as argue for these mediations across discipline, genre, history, and culture. Consequently, they are organized thematically rather than chronologically, and pair quite different texts to delineate and then progressively destabilize a series of neat oppositions between, for example, the literary and the historical, political theory and the *rihla*, Islamic and Western travel, and masculine and feminine mobility. As these texts can be productively read both in terms of and against the grain of these polarities, the point here is not to dispense with such distinctions but rather to suggest that attention to their instability, plasticity, and contingency brings into view all kinds of unexpected commonalities and ruptures.

Chapter 2 is a kind of prelude to the journey, as it adumbrates a conception of theorizing as an inherently comparative enterprise by recuperating the Greek practice of *theôria*, precursor to the English word *theory*, the Islamic emphasis on *talab al-ʿilm*, and the association between the acquisition of wisdom and the experience of travel both presuppose. This juxtaposition foregrounds an overlapping grammar in which travel becomes a metaphor for and a practice of the pursuit of knowledge about others and oneself by way of literal and imaginative contrasts with seemingly alien lands, peoples, and institutions. Such overlap, I suggest, works as a prism to refract the practice of theorizing across history and culture. As recent work in anthropology, cultural, and postcolonial studies has shown, however, an unqualified emphasis on travel collapses important distinctions between those who can and cannot travel, and those for whom mobility is a matter of survival rather than leisure. In contrast, my particular use of travel is an attempt to ground the acquisition of knowledge in those inescapable, ordinary, transformative if inevitably flawed practices of translation so often occasioned by exposures to the unfamiliar. I will argue that travel in search of knowledge is not only a practice of translation but a *term* of translation,[59] a conceptual bridge across traditions separated by culture or time in which the link between mobility and wisdom, as well the corruption or loss it risks, are explicit.

In chapter 3, I turn to Herodotus's *Histories* (ca. fifth century bce), for Herodotus provides one of the earliest known uses of the word *theôria* in the ancient West when he describes Solon's journey from Athens. By associating the wisdom for which Solon is famous with his intensive travels, and by characterizing those travels as a *theôria*, Herodotus is a bridge to an understanding of theory as inherently comparative. It is also a bridge to the *Rihla* of Ibn Battuta, the famous fourteenth-century Moroccan traveler whose narrative of his search for knowledge established many of the paradigmatic features of the *rihla* genre. In these terms, Ibn Battuta's travels may be characterized as a *theôria* and the *Histories* a *rihla*. Taken together, these two travelers and texts in many ways serve as templates for the analyses that follow, as they occasion the elaboration of three arguments central to this book. The first is that the association of travel and the pursuit of knowledge is not confined to any particular cultural constellation or epoch. The second is the claim that knowledge about what is unfamiliar and familiar is produced comparatively by way of what I call nested polarities—

for example, between Greek and non-Greek, Sunni and Shiʿite, barbarian and civilized, male and female, Muslim heartland and frontier. These recurring dyads are both plastic and persistent, serving to establish contrasts that alternately distort and enable understanding of what is familiar and unfamiliar. This leads directly to my third argument: the course and consequences of exposures to the unfamiliar are unpredictable, in part because they simultaneously serve to articulate and transform the parameters of home and the foreign, at once occasioning a perspective of critical distance productive of what I have called theoretical moments and enacting sharp closures in which prejudices harden and commitments congeal.

Turning to the nineteenth century, in chapter 4 I juxtapose the virtually contemporaneous journeys of Alexis de Tocqueville to America and an Egyptian by the name of Rifaʿa Rafiʿ al-Tahtawi, who was on one of the first student missions Muhammad ʿAli sent to Paris. Despite important differences between them, I argue that these two nineteenth-century texts can be characterized as pedagogical *theôriai* (plural of *theôria*) to unfamiliar lands in search of practical wisdom to bring home: al-Tahtawi sought in Paris knowledge of the sciences he saw as integral to the intellectual reawakening and material prosperity of Egypt, and Tocqueville sought in America instruction for France on the risks and rewards of a fully realized democracy. *Democracy in America* and al-Tahtawi's *Rihla* are particularly illuminating for my purposes as they illustrate a series of transhistorical and cross-cultural continuities in the meaning and practice of travel in search of knowledge, while also disclosing several evocative discontinuities. Like Ibn Battuta and Herodotus, for example, both travelers establish their credibility by reference to the authority of autopsy—here in the Greek sense of the word, meaning "seeing first-hand," and in Arabic *ʿiyan* (direct observation). Their journeys also illustrate the double-edged nature of travel detailed in chapters 1 and 2, that is, its risks and dangers, as well as its radical unpredictability. To the extent that their later travels became implicated in imperialist projects, these two cases also exemplify the longstanding interplay between travel and domination while illustrating the ways in which this nexus is in some ways distinctively articulated in the nineteenth century.

In chapter 5, I analyze questions of gender and genre through Montesquieu's *Persian Letters* (1721), a novel that tells of fictitious Persian travelers to Paris who call themselves "searchers after wisdom," and the writings of Princess Sayyida Salme bint Saʿid ibn Sultan, a nineteenth-century Arabian princess from East Africa. I argue that both texts destabilize a series of oppositions that not only sustain the coding of travel and travel writing as heroic, masculine, Western, and scientific, but also establish a boundary between those philosophical treatises considered the proper material of political theory and those genres—memoir, novel, *rihla*—largely considered beyond its jurisdiction. More specifically, I argue that the multivocality of the epistolary genre ultimately confounds rather than certifies a series of oppositions between West and East, male mobility and female immobility, domestic and political, novel and theory. The *Memoirs* of Salme, who not only physically traveled from Africa to Europe to the Middle East, but was herself a "translated person," negotiating multiple worlds, languages, and practices, illuminates the complex experience and multiple mediations occasioned by travel, and can thus be read both with and against the grain of the same binaries Montesquieu's novel subverts.[60] In particular, her writings bring into view the reach and limits of comparative theorizing, the political complexity of domestic realms often hidden from view, and the rough and gritty underbelly of what Said has called the "privilege of exile."

I conclude in chapter 6 by drawing out the implications of the previous chapters for theorists engaged in debates about a "new cosmopolitanism" and the challenges of a world in which identities are not only shaped by particular places and spaces such as nation and culture, but are also subject to the multiple cross-currents, displacements, and exposures created by rapid economic globalization. Theorists engaged in these debates tend to see in the features of the contemporary world an unprecedented level of contact and exchange among peoples and information and, correlatively, a distinct challenge: to rethink the scope and scale of moral and political obligations among human beings whose identities and loyalties are no longer coextensive with the modern nation-state. Yet the chapters in this book demonstrate that the fluidity of identities and boundaries associated with the postcolonial, increasingly globalized world has a long history and is not only the product of the spread of Western cultural and economic power. The travelers and narratives surveyed here thus underscore what is missed in an often overly presentist and culturally narrow debate about appropriate ways of being, acting, and encountering others in a deterritorialized world. More specifically, the Islamic ethos of travel in search of knowledge I trace throughout this book illuminates a genealogy of Muslim cosmopolitanism obscured by such European analytic and temporal frameworks, one woven from a variety of doctrinal sources and all the disparate practices, moments, and ideas that punctuate the history of Islamic societies and continually inform and transform the reimagining of the *umma* (Muslim community) as a moral, political, and even virtual *Oikoumene*.[61]

There is no doubt that some kinds of mobility cauterize critical reflection; it is instructive to recall, for example, that medieval chroni-
clers of what later came to be called the Crusades often referred to such
martial excursions as *via* or *iter* (path or journey) or *peregrinatio* (pilgrimage).[62] It is also clear that direct exposure to what is culturally unfamiliar is just as likely to engender alienation or antagonism as openness. In the concluding chapter, then, I draw out the ways in which
these narratives make possible a critical assessment of the expectation
that direct exposure to what is strange and estranging is conducive to
expansive rather than provincial solidarities and attachments. Taken
together, these narratives unintentionally show that direct observation
cannot guarantee depth of insight into one's own *nomoi* (customs,
laws) or that of others, and that vicarious or imaginative travel does
not by definition prohibit it. The kinds of blindnesses that attend physical travel on the one hand and, on the other, the insights available to
those who journey imaginatively, suggest that what is crucial to
"travel" is not bodily presence but the dislocating character of the encounter. Just as engagement with past theories that are strange and
estranging are crucial to what Wolin calls "political initiation" into the
complexities of political life and to developing the capacities for reflection, judgment, and exploration, texts that reflect and enact such
dislocating mediations between the familiar and unfamiliar can serve
as an invaluable resource for those who do not or cannot travel, in part
by enabling imagination of and reflection on modes of life other than
their own.[63]

As the following chapters show, juxtapositions of Muslim and European travels, both literal and figurative, point to numerous differences
within and across history and culture in the meaning, practice, and
narrativization of travel in search of wisdom. Yet they also reveal common patterns where perhaps only difference was expected. In light of
the current political purchase of arguments contrasting an insular Islamic civilization with a West characterized by boundless curiosity,
perhaps the most important (and seemingly obvious) commonality is
that Muslims and Europeans have long compared and understood
themselves in terms of a shifting panoply of others. Moreover, whether
the subject is Montesquieu's Persians or Ibn Battuta's Sudanese, such
journeys, either explicitly fictional or ostensibly factual, often serve less
as reliable geographical or anthropological documents of actual places
and peoples than as windows onto the dialectical process of acquiring
knowledge about others and about one's own cultural and political
world. Thus these juxtapositions disclose common mechanisms of
translation and mistranslation, transcultural and transhistorical patterns by which both Muslim and European travelers seek and produce

knowledge about others as well as themselves. They make visible the ways in which such knowledge is constituted through shifting sets of nested polarities—us and them, self and other, male and female—that are as much product as premise of a dialectical engagement with shifting terrain.

Such commonalities challenge the presumption that political theory is a field not only produced by but coextensive with the West, one recently reinforced by scholars anxious to secure a certain spirit of intellectual inquiry as a Euro-American possession and establish Islam in particular as the antithesis of critical reflection. At the same time, however, it suggests that despite the legacy of colonialist and imperialist enterprises, the West does not have a monopoly on what Maria Lugones and Elizabeth Spelman have called "imperialist theorizing," the kind of theorizing that happens when "I observe myself and others like me culturally and in other ways and use that account to give an account of you. In doing this, I remake you in my own image."[64] Representational power is an inescapable feature of translation—the women, Shi'ites, and Chinese of Ibn Battuta's *rihla* no more speak for themselves than did Herodotus's Egyptians—yet techniques of representation may also be said to constitute the very conditions of intelligibility across difference; they make it possible to locate reverberations between what is unfamiliar and familiar and negotiate the dislocation between rootedness and distance. Using travel as a term of translation, then, makes visible the extent to which the desire for new knowledge, the capacity for critical distance, curiosity about what is strange, and the will to remake another in one's own image are not the purview of any one cultural constellation or any particular historical epoch.

Chapter 2

TRAVELING THEORISTS AND

TRANSLATING PRACTICES

THEORY AND *THEÔRIA*

In his monumental history of India (1817), British philosopher James Mill devotes more than two-thirds of the preface to refuting the charge that a man who has never visited the subcontinent or learned its languages is unsuited to the task of writing Indian history. Mill insists that what some might regard as parochialism is in fact a virtue, for his critical faculties and judiciousness require insulation from the "partial impressions" and distortions characteristic of firsthand sense perception. He writes:

> Whatever is worth seeing or hearing in India, can be expressed in writing. As soon as every thing of importance is expressed in writing, a man who is duly qualified may obtain more knowledge of India in one year in his closet in England, than he could obtain during the course of the longest life, by the use of his eyes and ears in India.[1]

Mill's defense of insularity has many precedents and progeny in the West and elsewhere.[2] Consider, for example, the ways in which past and current invocations of Muslim authenticity link exposure to foreignness to the specter of moral, spiritual, and cultural corruption.[3] Yet as early as *The Epic of Gilgamesh* (transcribed 1900 bce), the pursuit of knowledge and the attainment of wisdom has been linked to travel and direct experience of the radically unfamiliar. Gilgamesh, the mythic Sumerian traveler and ruler,

> was the man to whom all things were known: this was the king who knew the countries of the world. He was wise, he saw mysteries and knew secret things, he brought us a tale of the days before the flood. He went on a long journey, was weary, worn-out with labour, returning he rested, he engraved on a stone the whole story.[4]

Indeed, the very roots of the Western tradition are often traced to the world of Homer, whose epic poem *The Odyssey* promises its listeners tales of a hero "who has traveled a great deal; he has seen the cities of men and learned their minds."[5] Similarly, the highly contested narrative of the life of the Prophet Muhammad includes a series of now legendary peregrinations—ranging from his nocturnal journey (*isra*) to Jerusalem in the company of the angel Gabriel to the *hijra*, the migration from Mecca to Medina that inaugurates the Islamic calendar. Such travels have served as both model and justification for past and present exhortations to Muslims to seek knowledge wherever it resides.[6]

The association between travel and experience is commonplace and is reflected in the etymological roots of the Indo-European words for travel, from the proximity of the German *Erfahrung* (experience) and *irfaran* (to travel, in Old High German) to the ways in which "experience" itself connotes a "passage through a frame of action."[7] The explicit connection between travel and knowledge is perhaps less common and, from a perspective such as Mill's, deeply suspect. Yet Mill's ostensibly solitary reflections on the history of India are dependent on the firsthand experiences of others; his work is thus parasitic on the very association between knowledge and autopsy (in the Greek sense of the word, to see with one's own eyes) he impugns.

In contrast to Mill, the association between mobility and the pursuit of knowledge is suggested by the Arabic root *k-sh-f*, from which both the words for explorer (*kashaf*) and inquiry (*kashf*) are derived, and the link is explicitly ratified in the Greek practice of *theôria*, the etymological precursor to the English word *theory*. In George Rawlinson's translation of Herodotus, *theôria* is rendered only as "to see the world," yet *theôros* has multiple meanings, including a spectator, a state delegate to a festival in another city, and someone who travels to consult an oracle.[8] *Theôria* is itself a compound of different etymological possibilities: the first half of the word suggests both vision (*thea*, meaning sight/spectacle) and God (*theos*), while -*oros* connotes "one who sees."[9] Unsurprisingly, then, *theôrein* is the verb meaning "to observe" and is connected to sightseeing and religious emissaries. This etymology posits a link among *theôria*, travel, direct experience, and vision, but it is in Herodotus's *Histories* that such practices are tied specifically to the achievement of knowledge: in one of the earliest known uses of the word *theôria* in the ancient world, Herodotus describes Solon the Lawgiver's journey from Athens for (among other reasons) the sake of *theôria* and explicitly links theory and wisdom (*sophia*) to travel across vast terrain (1.30.2). Herodotus reiterates the association among theory, travel, and knowledge when he describes Anacharsis the Scythian (4.76.2) as one who "had traversed much of the world on a *theôria* and throughout this had given evidence of his great wisdom."[10]

Herodotus provides a bridge between the Greek practice of *theôria* and the English word *theory*, most often understood as the systematic investigation and attainment of knowledge. But it is Plato who specifies the implications of this practice, and the knowledge such travel makes possible, for the course of political life. In book 12 of *The Laws*, the character of the Athenian contends that only men of good repute over the age of fifty will be allowed to travel abroad for the purposes of observing other practices and people, and then for a period of no more than ten years—the exact length of Solon's journeys (951c). Such sojourns are not only permissible but necessary, Plato writes, for without these carefully selected travelers, the polis "will never in its isolation attain an adequate level of civilization and maturity, nor will it succeed in preserving its own laws permanently, so long as its grasp of them depends on mere habituation without comprehension" (951b).[11] Such travelers must be rigorously examined on their return, however, the knowledge they bring home carefully vetted by those presumably capable of distinguishing between wisdom and contamination. Without specifying precisely how to differentiate between subversive and useful knowledge from afar, the Athenian concludes that if the *theôros* is improved by his journeys, he shall be honored both in life and in death. Should it be shown, however, that the *theôros* has been corrupted by his travels, the examiners may forcibly remove him from influence by isolation or death (952a–c).[12]

Plato's grim warning about the risks of travel for both the *theôros* and his polis is echoed in the story of Herodotus's Anacharsis, whose attempt to introduce a foreign religious practice on returning to his native Scythia occasioned his violent death (4.77).[13] Such narratives do indeed seem to "articulate a general truth about the dangers involved in contact between different societies,"[14] but this passage in the *Laws* also discloses the (literally) conservative dimension to the activity of the theorist, one with roots in the etymological connection between the suffix *-ôros* in *theôros* and "one who watches over, guards."[15] This is because travel and *theôria* are here rendered not only as practices of observation but also vehicles of wisdom and *political* wisdom in particular: exposures to other lands and the comparisons they make possible facilitate an epistemological journey from habit to knowledge on which the survival and excellence of the polis depends. The image of political wisdom this passage thus evokes is not the Philosopher-King's solitary contemplation of the eternal but rather the figures of Solon and Gilgamesh, the ancient traveler-King, whose wisdom derived from observation of more worldly things and places.

Herodotus and Plato's *Laws* disclose an often unacknowledged connection between the Greek practice of *theôria*, the attainment of knowl-

edge in general, and political wisdom in particular.[16] Without collapsing the distinction between *theôria* and theory, such linkages challenge
the equation of insularity and accuracy advanced by Mill by suggesting that the acquisition of knowledge requires not detachment
from the world but movement in and through it. Here, then, is a rejoin-
der to the epistemology generally thought to be captured in the image
of Plato's Philosopher-King who, having relinquished the world of
shadows and appearances, stands alone, in silent contemplation of
Truth. Such apprehension of Knowledge not only transpires beyond
the public realm but, as Hannah Arendt describes it, "has no correspondence with and cannot be transformed into any activity whatso-
ever, since even the activity of thought, which goes on within one's
self by means of words, is obviously not only inadequate to render it
but would interrupt and ruin the experience itself."[17] Yet it is not clear
that Plato himself endorses such an opposition between knowledge
and travel, for the *Republic* is itself a kind of journey, both literal and
epistemological: the opening of the book takes the characters "down
to the Piraeus" (327a) for a religious festival and then up to the streets
of Athens in which the discussion proceeds, a physical movement
echoed in the later "ascent" (517b) to enlightenment by following a
particular "route of learning."[18]

When conjoined with the *Laws*, these aspects of the *Republic* suggest
that the solitary contemplation of Truth necessary for wisdom is contingent on, rather than inimical to, such travels, illustrating what Rutherford terms the "semantic imbrication" between philosophical inquiry
and sacred journeys in ancient Greek.[19] Thus if we take Herodotus and
the *Laws* seriously, theorizing is a practice intimately connected to the
comparative insights firsthand observation often provides, political
wisdom a function of direct yet agonistic engagement with the world.
So understood, theory is not the opposite of the political, empirical,
and everyday, but actually arises from and in turn informs concrete
practices and experiences. More specifically, as I have suggested in the
previous chapter, theorizing involves examining and making explicit
the assumptions and commitments that underlie everyday actions, a
practice that at once presupposes and enacts a kind of journey to a
perspective of critical distance from daily engagements. So understood, literal or imaginative exposures to what is unfamiliar can inaugurate precisely the kind of dislocation from which it becomes possible
to learn about other people and practices, gain critical purchase on
one's own, and discern formerly unrecognized patterns and connections. In this context, then, "travel" signals both a metaphor for and a
practice of journeying, in Nietzsche's words, to "the other shore," to

worlds less familiar, and in terms of which a traveler may well come to understand his or her own more deeply and fully.[20]

As the *Laws* suggests, however, a practice of theorizing so rooted in the messiness of human affairs is potentially double edged: while exposures to other ways of living and arranging collectivities make possible the knowledge necessary for both politics and political excellence, it is also and simultaneously rife with hidden dangers and risks. This is less because direct experience and autopsy are inherently corrupting, but rather because the consequences for politics of the knowledge thereby gained are radically indeterminate. Unlike atoms of inert gases that collide and part unchanged, exposures to different and alien lands, institutions, and practices may well transform those who travel, those who are visited, and those who remain behind. As I have suggested, inasmuch as temporal and spatial travel occasion comparisons, and comparisons entail translation between what is unfamiliar and familiar, such journeys make possible not only greater awareness of other worlds but also a perspective of critical distance from home and the often unexamined commitments and attachments home entails. Such awareness can serve and has served to shore up self-serving prejudices and antipathy to difference, in some instances justifying ancient and modern imperialist ventures; it has also served as the grounds on which such ventures and "conceits of cultural superiority" are challenged.[21] Less obviously, such distance may unsettle the presumption that familiar political arrangements are natural, inevitable, and inherently coherent. Yet here too the outcome is highly unpredictable: it may engender either deeper allegiance or radical skepticism toward inherited political practices and cultural shibboleths. As Plato knew well, those who gather knowledge from afar render urgent questions to which there is no definitive a priori answer: "are these travelers ambassadors of certainty or of doubt? Do they confirm or destabilize notions of cultural identity? Do they make room for the 'other,' or do they put it in its place?"[22]

"Seeing the Entire World as a Foreign Land"

It has been suggested that to "travel and observe is characteristically Greek."[23] Yet from Bacon's characterization of travelers as "merchants of light," to Montesquieu's description of his fictional Persian travelers as searchers after wisdom, to Nietzsche's contention that "we must travel, as old Herodotus travelled" in part because "immediate self observation is not enough, by a long way, to enable us to learn to know ourselves,"[24] it is clear that the links between theory, travel, and knowledge is a subterranean premise of Western political and social theory long after the classical era.[25] It is thus perhaps no accident that a remarkable range of histories and political treatises have been composed under conditions of voluntary or coerced exile, of physical and intellectual distance from "home" and the attendant press of everyday affairs.

A classic case in point is Machiavelli, who wrote *The Prince* while in exile from Florence in 1513 and refers to it in the dedication as part of the many cruelties suffered at the hands of the Medicis. Yet in the same dedication, Machiavelli exhorts the prince to recognize the enlargement of vision made possible by dislocation, likening the task of an informed ruler to that of landscape painters who "station themselves in the valleys in order to draw mountains or high ground, and ascend an eminence in order to get a good view of the plains."[26] Herodotus traveled extensively after he left Halicarnassus, and the observations about Greeks and non-Greeks occasioned by his journeys comprise a substantial portion of the *Histories*.[27] Thucydides endured twenty years of exile from Athens following his reputed failure to save Amphipolis, yet such homelessness provided, in his words, the "leisure" necessary to access both sides of the war, the result of which was a history containing "exact knowledge of the past," a "possession for all time" rather than an exaggerated or rhetorically excessive story pitched to "win the applause of the moment."[28] Montaigne kept extensive journals of his European travels and the observations they occasioned, arguing that "travel is a very profitable exercise; the soul is there continually employed in observing new and unknown things, and I do not know . . . a better school wherein to model life than by incessantly exposing it to the diversity of so many other lives, fancies, and usances, and by making it relish so perpetual a variety of forms of human nature."[29] In an account of his own famous nineteenth-century travels, Alexis de Tocqueville exhorts his countrymen to look to America, not "in order slavishly to copy the institutions she has fashioned for herself, but in order that we may better understand what suits us; let us look there for instruction rather than models." He goes on to liken a theorist to a "traveler who has gone out beyond the walls of some vast city and gone up a neighboring hill . . . the city's outline is [now] easier to see, and for the first time he grasps its shape."[30]

The examples abound in many cultures and times. Thomas More wrote book 2 of his *Utopia* in 1515 while living in Flanders on a commercial embassy from England; Thomas Hobbes composed both *De Cive* and *Leviathan* during his eleven-year stay in Paris; "A Letter Concerning Toleration" was written while John Locke was in exile in Amsterdam; and although Rousseau identifies himself as a "citizen of Geneva" in the *Second Discourse*, his life after he was locked out of the city gates at age sixteen was characterized by political, geographical, and spiritual homelessness. al-Farabi, dubbed by many the founder of Islamic philosophy, traveled extensively for his studies, moving from his hometown in Turkestan to Baghdad, Aleppo, Cairo, and Damascus; one of the most influential scholars of the Islamic middle period, Abu Hamid al-Ghazali, was transformed by his travels from Persia to Jerusalem, Damascus, and Arabia; and Maimonides lived and wrote in a condition of double exile—the *Galut* (unredeemed dispersion) of the Jewish nation/people (*Am Israel*) and in exile from his childhood home in Muslim Spain.[31] Ibn Khaldûn—born to an Andalusian family displaced by the Christian *Reconquista*—retreated with his household to a remote area of Tunis after a series of ultimately unsuccessful political interventions.[32] During the ensuing four years of self-imposed exile he wrote the *Muqaddimah* (finished in 1377), the introduction to a much longer history of the world that sought to discern an underlying pattern connecting all discrete historical events.

In more recent history, Rifaʿa Rafiʿ al-Tahtawi (1801–73), considered the father of the "Egyptian Enlightenment," traveled to Paris in search of scientific knowledge to bring home to his native Egypt (see chapter 4), while Jamal al-Din al-Afghani [al-Asadabadi] (1839–97), one of the most influential proponents of pan-Islamic unity, forged his arguments against imperialism in a condition of perpetual itinerancy far from his native Iran.[33] Ayatollah Ruhollah Khomeini's famous tract on Islamic government was fully developed during his protracted exile from Iran, and the political thought of Sayyid Qutb, one of the most influential Sunni Islamist thinkers of the twentieth century, was transformed by his nominal exile from Egypt to postwar America, resulting in a *rihla* later titled *The America I Have Seen*.[34] The political thought of ʿAli Shariʿati, dubbed by some the ideologue of the Iranian Revolution, was transformed by his student years in Paris in the 1960s; the Tunisian Islamist leader Rachid Ghannoushi has advanced an argument for the democratic vetting of textual interpretations while in exile; Muhammad Arkoun, an Algerian Berber living in France, has produced a body of scholarship developing a poststructuralist approach to Islam; and Riffat Hassan effects a reworking of patriarchal interpretations of Islam while shuttling between Pakistan and the United States.[35]

Edward Said, "specular border intellectual"[36] par excellence, has stitched together by argument and example both the pain and privilege of homelessness: that "unhealable rift forced between a human being and a native place, between the self and its true home . . . [a] crippling sorrow of estrangement" that also makes possible the "privilege" of having "not just one set of eyes but half a dozen, each of them corresponding to the places you have been."[37] Said elaborates:

While it perhaps seems peculiar to speak of the pleasures of exile. . . . seeing the "entire world as a foreign land" makes possible originality of vision. Most people are principally aware of one culture, one setting, one home; exiles are aware of at least two, and this plurality of vision gives rise to an awareness of simultaneous dimensions, an awareness that—to borrow a phrase from music—is *contrapuntal*. For an exile, habits of life, expression, or activity in the new environment inevitably occur against the memory of these things in another environment. Thus both the new and the old environments are vivid, actual, occurring together contrapuntally. There is a unique pleasure in this sort of apprehension, especially if the exile is conscious of other contrapuntal juxtapositions that diminish orthodox judgment and elevate appreciative sympathy.[38]

Said's eloquent phenomenology of dislocation reveals the logic at work in the overlapping images and experiences of exile, distance, loss, travel, discovery, vision, and knowledge: to be of but no longer in one's own cultural home creates an "agonizing distance" from what was once second nature, an experience of loss often productive of extraordinary moments of insight.[39] What this particular formulation obscures and thus reinforces, however, are the ways in which the valorization of wandering, rootlessness, and perpetual itinerancy has often served to privilege a position of what Michael Walzer has called radical detachment, intellectual and emotional, characteristic of representational or correspondence theories of knowledge. Such is exemplified by Eric Leed's argument that

in the West, travel produces a science [for it makes possible a] self-conscious stripping away of an enculturated self [which] succeeds in erecting a new edifice of knowledge. . . . Travel has long been valued, in both West and East, because it annihilates the ego of the traveler, reduces patriotism, acquaints travelers with a common nature, fate and identity that persist beneath the diversity of cultural types and careers.[40]

As Donna Haraway has famously argued, this privileging of radical detachment presupposes a specific epistemology, one that expresses and reinforces particular power relations in which the "view from nowhere" signifies the "unmarked position of Man and White," a conquering gaze empowered to "see and not be seen, to represent while escaping representation."[41] More obviously, however, the course and consequences of travel far from guarantee the transformations Leed expects and extols. To return just for a moment to the examples of itinerant thinkers above: the occasions of mobility in these instances run the gamut from exile to diplomatic embassies to tourism, issuing in theories of soaring vision, ambitious handbooks for nationalist transformation, and doctrines of radical religious revolution. Such disparate examples simultaneously illustrate both the unpredictability of travel and a consistently agonistic engagement with the world best captured by the language of *dislocation* rather than *detachment*, an inescapably rooted estrangement akin to what Walzer has characterized as the "ambiguous connection" of those "in but not wholly of their society."[42] These features are interrelated rather than accidental, for such irreducible unpredictability is characteristic even of such "ambiguous" connections to the messiness of human affairs. As opposed to the language of rootlessness and parochialism, then, the image of dislocation brings into view the mutual implication of home and abroad, mobility and place, critical distance and local engagement that captures, for example, how it is that Tocqueville's account of his travels to America are reflections on France, and Ibn Battuta's exposition on the Maldives articulate his connections to home in North Africa.

Even utopian visions, released from fidelity to facts, are agonistically engaged with the realities they often purport to transcend, for as Ernest Bloch points out, "all possibilities only attain possibility within history; even the New is historical."[43] Thus, for example, the subject of Thomas More's *Utopia* is both a fictional island and sixteenth-century England and Naguib Mahfouz's *Rihlat Ibn Fattuma* is simultaneously a satire of Ibn Battuta's travels and a journey from one contemporary political regime to another.[44] In such instances, journeys to fantastic places become the vehicle for exploring the limits and imaginative potentialities of conventional and quite specific human arrangements. In this context, vision does not connote the observation of facts about the world as it "really is" but rather an antidote to the naturalizing of current social and political conditions, the tendency to project what happens to be at a particular moment and place onto both the past and future of the human condition. Utopian visions enlarge the boundaries of what we can imagine our world to be, thus providing in Wolin's words, a "sorely needed perspective of tantalizing possibilities" that neither "proves or disproves; it seeks, instead, to illuminate, to help us become wiser about political things."[45] Distinct from Said's privilege of exile, the vision entailed here is nevertheless contrapuntal in his sense, a contrast of the imaginary and the real, only in this case fanciful exaggeration compensates for the "fact that political theorists, like the rest of mankind, are prevented from 'seeing' all political things first hand."[46] Social utopias thus represent not a flight from politics but a location, as Bloch puts it, always capable of saying no to the despicable, even if it was the powerful, even if it was the habitual. The latter is in fact subjectively even more of a hindrance for the most part than the powerful, since it presents itself more continually and therefore less dramatically; since it numbs the awareness of contradiction, and reduces the cause of courage. But social utopias have almost always arisen in contrast to this numbness, in contrast to that kind of habit which among despicable acts, especially among intolerable ones, constitutes half of moral unimaginativeness and the whole of political stupidity. Social utopias function as part of the power to be amazed and to find the given so little self-evident that only changing it can clarify it.[47]

EXPOSURES AND CLOSURES

Scholarship on the mobilities and displacements involved in such disparate phenomena as diaspora, tourism, exile, and migration have demonstrated not only the virtues of travel but also its closures and exclusions. Abstracted from concrete contexts, the category of travel collapses crucial distinctions between, at one extreme, the power, privilege, and leisure that makes voluntary mobility (such as tourism) possible and, at the other, the pogroms, poverty, wars, sex traffic, and slave trades that have transformed entire peoples into immigrants, refugees, fugitives, or chattel.[48] Moreover, as I have suggested, travel as a metaphor for the search for knowledge has been criticized for valorizing mobility and aloofness over the concrete attachments to particular cultures and places arguably central to human life.[49] This is because the association of travel, imagination, curiosity, knowledge, and reflexive self-understanding simultaneously produces an image of the people who do not or cannot travel, whether they are those left behind or those "exotics" at the end of the journey. If immobility is implicitly linked to stasis, inertia, narrowness, and complacency, those who do not travel come to be characterized by an absence of curiosity, lack of philosophical reflectiveness, or both.

Much attention has been given, for example, to the intersection of travel and gender privilege: the travel metaphor tends to code the pursuit of knowledge as a distinctively male activity, for certain kinds of mobility are historically associated with men, while the "domain of women" is often associated with the particular places of home and hearth.[50] Such associations are often implicit but are occasionally spelled out, as in Montaigne's suggestion that 'tis the best time to leave a man's house, when he has put it into a way of continuing without him, and settled such order as corresponds with its former government . . . [for this reason] I require in married women the economical virtue above all other virtues; I put my wife to't, as a concern of her own, leaving her, by my absence, the whole government of my affairs.[51]

Indeed, what counts as travel—what James Clifford ironically refers to as "good travel," that which is "heroic, educational, scientific, adventurous, ennobling"[52]—is rarely the movement of servants, slaves, beggars, concubines, mistresses, and wives that represent either the detritus or trappings of the mobility of men of a certain class or race.[53] Travel is gendered, then, but not only because women have historically traveled far less than men. The very rhetoric of travel is "shot through with metaphors that reinforce male prerogatives to wander and conquer as they please" and so, as Janet Wolff argues, the "gendering of travel (as male) both impedes female travel and renders problematic the self-definition of (and response to) women who *do* travel."[54] The connection between theory and spectatorship/sightseeing has thus elicited from a variety of quarters a "systematic suspicion of the apparent transparency and naturalness of vision," ranging from feminist critiques of the objectivizing "male gaze" to a deepening skepticism toward positivism and the ideal of detached, impartial knowledge it has enshrined in fields such as anthropology, history, and philosophy.[55]

The link between literal and figurative mobility, critical distance, and philosophical reflection also tends to code "heroic" travel as a distinctively Western activity. Just as women are often rooted literally and metaphorically to the home left behind, peoples of the non-West are often those to whom men travel rather than travelers themselves, objects rather than agents of "discovery." At times gender is mapped onto geography and culture, resulting in the feminization of non-Western peoples located at the end of the voyage, as exemplified by a French traveler who described Japan as "opened to our view, through a fairy-like rent, which thus allowed us to penetrate into her very heart."[56] The epistemological implication of coding "heroic" travel as Western is actually made explicit in Jürgen Habermas's contention that "to gain distance from one's own traditions and broaden limited perspectives is the advantage of Occidental rationalism."[57] As Pratap Mehta points out, the underlying premise of Habermas's account is that members of other cultures are "prisoners of their mythic worldviews, their culture possesses them rather than they *it*."[58]

This is perhaps nowhere more evident than in both scholarly and popular accounts of Islam. Despite the fact that large numbers of Muslims live in Europe, that Islam is one of the fastest growing religions in the United States, and that there is a mutual cultural and intellectual debt between Europe and Islam dating back centuries, in popular imagination, Islam is often associated with a world "over there," home to an explosive anti-Western rage, the front line of conflict in a post–Cold War world increasingly defined by a clash of civilizations between "the West and the Rest."[59] In a post–September 11 world in particular, the most ubiquitous image of Muslim travel is the mobile *jihadi* who moves from Saudi Arabia to Pakistan to Africa to the United States and back with terrifying speed and ease. The deadly purposes of *al-Qaʿida* have mobilized a broader anxiety that when non-Westerners—and Muslims in particular—captured by their "mythic worldviews" *do* travel, it is less to learn than to disrupt and destroy. Such assumptions in many ways animate and explain the increasingly widespread conviction that, as Richard Rorty argues, "the idea of dialogue with Islam is pointless."[60]

The presumption that adherents of Islam are captured by a narrow worldview inimical to critical reflection has a particularly long lineage and distinguished pedigree: in his famous 1883 address to the Sorbonne, for example, Ernest Renan argued that the Muslim is constrained by an

> iron clasp around his head, which makes it completely closed to science, incapable of learning anything, or of openness to any new ideas. From the time of his religious instruction, around the age of ten or twelve, a Muslim child—until then somewhat receptive—suddenly becomes a fanatic, full of the deluded pride of holding what he knows as the absolute truth, happy as though privileged in possessing what actually makes him inferior.[61]

Yet even some contemporary scholars of the Middle East reinforce rather than trouble this presumption. For example, common to several scholars of the Middle East is an assessment of Islamic religious education as dull, static, and monotonous, constituted by, in Marshall Hodgson's words, "the teaching of fixed and memorizable statements and formulas which could be learned without any process of thinking as such."[62] As Dale Eickelman persuasively argues, however, the claim that Islamic education "deadens all sense of inquiry" simply does not square with the "considerable flexibility" exhibited even by intellectual traditions that emphasize memorization, and occludes from view the prismatic nature of learning during the classical period of Islamic civilization.

Such assumptions are particularly evident in a time-worn scholarly argument newly influential in post-9/11 American foreign policy: in

The Muslim Discovery of Europe, Bernard Lewis contrasts the insularity of Muslims with Europeans' relentless quest for knowledge of those beyond its borders. According to Lewis, Europeans sought to acquire Arabic and knowledge of the politics, culture, and economics of Muslim lands not only to fulfill the practical demands of commerce and diplomacy but also to "gratify the boundless intellectual curiosity unleashed by the Renaissance."[63] By contrast, he repeatedly notes the lack of curiosity or desire for knowledge among Muslims about languages, literatures, religions, or cultures beyond Islamic lands, a narrowness attributable to the Muslim world's "belief in its own self-sufficiency and superiority as the one repository of the true faith and—which for Muslims meant the same thing—of the civilized way of life."[64] Travel accounts by merchants, diplomats, and other Muslims provide much of Lewis's historical data, yet the extensive literature about Muslim mobility, both literal and imaginative, is attributed to a "great appetite for wonders and marvels" as distinct from a desire for knowledge.[65] It is only under duress that a Muslim world in the shadow of Western power begins to show interest in matters European, but then only for purely practical purposes.[66] It "was not until Renaissance and post-Renaissance Europe," Lewis concludes, "that a human society for the first time developed the sophistication, the detachment and, above all, the curiosity to study and appreciate the cultures of alien and even hostile societies."[67]

Lewis here equates curiosity about Europe with curiosity per se.[68] At the point in history when European interest in Islamic cultures was particularly unrequited, however, Muslims were in fact borrowing from China, suggesting a phase not of Muslim parochialism but of relative Western cultural stasis.[69] Equally troubling, Lewis's insistence that a sense of Muslim superiority prior to the nineteenth century meant that the "question of travel for study did not arise, since clearly there was nothing to be learnt from the benighted infidels of the outer wilderness," is directly contradicted by several studies of Muslim travels and travel narratives.[70] As Tarif Khalidi argues, for example, Muslims from the fifteenth to the nineteenth centuries demonstrated an "astonishing curiosity" about European geography and societies, although their wonder and admiration was often admixed with hatred and fear.[71] Nabil Matar's work on sixteenth- and seventeenth-century Arabic travel texts further suggests that while travelers to non-Muslim lands often felt the need to "temper exhilaration with denunciation" in their accounts for the consumption of Arab rulers, such strategic gestures did not, in fact, bespeak a general inability to value or appreciate all things "un-Islamic."[72] On the contrary, the texts Matar translates reveal not only the largely unrecognized extent of Arab travel writing about Europe, but also an intense curiosity about it on the part of the travelers themselves, along with a desire to record, measure, and evaluate their observations, and at times an ability to differentiate among rather than essentialize the peoples of *bilad al-nasara* ("lands of the Christians").[73] Ironically given Lewis's claims, Matar suggests that it was often Christian antipathy to "Mahumetans" that deterred or constrained the mobility of Muslims who wished to travel to Europe, ranging from English seamen unwilling to transport "infidels" on their ships to the fear of violence regularly unleashed by Christians against Muslims.[74]

Such scholarship affirms anthropologist Mary Helms's argument that curiosity about cultural others, as well as an emphasis on the intrinsic value of knowledge gleaned from travel to "geographically distant places," is common to a remarkably wide array of preindustrial cultural traditions and practices.[75] It also echoes Sanjay Subrahmanyam's emphasis on the regional breadth of non-European curiosity, and his argument that there were

> various attempts, often from conflicting perspectives and points of departure, to push back the limits of the world, as they were known to different peoples in about 1350. Rather than treat the European voyages of exploration as the sole or even the single most important focus, we need to bear in mind that the period witnesses the expansion in a number of cultures of travel, as well as the concomitant development of travel-literature as a literary genre, whether the routes explored are overland (trans-Saharan, trans-Central Asian) or maritime. The notion of "discovery" thus applies as much to Zheng He's Indian Ocean voyages in the early fifteenth century as those of Cabral or Magellan a century later. These voyages were accompanied by often momentous changes in conceptions of space and thus cartography; significant new empirical "ethnographies" also emerged from them.[76]

Further complicating Lewis's arguments, encounters with what is foreign have been accompanied as much by anxiety and ambivalence as curiosity within Western traditions.[77] But what is perhaps most striking in Lewis's argument is the almost offhand way he draws a distinction between an "appetite for wonders and marvels" and genuine knowledge: here the line between history-as-knowledge and fiction-as-fantasy is fixed and bright, a reiteration of the age-old epistemological distinction Cicero drew between history, which aims at truth, and poetry, the purpose of which is pleasure.[78] For Lewis, this epistemological distinction maps onto a civilizational divide between modern Islam and Christendom in particular. Muslims gather factual information about the unfamiliar for purely instrumental purposes, but their curiosity is reserved for the fantastic. By contrast, the pursuit of knowledge about others for its own sake—knowledge which is, to borrow from Clifford, scientific and ennobling—is a distinctively European phenomenon.[79]

ISLAM, TRAVEL, AND *TALAB AL-ʿILM*

A sharp divide between knowledge, truth, and history on the one hand, and fantasy, wonder, and pleasure on the other, misses the ways in which curiosity itself connotes a drive to know about what is novel or strange. Indeed, the pursuit of knowledge for its own sake is often characterized in terms of desire or love of wisdom, and the "architectonic vision" central to political theory encompasses perception of concrete phenomena and those possibilities mapped by political imagination. Moreover, the boundary between history and fiction in particular is "more open than closed, more often displaced than fixed, as much within each field as at the limits of each"; and history itself is often described as the privileging of one interpretation of the past over other possible interpretations.[80] As many philosophers of social science have pointed out, knowledge is not solely a matter of one-to-one correspondence between interpretation and "linguistically naked" things-in-themselves—between what, for example, Herodotus says about Scythia and what archeological research suggests Scythians actually were.[81] In the human sciences in particular, knowledge is an hermeneutically informed endeavor, an open-ended inquiry mindful always of the embeddedness of both scholars and subjects in linguistic and cultural worlds that constitute, constrain, and enable self-understanding and understanding of others. Knowledge, then, is not only that which meets the positivistic criteria of correspondence, but is also what is revealed in the translating practices of the traveler who purveys and represents what is unfamiliar by way of comparison with what is familiar, an activity that simultaneously discloses and articulates the shifting boundaries and content of other and self.

So understood, it is my contention that the connection between travel and knowledge is not confined to any particular culture or epoch and, as recent scholarship on Arab and Muslim travel amply demonstrates, is prevalent in both Muslim doctrinal sources and historical practice.[82] In a general sense, as historian Franz Rosenthal points out, the "ancient use of travel as a metaphor to describe man's sojourn on earth was widely accepted in Islam," and is in evidence in several Qurʾanic verses, including one (5:18) which states that "Allah's is the

Sovereignty of the heavens and the earth and all that is between them, and unto Him is the journeying (masîr / مصير)."[83] Some Sufi mystics would transform the metaphorical rendering of life as a journey into an embrace of perpetual homelessness, an exhortation to live as a stranger through constant travel.[84] The specific association between travel and knowledge, however, is evident in many Qurʾanic verses that exhort readers to "travel on the earth and see" (3:137; 6:11; 12:109; 16:36; 29:20; 30:9; 30:42) both how the end comes to the unjust and "how He origi-nated creation" (29:20).[85] As verse 22:46 asks: "Have they not traveled in the land that they could have the heart to understand, and ears to hear?"

The hadith literature, the reports of the words and deeds of the Prophet collected and recorded in the centuries following Muham-mad's death, elaborates on this Qurʾanic thread. Al-Suyuti (d. 1505) relates a now-famous narrative in which Muhammad is said to have exhorted his followers to seek knowledge as far as China. Several other ahadith (plural of hadith) link travel to God's pleasure, including three related by al-Tirmidhi (d. 892), one in which the Prophet characterized the search for knowledge as expiation for past deeds, and two others in which he reportedly said that "those who go out in search of knowl-edge will be in the path of God until they return" and "wisdom is the lost property of a believer, it is his, wherever he may find it."[86] Another hadith related by Ibn Majah (d. 886) states

> God makes the path to paradise easy for him who travels a road
> in search of knowledge, and the angels spread their wings for the
> pleasure of the seeker of knowledge. All those in heaven and earth
> will seek forgiveness from those who pursue knowledge, even the
> serpents in the water. The learned person is superior to the wor-
> shipper just as the moon has precedence over the rest of the stars.[87]

The knowledge (ʿilm) here is unquestionably religious, but a hard and fast distinction between secular and religious knowledge misses the scope of ʿilm.[88] Within the terms of Islam, all human knowledge—whether of things divine or purely mundane—ultimately derives from God, and thus all potential objects of human knowledge are them-selves aspects of divine creation.[89] Of course the scope of what humans can know is clearly delimited by the Qurʾan, which repeatedly invokes God's omniscience, cautioning believers to remember that "God knows, but/and you do not know" (3:66). Yet when joined to the ex-hortation to travel and learn, the invocation of God's omniscience serves not to arrest human inquiry but to insist on its limits; it pre-scribes humility rather than ignorance.[90] The insistence that only God knows the secrets of the universe presupposes, as does hermeneutics (for different reasons), the finitude of human understanding—and, by extension, that wisdom may reside not only in what one knows but also, as Socrates argued, in the recognition of what one does not know.

The translation of *ʿilm* as knowledge and learning broadly understood is supported by the *Encyclopedia of Islam*, and its connection to mobility is suggested by the very etymological commonality between *ʿilm* (knowledge) and *maʿlam* (road sign), both derived from the same Arabic root *(ayn-lam-mim)*.[91] Thus, one scholar of the *rihla* in Andalusia contends that those who traveled were concerned with secular and religious disciplines alike and, "far from being restricted to the search and study of Tradition . . . [the *rihla*] was a many-sided intellectual endeavor, true 'Wanderjahre' spent with the best scholars in various parts of [the] Islamic world." As a motive for travel, then, *talab al-ʿilm* "surpassed in significance all other incentives including the pilgrimage itself . . . the seeking of knowledge is a lifetime mission rather than a short term goal motivated by practicality."[92]

This rendering of *talab al-ʿilm* illuminates the ways in which pilgrimage, the religious journey par excellence,

> involves not only movement through space but also an active process of response as the pilgrim encounters both the journey and the goal. It is the experience of travel and the constant possibility of encountering the new which makes pilgrimage distinct from other forms of ritual.[93]

It also suggests how it is that journeys undertaken for explicitly religious reasons so often shade in practice into quests of a more mundane nature, occasion the emergence or transformation of political and social identities, or serve as a cultural marker over which governmental and popular forces discursively struggle.[94] Far from signaling some radical epistemological difference between cultural traditions, then, *talab al-ʿilm* recalls the many connotations of the Greek *theôria* in which religious embassies, pilgrimage, sightseeing, knowledge, and observation of others are closely connected, and may in this sense be continuous with practices of pilgrimage in other cultural traditions, for example, *darśan* in Hinduism.[95] Indeed, an early meaning of *theôros* was an envoy dispatched to consult the Delphic Oracle and so "from the very beginning the theorist was sent to bring back the word of a god."[96] The sense in which the Greek practice of *theôria* could in this way become a "divine vocation" is thus mirrored in the identification in Islam of travel with "pious activity," the achievement of which was thought to constitute a "sign of divine approval and munificence."[97]

The scope of *ʿilm* in the exhortations to travel in search of knowledge is reflected in the extensive and varied types of Muslim travel, every

one of which may entail both physical movement and spiritual transformation: the *hajj* (pilgrimage to Mecca, one of the pillars of Islam),
hijra (emigration, modeled on the Prophetic journey), *rihla* (travel in
pursuit of knowledge) and *ziyara* (visits to shrines, often associated
with popular Islam). These categories encompass many kinds of Islam,
from what is often called orthodox to mystical, popular to elite, and
thus any single journey may well incorporate all four of these purposes
and traverse different religious expressions.[98] Indeed, such carefully
differentiated categories and terms can never fully capture the varieties
of historical experience, for "the practice and significance of Islamic
faith in any given historical setting cannot readily be predicted from
first principles of dogma or belief."[99] In fact, many Muslims undertook
journeys for such mundane and less religiously specific purposes as
job-seeking, trade, diplomatic missions for sultans, desire for status, or
just plain curoisity, and wanderers throughout the *Dar al-Islam* included beggars, slaves, soldiers, crooks, and entertainers, as well as
pilgrims, merchants, students, poets, and fortune-hunters.[100]

Yet it is also the case that the plural purposes of Muslim travel can
be usefully understood in terms of a vast web of transnational networks whose content and reach has been established through "trade,
language, Sufism and scholarship but above all . . . common moral ideals and social codes" that at once facilitate and are themselves re-
shaped by mobility.[101] Such common codes and norms range from the
religious imprimatur for travel in search of knowledge I have outlined
to the Islamic exhortation to extend protection (*ijara*) and hospitality to
strangers and travelers, an exhortation captured in a hadith that states,
"Islam began as a stranger and it will return as it began, [as] a stranger.
Blessed are the strangers."[102] Indeed, as Miriam Cooke and Bruce Lawrence argue, Muslim networks can be understood simultaneously as a
medium of travel, a method for analyzing the constant refiguring of
the transnational *umma,* and a metaphor for the fluidity, contingency,
and variety of exchange among Muslims across time and space, from
traffic along fourteenth-century trade routes to cybernauts engaged in
electronic *ijtihad* (interpretation) or virtual *hajj.*[103]

Understood in these terms, Muslim networks are particularly evident in the mobility of those, such as Ibn Battuta (see chapter 3), whose
travel proceeds along well-established routes of trade, study, and pilgrimage: his voyage was punctuated by the many brotherhoods (*turuq,*
plural of *tariqa*), associations, and hospices (*manazil*) dedicated to ex-
tending travelers hospitality, and his emergence as a *qadi* (Muslim
judge) initiated him into a "shared and longstanding language of discourse and meaning, of shared ideas about what constituted valuable
knowledge and how such knowledge was articulated, preserved,

transmitted."[104] Yet the networked nature of Muslim mobility extends well beyond such established routes and purposes to "privilege travel of all kinds to many places," as is evident in the voyage of al-Tahtawi (see chapter 4) beyond the world of Islam in search of knowledge abroad.[105] Viewed through the prism of Muslim networks as medium, method, and metaphor, then, travel in pursuit of knowledge may be said to constitute a central component of mainstream and popular Islam past and present, and follows Muslim travelers within and beyond the *umma*. Sanctioned by divine exhortations, tied to the promise of *baraka* ("blessings," but also charisma), and nourished by a complex and cosmopolitan civilization "which in the fullest sense owed its vibrancy to constant movement,"[106] travel in pursuit of knowledge is more than merely a recurrent theme in Islam or an occasional practice of Muslims. It is, rather, an ethos.[107]

THE DOUBLE-EDGED NATURE OF TRAVEL

The foregoing suggests that what are often called Western and Islamic traditions, both past and present, share an emphasis on the connection between travel and the pursuit of knowledge. What this means is that despite the ways it may elide important distinctions of privilege and marginality, power and powerlessness, travel here operates as a bridge that opens a realm of comparative inquiry across culture and history without presupposing any particular content.[108] Importantly, this focus discloses not only a transcultural association of mobility and knowledge but also a remarkable range of common anxieties and ambivalences occasioned by travel. Such anxieties are tied in part to the inevitable risks a traveler may court—Ibn Khaldûn lost his family and all his belongings in a shipwreck and Ibn Battuta was robbed and barely outran the Black Plague—risks reflected in the etymological connection of "travel" to "travail" by way of its roots in the Latin *trepalium*, an instrument of torture.[109] Indeed, as Mary Helms suggests, the prestige a traveler may enjoy is often dependent on the inaccessibility of what is faraway and the danger associated with reaching it.[110] Moreover, as the passage in Plato's *Laws* details, there is an ever present possibility that the knowledge a traveler brings home will occasion disaster, as when Herodotus's Croesus misunderstands the message of the Oracle at Delphi, assuming that the empire he was prophesied to destroy would be that of Persia rather than his own.[111]

The traveler also courts the psychic, physical, social, and economic miseries separation from home may entail. Thus, a late-fifteenth-century English guidebook for pilgrims warns against the dangers of "shrewes," the "blody fluxe," robbers, and the ever present possibility of death from corrupt air and water.[112] Medieval Arabic literature links travel, on the one hand, to renewal, opportunity, a broadened perspective, and a useful education and, on the other, to poverty, humiliation, the loss of prestige entailed by the abandonment of familiar connections with family and friends, as well as the homesickness and loneliness of the foreigner who, "far away from his country and people is like a runaway bull which is a mark for every hunter."[113] Travel, in short, signals estrangement from the moorings that impart solidity and definition to human life; a loss, not just of a familiar place but of a world comprised of family, friends, customs, and institutions, which both nurture and sustain its inhabitants. Such loss is captured by Descartes when he cautions that "when one spends too much time traveling, one finally becomes a stranger in one's own country." Indeed, the Socrates of *The Crito* envisions the Laws of Athens speaking to him as parent to child, reminding him of why he did not "travel abroad [*theôria*, 52b] as other people do," and spelling out the moral and practical futility of attempting to take refuge elsewhere when his own fellow-citizens have condemned him to death.[114]

Inasmuch as travel makes possible and often reflects a desire for new experience and knowledge, there are also those who have identified a latent affinity between travel and disorder, who see in all that is unprecedented or innovative the potential for disruption of stable boundaries, conventional arrangements, settled customs, or established authority. The association between novelty and danger is captured, for example, by the Arabic word, *bid'a*, a term that means both innovation and heresy.[115] According to Rosenthal, in Muslim scholarship of the "manuscript age" this association meant that

> the ultimate success of new ideas, which did not fit in with the dominant systems of thought, was unusually uncertain. If a new idea did not find the approval of a comparatively large group of scholars in a comparatively short interval of time, it was likely to be buried in a library, with an infinitesimal chance of subsequent rediscovery.[116]

A similar affinity among travel, novelty, and transgression is expressed by Thomas à Kempis in his *Imitation of Christ*, when he warns that journeys to marvel at the deeds of the saints, to satisfy curiosity, or seek the "novelties of things not yet seen" may be inimical to salvation.[117] St. Augustine characterizes the pursuit of learning and science, and curiosity about the world it expresses, as "lust of the eyes."[118] Given the dangers of worldly curiosity, he continues, the ideal pilgrim "would have traveled . . . with his eyes upon the ground to shut out the glories of the world."[119] The *political* disruption latent in such mobility is perhaps best captured in the person of the vagabond, the perpetual wanderer who represents the danger of masterless men. Thus in the seventeenth-century, Puritan William Perkins writes that those who "passe from place to place, being under no certaine Magistracie or Ministerie, nor joyning themselves to any set society in Church or Common-wealth, are plagues and banes of both, and are to be taken as maine enemies of [the] ordinance of God."[120] The disruptive potential of perpetual itinerancy was recognized not only by civil authorities but also by religious ones: urban bishops in late antiquity, for example, often regarded wandering monks not as exemplars of ascetic virtue but as rivals and challenges to their power.[121]

To the extent that travel entails encounters with what is foreign, it has also been associated with corruption of several kinds in both Muslim and European thought. In contrast to those Sufis who have valorized the life of the fugitive to avoid "contamination by the worldly concerns of the homebound," encounters with what is alien, that is, what is not Muslim, have repeatedly raised the fear that the purity of the Islamic message will be contaminated or debased.[122] Such anxieties are expressed in many ways, ranging from the Maliki injunction (see note 3 in this chapter) against traveling to non-Muslim lands to objections regarding the foreign provenance of Greek philosophy and rationalism in the work of al-Ghazali (d. 1111) and Ibn Taymiyya (d. 1328) to the more recent arguments of "conservative modernists"[123] such as Tariq al-Bishri about the threat to Islam from "that which is imported [*al-wafid*]." The connection between such exposures and corruption reaches its apotheosis in the work of twentieth-century Islamists, as exemplified by Khomeini's well-known invectives against "Westoxification" and Sayyid Qutb's insistence that the rise of Western cultural, political, and economic domination has occasioned a new *jahiliyya*, a modern age of ignorance in which the truths of Islam are either corrupted or occluded.[124]

Just as Mill worried about the perceptual distortions latent in exposure to foreignness, there are untold others anxious about the ever present danger of "going native," of losing one's sense of self, place, and even time in exotic worlds (Rifaʿa Rafiʿ al-Tahtawi, the Egyptian traveler discussed in chapter 4, is a case in point). Inasmuch as travel becomes implicated in imperialist ventures, moreover, there are also those, such as Denis Diderot, who argue that *both* the European traveler to "uncivilized" worlds and those he encounters there are disfigured by the experience. For Diderot, European travel to the Americas or India signifies a kind of time travel in which civilized man is transformed into a savage, a reversal, in Anthony Pagden's words, of the "journey that his ancestors once made from the state of nature to civil society."[125] Such excursions, Diderot writes, "reared a new generation of savage nomads. . . . Those men who visit so many countries that they end up belonging to none."[126] Far from being men to admire, for Diderot, there is "no state more immoral than that of the continual traveler." Taking his home for granted, the European traveler is driven by a "potentially destructive restlessness," seeking not only to see but also possess what he sees, an expression, in Michel de Certeau's words, of the "conquering and orgiastic curiosity, so taken with unveiling hidden things" at the heart of European discovery.[127] Thus the traveler, for Diderot, is "always, potentially, a colonist," those he encounters always, potentially, the colonized.[128]

The preceding panoply of fears may be aptly characterized as a "form of dystopic transgression," for they reveal how exposures to the unfamiliar have provoked a riot of fantasy about the grave dangers for and of those who travel, those traveled to, and those left behind.[129] The intensity of these anxieties as well as the wide array of those across history and culture who share them attests not only to the unpredictability of travel but also to its capacity to radically refigure people and politics; its transformative power is revealed as much by the political, religious, and discursive energy mobilized to contain or discredit travel and travelers as by actual travel accounts. Here again is the threat Plato's Athenian sought to identify and cauterize: haunted by the impossibility of guaranteeing in advance that knowledge and experience from afar will improve rather than destroy, the Athenian argues that only the potentially lethal quarantine of a "corrupted" *theôros* can permanently secure the city from its uncharted dangers.[130]

TRAVEL AS TRANSLATION

Inasmuch as the explicit link between travel and the pursuit of knowledge is itself mobile, transcending cultural and historical boundaries to evoke resonances and anxieties across language and time, travel is, in Clifford's words, an invaluable term of translation.[131] Not only is travel a term of translation, reports of such travels are also *acts* of translation, practices, as François Hartog shows, of both "seeing and making seen" and, I would add, of hearing and making heard.[132] Importantly, however, those who are seeing and hearing, and *what* it is that is seen and heard, are in constant flux. This is in part because the categories of contrast are not fixed or stable; each new encounter discloses different vectors of comparison for the traveler. For example, Ibn Battuta, the fourteenth-century North African who traveled throughout the Middle East, the Asian steppes, India, China and sub-Saharan Africa for almost thirty years, classifies the unfamiliar by way of gradations of distance from the features of his home in the Maghrib,[133] yet the categories of contrast shift, enlarge, and constrict as his itinerary brings him into proximity with various geographic, religious, linguistic, cultural, and racial frontiers. Thus the audience for whom he translates his observations are alternately Maghribis, Malikis (adherents of a particular school of Islamic law), Sunnis, Arabs, people with white skin, scholars of his class, or in his encounters with Jews, Christians and Hindus among others, simply "Muslims" (they are, however, always male).

The fluidity of what is translated, by whom, and for whom is also due to the fact that travelers are not only receptacles of knowledge but agents of its dissemination. As James Redfield points out, for example, Greeks carried a certain moralism with them and traveled as much to teach as to learn; thus in the *Histories*, Herodotus writes of a Solon who is at once a traveler and purveyor of wisdom to those who seek it.[134] Similarly, Ibn Battuta both gathers and conveys knowledge to curious sultans in far-flung locales; indeed, his stature as a learned man is itself the product of travel. There is, moreover, a certain indeterminacy to such practices of translation over time, as the status and content of the knowledge gleaned from such encounters changes with each new generation of readers. The narrative is thus always a collaboration between at least two "authors," the travel writer and her reader.[135] In this way, the act of translation is double: the traveler "sees and makes seen" for those in his own world, but to audiences in a variety of cultural and historical locations the travels may disclose different kinds of knowledge. The very claim that tales of "wonders and marvels" are translating practices that constitute a nonpositivistic source of knowledge rather than a mere repository of fantasy is a case in point.

Among others, Said has exposed the inequalities of power implicated in the imposition of Western language, concerns, and categories on the rest of the world, and emphasized in particular the distortion of the "Orient" such power has produced. The danger of recuperating this comparative understanding of theory, then, is a reimposition of Western preoccupations, now under the sign of the comparative rather than the universal. However, travel is a term of translation for the practice of theorizing precisely because its association with the pursuit of knowledge arises from within the cultural traditions commonly designated as Muslim as well as within those that are called Western. Attending to the Islamic emphasis on *talab al-ʿilm* discloses linkages and anxieties about mobility, knowledge, travel, and translation that overlap sufficiently with Western preoccupations to make comparisons possible without presupposing a particular outcome.

Such linkages not only make possible comparisons among cultures but also within cultures across time; indeed, *intracultural* juxtapositions demonstrate that the operations of representational power against which Said warns are discernible not only between cultures but within them. All comparisons entail acts of translation—of seeing and making seen, hearing and making heard—which are at once invaluable to "make sense of an otherness which would otherwise remain altogether opaque" and suspect for the cultural grammar they inevitably impose.[136] This is because representation through translation at least initially organizes the unfamiliar by way of linguistic strategies and devices derived from the world of the translator, techniques by which what is foreign is charted, decoded, and domesticated for an audience at a cultural or historical remove. It is dramatically evident in those efforts, for example, to translate something called Christianity for Hindus, but it is also evident in less obviously loaded practices of translation across time, such as twenty-first-century Christian efforts to translate Jesus' teachings within a radically altered context,[137] or the use of analogical thinking by intellectual historians to bridge the "otherness of the past."[138] It may even be the case, as Carol Gilligan suggests in her classic book, *In a Different Voice*, that it is precisely when languages share an overlapping vocabulary that there is a "propensity for systematic mistranslation."[139]

Such instances show that the ideological impulse Said emphasizes does not exhaust what is going on in translation. As Catherine Gimelli Martin argues persuasively, while translation "presumes the hegemony of self over other," it does so dialogically in the quite specific sense that it is "polysemic and multivocal rather than monological or unidirectional."[140] A model of translation that implies approximation rather than correspondence means that "interpretative 'facts' must be represented as acts, partial recognitions, which are never either fully translatable or fully comprehensible."[141] Good translation, then, is not a matter of reproducing meaning but rather of locating echoes, as Walter Benjamin argues:

> The task of the translator consists in finding that intended effect upon the language into which he is translating which produces in it the echo of the original. . . . Unlike a work of literature, translation does not find itself in the center of the language forest but on the outside facing the wooded ridge; it calls into it without entering, aiming at that single spot where the echo is able to give, in its own language, the reverberation of the work in the alien one.[142]

Translation can be bad translation—mistranslation—but if it is understood as a process of approximation, the criteria by which better translations are distinguished emphasize opacity and translucence rather than
coherence and transparency. What Emmanuel Hocquard characterizes
as a "'white spot' makes translation a 'present territory' halfway between two languages, a hedge between two fields of literature."[143]

In contrast to the translator who presumes to float, tabula rasa,
above a linear process culminating in the faithful and complete reproduction of the original in a new language, the translator is here understood to be dialogically implicated[144] in a jagged and perpetually
unfinished endeavor constrained by power inequalities and social institutions, characterized as much by moments of incomprehension as
illumination, and where the translator, translated, and language of
translation are transformed in the process.[145] The practices travel occasions thus entail the search for those echoes and reverberations across
spatial or temporal difference that make some measure of understanding possible.[146] Indeed, the familiar lament that something is always
"lost in translation," is a recognition that translations are "necessarily
faithless appropriation(s)," that a degree of distortion is intrinsic to the
endeavor rather than an occasional feature of bad translation or an expression of only historically specific inequalities of power.[147] As opposed to the claim that there is a fully accessible universality (psychological, moral, or otherwise) lurking just beneath "surface" differences,
then, better translations register rather than efface the untranslatable
and, in so doing,

> help preserve the linguistic and cultural difference of the foreign
> text by producing translations which are strange and estranging,
> which mark the limits of dominant values in the target-language
> culture and hinder those values from enacting an imperialistic do-
> mestication of a cultural other.[148]

This understanding of the connection between travel, theory, and vision grounds the acquisition of knowledge in those concrete, inescapable, and inevitably flawed practices of translation that are part of the
realm of ordinary rather than extraordinary experience. If travel is both
a term and a practice of translation, and translation entails the "paradoxical duality of blindness and insight" that is, in turn, the precondition of all knowledge, there is a simultaneous embrace of and resistance to what is radically unfamiliar built into the metaphor and the
practice, a simultaneous opening and closing.[149] Those moments in
which prejudices (in Gadamer's sense) congeal are thus not necessarily
a matter of bad faith or malicious intent but are part and parcel of an

inescapably intermittent myopia captured by Socrates' insistence that "he will carry part of his native city with him wherever he goes."[150]

This way of rendering the link between mobility and knowledge does not rest on an ideal of disembodied objectivity but rather derives from the multiplication of vision—and the recognitions and misrecognitions it inevitably entails—made possible by a condition of simultaneous rootedness and estrangement. As such, it is part of a broader reconsideration of knowledge and vision effected by various feminist, social, and cultural theorists who emphasize, for example, the mutual implication of the visual and linguistic "turn," and develop a nonimperialist conception of travel that substitutes the association of travel/connectedness/understanding for travel/detachment/domination.[151] Such reconsiderations suggest that, far from privileging a disembodied "gaze," travel as both a metaphor and practice makes possible knowledge that is necessarily partial and contingent yet constitutive of both self-understanding and understanding of others. Indeed, despite the ways in which Islam and the West in particular are increasingly portrayed as hermetically sealed and antagonistic civilizations, this investigation suggests that such "civilizational" borders are doubly permeable, traversed by travelers from many directions whose wanderings disclose commonalities in the cross-cultural production of knowledge. Rather than coding travel as "scientific and heroic," a symptom and symbol of certain kinds of gender, racial, and cultural privilege, the preceding arguments about travel, theory, and translation pluralize the locations, genres, and agents that occasion or engage in the practice of theorizing. The explorations in the following chapters are an attempt to enact as well as illustrate these arguments.

Chapter 3

LIARS, TRAVELERS, THEORISTS: HERODOTUS
AND IBN BATTUTA

> [Ibn Battuta] used to tell about experiences he had
> had on his travels and about the remarkable things
> he had seen in different realms . . . people in the
> dynasty (in official positions) whispered to each
> other that he must be a liar. During that time, one
> day I met the Sultan's famous wazir, Faris b. Wadrar.
> I talked to him about this matter and intimated to
> him that I did not believe that man's stories, because
> people in the dynasty were in general inclined to
> consider him a liar. Whereupon the wazir Faris said
> to me: "Be careful not to reject such information . . .
> because you have not seen such things yourself."
> —Ibn Khaldûn, *The Muqaddimah*[1]

THIS IS A CHAPTER about liars. Or at least about two travelers, Herodotus and Ibn Battuta, consistently accused of lying. Cicero may have dubbed Herodotus the Father of History, but Thucydides repudiated entirely Herodotus's approach to the past, accusing him of fabrication and telling tall tales.[2] In the wake of Thucydides' damning verdict, impugning Herodotus's reliability became, for a time, a veritable cottage industry. Some characterized him as ignorant or overly credulous; others would accuse him of malicious intent. Plutarch, for example, charged Herodotus with undue partiality to both the non-Greeks (*philobarbaros*—lover/friend of barbarians) and Athens, along with an egregious lack of veracity and balance.[3] Even more recent commentators on Herodotus's *Histories* have spilt an enormous amount of ink attempting to reconcile the historian of the Persian Wars with the "father of lies," the traveler who conveyed myths and fables. Herodotus, Edward Gibbon wrote, is one "who sometimes writes for children and sometimes for philosophers."[4] Herodotus's newest honorific as the "Father of Anthropology" has hardly put the matter to rest: the charge of Orientalism has now been added to the list of complaints about the *Histories* general lack of trustworthiness.[5]

This is no less true of Ibn Battuta, the fourteenth-century Maghribi traveler who wrote his *Rihla* (with the substantial help of editor and ghostwriter, Ibn Juzayy) after almost thirty years of wandering throughout the Middle East, Asia, Europe, and Africa. As his later contemporary, Ibn Khaldûn, would write, many who heard Ibn Battuta's stories assumed he was lying, particularly when it came to radically unfamiliar lands, people, and practices. There were those who doubted his talents altogether: one rather ungenerous contemporary remarked that Ibn Battuta possessed no more than a "modest share of the sciences."[6] More recently, Ibn Battuta has been celebrated in popular and scholarly work as "the Marco Polo of Islam," and the "Prince of Travelers," although serious questions about his reliability persist.[7] Attempting to make sense of his often inconsistent dating and confusing chronologies, for example, some scholars have concluded on the basis of historical, geographical, and archaeological evidence that Ibn Battuta (and/or Ibn Juzayy)[8] simply lied about several of his trips,[9] fabricated encounters,[10] and heavily plagiarized earlier travel accounts.[11] One scholar has attributed these failings to a combination of laziness, dishonesty, and a "certain slovenliness of mind."[12] Others suggest that for Ibn Battuta, accuracy was simply less important than adhering to certain literary rituals, exaggerating his own accomplishments, or providing a Maghribi audience with the range of tales and journeys they would expect and enjoy.[13]

As Joseph Spence pointed out in 1739, "all travellers are a little noted for lying."[14] But what accounts for the close proximity of the telling of travels to the telling of lies? In the case of the *Histories* and the *Rihla*, the obvious answer is that Herodotus and Ibn Battuta do not always tell the truth, but this also begs a central question: inasmuch any invocation of truth presupposes a particular epistemology, what counts here as reliable and valuable knowledge, and how is such reliability and value defined and measured? This question is particularly crucial given the dramatic shifts in reception and reputation that have characterized the literary lives of both the *Histories* and the *Rihla*, transformations that at once underscore and refract the historical contingency of what counts as truth and falsity, and the mutual implication of questions about what counts as knowledge and knowledge for whom. While the specific explanations given for each traveler's supposed unreliability are different, in both cases, the accusations are clearly tied to the promiscuous blurring of the literary and historical, the fantastic and ethnographic endemic to the genre of travel writing. This may seem transgressive only from the vantage of a contemporary academic territorialism sharpened by recent attempts to transform the human sciences from "soft" qualitative work into an exact science comparable to the study of markets or protons.[15] Yet it was Cicero who articulated the distinction (which Thucydides before him presupposed) between history, which aims at truth, and poetry, the purpose of which is pleasure.[16]

Such transgression is evident from the famous opening lines of the *Histories*, where Herodotus states for his readers the purpose of his book: he writes in the hope of "preserving from decay the remembrance of what men have done, and of preventing the great and wonderful actions of the Greeks and the Barbarians from losing their due meed of glory; and withal to put on record what were their grounds of feud."[17] On the one hand, scholars wedded to a conception of history as an impartial record of the past have found an admirable precedent in Herodotus's attempt to locate the precise cause of the Persian Wars, as well as his attention to the bravery of "barbarians" and Greeks alike.[18] Yet to the dismay of many such historians, the *Histories* is also full of myth; Herodotus often traces the origin of worldly events and phenomena to the intervention of the gods; his account of the great deeds of men owes as much to the epic genre as to actual events; and many of Herodotus's anthropological observations are organized in terms of *thauma*, meaning a marvel and curiosity, but also a "miracle as an object of stupefaction."[19] Such marvels range from a "goat coup[ling] openly with a woman, in full view" in Egypt (II:46); to an oversize footprint attributed uncritically to Heracles (IV: 82); to the intervention of the goddess Demeter, who is said to have protected consecrated ground from Persian intrusion (IX: 65).

The *Rihla* is similarly transgressive. Ibn Battuta writes that his extensive journeys were motivated by a desire to make the *hajj* to Mecca, and that he was "spurred by a powerful impulse and longing"[20] within himself not only to visit religious sites but also simply to "travel throughout the earth."[21] Yet Ibn Battuta composed these reflections only after he returned to Fez in 1354, and then only at the behest of the sultan of Morocco, Abu ʿInan Faris, who sought from Ibn Battuta a narrative to "amuse minds and delight the ears and eyes," and who even assigned Ibn Battuta a scribe, Ibn Juzayy, to assist.[22] From the outset, then, the *Rihla* straddles several domains now carved up into separate genres and disciplines. To the extent that it reliably chronicles actual peoples, practices, events, architecture, climates, and locales that might otherwise have disappeared into the past, many have regarded the *Rihla* as a work of geography and history.[23] Yet it is also an example of the literature of "witnessing" (ʿiyan, direct observation),[24] of *hajj* literature, of medieval tourist *adab*,[25] a tale told for the pleasure of a sultan's court, and more simply, a "human diary."[26]

Importantly, these historical and literary aspects of the *Rihla* do not represent sequential, discrete parts of the book but are contemporaneous, for an account of the world through which a traveler moves is shaped by the grammar of understanding by which he or she translates and understands it. Thus, for example, Ibn Battuta's observations are often expressed by way of a style of prose known as *saj*, which is perhaps best defined as "exploiting the potentialities of Arabic morphology to produce rhyming patterns, often with great lexical virtuosity."[27] The text is also replete with *ʿajaʾib* (literally "marvels"), which refer both to those wonders of antiquity and miracles of the Creator—indeed, the complete title of the *Rihla* is *Tuhfat al-nuzzar fi gharaʾib al-amsar wa-ʿajaʾib al-asfar* [A Donation to Those Interested in the Curiosities of the Cities and Marvels of Travels]. *ʿAjaʾib* are particularly evident in Arabic accounts of embassies and geographical texts which, in the Islamic classical period, were often "characterized by an equilibrium between erudition and aesthetic creation."[28] In Ibn Battuta's *Rihla*, *ʿajaʾib* function much as *thaumata* (plural of *thauma*) do in the *Histories*, for they provide the rhetorical terms in which Battuta translates what is extraordinary, unbelievable, or even untrue, whether of divine or mundane origin, for his expected audience—that is, those who presumably share his linguistic, cultural, and historical understanding of the world.

Cicero himself was well aware that his distinction between history and poetry might not always apply: he acknowledges that as Herodotus is both the "Father of History" and the author of "innumerable fabulous tales," his book is at once a work of truth and of pleasure.[29] Herodotus appears as an exception in Cicero. Yet if, as François Hartog argues, the historical, literary, and ethnographic aspects of Herodotus's *Histories* are an integrated whole, a text that is at one and the same time a construction of the Greeks' own recent past and an attempt to "translate 'others' into the terms of knowledge shared by all Greeks," the distinction founders because a sharp divide between history and fiction may be misplaced, serving in this instance to delegitimize rather than disclose significant knowledge about the ancient world.[30] Such is suggested, on the one hand, by Henry Immerwahr's insistence that history is

is not solely a rational construct based on evidence, but, more than that, a collective memory in which men acquire self-knowledge by the contemplation of the past. History is, as it were, mankind's autobiography, and thus, at any one moment, it reaffirms the relation between past and present in a new way. The historian, in noting and defining these connections, is not a scientist working in isolation, but participates in the "stream of consciousness" of his own generation. . . . The historian reconstructs the past by using all the aspects of imagination except invention. All history, like poetry, is myth, for history is representation and interpretation in concrete form.[31]

Conversely, Carol Dougherty's work demonstrates that the epic tradition of heroic travel exemplified by Homer bleeds myth, poetry, and ethnography in texts that are at once literary and profoundly revealing of the cultural and historical context they presuppose and reflect. In a passage that captures Herodotus and Ibn Battuta as well, Dougherty writes: "Homer's fabulous tales of savage lands and magical palaces are more than folktale or fantasy; they are also steeped in the social, political and cultural transformations taking place in the early archaic Greek world" and thus, among other things, articulate the "complexities of cross-cultural identity and contact at a time of particular upheaval and change."[32] These arguments suggest that inquiries into if, where, why, and by what measure certain travelers are liars in many ways presume and reinforce a sharp opposition between history and literature that occludes from view invaluable knowledge located in that murky domain between fact and fantasy. In an effort to bring precisely such knowledge into focus, here I want to skirt well-trodden ground regarding Herodotus's and Ibn Battuta's reliability in favor of questions that expose who it is that is hearing and seeing, what it is that is seen and heard, and for whom such sights and sounds are surveyed, processed, and approximated.

Given the sheer number of travel writers of all origins—not to mention genres in which travel figures prominently, such as early Arabic geography, utopian literature, guidebooks, and diplomatic histories, among others—the question inevitably arises: why choose these travelers and texts as opposed to others and why juxtapose these two particular accounts? To begin with, as I suggested in the introductory chapter, Herodotus's invocation and enactment of *theôria* as a journey associated with the acquisition of wisdom provides a bridge to an understanding of theory as inherently comparative. In this chapter, moreover, *theôria* also becomes a *term* of comparison, as it links Herodotus's travels with those of Ibn Battuta, whose journey in search of knowledge (*talab al-ʿilm*) can be characterized as a *theôria*—just as the *Histories* can be understood as a *rihla*. This conceptual bridge between travelers separated by time, language, and culture foregrounds one further commonality: in contrast to the instances of travel in the chapters that follow, Herodotus and Ibn Battuta both moved through worlds unbounded by the modern nation-state. Their texts thus bring into particularly sharp relief a dialectic between local urban allegiance and attenuated membership in a transregional *Oikoumene* particularly evocative of the "postnational" implications of globalization, an argument to which I will return in the concluding chapter.[33]

Juxtaposition and an occasional parallel are not equivalence, of course; the *Rihla* and *Histories* capture radically different journeys and were composed under very different historical and cultural conditions, in different languages, and for different purposes. Yet both texts are "foundational" in the sense that each, by virtue of breadth, richness, and sheer longevity, has helped establish the genres they exemplify; both paradigmatic and exceptional, they serve as templates for the texts and analyses that follow. This particular pairing is designed to foreground echoes rather than establish correspondences, and the echoes that emerge illustrate three arguments that are central to this book. The first claim, advanced in detail in the previous chapter, is that the association of travel and the pursuit of knowledge is not confined to any particular cultural constellation or epoch. The second is the argument that knowledge about what is unfamiliar and familiar is produced comparatively by way of what I have called nested polarities—for example, between Greek and non-Greek, Sunni and Shi'ite, barbarian and civilized, male and female, Muslim heartland and frontier. These recurring dyads are both plastic and persistent, serving to establish contrasts that alternately distort and enable understanding of what is familiar and unfamiliar. Herodotus, for example, reveals as much about the "shared understanding" of the Greeks for whom he wrote as he does about the Scythians and Egyptians that are his ostensible subject. Similarly, when writing about the *bilad al-Sudan* (lands of black people), Ibn Battuta reveals as much about a perspective of a Sunni Muslim from the Maghribi frontier of the *Dar al-Islam* as he does about those he visits. What is available to the reader, then, is simultaneously the mediated knowledge of those Other to the traveler, and the "absent model" of the traveler's own culture in terms of which the rest of the world is measured—the "grid" to use Hartog's language, that governs the substance and course of such mediated understandings as well as the distortions, occlusions, and misunderstandings that are their inescapable accompaniment.

This leads directly to my third argument, that is, that the course and consequences of exposures to the unfamiliar are unpredictable, in part because they simultaneously serve to articulate and transform the parameters of home and the foreign, occasioning along the way both the kind of reflective consciousness central to theorizing and moments in which prejudices harden and commitments congeal. As I have suggested in the previous chapter, this is often less a matter of bad faith or malicious intent than a function of the inescapable conditions and limits of translation. The following analysis is thus a triple act of translation in the sense described by Benjamin: it is a negotiation between two texts that are themselves organized by practices of translation between the familiar and unfamiliar. This analysis is then translated for contemporary readers by way of the language, rhetoric, and concerns that constitute my work as a situated interpreter. The evidence for all these arguments, however, cannot be adduced in advance; the "proof" is, in essence, the analysis that follows.

HERODOTUS

The voluminous literature on Herodotus reveals little agreement and much that remains unknown. Of Herodotus the man the facts are scanty: he was born to upper-class parents in Halicarnassus, in Asia Minor, in what is now the Turkish town of Budrum, probably in 484 bce.[34] This birthplace of the historian of the Persian Wars could be described as a frontier of sorts, on the boundary between Ionia and the western edge of the Persian Empire. It was alternately subject to Greek and Persian dominion—Herodotus's own family may have had non-Greek origins—its politics often roiled by the clash of "Medizing" and "Hellenizing" factions.[35] While still a young man, Herodotus became involved with the opposition to the tyrant of Halicarnassus, Lygdamis, and subsequently left. He seems to have participated in the coup that eventually overthrew Lygdamis, but rather than returning home, traveled extensively throughout the ancient world, including to Egypt and Scythia. He settled for a time in Athens, and during this period, gave recitals of parts of what would later become the *Histories* (and he may have given such readings at various Greek festivals). He is said to have left Athens in 444/443 and settled in Thurii, a new Pan-Hellenic colony in southern Italy. While it is clear that his life was framed by the Persian Wars on the one hand, and the outbreak of the Peloponnesian War on the other, it is actually uncertain when he died (some historians loosely date it to the early 420s) and where he died (Thurii, Athens, and Pella in Macedonia all appear to be candidates).

It is largely agreed that Herodotus delivered parts of the *Histories* orally, thus confounding attempts to pinpoint a fixed date of publication, let alone specify the order of composition, the dates of revision, and the precise makeup of his audiences.[36] The *Histories* contains nine books, each of which bears the name of one of the nine muses, but Herodotus did not himself divide up the book this way.[37] There is not much agreement among scholars on the structure of the book or, indeed, if the *Histories* exhibits any structure at all: it has been alternately characterized as kaleidoscopic, incoherent, or as an example of "ring composition."[38] Debates about whether Herodotus is primarily an historian, ethnographer, geographer, artist, journalist, or entertainer continue, fueled in part by disagreements about the relationship, if any, among the various parts of the book, why he ended it where he did, whether his travels and interest in the Persian Wars may be subsumed under a single grand design and, if so, at what point in his life and in what locale the future author was first seized by his idea or, alternatively, under what conditions it gradually evolved.[39] Herodotus refers to his work as *histories apodexis* (publication/exposition of the *histories*) which, of course, suggests a close connection to what is meant today by history. Yet *historiê* means literally "investigation by inquiry," and its etymology links it to the role of a legal arbiter or umpire, that is, one who knows or has a skill.[40] In a sense, then, *historiê* "implies more than mere inquiry; it suggests both the witnessing of actions and the exercise of judgment about what is seen and heard."[41] One scholar argues that for Herodotus in particular it meant "oral inquiry, the examination of the *logioi* [chroniclers, annalists, eloquent story tellers] who kept and maintained oral tradition."[42] Yet the sources for the *Histories* are a complex combination of oral traditions, written documents (from epigraphs to epic poetry), archaeological evidence, eyewitness accounts, and direct personal observation (*autopsy*).[43]

There is very little about the *Histories* that has not been parsed, debated, examined, and reconsidered by scholars in the nearly twenty-five hundred years since it appeared, a fact due not only to the richness of what is by now a very old text but also to its apparently inescapable indeterminacies. My interest in Herodotus, however, is not that of a classicist, nor is this an intervention into the interpretive debates about the stature or meaning of the *Histories*. Rather, I take the very richness and vitality of such debates as a measure of Herodotus's continuing significance, even if what is at issue is the very nature of that significance. The import accorded the *Histories* lends a particular authority to what it says, or what scholars claim it says, about history, theory, and ethnography. As so many before me have done, then, I approach Herodotus with a particular set of purposes justified in part by the very canonical stature the *Histories* enjoys: here the connections among theory, travel, and wisdom are given their first explicit, if unsystematic, expression, both in the figure of Solon who ventures forth from Athens for the sake of *theôria*, and in Herodotus himself, whose extensive wandering occasioned the study he has bequeathed to generations of subsequent readers. In this way, Herodotus serves as a paradigmatic traveler and translator, and the *Histories* may be read as a kind of template for several of the journeys in the chapters that follow.

The Mirror of Herodotus

A particularly instructive analysis of the connection between travel
and translation in the *Histories* is François Hartog's *Mirror of Herodotus.*
Hartog's analysis is concerned primarily with the ethnographic aspects
of the *Histories*, those parts of the text that deal with non-Greeks, including Scythians, Egyptians, and Persians. He deploys an essentially
structuralist approach to shift the terms in which the *Histories* has been
analyzed, challenging in particular the positivist preoccupation with
fidelity to archaeological remnants and the concomitant tendency to
locate the book's value in those moments when the "text and the excavations . . . tally."[44] Correlation of the *Histories* with supposedly reliable
archaeological or poetic evidence external to it makes the text "validate
the excavations, providing a kind of supplementary soul for them
while, conversely, the excavations . . . validate the text, on which they
. . . confer, if not reality, at least a kind of supplement to reality."[45] Excluded from such analyses are bits of information that do not tally, yet
such seemingly irrelevant details may be integral to Herodotus's representation of non-Greeks when situated within the logic of the narrative. Hartog thus seeks to displace the tendency to measure the trustworthiness of the *Histories* by its internal coherence or by the extent
that it captures the real Scythians, Egyptians, and Persians. He seeks
instead an account of what the semiotics of the text reveals about the
shared understandings of the ancient Greeks regarding "otherness"
and their own history. For Hartog, Herodotus is a mirror that refracts
debates about the nature of truth and history across the centuries; reveals the particular "rhythms, emphases and discontinuities" of classical ethnography; and reflects the contours and content of Greek knowledge about cultural others and themselves.

> The mirror of Herodotus is also the eye of the *histor* who, as he
> traveled the world and told of it, set it in order within the context
> of Greek knowledge, and, in so doing, constructed for the Greeks
> a representation of their own recent past; the *histor* became both
> the rhapsode and surveyor. But beyond himself, he is also the mir-
> ror through which others, who came later, tended to see the
> world.[46]

Hartog's inquiry into the rhetorical strategies of the text is organized
in terms of a comparison that is at once internal and external: his analysis is framed by the relationship between what he calls "addresser and
addressee," or more precisely between Herodotus the narrator and the
Greeks to which his *Histories* was addressed.[47] This is not reducible to
the general relation between writer and reader, in part because portions

of the *Histories* were delivered orally, but also because Hartog presupposes a particular audience, fifth-century Greeks, who function in this analysis not simply as ghostly spectators but as a body of shared knowledge constitutive of and, in turn constituted by, the terms of the text.

> The possibility of such a comparison rests on the idea that a text is not something inert but is circumscribed by the relationship between the narrator and his addressee. Between the narrator and his addressee there exists, as a precondition for communication, a whole collection of semantic, encyclopedic, and symbolic knowledge common to both sides. And it is precisely on the basis of this shared knowledge that the text can be developed and the addressee can decode the various utterances addressed to him.[48]

The interdependence of this narrator and this particular audience means that the semiotics and architecture of the *Histories*—including its famous "digressions" (VII:171) into the histories of Media, Persia, Ionia, Egypt, Scythia, Libya, and Thrace, its techniques of understanding, the marvels measured, and the tales "worth telling"—can reveal something of how fifth-century Greeks understood non-Greeks, their own history, and the interrelationship between them.[49] Thus comparisons *within* the text between say, Herodotus's representation of the Egyptians and his construction of the Scythians, disclose complex strategies of understanding that may reliably capture aspects of the Greeks' shared knowledge of the world independent of the question of whether Herodotus is at the same time a trustworthy source on the actual Scythians and Egyptians.

This approach makes Herodotus more translator than historian, and Hartog his decoder: the *Histories* is here read as an assemblage of textual strategies and rhetorical devices in terms of which Herodotus translates non-Greeks for Greeks and Hartog decodes the shared knowledge of the Greeks thereby disclosed for us. Hartog takes on a particularly difficult task, for in seeking to chart the "symbolic effects" of Herodotus's representations he is trafficking in codes that are at once long gone and largely implicit.[50] This is made more difficult by the fact that, while many scholars argue that the *Histories* is structured by way of Greek categories and presuppositions, Herodotus often complicates or reworks them. For example, some scholars have argued that the Greeks organized what was foreign into binaries by which the unfamiliar was simply the inversion of what was Greek, and by extension, "the more remote the area, the more thoroughly it reversed Greek customs."[51] The use of polarity and analogy is evident, for example, in Herodotus's well-known description of the Egyptians:

Not only is the climate different from that of the rest of the world,
and the rivers unlike any other rivers, but the people also, in most
of their manners and customs, exactly reverse the common practice of mankind. The women attend the markets and trade, while
the men sit at home at the loom; and here, while the rest of the
world works the woof up the warp, the Egyptians work it down;
the women likewise carry burthens upon their shoulders, while
the men carry them upon their heads. The women urinate standing up, the men sitting down. . . . In other countries the priests
have long hair, in Egypt their heads are shaven; elsewhere it is
customary, in mourning, for near relations to cut their hair close:
the Egyptians, who wear no hair at any other time, when they lose
a relative, let their beards and the hair of their heads grow
long. . . . Dough they knead with their feet; but they mix mud, and
even take up dung, with their hands. . . .When they write or calcu-
late, instead of going, like the Greeks, from left to right, they move
their hand from right to left.[52]

Here the *Histories* appears to affirm the Greeks' supposedly symmetri-
cal rendering of the world. Yet in contrast to the prevalent assumption
that the ocean encircled the earth, Herodotus notes that the "boundaries of Europe are quite unknown, and there is not a man who can
say whether any sea girds it round either on the north or on the east"
(IV:45).[53] Similarly, while the Greeks coded Scythians as nomads, the
inversion of their own agriculturally based civilization, according to
Hartog, "compared with other nomads, [Herodotus's] Scythians seem
relatively 'un-nomadic.' Their mode of life is not the one that is the
most different (from the Greek model of existence): they are monoga-
mous, cook their food, and make sacrifices."[54]

Here I am less interested in Hartog's specific argument, for example,
that Herodotus's Scythians are not the inversion of all things Greek but
actually represent "Athenians of a kind" because of their resistance to
the Persians.[55] It is, rather, his reading of the *Histories* through the lens
of translation that is particularly useful for this inquiry into the doubled character of comparative theorizing I have outlined in the previous two chapters. In Hartog's analysis, translation refers to those rhetorical procedures by which comparisons between Greeks and various
non-Greeks are managed, or what Hartog calls Herodotus's "rhetoric
of otherness." This rhetoric exhibits particular patterns grouped
around mechanisms of inversion, imitation, comparison, analogy, and
thauma, among others. The rhetorical strategies are multiple, but governing all is a dyadic rhythm running like a beat through the narrative;
in the end, Hartog contends, "in its effort to translate the 'other' the

narrative proves unable to cope with more than two terms at a time."[56] This is in some senses unsurprising given the common assumption that the Greeks tended to order the world into neat polarities, Greek and non-Greek, a net that brings "what is 'other' into proximity with what is the 'same.'"[57] Yet Hartog burrows deeply into the semiotics of the text to disclose the mechanisms by which narrator and audience (here understood as mutually constitutive) ordered and understood the ancient world, the "grid" that not only maps non-Greeks but also establishes the Greeks as the "absent model" in terms of which all others are measured.

A central feature of this grid are the rhetorical techniques Herodotus employs to establish his own credibility, to buttress the standing of his material and render his stories sufficiently trustworthy. For it is not enough to tell tales of *thaumata*, serve up a history of Lydia for Greek consumption, reconstruct debates among Persian rebels, or intuit the intentions of a barbarian king; Herodotus pursues several strategies to enact his authority as purveyor and translator of knowledge. It has been argued, for example, that Herodotus implicitly establishes his own credibility in contrast to his predecessors, most notably Hecataeus of Miletus, who had also reported on Egypt.[58] But a more pervasive strategy concerns *autopsy*, the claim to have seen something with one's own eyes. Just as Aristotle argued that "we prefer seeing to everything else [because] this, most of all the senses, makes us know and brings to light many differences between things," and Heraclitus contended that "the eyes are more exact witnesses than the ears," Herodotus has Candaules in book I contend that "men's ears are less credulous than their eyes."[59] Unsurprisingly, then, in the *Histories*, firsthand observations are distinguished from all others by their greater claims to credibility (for example, I:183). Those instances where Herodotus relates what he hears from others occasion much more caution; he often seeks to establish distance between his own judgment and that of his sources, as when he recounts how the Assyrians declare "that the god comes down in person into this chamber, and sleeps upon the couch," but avers that "I for my part do not credit it" (I:182; also I:51; I:75; I:172; II:63; II:73).

When Herodotus intrudes in the narrative, it is often to reveal the operations of his own critical judgment. He sifts through competing explanations to settle on what "appears to me most worthy of credit," conveying only those stories "worthiest of mention" (I:214, 177); details his criteria for accepting or rejecting the claims of his sources (II:4, 12; I:120; II:147); resigns himself to the incredulity with which his observations will be met (I:193); flags those instances where he seeks simply to record traditions that may very well be false (II:123; IV:195; V:86);

and testifies to his own efforts at corroboration ("though I have taken vast pains, I have never been able to get an assurance from an eyewitness that there is any sea on the further side of Europe," III:115, also IV:16). He declines to relate tales that strain credulity (IV:36), establishes himself at one moment as arbiter of "the truth in this matter" (IV:36; V:57) and at another, stands like an umpire well above the interpretive fray, declaring that "such are the testimonies which are adduced on either side; it is open to every man to adopt whichever view he deems the best" (V:45). Such intrusions function to establish the authority, credibility, and trustworthiness of the narrator and the travels he relates in terms persuasive to a largely spectral Greek audience.

This epistemological grid also makes possible a taxonomy of cultural Others in which the Greeks are situated at the center of the ancient world. For example, one of the central polarities of the *Histories* is between center and frontier, or what also may be rendered as an opposition between an urban based, agricultural civilization and "savage" nomads, such as the Scythians, who exist in a cultural wilderness at once evinced and reinforced by their geographical distance from heart of the Greek Empire, Athens. Indeed, as Scythians figure as the nomads par excellence, and as Scythia exists at the border of the Greeks' known world, the contrast here is between fixed boundaries and what is seen as the absence of any cultural and geographical frontier at all.[60] This contrast is mapped onto another comparison between Greeks and Persians, but the features of the polarity change in crucial ways: Persians are not nomads but "barbarians." Scythians are also barbarians but Persians, by contrast, exist in a known geographical space with institutions and practices that register as "culture." Here, then, the contrast is not between civilization and a nomadic wilderness but between one civilization supposedly characterized by democracy and the other characterized by royal—which is to say despotic—power that renders the relation among barbarians akin to that between a master and his slaves.[61]

The polarity between Greece-democracy/barbarism-despotism encompasses yet another, this one between male and female, but in ways that both reinforce and undermine the primary opposition between Greek and non-Greek. On the one hand, as Vivienne Gray points out, a consistent (though not exclusive) feature of Herodotus's portrayal of royal power is the figure of the vengeful queen whose masculinity forms part of the code of barbaric otherness.[62] In the stories of Candaules and of Xerxes that frame the *Histories*, for example, two different queens are provoked by the despotic acts of their husbands to take vengeance. They are thus at once subjected to the king's tyranny but

come by their acts of violent reprisal—which include victimizing innocent subordinates—to participate in the features of barbaric royalty.[63]
Yet it is also clear that for Herodotus, as for his Greek audience, democratic freedoms are the purview of free-born males; the natural order
of gender is hierarchical, justified in part by a gender ideology that, as
Roger Just argues, tends to place women closer to nature while making
men the epitome of culture. Thus while women were accorded a position of some honor in Athenian society "since they bore its progeny,"
"transmitted political rights among them," and furnished and maintained a domestic retreat, they also had to be "restrained, controlled,
and subjugated if civilized life was to be maintained."[64] It is on the
behavior of women, then, that the possibility of an ordered and civilized polis depends, for uncontrolled, women's natural characteristics
place her "quite literally beyond the bounds of the civilized world . . .
the inhabitants of a natural, barbaric and alien world beyond man's
dominion."[65] While non-Greek queens may participate in the particular
features of barbaric despotism, this gender ideology cuts across the opposition between Greek and barbarian—hence the fear of domination
by women and of being called "womanly" shared by Greek and non-
Greek alike (I:155, 207; II:102)—and, in so doing, constitutes the "absent model" as distinctively male.[66]

A contrast *among* non-Greeks similarly operates by way of polarities
implicitly defined by gradations of distance from all things Greek:
Egypt and Scythia are grouped together as non-Greeks noted for es-
chewing Greek *nomoi* (customs, laws: II:79, 91; IV:76–80) and are ruled
by kings, but constitute the inverse of one another. Both represent extremities from the Greek vantage: Scythia is northern and cold, its peoples hardened by the austerity of the place; Egypt is southern and hot,
its peoples softened by luxury. The Scythians are the youngest peoples
(IV:5), Egyptians the oldest (II:15). The nomads are largely ignorant,[67]
whereas Egypt is the repository of the most ancient of wisdom (II:160).
The country of Egypt is dominated, engineered, irrigated (II:108–9),
and there is

> no country that possesses so many wonders, nor any that has such
> a number of works which defy description. Not only is the climate
> different from that of the rest of the world, and the rivers unlike
> any other rivers, but the people also, in most of their manners and
> customs, exactly reverse the common practice of mankind.[68]

By contrast, Scythia is wild, deserted, unmastered, bounded by the unknown or forbidding mountains (IV:25), the wonders it holds more by
accident than design (IV:30, 82).

These polarities and the mechanisms of analogy, inversion, and symmetry that sustain and produce them represent what Hartog calls a "code of power," for they function much as the "watercolorist's grid cuts up and organize the space of his painting," only in this instance, the grid is "formed not by threads or lines, but by language."[69] More specifically, these techniques at once map, classify, and order the non-Greek ancient world and establish a central point of reference, the "absent model" of fifth-century Greece, the culture for whom these various Others are produced. This is reinforced by those rare occasions when this otherwise "absent model" materializes abruptly into the text, as when Herodotus states that "as the Greeks are well acquainted with the shape of the camel, I shall not trouble to describe it; but I shall mention what seems to have escaped their notice" (III:103). Moreover, as Martin aptly puts it, since "Herodotus counts, measures, surveys and charts the entire world of the Other in his travels, and since Greece is not rendered up in this fashion, it implicitly becomes the center of the numerically partitioned world."[70] Thus Scythia is periphery to the Athenian center, and it and Egypt represent the extreme poles of climate, geography, age, wisdom, and civilization from an Hellenic perspective: "each people marks the limit of the other's history," and in between is a cultural and geographical center characterized not by extremes but by balance and blending.[71] Persians are slaves to despotic power, their barbarism measured in terms of distance from Hellenic freedoms, although they are capable of great bravery, "the same as" the Greeks. In the hands of Herodotus, they are also capable of powerful arguments for (Hellenic) democracy, oligarchy, and monarchy (III:80–84). Indeed, although Greeks may well doubt the existence of democratic Persians, Herodotus writes, the "marvel" is that one of Darius's generals "put down all the despots in Ionia, and in lieu of them established democracies" (VI:43).

Inasmuch as non-Greeks do not speak for themselves but are represented, mapped, classified, and understood in exclusively Greek categories and terms, the *Histories'* "rhetoric of otherness" seems an apt illustration of Said's account of Orientalist practices, where translation is a practice of domestication, representation enacts domination, and the production of knowledge about cultural Others is deeply implicated in disciplinary purposes. Yet both Hartog and the Orientalist analysis miss the ways in which Herodotus's own standing at this epicenter is itself suspect: he was, after all, born on the frontier of the Hellenic world, raised at a cultural crossroads of two empires, and most likely came from a family with both Greek and non-Greek blood. Moreover, after his departure from Halicarnassus, he was permanent citizen of no single polis, a traveler throughout the ancient world until he ultimately settled in a newly founded, pan-Hellenic state. It is often noted that the Persian Wars significantly sharpened collective Greek identity over and against the barbarian world and "what were perceived as barbarian characteristics of cowardice, effeminacy, and slavery. . . . [concentrating] both local and national patriotic feelings, magnifying the self-images of both the city-states and the Greek 'nation' as a whole."[72] But Herodotus's identification with the Greeks seems neither complete nor uncomplicated; at one point he appears to make fun of mainland Greeks for imagining that all beyond Delos was "full of danger," "to their fancy swarmed with Persian troops; as for Samos, it appeared to them as far off as the Pillars of Heracles" (VIII:132).[73] On the occasion when Herodotus invokes "we Greeks," (II:154) one then wonders, what kind of Greek was Herodotus? Where, precisely, is this itinerant of mixed blood from Ionia located such that "home" and "frontier" are the same for him as for Athenians? What is the nature of his "Greek identity" given the centrality of the polis as the locus of political membership and the fluidity and instability of larger, pan-Hellenic loyalties in a region on the cusp of civil war?

Given how little is known about Herodotus himself, these are ultimately unanswerable questions. What is clear is that the barbarians that flicker on his pages are, in the end, far from barbaric. Alongside conventional stereotypes of barbarians as prone to sexual excess, despotism, softness (or in the case of Scythia, wildness), Herodotus's non-Greeks are neither the innate enemies Plato described nor the natural slaves Aristotle presumed.[74] They are at once cowardly and brave, wise and ignorant, noble and petty, and despite conditions of despotism, subject just as the Greeks are to the larger patterns and truths Herodotus suggests are characteristic of the human condition: human beings are everywhere subject to mortality and necessity (VII:46; I:86); all must concede that "chances rule men, and not men chances" (VII:49); that "'tis the sorest of all human ills, to abound in knowledge and yet have no power over action" (IX:16); that everywhere "freedom is an excellent thing" (V:78); and that all men—including, presumably, Herodotus himself—deem their own *nomoi* superior to others (III:38).

Even Hartog's central polarity between Greece/democracy and barbarism/despotism bleeds at the edges. Just as there is an occasional Persian championing democracy, there are several Greek tyrants stalking the pages whose characteristics "include promiscuity and lust, pride and oppression, secret operations, violation of *nomoi*, physical mutilation. . . . [thus sharing] the excessive hierarchy, luxury, and emotion of the tragic barbarian."[75] Moreover, while Herodotus's binaries may establish the centrality of the Greeks, they do not always serve to affirm the superiority of the Greek "way," and at times suggest quite

the opposite. Herodotus notes the Greeks' religious debt to Egypt
(II:43), refers with contempt to the Hellenes' ignorance and credulity
(II:45), and on occasion records achievements that far surpass those of
the Greeks (II:148). Nor does Herodotus presume that Hellenic *nomoi*
are the model to which barbarians must strive or toward which they
will inevitably evolve, and nomads are nowhere made to represent an
early stage of Greek development.

While it perhaps goes too far to argue that Herodotus's attitudes toward Greek *nomoi* and relative "open-mindedness" toward non-
Greeks are due to his mixed lineage and background, it is plausible to
argue that his experiences of homelessness, travel, and exposures to
unfamiliar people inflect the representations of Greeks and non-Greeks
in the *Histories*. This does not mean that Herodotus's ethnography is
innocent of power; this is, after all, a book governed by serious closures. Early in the text, for example, the Greeks are distinguished
"from the barbarians by superior sagacity and freedom from foolish
simpleness" (I:60). Yet such expressions of ethnocentrism and the
mechanisms of representation they sustain do not exhaust all that transpires about Otherness in the *Histories*. For Herodotus is a traveler as
well as a "Greek," and as a result, the *Histories* suggests not only that
there are limits to Greek knowledge, but also that there are certain
commonalities of human experience—foremost among them, the tendency to privilege one's own *nomoi* over all others.

Perhaps nowhere are these particular complexities more vividly captured in the *Histories* than in the figure of Solon, the Athenian lawgiver
whose wanderings are inaugurated, at least in part, "for the sake of
theôria," and whose journeys are explicitly linked to wisdom. Described as one of the great "sages of Greece," Solon traveled for ten
years, not only to "avoid being forced to repeal any of the laws which,
at the request of the Athenians, he had made for them," but also to
"see the world" (I:29–30). The character of Solon initially appears in
the *Histories* as a dispenser of wisdom: in response to a query from
Croesus of Sardis, Solon delivers a lecture about the nature of true happiness and a caution about the uncertainty of fate. Solon's words immediately prove prophetic, as divine vengeance is soon after visited
upon Croesus, punishment for the arrogance of "deeming himself the
happiest of men" (I:34). Perhaps for this reason, James Redfield sees
Solon primarily as "tourist and lawgiver," the embodiment of a characteristic Greek moralism "critical of barbarian values," and thus is one
who "travels not so much to learn as to teach."[76] Yet Solon's next appearance in the narrative links the role of lawgiver not to that of
teacher but of student: he borrows a particularly wise custom from
Amasis of Egypt, imposing it on Athens to great effect (II:177). In part,

then, Solon is one who "travels in order to be a foreigner, which is to say he travels in order to come home. He discovers his own culture by taking it with him to places where it is out of place, discovers its specific contours by taking it to places where it does not fit."[77] But Solon does not only travel to domesticate the unfamiliar; he also seeks to learn about and from it, and thus, like Herodotus himself, is both traveler and translator, tourist and student.

This doubled aspect of travel suggests that the representational power exercised as a function of translation does not exhaust what is disclosed in the text, nor is it reducible to political and ideological domination. As Martin argues, "Power in the sense of mapping cannot be meaningfully detached from the process of 'making seen,' and to chart the stars is not to conquer them in the same sense as to chart, rule, and hence conquer a neighboring or at least an accessible territory."[78] So understood, the process by which Herodotus both sees and makes seen is rooted not in exceptional exercises of power but rather in those unremarkable and inescapable practices of translation that simultaneously enable knowledge of and distort what is unfamiliar. A case in point is the classification of wonders, marvels, and oddities central not only to the *Histories* but to virtually all the narratives that follow. Such classification is certainly an ethnocentric mode of representation, for something is only odd to one for whom it is different rather than natural. But *thaumata* are simultaneously "operators of intelligibility," serving to "classify phenomena and set them in order. . . . [making] it easier to understand the world, operating almost as instruments of thought, even tools of logic."[79] Thus each technique of representation makes it possible to understand unfamiliar terrain, "to explain, to make sense of an otherness which would otherwise remain altogether opaque . . . [each] is a fiction which 'shows how it is' and makes it possible . . . to elaborate a representation of the world."[80]

Ibn Battuta

The move from the world of Herodotus to the journeys of Ibn Battuta not only involves a dramatic jump in time but also a somewhat jarring cultural and linguistic shift to the genre of the *rihla* as elaborated in the Islamic middle periods.[81] Ibn Battuta's *Rihla* was not the first of its kind; at a minimum, it was preceded by the *rihla* of Ibn Jubayr, whose account of his *hajj* to Mecca in 1183–85 is often characterized as a model for many that followed.[82] But while Ibn Jubayr's limited journey was undertaken for the specific purpose of expiation (*kaffara*) for drinking wine, Ibn Battuta's *hajj* ultimately led him far afield of both Arabia and his initial purpose in a series of travels that would be remarkable for both their length and breadth: his voyage lasted almost thirty years and traversed the heart of the Middle East, the Asian steppes, India, China, and sub-Saharan Africa for a total distance of more than seventy thousand miles.[83] Indeed, while Ibn Battuta's account begins as a conventional *rihla hijaziyya* (pilgrimage to the Hijaz in Arabia),[84] he himself testifies that it "was my practice on my journeys never to return by way of a road I had already traveled whenever possible," and concludes with satisfaction that "I have indeed, praise God, realized my desire in this world, which was to travel throughout the earth and, in so doing, I have accomplished what no other has accomplished, as far as I know."[85]

Much of what is known about Ibn Battuta's life comes from the *Rihla* itself, either from Ibn Juzayy's introduction or what is revealed in the course of the text.[86] He was born in 1304 into a Berber family of sufficient means and standing to provide him with an education in the religious sciences in general and Maliki law in particular. As described in the *Rihla*, in 1325, at twenty-two years of age, Ibn Battuta resolved to leave his parents, "part from those dearest to me, female and male, and take leave of my home just as birds fly from their nests," and set out on a *hajj* to Mecca.[87] He endured enormous hardships over the course of what turned out to be almost thirty years of traveling—he was robbed, shipwrecked, captured by bandits, attacked by pirates, and often gravely ill—yet by the end had also acquired (then lost, and gained again) a small fortune and a reputation as a learned man. While he set out alone, "without the companionship of a friend or even of a caravan whose company I could join," as his stature grew over the course of his journeys, he acquired numerous male and female slaves who often traveled with him, as well as several wives (ten are mentioned in the *Rihla*, but there may well have been more), and fathered an unknown number of children (five are mentioned, but there may have been more).[88] After an extraordinary series of journeys, the forty-five-year-old Ibn Battuta found himself in Cairo as the Black Plague raged around him. He had already heard of the death of his father but assumed his mother was still alive; at long last, he decides to return to Morocco, writing that "the memory of my homeland moved me, affection for my people and friends, and love for my country which for me is better than all others," although it is also clear that reports of increasing prosperity back home beckoned. He did not stay put for long after his return to the Maghrib however: he made two more journeys—one to Andalusia, a second to Mali—but then returned for good in 1354, at which time the sultan of Morocco commissioned the *Rihla*. Of his later life all that is known is that he served as a *qadi* (judge) in an unidentified town and died somewhere in Morocco in either 1368 or 1369.[89]

Composed in the epoch of the plague that decimated entire communities, the *Rihla* was not widely known in Muslim societies[90] in the centuries that followed Ibn Battuta's death, but copies of it were preserved in various places throughout the Middle East.[91] Dunn traces Ibn Battuta's eventual renown to the interest of nineteenth-century European scholars, although the interest was admixed with impatience and some contempt for the *Rihla's* predilection for "unscientific" digressions into miracles and magic.[92] Samuel Lee, who produced the first English abridgement of the *Rihla* in 1829, states that his "principal object in making these inquiries, was to ascertain the accuracy and fidelity of my author" and notes with satisfaction that Ibn Battuta "is worthy of all credit."[93] Lee's approach set the stage for much of what followed: with some recent exceptions, the bulk of scholarship on the *Rihla* in both Arabic and English has been governed by positivistic preoccupations, such as fixing Ibn Battuta's chronologies and tallying his observations of far-flung locales with archaeological, geographical, anthropological, and historical evidence.[94] While some scholars still echo Lee's confidence, many others have cast serious doubts on the veracity of several of Ibn Battuta's journeys and, as with scholarship on Herodotus, very little agreement has since emerged. Several scholars insist Ibn Battuta never went to China; others insist he did;[95] one scholar claims that Ibn Battuta's account of India is not trustworthy, another says it is;[96] one states he most certainly did not go to Constantinople, another says he most certainly did.[97] The *Rihla* is described as a fount of historical, geographical, ethnographic, and sociological information, yet his journey to Bulghar is said to be made up, his account of Palestine plagiarized, and his visit to Syria factual but incorrectly dated.[98]

Closely related to the varying assessments of the *Rihla's* accuracy are the radical disagreements about Ibn Battuta's intellectual talents and sensibilities, provoking at least one observation about a timeless "bitchiness among scholars."[99] His intellect is said to be either modest or capacious, his education and training limited or deep, rigid or flexible. At one moment, the *Rihla* is said to be unusually free of bigotry and fanaticism,[100] and Ibn Battuta described as a "shrewd and careful observer" with a "keen sense of humour."[101] At another, he is characterized as a "Muhammadan fanatic" or as a humorless and "puritanically self-righteous, even sanctimonious, Maliki zealot," who must have in addition been a "tiresome traveling companion."[102] One scholar characterizes him as a theologian (*mutakallim*), while another argues that he was not particularly interested in "scholastic theology."[103] Ibn Battuta's primary motivation for travel is alternatively said to be wanderlust, pursuit of *baraka*,[104] sheer ambition,[105] or all of the above.[106] Others foreground more mundane interests, particularly in the opposite sex and in food; Ibn Battuta is even credited with providing a "gastronomical atlas of the Orient."[107] Scholars further disagree about the actual miles Ibn Battuta covered,[108] when and if he conceived of the idea of the *Rihla* while still on his journeys,[109] and whether or not he took notes along the way that would form the basis of the text he later dictated to Ibn Juzayy.[110]

As with scholarship on the *Histories*, many of these disagreements say more about scholars' historically contingent understanding of what constitutes relevance and knowledge than about Ibn Battuta or the "essence" of the *Rihla*. But like Hartog in his analysis of the *Histories*, I am concerned less with what the text reveals about, for example, actual fourteenth-century Sudanese than how Ibn Battuta purveys and represents the world he experiences for his Muslim audiences. As André Miquel suggests in connection with ninth- and tenth-century Arab travel literature, much about the cultural and sociological world of a *rihla*'s audience is revealed not despite but *because of* the precise ways it deviates from fidelity to sources and facts.[111] The following is thus an inquiry into the ways in which Ibn Battuta represents the world and himself, how these techniques of representation disclose a shifting sense of home and frontier, self and other, and what such practices of seeing and making seen, hearing and making heard, disclose about theorizing comparatively.

From West to East

At the time the *Rihla* was composed, Ibn Battuta had spent more of his life away from home than in it. In the text, then, "home" is perhaps best understood less as a fixed place and locale than a set of nested polarities, overlapping portable allegiances defined by contrasts that emerge, attenuate, transform, and recede as he moves from familiar to strange terrain and back again. As is clear at the beginning of the *Rihla*, for example, Ibn Battuta's most immediate sense of home is defined by Tangier, a frontier port town that served as a crossing for multiple currents and peoples of African, European, Atlantic, and Mediterranean origin.[112] Ibn Battuta frequently identifies himself as from Tangier and, reflecting common practice, the city is part of his full name: Ibn Juzayy identifies him Abu ʿAbdallah Muhammad ibn ʿAbdallah ibn Muhammad ibn Ibrahim al-Lawait [a Berber group] ibn Battuta al-Tanji ("of Tangier").[113] The *Rihla* relates a small incident when, during Ibn Battuta's travels in China, he encounters a man he feels is familiar and asks him where he is from: "He replied, 'From Ceuta.' I said to him, 'and I am from Tangier,' at which point he greeted me anew and wept until I wept with him."[114] Ibn Battuta's sense of "home," however, is perhaps most explicit at moments of loss: early in his travels, for example, the *Rihla* relates his arrival in Tunis and his initially sharp sense of estrangement in this North African city. He is forlorn until welcomed by a fellow pilgrim:

> [The people of the city] received us and greetings and questions were exchanged all around, but no one greeted me, as I did not know a single person there. I was so distressed by my loneliness that I could not contain myself and wept bitterly. But one of the pilgrims, realizing my state, came up to me and greeted me warmly, and did not cease his friendly conversation until I had entered the city.[115]

Ibn Battuta's powerful ties to Tangier reflect, in part, the ways in which cities rather than larger political units, such as states, served as first source of identification and allegiance. Although the world in which Ibn Battuta lived was composed of numerous dynasties and kingdoms with at times broad territorial claims, "one has to think of a Muslim ruler as . . . being rather like a lantern stood down in a field at night: it is a centre of light, a centre of influence, which will extend farther in one direction or another because in one direction there is an obstacle in the way and in another direction there is not."[116] Individual kingdoms, their borders porous and authority often uncertain, commanded the attention of Muslim travelers largely in passing, only one of several sources of authority that included religious scholars, "tribal notables, merchant guilds, Sufi orders and vast networks of extended families."[117] Thus as Ibn Battuta travels beyond North Africa, he comes to identify himself not only as from Tangier but as *Maghribi* (from Northwest Africa), and Ibn Battuta was often known by others as al-Maghribi.[118]

Literally meaning "the place of setting sun" or more generally, "the West," the *Maghrib* operates in contrast to the *Mashriq*, the Islamic heartlands of "the East" and this distinction is crucial for understanding the very impetus for Ibn Battuta's travel. As scholars have argued, *talab al-ʿilm* was particularly prevalent among those living on the western frontier of the medieval *Dar al-Islam*, in the lands remote from the historical centers of Islamic civilization and in closest proximity to the advancing Christian *Reconquista*.[119] More specifically, those in al-Andalus (Muslim Spain) and northwest Africa—the so-called Island of the West (*Jazirat al-Maghrib*)— journeyed, often at great risk, across both sea and desert to make the *hajj* to Mecca, and "literate frontiersmen" such as Ibn Battuta turned to the East to find established centers of Muslim learning.[120] By contrast, educated Egyptians, Syrians, and Persians at the time were less inclined to journey to Islam's "back country" in search of knowledge, a reluctance captured in the Arabic root of *maghrib* (*gh-r-b*), from which are derived the words for foreign, strange, and remote.[121] Treks from the western edge of the *Dar al-Islam* thus facilitated a sense of membership in a cosmopolitan civilization and provided a contrast in terms of which regional identity and a sense of frontier coalesced.[122]

Within the *Rihla*, the distinction between West and East is not only geographical but intellectual and religious: at one point, Ibn Battuta exhibits what H.A.R. Gibb characterizes as a Maliki distrust of the "over-subtle theologians of the East" when he disparages the obfuscatory scholasticism of those intellectuals/thinkers (المتفكّرين) who seek to dissect or explain religious devotion.[123] Ibn Battuta even locates the proximate cause of the Mongol invasion of Muslim lands, not in the blood-thirsty character of Genghis Khan, but in the bad judgment of Eastern rulers who, in a now infamous incident, deliberately mutilated a party of Mongol merchants and seized their wares.[124] Indeed, the contrast between West and East provides the terms in which Ibn Battuta translates much of the world, for the audience for whom he "sees and makes seen" is first and foremost Maghribi. Much as a local newspaper would, Ibn Battuta converts local exchange values into Maghribi money; identifies the presence of Maghribis in stories he hears; duly notes any connections the locals have to the Maghrib; translates unfamiliar terms into language specific to Morocco; and measures all rulers against the virtues of Abu ʿInan, the Moroccan sultan who commissioned the *Rihla*. Moreover, he deploys a technique of symmetry to organize comparisons in terms of shared Maghribi knowledge, whether it is the workings of rivers (in al-Basra the tides are "the same as in Wadi Sala in the Maghrib");[125] the appearance of unfamiliar peoples ("their men are like us in appearance except that their mouths are like the mouths of dogs");[126] methods of preserving food; the structure of mosques; the treatment of prisoners; or religious practices. In a city in Yemen, far from home, he exclaims that

> among the marvels [here] is that the people of this city resemble more than any other the people of the Maghrib in their customs . . . [the Khatib] had slavegirls whose names were the same as female servants in the Maghrib . . . I have not heard these names in any other country. . . . and the master of each house prays exactly like the people of the Maghrib.[127]

In his reflections on what he regards as the inferior organization of Syrian and Egyptian markets and the fruits and meats available there, he writes:

If you consider all this, it will become evident to you that the lands of the Maghrib have the least expensive prices, the greatest abundance of resources, and the most conveniences and advantages. Indeed, God has amplified the glory and eminence of the lands of the Maghrib through the Imamate of our master, the Commander of the Faithful [the ruler of Morocco], who has spread the mantle of protection over all its territories, caused the sun of justice to rise over all its lands, the clouds to inundate the inhabitants of both country and city with good fortune, and has purged it of evildoers and established in it the practices of religious and secular life.[128]

Religious Frontiers

Crucial to Ibn Battuta's identification as *Maghribi* is his adherence to Islam, although what he regards as Islam proper is regionally and historically specific. Born into the notable class of Tangier, Ibn Battuta was a Sunni Muslim educated in the Maliki legal school that dominated the Maghrib at the time, and his *Rihla* also reveals an affinity for Sufism evident among both nonelites and ʿulama in Marinid-era Morocco (thirteenth to fifteenth centuries).[129] Ibn Battuta occasionally has generous things to say about Shafiʿi, Hanafi, or Hanbali (the other three schools of Sunni law) Muslims, but his interest lies elsewhere: he makes a point of identifying for his audience the Maliki jurists buried at a shrine in Cairo, and the Malikis he meets or hears about on his journeys.[130] He exhibits, moreover, a profound distaste for what he regards as the loathsome practices of Shiʿite Muslims; he repeatedly refers to them as *rafidis*, a term of contempt that literally means turncoat, renegade, or fanatic.[131] Such antipathy is not all that surprising in a Sunni traveler, but is perhaps sharpened in this instance by Malikism, which some regard as stricter than other *madhhabs* (legal schools), as well as by a history of struggles between Malikite and Shiʿite (Fatimid) dynasties in the Maghrib.[132] Although he does his best to avoid them on his journeys—at one point, he refuses to enter a town because its population is Shiʿite[133]—Ibn Battuta nevertheless insists on describing Shiʿites as extremist heretics with despotic and criminal tendencies. Relating a visit to a Shiʿite district in a Syrian city, for example, he characterizes the inhabitants as an "loathsome people who hate the Ten Companions, God be pleased with them and curse those who hate them."[134] Yet the extent of the "abominations" he generally encounters are the failure of a particular Shiʿi to wash himself ritually in the proper (i.e., Sunni) sequence, prayers that mention ʿAli, and the eating of hare.

The contours and content of Ibn Battuta's home are thus constituted by what is perhaps best described as concentric circles of geographical

and religious allegiance: to the city of Tangier, to the region of the
Maghrib, to Malikism in particular, and to Sunnism more generally.[135]
Such nested allegiances and the contrasts that give them definition
disclose the grid that governs his observations and provides, among
other things, the criteria by which he organizes, classifies, and judges
all that is familiar and unfamiliar. As in Herodotus's *Histories*, one of
the ways this grid surfaces is by way of those *ʿajaʾib* (marvels and wonders) Ibn Battuta singles out for notice. Early in his journey, for example, he refers to the wonders of the Pyramids and the many marvels
that unfold in Alexandria, but forbears to describe them, as they
would have been well known to his readers, and his description of
his later travels in al-Andalus is similarly brief. By contrast, near Sa-
wakin (in Sudan), Ibn Battuta relates the "wondrous" way the local
people catch fish by holding a large cloth across a sea-water channel;
describes in detail the people and practices of the Maldive islands,
"one of the wonders of the world"; extols at length the benefits of
the coconut, particularly its aphrodisiac properties; and anatomizes at
great length the behavior and reign of the Indian sultan Muhammad
ibn Tughluq, knowing full well that "some of these deeds will seem
impossible to the minds of many people and they will deem them as
quite implausible under normal conditions."[136]

Like a shadow of the worldly marvels he maps, there is also a sacred
geography in the *Rihla*, a record of all those *ayat* (literally "signs," but
here meaning divine marvels and miracles) Ibn Battuta experiences or
about which he hears from others. Following Miquel, this may be characterized as the move from a profane topography of what is visible to
a spiritual geography of the invisible, although again, such a "move"
is not a linear transition but rather a jagged dynamic that runs
throughout the *Rihla*.[137] Thus in keeping with his interest in mysticism,
from the very outset of the narrative, Ibn Battuta actively pursues *baraka*, a rich and complex term that not only means "blessing" but also
holiness and the charismatic and saintly power to confer blessings on
a supplicant, a people, or even an entire community.[138] Toward this
end, he seeks out holy men, shrines, and places associated with *baraka*
wherever he goes, and regards the experiences and blessings thereby
gained as a primary purpose for his travels. Yet the many "miracles"
he relates of this or that local *shaikh* or religious site are not only meant
to convey the piety of a holy man or the blessedness of a particular
place but also to certify Ibn Battuta as a trustworthy transmitter of such
sacred geography for his audience.

While many such miracles are reported to Ibn Battuta rather than experienced directly, there are several he claims to have seen for himself,
from a yogi levitating above the ground to a magical sandal he claimed

rose into the air and at the will of its master began beating another man on the neck.[139] The holy men whose abilities Ibn Battuta says he experienced directly include a *shaikh* in Alexandria who predicted Ibn Battuta would journey to India and China well before the traveler himself knew; another who foretold Ibn Battuta's itinerary by way of interpreting a dream; a *shaikh* whose prediction that Ibn Battuta would not be able to go to Mecca by way of Jedda was borne out; and yet another who advised Ibn Battuta to relinquish a slave boy who later killed his new master.[140] By contrast, he takes a stance of deliberate skepticism about what is related by or about Shiʿites—he ostentatiously declines, for example, to endorse the claim by the Shiʿites of Najaf that their mausoleum contains the grave of ʿAli,[141] being careful to note that while reputable people told him of cripples being cured there on a particular night, "I was not actually present on any such night."[142] He reports without qualification, however, the "miracles" related about numerous Sunni holy men, from one who foretold the exact moment of his own death to a story about a clean shaven *shaikh* who made a beard appear and disappear on his face in quick succession.[143]

Worldly and Otherworldly Entanglements

Commentators on the *Rihla* frequently argue that the desire for status and wealth must be counted among the central motivations for Ibn Battuta's travels. In this pursuit, he was hardly alone. As Lenker shows in his study of the *rihla* in Andalusia, travel to the learning centers of the East was so highly regarded it virtually became a requirement for ascending to the most coveted of public offices. Individuals were often anxious to establish themselves as 'seekers of knowledge' in part because "most of the public offices in Islamic Spain belonged to the *ahl al-rihla* [people who travel]."[144] By the same token, an Arab *qadi* of 'the Prophet's race' without extensive experience such as Ibn Battuta could ascend to much higher offices on the frontiers of the *Dar al-Islam* than closer to its venerated centers of learning.

In the *Rihla*, the extent to which travels confer on Ibn Battuta a certain elevated stature is evident in the amount of gifts and regard he accrues in the course of his journeys. As a Muslim traveler, of course, Ibn Battuta was often the recipient of those alms the Qurʾan and *hadith* exhort Muslims to confer on the neediest, including beggars, orphans, wayfarers, and *mujahidin* (those who struggle for *jihad*).[145] Yet in both the *Rihla* and in the Arabo-Islamic tradition in which it is embedded, voluntary offerings have multiple and overlapping political, psychological, material and religious valences, which are reflected in the multiple Arabic terms for "gift" itself, including *hiba, hadiyya*, and ʿ*ata*.[146] Thus as

Ibn Battuta's reputation as a learned *qadi* grows in the *Rihla*, he becomes progressively conscious of his reputation, protective of the prerogatives it confers, and insistent that the size and quality of the gifts he receives adequately reflect his worldly standing.[147]

He repeatedly assesses the virtue of local leaders and sultans in terms of generosity to him or lack thereof: he describes the *qadi* of Mecca as a man of excellent and generous character but complains elsewhere of kings who pretend to honor visiting scholars but offer meager donations.[148] Later he vilifies the son of the caliph in India as "the stingiest of God's creatures," relating the following exchange: "I said to [the caliph's son] 'It is incumbent upon you to praise God for His favor to you and to give alms to the poor and the needy . . .' But he said 'I am not able to do that,' and I never saw him being liberal with anything or doing a generous action—may God protect us from such miserliness!"[149] While couched in the language of piety, as Ibn Battuta's sense of his own importance grows, he comes to regard large gifts of money as part of a ritual of exchange that ratifies his self-image, in one instance turning down a gift deemed too small.[150] When the sultan of Mali presents him with a modest gift of food rather than the money and robes he expects, Ibn Battuta laughs derisively, "astonished at their feeble-mindedness and their overestimation of something so paltry."[151] When he finally gains an audience with the sultan, Ibn Battuta says: "I have traveled throughout the countries of the world and I have met their kings. I have been in your country for four months, but you have not treated me hospitably, and you have not offered me anything. What shall I say about you to (other) Sultans?"[152]

Ibn Battuta's expectations reflect and reinforce a deeper shift in his stature from pilgrim to power-broker over the course of his travels. In the early parts of the narrative, for example, Ibn Battuta often seeks out the local *shaikhs* and *amirs*, but as his reputation for learning grows, sultans and rulers increasingly send for him on his arrival to ask him about his adventures and what he has learned. He not only comes close to political power, on several occasions he ascends or aspires to significant rank himself: he is appointed *qadi* of Delhi, sent by the sultan as an ambassador to the Mongol rulers of China, and is made *qadi* in the Maldives, where he intrigues against the local *wazir*, stirring up a revolt against him. As his stature grows so does his sense of his own expertise in matters of Islamic law—at one point he claims about a local *qadi* that "he never did anything properly"—and his feeling of entitlement.[153] As he is about to set sail on his embassy to China, for example, Ibn Battuta refuses accommodations aboard a junk as inadequate for himself and his slave women to travel in privacy and comfort.[154]

Yet despite Ibn Battuta's manifest appreciation of money and the luxury it affords—his spending even prompts the sultan of Delhi to warn
him to regulate his finances and avoid more debts—he is repeatedly
tempted to withdraw from his participation in the world for a life of
austerity and reflection.[155] Indeed, a consistent feature of the *Rihla* is Ibn
Battuta's abiding interest in the ascetic life, part of the Sufism which,
along with Malikism, was central to his religious life and that of many
of his contemporaries with similar backgrounds, origins, and training.
At the outset of the *Rihla*, Ibn Battuta describes in unusually vivid terms
the intense yearning God has implanted in humans to seek "blessed
sights," and it is this very desire for spiritual wisdom that leads him to
seek out far-flung mystics and shrines, and to describe the voluntary
poverty, devotion, and asceticism of various holy men he meets or hears
about with great reverence.[156] At one point, for example, he is so overcome by the wisdom of a famous holy man residing in a cave outside
Delhi (the very man who had advised Ibn Battuta to dispense with the
slave who later killed his master) that "I pledged myself to him, with-
drawing from the world and giving away all that I had to the poor and
needy. I stayed with him for some time and I used to see him fast for
ten and twenty days at a time and remain standing most of the night."[157]
Later, chagrined at his financial mishaps, and shaken by a term of imprisonment for incurring the displeasure of the sultan of Delhi, he becomes a disciple of a famous holy man for a period of five months,
ridding himself of all his possessions and taking on the devotional rigors of a Sufi mystic.[158] Yet despite describing himself on one occasion as
envious of a man who was, with his wife, the sole inhabitant of an entire
island, Ibn Battuta's periods of withdrawal are short lived: he is drawn
back from a life of pious asceticism, repeatedly (in his words) "entan-
gled in the world" by the call of sultans, curiosity, love of pleasure, and
what he refers to as the "restiveness [*lajuj*] of my spirit."[159]

Credulity and Credibility

Ibn Battuta's worldly and other-worldly commitments not only constitute his home as the absent model in terms of which he selects and
translates his observations, they also establish the conditions of his credulity and credibility. Franz Rosenthal argues that, for Muslim travelers of the middle period, knowledge gained through firsthand experience had a virtually unmatched reliability, a presumption captured by
Ibn Khaldûn's assertion that the "transmission of things one has observed with one's own eyes is something more comprehensive and
complete than the transmission of information and things one has
learned about."[160] Much like Herodotus's use of autopsy, then, one of

the primary techniques by which Ibn Battuta attempts to establish himself as a trustworthy purveyor and translator of knowledge is direct
observation (ʿiyan), expressed variously and repeatedly in the text as
"I witnessed," "I myself saw," and "I was present" as a preface particularly to stories about places, peoples, and events his audience would
not have known. A particularly telling illustration is Ibn Battuta's repeated claim to have seen with his own eyes the behavior of the Indian
sultan, Muhammad Ibn Tughluq. Knowing full well that his audience
will not believe him, he claims more than once that his descriptions of
the bizarre behaviors of the sultan are based on "what I myself witnessed," and calls on every authority in the universe to buttress his
account:

> I call God and His Angels and His Prophets to witness that every-
> thing I will relate about his unsurpassed and extraordinary gener-
> osity is absolute truth, and God is a sufficient witness. I know that
> some of these deeds will seem impossible to the minds of many
> people and they will deem them as quite implausible under nor-
> mal circumstances; but in a matter which I have seen with my own
> eyes and which I know to be accurate, I cannot but speak the truth
> about it, and most of this is established by many independent au-
> thorities in the lands of the East.[161]

This passage not only evokes the authority of direct observation but
is also, as Gibb points out, "loaded with technical terms of the science
of transmission of the Prophetic tradition" designed to enhance the reliability of his observations and his stature as a purveyor of knowledge. Along with ʿiyan, oral transmission is a primary source of knowledge in the Rihla, one that would have been more than familiar to any
Muslim reader acquainted with the process by which hadith [reports]
about the words and deeds of Muhammad are authenticated by tracing
an unbroken chain of authorities (isnad) back to the Prophet himself.
As Matar points out, "the tradition of tawaatur (repetition with the
same content), which has been used in the establishment of Islam's
religious canons, widely served in the authentication as well as dissemination" of information through travel texts.[162] Along with those
things seen with one's own eyes, then memorized knowledge orally
transmitted directly from student to teacher was held in particularly
high regard, an esteem captured in the story told by the eleventh-cen-
tury traveler al-Beruni, in which Socrates is said to have replied to the
question of why he did not write books: "I do not transplant knowledge from the living hearts of human beings to the dead skins of
sheep."[163]

When Ibn Battuta relates an event he has not experienced directly,
he invokes this model of knowledge to establish the authority of what

he says or of what he has learned, repeatedly prefacing his accounts with "I was told by trustworthy people," "I heard from reliable sources," "it is related on the authority of this *shaikh*" or, in some cases, by explicitly tracing a chain of authorities, for example, back to the original author of a book to establish its value, or to demonstrate the stature of a *shaikh* who incorporated him into the Suhrawardi order.[164] At one point, Ibn Battuta asks a learned man about the authenticity of the sacred graves in Hebron: "He said to me: 'All the scholars I have met attest to the fact that these graves are indeed the tombs of Abraham, Isaac, and Jacob and their wives. No one challenges this but heretics; it has been passed along without question from generation to generation.'"[165] For Ibn Battuta, even the most extraordinary of miracles are worthy of unqualified retelling provided they are transmitted to him by learned holy men whose piety, knowledge, lineage, stature, and *baraka* render their reliability beyond question.

Along with testimony of direct observation and reliable oral transmission, like Herodotus, Ibn Battuta also attempts to establish his credibility by deliberately disclosing the operations of his own critical skepticism for the benefit of his audience, as when he states that a story he has related is clearly false but worth reporting because it is widely told; distrusts a story of a yogi who could transform himself into a tiger; and in Ceylon reports quite bluntly that those who claim the leaves of an ancient tree can confer youth on even the oldest of men are lying.[166] On several occasions, Ibn Battuta distrusts what he hears because his own direct observation contradicts it, as when he meets a Turkish holy man who is said to be 350 years old but sees for himself that "his body is as fresh and smooth as any that I have seen" casting doubt on all the *shaikh* says thereafter.[167] Or on another occasion Ibn Battuta adjudicates between two different stories about the sultan of Turkestan, saying that the story of his death is clearly false for "I saw him, in fact, in the land of India."[168] On many other occasions, however, Ibn Battuta's consistent distrust of myths, miracles, and facts related by Christians, Jews, Shi'ites, and most other "infidels" mirrors closely the perhaps less-well-known theological partisanship of his fellow Maghribi Ibn Khaldûn, who cautions in the *Muqaddimah* against the "insincerity and trickery" of the Jews and repeatedly invokes al-Mas'udi, a Shi'ite, as the prime example of someone who transmits ridiculous tales.[169]

Nested Polarities, Multiple Frontiers

Ibn Battuta's adherence to strict Malikism, coupled with his preference for Maghribi *nomoi* and a reverence for the austerity and devotional rigors of mysticism, constitute the specific features of what he regards simply as "Islam," and provide the criteria by which he differentiates between virtue and immorality, justice and tyranny wherever he goes. He characterizes the virtue of an individual, for example, in terms of generosity, affection for strangers, asceticism, piety, cleanliness, courage, rigorous devotion to and knowledge of what are to him the only correct precepts of Islam. Singled out for criticism are those who are ambitious, greedy, who deny the authority of Islam, voice heretical thoughts, sow discord among Muslims, steal from others, or engage in violence for personal gain. He establishes the features of just rule by way of similar standards: sultans worthy of his praise include those who are generous (particularly to Ibn Battuta), humble, welcome foreigners (particularly Ibn Battuta), respect holy men and descendants of the Prophet, suppress factionalism, reject bribes, attend directly to the needs of the people (particularly the poorest among them), apply (Sunni) Islamic law rigorously, fight infidels successfully, and have knowledge of government affairs. Conversely, unjust are those rulers who are miserly, arrogant, brutal, and ambitious; fail to protect Muslims and pilgrims; indulge in wine, music, and dance; are too solicitous of infidel practices or adhere to or impose the wrong version of Islam.[170] The responsibility of the ruler to the ruled and ruled to ruler is thus measured by adherence to the letter or spirit of the *shari'a* and not, for example, to the terms of a political contract. Thus in one instance, Ibn Battuta tells of the virtuous citizens of Herat who, under the leadership of a particular *shaikh* they revered, took it upon themselves to punish their own king for having consumed wine contrary to law.[171]

Ibn Battuta's judgments are informed by this grid wherever he goes, but his observations are refracted through nested polarities organized around increasingly broader allegiances the closer he comes to the borders of the *Dar al-Islam*. I have suggested that, in the heart of the Muslim world, the primary (although not exclusive) terms of comparison are East/West, Maliki/non-Maliki, and Sunni/Shi'ite; there is even, pace Herodotus, a differentiation between nomads and sedentary peoples, a distinction also central to Ibn Khaldûn's arguments about the dynamic by which dynasties rise and fall.[172] But beyond and along the very borders of the *umma*, the binaries that increasingly come into play are those of Muslim and infidel, Arab and non-Arab, white and black. In Ceylon, for example, Ibn Battuta points out the absence of any Muslims at all; in India he notes that while in "Muslim lands every tree is owned, in the infidel lands most of them are not"; and by the time he gets to Bengal, he is comparing the locals not to Maghribis and Malikis, but to Turks and Egyptians.[173] Indeed, Ibn Battuta relates an exchange where a local Bengali *shaikh* of some repute identifies him as no less than "the traveler of the Arabs." This prompts one of the *shaikh's* companions to add, "'And of the non-Arabs/barbarians, my master.' He said, 'And of the non-Arabs/barbarians. Treat him with respect.'"[174] In China, the *Rihla* identifies Ibn Battuta simply as one who has "come from the lands of Islam."[175]

For a Maghribi raised in the shadow of the Christian *Reconquista*, the frontier between Muslim and non-Muslim—or in Ibn Battuta's words, infidel and Muslim—is both proximate and bloody; early parts of the *Rihla* are haunted by recollections of Crusader violence and fear of fresh attacks from the north or east. Yet as the *Rihla* reveals, such frontiers are not only at the edges of the *Dar al-Islam* but also within it: the radical shifts in borders occasioned by Christian and Muslim incursions, coupled with the mobility of merchants of all faiths, produced many sites—cities, ships, holy places—in which Christians and Muslims coexisted, mingled, and collaborated. As Netton notes in analyzing the *Rihla* of Ibn Jubayr, here was a "strange age of real intercultural *travel and trading* produced by centuries of co-operation, on the one hand, co-existing beside very real intercultural *military* strife produced by the Crusades, on the other."[176] Thus the *Rihla* is full of encounters with Christians both beyond and within the *Dar al-Islam*, and Ibn Battuta makes clear exactly what he thinks of them and their beliefs. He accuses them of lying outright about, for example, the Church of the Holy Sepulchre containing the grave of Jesus.[177] And he is on occasion repulsed by European appearance: of the Rus (Russians) he says, "They are Christians, and they have blonde hair, blue eyes, a repulsive appearance and are treacherous people."[178]

Yet Ibn Battuta also notes the coexistence of Muslim and Christian traders in Alexandria, acknowledges Christian hospitality to all comers in Bethlehem, travels in a Genoese vessel where the "Christians treated us honorably and took no payment from us," is moved by the sight of Christians who had renounced worldly pleasures for an ascetic life, and impressed by the ecumenism of a monk in Constantinople who greets Ibn Battuta not as an alien but as a fellow traveler in faith.[179] Ibn Battuta not only registers such differences among Christians but is also sufficiently well aware of Jews, many of whom spoke Arabic, to dislike them: while he relies, for example, on a Jewish translator in Constantinople, he distrusts the words of a Jewish traveler and expresses hostility about the elevated status of the Jewish physician to a Muslim sultan.[180] Such distinctions may be contrasted, for example, with an apparent lack of awareness on Ibn Battuta's part of the difference between Hinduism and Buddhism in India.[181]

Yet even the opposition between Muslim and non-Muslim is fluid and is mapped in several ways in the *Rihla*. It is rendered as geographical frontier, as when Ibn Battuta, spurred by insatiable curiosity to "see Constantinople the Great for myself," travels to the edge of the *Dar al-Islam* in the company of Princess Bayalun.[182] Christian daughter of the Byzantine emperor, Bayalun had been married off to a Mongol khan for strategic reasons and sought to return to Constantinople to give birth to her child in the land of her father. In the company of the princess and her entourage, Ibn Battuta writes of leaving the last town populated by (Muslim) Turks, and of entering into a protracted journey through "uninhabited waste" that marks entry into the land of the *Rum*, by which Ibn Battuta here means (Christian) Byzantine Greeks, but which he often uses to refer to Christians in general (rather than *al-ifranj*, Latin Christians, see chapter 4).[183] This geographical "wasteland" is a prelude to a wilderness of a more profound nature, however, for no sooner had the company entered Byzantine land than the princess, having had to adopt Muslim ways in her husband's household, immediately reverts to Christian practices, much to Ibn Battuta's great distress:

> She left her mosque behind at this fortress, and the regimen of prayer came to an end. Alcohol was brought to her as hospitality, and she would drink it; pork [was brought to her as well] and one of her slaves told me she ate it . . . once we entered the land of the infidels, deep feelings [long] concealed were disclosed.[184]

On reaching Constantinople, he is initially denied entrance at the city gates. Admitted by intervention of the princess, and then granted permission by King Andronicus III to "see with my own eyes its wonders and marvels and tell of them back in my own country," Ibn Battuta experiences the city as a succession of multiple if unseen barriers: he is hemmed in by the unwelcome peal of church bells, nonplused by pictures of "creatures, both animate and inanimate," and denied entry to the Hagia Sophia, by his account because he refuses to "prostrate himself before the mighty cross."[185]

Racial Frontiers

Such frontiers are also mapped by skin color, as becomes particularly clear during his two trips to sub-Saharan Africa, the first a journey of only a few months down the coast of East Africa (in either 1329 or 1331) and the second a two-year visit to the Mali Empire in West Africa (about 1352–54).[186] As Dunn points out, the towns of West Africa, like those of East Africa "occupied a geographic frontier; in this case the transitional zone between the great desert and the quite densely populated grassland belt of West Africa that the Arab geographers called the *bilad al-Sudan,* or lands of black people."[187] Yet for Ibn Battuta, *bilad al-Sudan* also constitutes a kind of racial frontier. Throughout the *Rihla*, Ibn Battuta identifies a people or a particular person he encounters as being black in color, but it is in Africa that a black/white distinction emerges explicitly: here he identifies himself and others as "white people" [*al-bidan*] in contrast to many others he refers to alternately by specific names (e.g., Barbara, Zunuj, Massufa) and more often, simply as black people [*al-Sudan*].[188] He notes, for example, that the "black people [*al-Sudan*] do not meddle with the possessions of a white person [*al-abyad*]" in Niger and identifies a particular man as "imam of the mosque of the white people."[189]

The language Ibn Battuta uses largely suggests that skin color is a difference without distinction: he writes of black rulers he likes and dislikes, relates the story of a black man who saved him from a crocodile and describes the *qadi* of Mali as "a black person, a *hajj* [one who has made the pilgrimage], distinguished and with a noble character."[190] But it is also the case that he often rests his judgment of various African townspeople on their treatment of (largely Arab) whites. In his visit to the northernmost province of *bilad al-Sudan*, for example, Ibn Battuta "regretted having come to their country, because of their lack of manners and their contempt for white people."[191] He describes as generous and virtuous a ruler of Mali who "loved white people and did them favors."[192] And at the conclusion of his extensive reflections on Mali, he notes with appreciation the fact that "they do not meddle with the possessions of white people who died in their lands . . . rather they leave it in the hands of a reliable white person until the legitimate heir takes it."[193]

It is tempting to see in these sections of the *Rihla* the racialization of identity characteristic of much modern and contemporary politics, one that begins to emerge, for example, in the nineteenth-century *rihla* central to the following chapter. Indeed, Eve Troutt Powell's analysis of the ways in which nineteenth-century Egyptian nationalism came to be linked to race seems in some ways applicable to Ibn Battuta's fourteenth-century observations. She writes: "race is an important marker of difference [for these writers], who painstakingly noted racial differences in skin color, sexual behavior and religious attitudes among the Sudanese" thereby illustrating "how an increasing sense of racial difference could be incorporated into a sense of political and cultural boundaries."[194] Yet there are important differences between the significance Ibn Battuta seems to attribute to variation in skin color and the contemporary meanings of "race" and "racialize."

Ibn Battuta's reactions to *bilad al-Sudan* are always doubled, reflecting a complex dialectic of racial, ethnic, and linguistic difference and religious and moral commonality. On the one hand, as Ibn Battuta moves from town to town, he notes various black Africans' "lack of manners and their contempt for white people" along with their "disgusting practices"; expounds the view that they are "of all people the most submissive to their king and the most obsequious to him"; and comments with disdain on a number of their customs, particularly with regard to Sudanese women who are not only uncovered but brazenly naked, without modesty and, by implication, lacking in virtue.[195] Many of his responses reflect the shock and somewhat priggish disapproval of a Maghribi trained in Maliki law to the syncretic blending of Islamic rituals and local cultural practices, and to "infidel" behavior of any kind. Such reactions are fully consistent with an antipathy to any religious heterodoxy he does not himself practice generally characteristic of the entire *Rihla*.[196] On the other hand, rather than serving as a consistent marker of political and cultural borders, race recedes in the *Rihla* amidst the commonality of religious practice; Ibn Battuta expresses unreserved admiration for those peoples of *bilad al-Sudan* who are not infidel, Shiʿite, or insufficiently rigorous adherents to the letter of Sunni law. For example, he appreciatively notes the unusually strong sense of justice he sees there, the security of their lands, the cleanliness of their garments on Friday, their careful observance of the details of prayer and commitment to memorizing the Qurʾan.[197] For Ibn Battuta, then, religion rather than race is largely the measure of civilization and humanity, where religion and (his version of) Islam are, of course, synonymous.

Decoding Culture through Gender

In *bilad al-Sudan*, Ibn Battuta's comments on women reflect the intersection of gender and cultural differences, but throughout the *Rihla*, he repeatedly measures strangeness by way of the appearance and behavior of the women he encounters. Indeed, Ibn Battuta's representation of women in part constitutes the contours of all other polarities governing the narrative, for they often function as a kind of legend, as on a map, by which his male audience can decode the *Rihla's* taxonomy of peoples and cultures.[198] One dimension of this legend is disclosed by when and where women remain largely absent: early in the *Rihla*, wives and slave-women flicker only briefly at the edges of the narrative, quickly disappearing without further mention. According to Remke Kruk, medieval Arab authors showed little interest in women's affairs and were particularly reticent about "women that belong to the family circle, those who were, by various devices and more or less strictly (depending on social position, period and place) screened off from the public sphere to which literature by its very nature belongs."[199] While the early parts of the *Rihla* largely conform to this convention, as Ibn Battuta travels farther afield, any reticence about the women attached to him gives way to ever lengthier disquisitions on the subject, as in his description of one of his wives in the Maldives as "the most wonderful of women, so mature in [sexual] intimacies that when I married her, she used to perfume me and suffuse my garments with incense while laughing and not showing any discomfort."[200] When women do appear, and they increasingly do, they are largely refracted through sets of binaries—veiled and naked, visible and secluded, aristocrats and slaves, learned and illiterate, rich and poor, autonomous and obedient—that overlap and intertwine.[201]

In the representation of high-born women or those known to be particularly pious or holy, it initially seems as if the same grid is being brought to bear on women as on men: Ibn Battuta has only praise for the various princesses and high ranking women he meets who are particularly generous with their money and devout in their adherence to Sunni Islam, and instantly dislikes those who are "tight-fisted," linking, as usual, miserliness to impiety. He relates with deference the occasional reports he hears about learned female mystics and pilgrims, in one instance telling the story of a woman so pious she refused to wear a robe looked upon by any man other than her husband and family.[202] Yet Ibn Battuta's focus on what he regards as proper religious observance also fuels a consistent preoccupation with women's sexual behavior and appearance, and a concomitant tendency to transform women into an index of the virtue or value of an entire people, as when he deems the citizens of Shiraz particularly pious because of the modesty and purity of their women.[203]

While women are largely reduced to bodies whose very piety is measured by their sexual unavailability—often measured by their physical occlusion (by clothing) or seclusion—as Ibn Battuta's interest in sexual pleasure becomes central to his experiences of unfamiliar places and cultures, the emphasis shifts, and women's sexual availability as well as their unusual erotic skills become increasingly paramount. Thus he takes four wives in the Maldives (the maximum allowed by Islamic law), swears that he lived only on coconuts known as aphrodisiacs for his entire year and a half stay there, and describes the women of Marhata as having "in sexual intercourse a deliciousness and a knowledge of erotic movements that other women do not have."[204] There is a concomitant decrease in attention as to whether or not the women in question are his wives or slaves, non-Muslims or Muslims; at one point he even seems to forget his dislike of infidels when he reports that the women of a particular Hindu people are "of surpassing beauty, and famous for their deliciousness in sexual intercourse and the abundance of pleasure that they give."[205] Unconstrained by any purported opposition between body and soul, Ibn Battuta frequently represents women as objects of sexual pleasure, indices of piety, or both at once. Indeed, women's piety, generosity, and beauty (or lack thereof) often seem mutually constitutive, as in one instance when he describes Meccan women as "strikingly beautiful, pious, and chaste," the sanctuaries they visit suffused with their intoxicating perfume, and at another describes Yemeni women as particularly virtuous, beautiful, and willing to marry strangers, unlike Maghribi women.[206] By contrast, when Ibn Battuta conceives a dislike for the favorite wife of a sultan he deems miserly, he disbelieves reports that the sultan prefers her because of her unusually configured vagina, which makes him "experience her every night like a virgin."[207]

Delighted to benefit from women's sexual services in private, Ibn Battuta heaps disdain on those people, places, and cultures whose women exhibit what he regards as immodesty, ambition, or inappropriate levels of public autonomy and control. Ibn Battuta notes with distaste, for example, the uncovered Mongol ladies who openly contribute to the enterprise of governing alongside the men and remarks with contempt of a well-heeled and unveiled Turkish woman and her husband that "anyone seeing him would take him for one of her man-servants."[208] He is scandalized by women allowed to go unveiled in Sumatra and by naked women in Mali; disgusted by the wives of Turks [al-atrak] who seek to outbid each other for jewels in the local market ("what I saw of all this was shameful—may God protect us from it!") while their husbands look on; and refuses invitations to visit a man who cultivates friendships with women who are not his family members.[209] Such representations are repeated in the Rihla's many stories detailing the havoc wrought by uncontrolled women who, like the lustful women of some Arabo-Islamic medieval literature, "stop at nothing [and] . . . violate spatial and other boundaries to satisfy their desires."[210] This is evident in one story in the Rihla in which a pious man castrates himself rather than submitting to a woman's lust, and another in which a jealous wife of a sultan poisons him for marrying another woman and is beaten to death for it. Yet another tale is of a woman who is made sultana because of her wisdom, and rides among her men unveiled, only to be deposed and married off after being accused of sleeping with her slave.[211]

While women operate in the Rihla as a legend to decode the unfamiliar, the terms of the legend are not always consistent as this is, after all, a travel narrative populated by actual friends, family, wives, teachers, slaves, robbers, kings, and princesses as well as by literary tropes. For example, Ibn Battuta's early reticence about women and his highly sexualized representation of them throughout is tempered by the opening lines of the *Rihla* that refer to his dear ones "both female and male," his repeated expression of concern for *both* his father and mother, and his celebration of the birth of a daughter. As Kruk argues, the invocation of both father and mother here is fairly unusual, and the "birth of a girl is rarely mentioned in Arabic sources in a positive connotation."[212] Moreover, there are occasions in the narrative that offset somewhat the relentless emphasis on women's (mis)behavior, as in one story about a sultan's sister who dies by her husband's violence after her numerous complaints about him were ignored. There are still other such moments, from a story Ibn Battuta tells in which a *qadi* successfully intervenes on behalf of a mistreated wife to Ibn Battuta's description of the practice of *suttee* (widow burning) he witnesses in India as transpiring in a "place in hell—God protect us from it."[213]

Techniques of Representation

Along with the classification of ʿajaʾib and *ayat*, all of these nested polarities—East/West, infidel/Muslim, Shiʿite/Sunni, women/men, black/white—comprise the grid in terms of which Ibn Battuta represents a shifting panoply of others for his audience of primarily literate Maghribi Muslim men. They constitute the *Rihla's* conditions of intelligibility, for they determine both the principle of selection—what is worth telling and what is not, what is trustworthy and what is not—and the strategies Ibn Battuta deploys to establish his own authority and the reliability of the narrative he conveys. In other words, the grid disclosed by Ibn Battuta's techniques of representation provide the terms in which the narrative's practices of translation operate: they organize and delimit what he sees and how he sees it. As in his representation of women, much of this grid is disclosed not only by how he represents those peoples and places worth relating, but also by what he fails to see or represent, including those moments of blindness occasioned by mistranslation or by practices of translation that render entire classes of people all but invisible.[214]

Most obviously, as a *qadi* of the legal class concerned with miracles, curiosities, money, and status, Ibn Battuta scarcely notes the poor, ordinary, and powerless in his narrative, even when it is evident that his own comfort is predicated on their existence, mobility, and labor. Despite his extensive stay in India, moreover, Ibn Battuta registers little awareness either of the distinction between Hindus and Buddhists, or of the existence of the caste system all around him. He grossly misunderstands African customs, interpreting conflict over an attempt by one sultan to displace a queen of royal blood in favor of his (younger) consort as the jealousy of wives competing for a man's favor, and ridicules the behavior and appearance of what he terms the "poets" at the court in Mali when, as Noël King argues, these "'poets' are none other than the great Manding *griots*, bards, remembrancers, who recall to the king his ancestors and their deeds, who by *anamnēsis*, make the ancestors really present; their costumes give them the corporate *personae* of their role as persons bodying forth spirits."[215]

Such "blindness" reaches a crescendo during Ibn Battuta's stay in China, at which time he literally retreats into his abode in an attempt insulate himself from what he does not wish to see:

> Despite all that is good in it, the land of China did not appeal to me. On the contrary, I was profoundly offended that unbelief was so widespread there. Whenever I left my house, I used to see many abominable things and that so upset me that I used to stay at home and would not leave unless it was absolutely necessary. When I would see Muslims, it was as if I had come across my family and kin.[216]

Yet this passage also demonstrates that it is precisely in the context of widening ethnic, religious, and linguistic differences that moments of intense identification with other Muslims in far-flung locales can and do erupt, as in his encounter with a group of otherwise unfamiliar Turkish-speaking Muslims: "the delight and joy they displayed at our presence was remarkable, even though we did not know each other's language and no one was there who could translate for us."[217] Elsewhere in the lands of the Turks where large Christian and Muslim populations mingled, he encounters Hanafi Muslims who, despite linguistic and cultural barriers, clearly touch Ibn Battuta deeply:

> This region known as *Bilad al-Rum* is one of the loveliest in the world; in it God has gathered together the virtues scattered throughout other lands: its people are the most beautiful, their clothes the cleanest, their food the most delicious, and they are the kindest of God's creatures. . . . Wherever we stayed in this land, whether in hospice or home, our neighbors, both men and women who do not veil themselves came to check on our comfort. When we departed, they took leave of us as if we were their relatives and of their people, and you could see women weeping with sorrow at our departure.[218]

One could argue that these instances evince more xenophobia than xenophilia, that Ibn Battuta's vision is so constrained by an unexamined allegiance to a particular version of Islam that he ignores or flees from all that is not Muslim because, in one scholar's description, he is "incapable of conceiving that that which he does not know or has not seen could be a different world, alongside that of Islam. That world can only be foreign and negative, sometimes even the reverse of Islam which is his only reference."[219] Yet just as Herodotus's *Histories* is not simply organized by way of a fixed opposition between Greeks and barbarians, the *Rihla's* representation of others is not exhausted by the polarity between Muslim and non-Muslim, nor are these categories uniform, static, or unyielding. For example, Ibn Battuta's representation of those cultures in which women behave inappropriately is complicated by very different moments, particularly toward the end of the *Rihla*. Such moments range from a generous account of a brave warrior princess who rides forth among her men unveiled, to his description of the practices of the Massufa people (in Sudan) only as "remarkable" and "strange," despite the fact that there he witnessed women unveiled, friendships among unmarried men and women, and a heterodox mixing of Sunni law and matrilineal practices.[220]

Or to take another example: inasmuch as Ibn Battuta takes sexual companionship along his journeys for granted, wives and slaves often appear in the narrative as just so much baggage, mere markers of his status whose own wishes are beyond consideration. To this extent, the *Rihla* appears to disclose a pattern of female travel forced or occasioned by male mobility that scholars have located throughout history and across culture, which I will discuss in chapter 5.[221] Yet there are many instances where the *Rihla* records the refusal of a woman to travel against her will, as in the Yemeni women who "never leave their communities and even if one of them were offered a sum if she would leave her land, she would not do it,[222] and one of Ibn Battuta's Indian wives whom he divorced when she was unwilling to leave her home. The narrative also tells of an occasional woman, usually of high rank, who travels of her own volition, from a woman who made the pilgrimage, to another who traveled extensively for learning to the Princess Bayalun, who travels back from the Mongol court of her husband to her family in Constantinople.[223]

There is no question that the narrative discloses a palpable discomfort when Ibn Battuta moves into lands beyond the *Dar al-Islam*. Yet as a deeply devout Muslim with a particular deference for the ascetic life, he is also able to recognize in the Christian ascetics of Constantinople a beauty and commonality amidst radical difference.[224] He further shares a moment of tremendous sadness with the Christian *khatun* married to the Mongol sultan, who weeps in sympathy and compassion for his experience of homelessness which she knew so well.[225] He conveys how the entire population of Damascus—Jews, Christians, and Muslims—joined together in a mosque to grieve and pray for relief from the Black Death ravaging the city.[226] And much like Herodotus,

Ibn Battuta's experiences and exposures along his travels occasion reflections about the power of destiny and the uncertainty of fate that
commands all human existence, as in his observation that "here is a
lesson one should contemplate: mighty is He who changes [all] things
and transforms [all] conditions."[227] Finally, despite his intense awareness of the frontiers between the *Dar al-Islam* and the lands of Christendom, for example, the *Rihla* groups Muslim and infidel alike within
a common humanity itself bordered by a final frontier beyond which
exist only cannibals and unrecognizable wasteland.[228]

Conclusion

Analysis of Herodotus's *Histories* as a window onto the Greeks' representation of the world rather than as a document about actual non-
Greeks is part and parcel of a burgeoning inquiry into the political,
ideological, linguistic, and material mechanisms by which the West has
at once constituted and silenced a diverse array of cultural Others. As
I have suggested by argument and example in the previous chapters,
the *rihla* genre is an occasion to invert and thus expand the questions
that have governed such inquiries, transforming analyses of the various Others produced by Western travel writing into an exploration of
the features of travel, translation, and theory from multiple directions.
Yet this chapter has also illustrated how and where the very terms with
which I have framed this inquiry become unstable: Herodotus's status
as Greek and Western is not quite secure; the non-Greeks in his *Histories* are far from consistently "barbarian"; the *Rihla*'s opposition between Muslim and non-Muslim dissolves into other polarities that
shift and recombine; *theôria* and *rihla* serve less as markers of fixed and
discreet cultural traditions than conceptual bridges across time and
space; and the techniques of representation constitutive of what Hartog terms Herodotus's "code of power" are just as crucial to the *Rihla*
as they are to this foundational text of "Western History."

    One crucial implication of these arguments, then, is that the mecha-
nisms by which travelers make sense of and domesticate the world are
no more Western than mobility itself. Indeed, the juxtaposition of these
two travelers and narratives in particular brings into sharp relief the
multiple and varied sites, occasions, and conditions under which practices of translation emerge. In this connection it is worth considering
that, in the annals of great travelers, Ibn Battuta is often given second
billing to Marco Polo, who ventured far afield of his Italian home and
"Christian lands."[229] Unlike the Venetian traveler, Ibn Battuta's journeys
were largely within and along the borders of the *Dar al-Islam*, literally

the "whole territory in which the law of Islam prevails," but in practice encompassing those lands in which there was a significant Muslim population, and particularly those ruled by Muslims.[230] Much as ancient Greek pilgrimage facilitated the emergence of a sense of pan-Hellenic unity never realized politically, it is often argued that Muslim pilgrimage in general, and Ibn Battuta's *Rihla* in particular, illustrate how travel within the *Dar al-Islam* facilitates identification with a larger *umma* at the expense of allegiances both to local potentates whose authority was often limited and unstable and to a wider humanity beyond the Muslim world.[231] An account of travel *within* Muslim lands for a Muslim audience might seem to obviate the need for those practices of translation across radical difference that are so evident in Herodotus's representation of non-Greeks for Greek consumption.

Yet at the time of Ibn Battuta's travels, the *Dar al-Islam* in many ways represented a highly cosmopolitan civilization, loosely linked territory through which a remarkable array of peoples moved and interacted without the hindrance of the fixed borders of the modern nation-state. Indeed, historian Marshall Hodgson provides a periodization of Islamic history that dates the greatest expansion of Islam as both a creed and a social order from ce 1000 to 1500.[232] Spurred in part by the advance of Turkic-speaking Muslims into Asia Minor and India and extensive migration of Muslim merchants in all directions, by the sixteenth century, the area of the *Dar al-Islam* had tripled, eventually incorporating lands as seemingly far-flung as Southeast and Central Asia, India, China, Europe, and sub-Saharan Africa.[233] Historians have identified in the *Dar al-Islam* of this time a transhemispheric Afro-Eurasian civilization in almost continuous intercommunication by way of an extraordinary fluidity of people and knowledge across political, cultural, and linguistic boundaries.[234] The result was an association of diverse peoples that "came closer than any other medieval society to establishing a common world order of social and even cultural standards."[235] "Almost everywhere," Hodgson writes, "political boundaries, never fundamental within the *Dar al-Islam*, were of even less importance in this period than ever before or after."[236] If extensive mobility and exchange characterized this epoch in general, Ibn Battuta journeyed in a period of time when conditions were particularly conducive to transregional travel: the carnage of the Mongol invasions had given way to relatively stable rule by khans voluntarily converting to Islam, and the bubonic plague had not yet ravaged the medieval world.[237]

Thus just as the features of contemporary globalization are often said to sharpen experiences of difference and commonality simultaneously, the *Dar al-Islam* of this period signaled not cultural or linguistic

homogeneity but a common framework of faith in which radical heterogeneity flourished—what Bamyeh has described as a heteroglossic
global civil society characterized by "unity imagined" rather than
"disunity proclaimed."[238] Although many studies of the intersection
of travel and identity formation tend to focus on the engagement of
non-Western cultures with the West, here is a crucial moment in which
we see how the "encounter with the Muslim 'other' has been at least
as important for self-definition as the confrontation with the European
'other.'"[239] More specifically, Ibn Battuta's journeys within and along
the boundaries of the *Dar al-Islam* provide an opportunity to see the
ways in which critical reflection as well as narrowness of vision is
borne of encounters with multiple "Others," where otherness is defined both *against and through* regional, racial, religious, ethnic, linguistic, and sexual differences somewhat closer to home. Here "the
West" is neither Europe nor America, but the "strange" and "remote"
Maghrib; here center and periphery, heartland and frontier are
mapped in relation to the historical seat of Muslim learning, creativity,
and power in the "Islamic East," rather than in relation to Europe;
here Christians, Jews, various Europeans and other non-Muslims
"from the outside" meld into flows of traffic within the *Dar al-Islam*
just as Muslim travelers are regularly conveyed by eddies of movement beyond its familiar environs.[240]

It is against this backdrop and in these terms that Ibn Battuta translates a shifting panoply of unfamiliar peoples and practices for his audience, and the techniques of representation he employs discloses
what I have argued it means to theorize comparatively. Ibn Battuta has
been characterized as a "geographer in spite of himself,"[241] and the
Rihla described as everything from history to literature to a compen-
dium of lies. The point here is not to now claim that the *Rihla* is above
all a text of political theory; rather it is a window onto what I have
called those theoretical moments that erupt erratically in ordinary
lives, those less than grand encounters with what is strange and estranging that occasion practices of mediation between rootedness and
distance, familiar and unfamiliar. As I have argued that theory is inherently comparative, and comparisons entail acts of translation that simultaneously make sense of and distort the unfamiliar, the *Rihla* is an
instance "when the subdued counterpoint between the external and
internal worlds becomes sufficiently audible for us to listen in."[242] As
in the *Histories*, what is audible in the *Rihla* is a dyadic rhythm, a recurrent juxtaposition of two terms, the nature and content of which shift
depending on context. These features express a form of representational power—the Turks, Shi'ites, and Chinese of the *Rihla* no more
speak for themselves than do Herodotus's Scythians—yet such dyads

also constitute the *Rihla's* conditions of intelligibility: they constrain Ibn Battuta's view of the world but also make it possible to locate echoes between the known and unknown, between new terrain and the features of "home" the traveler carries wherever she or he goes.

More specifically, fidelity to a regionally and historically specific version of Islam presumed to be "Islam proper" is one of the primary techniques Ibn Battuta employs to classify, compare, and judge other Muslims and designate outsiders, whether it is the rule of a sultan, the comportment of a small town *shaikh*, or the behavior of the local women. The strategies by which Ibn Battuta classifies the unfamiliar by way of gradations of distance from the "real Islam" thus constitute his home at the epicenter of the known world, and his Maghribi audience as the absent model in terms of which all others are compared. In a sense, then, the *Rihla*, like the *Histories*, affirms and enacts Herodotus's admission that all men deem their own *nomoi* superior to others (III:38). Yet just as the *Histories* reveals a much more complex, polyvalent, and dynamic understanding of Greek *nomoi* and Herodotus's relationship to them than Hartog's structuralist analysis allows, so do the very contours of Ibn Battuta's home change as his itinerary brings him into proximity with various geographic, religious, linguistic, cultural, and racial frontiers. This interplay between home and frontier, moreover, takes a jagged rather than linear course, an exemplification of what Abderrahmane El Moudden aptly calls the "ambivalence of *rihla*," that is, the ways in which *rihla fi talab al-ʿilm* simultaneously links travelers to the larger Muslim community and intensifies a sense of locality. Ibn Battuta's *Rihla* discloses precisely this dialectic of local and cosmopolitan identity, and in particular expresses those centripetal forces that enable a learned native of Tangier to feel united in a single community with Muslims in Delhi, and the centrifugal forces that define and sharpen his sense of place and attachment to "home."[243]

Chapter 4

TRAVEL IN SEARCH OF PRACTICAL WISDOM

THE MODERN *THEÔRIAI* OF AL-TAHTAWI

AND TOCQUEVILLE

IN ALEXANDRIA on April 13, 1826, a twenty-four-year old Egyptian by the name of Rifaʿa Rafiʿ al-Tahtawi boarded the French ship *La Truite* bound for Marseilles.[1] Al-Tahtawi was joined on board by forty-four others selected by Egypt's leader, Muhammad ʿAli (d.1849), to be part of a student mission to Paris. Due to the efforts of a well-placed mentor, al-Tahtawi had landed the enviable position of *imam* (religious leader) to the mission, one of the first of many such excursions engineered by the ambitious Muhammad ʿAli in his quest to acquire new European knowledge. Trained at al-Azhar, Egypt's preeminent mosque and university, al-Tahtawi's function was to provide religious guidance to his young, predominantly Muslim, fellow travelers as they delved into the alien cultural world of postrevolutionary Catholic France.[2] In the course of his sojourn in Paris, however, al-Tahtawi transformed himself from *imam* to avid student: without prior knowledge of French, he immersed himself in the language, politics, and culture of the city, an effort that culminated in the only firsthand account of the mission, a *rihla* titled *Takhlis al-Ibriz ila Talkhis Bariz* (The Extraction of Gold from a Distillation of Paris, 1834). *Takhlis* marked the beginning of what would ultimately be a long and productive career in government service in which al-Tahtawi eventually oversaw two thousand translations of European and Turkish works into Arabic, earning him posthumous descriptions as "father of modern Arabic literature," pioneer of the Arab/Muslim *Nahda* (Renaissance), a leader of the Egyptian "Enlightenment," and a "citizen of the world" who helped initiate the "nineteenth century's growing Arab awareness of the West."[3]

At about the time of al-Tahtawi's return to Egypt in 1831, another young man, this one a twenty-five-year-old French aristocrat by the name of Alexis de Tocqueville, waited at a French port to board the American ship *Le Havre* bound for New York. Tocqueville and his good friend, Gustave de Beaumont, had been engaged for several years in the rather deadening work of unpaid magistrates. When the occasion arose, then, both eagerly obtained an eighteen-month leave from the minister of justice to study firsthand American methods of incarceration and bring home their observations for use in efforts to reform the French penal system. The brief sojourn enabled them to produce a report on American penitentiaries, but more famously, the trip served as both the occasion and inspiration for Tocqueville's *Democracy in America*, published in two volumes separated by five years (volume 1 in 1835 and 2 in 1840).[4] The book, particularly the first volume, earned Tocqueville critical acclaim in France, launching a life of serious scholarship and a long if not illustrious career in the rough and tumble of nineteenth-century French politics. In the United States, the two volumes have gradually achieved the stature of "secular scripture,"[5] evoking from both sides of the political spectrum intense claims of ownership as well as scholarly paeans to the treatise as "at once the best book ever written on democracy and the best book ever written on America."[6]

Al-Tahtawi and Tocqueville share little in terms of class origin, education, religion, or political commitments. Moreover, while Tahtawi's journey took him to a radically different political, cultural, and linguistic world, Tocqueville saw himself as traveling to a people that were, in an extended sense, a variety of English culture fairly familiar to him. In addition, while the popularity and endless analysis of *Democracy in America* have transformed it into a virtual bible of all things democratic, al-Tahtawi's *Rihla* has largely remained the purview of specialists in Arabic literature, Egyptian history, and Muslim intellectual thought. This is in part due to its initial reception among prominent French scholars, including Ernest Renan, who famously (mis)characterized the *Rihla* as emblematic of Muslims' "hatred of science."[7] It is also due to linguistic barriers, as well as to the method, style, and genre of *Takhlis*, all of which are fairly unfamiliar to the (largely EuroAmerican) gatekeepers of social science in particular.[8] By contrast, Tocqueville describes his inquiry as indicative of a "new political science . . . for a world itself quite new."[9] He thus explicitly locates himself within what has now become a well-established field of inquiry, leading many scholars to declare him the forerunner of contemporary social science, despite *Democracy's* obvious literary richness, empirical lacunae, aphoristic style, indebtedness to English and French travel literature,[10] and the tendency of several other disciplines to claim his work as their own.[11]

In spite of such radical differences in background, genre, discipline, and reception, these virtually contemporaneous journeys constitute what might be called pedagogical *theôriai* (plural of *theôria*) to unfamiliar lands in search of practical wisdom to bring home: al-Tahtawi sought in Paris knowledge of the sciences he saw as integral to the intellectual reawakening and material prosperity of Egypt, and Tocqueville sought in America instruction for France on the risks and rewards of a fully realized democracy. While both explicitly character-ize their journeys in terms of a pursuit of instruction, moreover, each is pedagogical in a much broader sense than what is suggested by such explicitly practical aims to acquire "useful" knowledge. For along the way, both *theôriai* occasion and express the enlargement of experience, pleasures of curiosity, and wonders of newness that have simultane-ously instrumental, intellectual, aesthetic, and even erotic dimensions. The narrow and broad meaning of "pedagogical" here echo the double motivations for Solon's travels, undertaken both for the practical pur-pose of avoiding the repeal of Athenian laws and pursuit of wisdom for its own sake.

For a variety of technological, economic, political, and historical rea-sons, travel across long distances by both Muslims and Europeans from diverse regions and backgrounds proliferated exponentially in the nineteenth century.[12] Among the written records resulting from such journeys, Tocqueville's and Tahtawi's *theôriai* are particularly illu-minating for my purposes because they illustrate a series of historical and cross-cultural continuities in the meaning and practice of travel in search of knowledge, while also disclosing several evocative disconti-nuities. In the first instance, I want to suggest that these travels and the written reflections on them rearticulate many of the features of *theôria* explored in the previous chapters: the connection among travel, direct experience, vision, and curiosity, as well as the claim that knowledge from afar contributes to the edification of the traveler's homeland, much as Plato's Athenian connects literal travel to the journey from habit to understanding a maturing polis must make (951b). Along with Ibn Battuta, then, this nineteenth-century Frenchman journeying to America and Egyptian journeying to France at once rebut the claim that to "travel and observe is characteristically Greek"[13] and demon-strate more generally that travel in pursuit of knowledge as well as curiosity about what is strange are not the monopoly of any one partic-ular culture or limited to any specific historical epoch.

Moreover, in contrast to Mill's suspicion of autopsy (or, in Arabic, ʿiyan, seeing with one's own eyes) both Tocqueville and Tahtawi ex-plicitly locate their own authority and the value of their narratives in the breadth of vision made possible by a dislocation that is simultane-ously physical, cultural, and temporal. Like the *theôriai* of the previous chapter, then, their texts may be said to reflect and reenact for the reader a series of "contrapuntal juxtapositions that diminish orthodox judgment and elevate appreciative sympathy."[14] Inasmuch as both Tahtawi and Tocqueville explicitly attend not only to the utility and promise of such knowledge from afar but also to its hazards, their *theôriai* further illustrate the double-edged nature of travel detailed in the previous two chapters. Here exposures to the unfamiliar occasion a host of concerns, including anxieties about the corrosive or despotic dangers to "home" rendered visible in the sojourn abroad. Such concerns are shaped, of course, by the very different challenges each faced; unlike Tocqueville's voyage through America, Tahtawi's *theôria* demonstrates the risks to travelers journeying to a radically different political and cultural world, from the danger of losing one's sense of self in a foreign land to incurring the wrath of one's compatriots on returning home.

Yet in a departure from the previous chapter, Tahtawi's and Tocqueville's *theôriai* are both anchored in national projects in ways that are historically and conceptually distant from those of Herodotus and Ibn Battuta. These earlier travelers move through worlds unbounded by the modern nation-state, and their extensive wanderings express not a drive to bring home practical knowledge but (among other things) a powerful curiosity about the world and a desire to record its wonders for anyone who might wish to know them. Indeed, for Herodotus and Ibn Battuta, "home" largely registers as an attenuated lens through which they see the world rather than a fixed point of origin and return. By contrast, these nineteenth-century travelers explicitly see themselves and their excursions as serving a national project (in Egypt's case, newly emerging).[15] This is evident not only in the political purposes framing both voyages but also, and less obviously, in the pervasive preoccupation with France and Egypt that, like an invisible grid, frames the course and substance of their observations, and which at once reflect and help define what it meant to be French or Egyptian in the nineteenth century by way of contrasts with Americans and Parisians. In this sense, then, Tahtawi and Tocqueville illustrate Benedict Anderson's argument about the crucial role of traveling functionaries in the emergence of a framework of specifically national "imagined communities."[16]

The following discussion is largely organized around these two specific excursions, yet here it is instructive to consider for a moment the extent to which Tocqueville and Tahtawi's subsequent endeavors and travels were not only grounded in but also helped *articulate* the aspirations and boundaries of the nation-states each served. In his capacity as a French statesman later in life, for example, Tocqueville became quite engaged in the question of the French role in Algeria and traveled there twice despite ill health. In place of the wonder at newness and the enlargement of experience that characterized his travels to America, however, what emerges is a narrowly instrumentalist French imperial agenda.[17] Ever interested in statecraft, Tocqueville now concerned himself, in Melvin Richter's words, with "how to subjugate, how to administer efficiently, how to colonize a vanquished territory."[18] Having always identified civilization with the fate of "Christian nations," Tocqueville's firsthand observation of Algeria served to solidify a series of nationalist justifications for the territorial conquest of Muslim lands, an argument he would extend to Hindus when discussing British colonialism in India.

Unlike Tocqueville's journeys as a statesman, Tahtawi's later travels occurred under more ignominious circumstances, yet they culminated in an equally significant departure from the relatively ecumenical sensibility of his earlier voyage. After flourishing for some fifteen years in government service following his return from France, al-Tahtawi was banished to the Sudan for four years (1850–54) when Muhammad ʿAli's grandson, ʿAbbas I, came to power in Egypt. The official explanation for Tahtawi's marching orders was the need to establish a primary school in Khartoum, an expression of longstanding Egyptian colonialist aspirations in Sudan.[19] But it is clear that there were other reasons for the exile, chief among them the hostility of the ʿulama to al-Tahtawi's challenge to their monopoly on knowledge and instruction, and the antipathy of ʿAbbas both to French influence and the implied criticism of autocracy in the *Rihla*.[20] Like the story of Anacharsis, whose attempt to introduce a foreign religious practice on returning to his native land occasioned his violent death (Herodotus, 4.77), this episode serves as a cautionary reminder that "coming home," in an extended sense, can be a risky affair.

Festering in Sudan, Tahtawi decided to translate Fénelon's *Telemachus*, a text in which he sought "an allegory which perfectly fitted his case and the injustice done to him."[21] Tahtawi writes in the introduction that "I undertook this translation into Arabic in that Sudanese land with a troubled mind, clouded with sorrow, remote from family and home, and bowed by the misfortunes and mishaps of destiny."[22] When ʿAbbas I was assassinated in 1854, Tahtawi was recalled to Cairo under the auspices of ʿAbbas's successor, Saʿid Pasha, Muhammad ʿAli's last living son. Yet the misery of his exile in Khartoum left an indelible mark on him. Tahtawi's *Takhlis* had already demonstrated a certain contempt for *bilad al-Sudan*, which appears in it as an illustration of the most primitive of civilizations, its inhabitants characterized as barbaric, like savage, roaming ignorant animals.[23] Tahtawi's involuntary sojourn in Sudan occasioned not a revision of these judgments but a hardening of them. In a *qasida* (a kind of Arabic poem) he would ultimately publish in a later work on the history of Egypt, Tahtawi rails against the Sudanese, characterizing them at one moment as

insensible objects, at another as wild beasts who are sexually promiscuous and indifferent to the prescriptions of Islamic law; if not for the
(white) Arabs among them, he writes, all would be nothing but black-
ness.[24] Gone is the appreciation of what is different and foreign in the
Rihla. In its place is a justification of colonialism in terms of how it
benefits the welfare of both the conquered and the conquerors, a rationale in part facilitated by a profound hostility to people

> who were basically inanimate objects to him, or wild barbarians
> unable or unwilling to participate in the culture that al-Tahtawi
> had brought with him. . . . His sense of nationalist connection to
> Egypt was powerful enough for him to argue that bringing Sudan
> more closely into the Egyptian sphere would create one country,
> with links to both the glories of the ancient Egyptian past and the
> future power of Europe.[25]

I argued in chapter 2 that translation captures the process of mediat-
ing among worlds that travelers straddle; I also suggested that such
acts of translation entail the exercise of representational power,
whether the cross-cultural mediation in question is enacted by a
"Greek" traveling to ancient Egypt, a fourteenth-century Maghribi
venturing through *bilad al-Sudan*, a nascent Egyptian nationalist journeying to Paris, or a nineteenth-century Frenchman traveling to the
New World. As with the previous chapter, then, the following discussion demonstrates that direct observation of what is foreign, and the
mediations such exposures occasion, can at one and the same time clarify and distort, illuminate and domesticate. The extent to which
Tocqueville and Tahtawi were later implicated in colonial projects further suggests how representational power and the exercise of political
and territorial domination ably serve one another, a reminder that journeys to unfamiliar lands can serve either as the grounds on which conceits of cultural superiority are challenged, or as the precursor to and
justification for all kinds of imperialist ventures, ancient and modern,
European and Muslim.

At the same time, these two *theôriai* illustrate how the longstanding
interplay of travel and domination is in many ways distinctively articulated in the nineteenth century. More specifically, the self-consciously *scientific* character of the knowledge both sought to put at the
disposal of their compatriots back home illustrates how ethnographic
classifications of race, culture, and religion produced by travelers
could become crucial to elaborating emerging national borders and
colonial aspirations.[26] Tocqueville claims that both his inquiry and insights are productive of a new political science, one in which, as I will
show, spatial and temporal travel converge to instruct France on the

present and future of democracy, indigenous nobilities, and races. Despite the fact that Arabs, Muslims, and Egyptians were often the *object* of such European ethnographic classifications, Tahtawi regards his own endeavor as similarly scientific and doubly so: his is the pursuit of knowledge produced by the scientific method that itself exemplifies a particular spirit of inquiry, one characterized by impartiality, pragmatism, empiricism, antipathy to rote imitation (*taqlid*), and curiosity about new wonders and marvels. In both the *Rihla* and his later writings, these "scientific" endeavors are productive of a taxonomy of civilizations that racialize the political and cultural borders of the Egyptian nation-state. Thus, while the categories of black/white largely operate as a distinction without a difference in Ibn Battuta's *Rihla*, here they are transfigured into a painstaking classification of "racial differences in skin color, sexual behavior and religious attitudes among the Sudanese," thereby illustrating "how an increasing sense of racial difference could be incorporated into a sense of political and cultural boundaries."[27]

Finally, these nineteenth-century journeys reveal a crucial shift in the character of "wonders" and "marvels" from those of the previous chapter. Seeking to document epic deeds and magical wonders, Herodotus and Ibn Battuta went to great lengths to establish their credibility as purveyors of knowledge and marvels—from the earthly imprint of Heracles' foot to a levitating yogi—they knew their audiences might find suspect. There are moments when Tahtawi and Tocqueville anticipate just such incredulity, but not because they traffic in stories about objects suspended in mid-air. *Takhlis* and *Democracy* are full of "marvels and wonders," yet their *character* has shifted to the realm of the historical, scientific, and political: for al-Tahtawi it is the spectacle of nineteenth-century French society, knowledge, and organization that is a "wonder," and for Tocqueville, it is the "marvel" of American democracy on view that shows to the present the contours of the future.[28]

Narratives of modernization tend to presume that development from the "premodern" entails the ascendance of rationality in its many valences—from a principle of organization to the measure and substance of intelligibility—an advance that at once presupposes and reinforces the retreat of an authoritative transcendental order from the public realm, and concomitantly, the eclipse of the epistemological and theological certainties such an order was thought to have sustained.[29] It is thus worth making explicit that this shift in the character of wonders neither presupposes nor demonstrates a process of Weberian "de-magification"[30] whereby scientific and rationalist accounts of the world inevitably displace those filled with magic, gods, and nonrational miracles.[31] Gods may not walk the earth or send humans prophetic dreams in *Takhlis* and *Democracy,* but both Tahtawi and Tocqueville see Divine Providence at work in the extraordinary reconfiguration of society, knowledge, time, and space on view. The "this-worldly" nature of the marvels they emphasize thus derives not from "disenchantment" but from the explicitly pedagogical purposes of both journeys: to seek in other places and nations knowledge which is useful at home, where "useful knowledge" includes not only practical information but also wonder at what is new and different.[32]

These *theôriai* do, however, reflect a transformation of a different kind: a shift in the perception of space and distance engendered by an increasing *awareness* of regions and peoples separated by vast oceans and thousands of miles. Herodotus's *Histories* and Ibn Battuta's *Rihla* demonstrate the antiquity and extent of cross-cultural mobility, yet the domains of intelligible experience for both travelers largely remain the Greek world and the *Dar al-Islam* respectively, beyond which "barbarians," "wastes," or "wilderness" sprawl. "Othering" what is unfamiliar is hardly a thing of the past, of course, but it is only in a world grown smaller by the combined impact of European colonialism and innovations in transportation and communication that, despite great distances, American democracy would so readily present itself as an exemplar to a Frenchman and the acquisition of European science could appear so urgent to an Egyptian. Here the contours of a world we now associate with globalization come into view, one in which, to paraphrase Anthony Appiah's characterization of the twentieth century, ideas, objects, and people from "outside" are becoming more— and more obviously—*present* than they ever were before.[33]

As with much of the literature on Herodotus and Ibn Battuta, there is a wealth of secondary scholarship that seeks to tally *Takhlis* and *Democracy* with established archeological, geographical, and historical facts about the worlds from which Tocqueville and Tahtawi came and through which each traveled. Rather than anatomizing a set of empirical accuracies or factual missteps that add to or subtract from the overall persuasiveness of each text, in the following analysis I take as my point of departure Tocqueville's and Tahtawi's common concerns with instruction and political transformation—what I have called pedagogical *theôria.* Indeed, I want to suggest that these travelers and texts work as a prism to refract the features of *theôria* across both history and culture and, in so doing, bring new dimensions of well-traveled terrain into view. More specifically, the contemporaneousness of these two nineteenth-century voyages makes possible a modern rearticulation of the notion of *theôria* advanced in the previous chapters as well as an elaboration of what it means to be a *theôros* in two different cultures.

Such an approach provides a window onto those techniques by which what is foreign is charted, decoded, and domesticated for an audience at a cultural or historical remove *within* each text. This brings into sharp focus the doubleness of what I have called theoretical moments, those occasions in which cultural and temporal dislocation issues in flashes of insight and reflexive closure endemic to the comparative practice of seeking to make sense of the unfamiliar by recourse to the familiar. At the same time, this approach foregrounds a set of remarkable methodological, substantive, and experiential convergences *between* these two texts, intersections that are clearest when explored by way of shared themes rather than the serial exposition of two journeys and texts in the previous chapter. In addition to those accidental moments when their worlds quite literally overlap,[34] such convergences include parallels in purpose, a common reliance on the authority of autopsy *"ʿiyan,"* a shared attitude of "appreciative ambivalence" toward republican politics, and the multiple and nested cultural, political, aesthetic, linguistic, temporal, and epistemological mediations both texts at once reflect and enact.

Authorizing Autopsy

The student mission memorialized in Tahtawi's *Rihla* was but one component of the ambitious agenda of Muhammad ʿAli, the Ottoman governor-general whose absolutist rule (1805–48) left an indelible if highly controversial stamp on Egypt.[35] Egypt had been a province of the Ottoman Empire since 1517, although the Mamlukes—meaning slave, but here referring to the military slave institution that had ruled Egypt since the thirteenth century—continued to excerise substantial political power until the arrival of Napoleon in 1798.[36] Napoleon's abrupt departure in 1801 inaugurated four years of instability and political fragmentation, out of which Muhammad ʿAli emerged triumphant through a combination of brutality, strategic manipulation, and the military might of the Albanian garrison he led:

> Bonaparte's adventure in Egypt ended as suddenly as it had begun. When the French withdrew, they left Egypt without any constituted authority, and four years of chaos followed. The Mamelukes tried to restore their pre-Napoleonic supremacy; the Turks on the other hand wanted to put an end to them and re-impose their own rule. The people of Cairo hated them both. . . . Neither of these had enough power to establish itself in the face of the other two, and in the final event it was a fourth group which suc-

ceeded in winning power. This was the Albanian garrison, with Muhammad ʿAli at its head. In the tangled history of these years we can see Muhammad ʿAli skillfully playing off one group against another in order to weaken each in turn. . . . It was indeed his skillful manipulation of the people and of popular feeling in Cairo which showed his originality as a politician . . . Muhammad ʿAli's ascendancy was part design and part chance. During the convulsive events of the four years preceding his rise to power, the collective will of the Egyptians gathered strength and focused on his person.[37]

Once ascendant, Muhammad ʿAli sought to wrest control of Egypt from Ottoman sovereignty and "modernize" it by way of the acquisition and application of European scientific knowledge, ranging from military administration to political science, chemistry to natural history, mechanics to typography.[38] Both purposes reinforced one another: acquisition of the military and scientific knowledge conducive to modernizing Egypt's bureaucracy, economy, educational system, and military centralized the power of the Egyptian state and placed it squarely in the hands of the *wali* (governor), strengthening his position against a restive populace, the native ʿ*ulama*, and the Ottoman sultan living in distant Constantinople. The student missions to Europe and the School of Translation were two of the institutions by which Muhammad ʿAli sought to acquire the practical knowledge necessary to realize his ambitions, and Tahtawi was to play a prominent role in both.[39]

Yet there is little in Tahtawi's life story that foreshadows the crucial role he would play in Muhammad ʿAli's designs. He was born in a small town in upper Egypt in the year of Napoleon's departure, and while his family was from a noble lineage and had once had been wealthy, their fortunes were decimated by Muhammad ʿAli's abolition of the system of tax farming (*iltizam*) while Tahtawi was still young. Moreover, the highest levels of Muhammad ʿAli's Turco-Circassian administration were largely closed to native-born Arabs such as Tahtawi; he thus gravitated toward the religious education that would grant him entry into the teaching profession. There his evident intellectual talents brought him to the attention of a well-placed ʿ*alim* (religious scholar), Hasan al-ʿAttar (1766–1835), who secured the young teacher the position of *imam* to the student mission. The publication of *Takhlis* would radically reshape Tahtawi's professional prospects, despite the fact that at least one Cairo local at the time dismissed it as an account of how the author got drunk, womanized, ate pork, and just generally qualified himself "for an eminent place in Hell."[40] Muhammad ʿAli received the *Rihla* with great enthusiasm, however, and promptly had it translated into Turkish (the lingua franca of his administration), distributing copies to his officials, Egyptian students, and even the Ottoman sultan in Constantinople.[41] Having found favor with Muhammad ʿAli, wealth and a series of promotions within the Egyptian state educational system quickly followed.

The long shadow Muhammad ʿAli cast over Tahtawi's life and career does not, however, reduce *Takhlis* to a mere expression of the *wali*'s will and policies. For al-Tahtawi's *theôria* in many ways reflects the influence of his mentor, al-ʿAttar, a progressive ʿ*alim* who was himself an avid traveler and had developed extensive contacts with French scholars in Egypt. Al-ʿAttar was appreciative of the new knowledge coming from Europe and deeply concerned about what he saw as his fellow Egyptians' antipathy to innovation and stubborn reliance on ideas of the past.[42] It was al-ʿAttar who secured for his protégé a place on the student mission, and by Tahtawi's own account in the *Rihla*, the very idea of recording every observation originated with the curious ʿ*alim* "who adored listening to stories of marvels and learning about wonders," and instructed the young man to "pay close attention to what happened on this journey, and to the strange and curious things" he encountered.[43]

With al-ʿAttar's guidance and interests as inspiration, then, al-Tahtawi defines the purpose of his *Rihla* in terms neither entirely instrumental nor exclusively intellectual but rather evocative of what I have called a pedagogical *theôria* to seek instruction abroad for use at home. In *Takhlis*, the young *imam* exhorts his compatriots both by example and argument to pursue, not wholesale imitation of France, but rather the knowledge of modern science and the arts he deemed necessary for Egyptian prosperity and greatness. "One who is ignorant of something is inferior to one who has mastered it," Tahtawi writes, "and in the same measure a man disdains such knowledge, will he regret it unto death."[44] Writing for an Egyptian audience for whom science was largely synonymous with those "religious sciences"[45] over which the ʿ*ulama* had an instructional monopoly, however, al-Tahtawi could take neither the importance of European science nor his own legitimacy as purveyor of them for granted.[46] *Takhlis* can thus be understood as functioning rhetorically and substantively as an overview and introduction to these new sciences, as well as a justification of their value and of his own travel to acquire them.

In the introduction to the *Takhlis*, then, al-Tahtawi goes to great lengths to establish the scope and significance of modern European science without jeopardizing the relevance of religious knowledge, or the primacy of Islamic civilization. This he does by, first, making clear that he will "condone only that which does not transgress the provisions of Muhammadan law," and second, attempting to decouple the discoveries of modern science from the culture in which they "happened" to be located.[47] Much as later reformers such as Jamal al-Din al-Afghani [al-Asadabadi] (d.1897) and Muhammad ʿAbduh (d. 1905) would attempt to characterize science and modernity as universal rather than Western, al-Tahtawi casts European scientific advances as a "modern extension of Islam's lost heritage" in nonreligious knowledge.[48] Travel for instruction in modern science is thus simply a matter of following the truth where it resides, seeking for Muslims the progress and prosperity they once had and again deserve.[49] Muslims need not feel humiliated by the endeavor, Tahtawi reassures his readers, for Europeans well know that "we were their teachers in all the sciences and we had an advance on them. It is obvious, and intellect has determined, that credit goes to the pioneers, for surely it is the case that he who lags behind draws from what preceded him and is guided by this influence."[50]

Given this rich intellectual bequest, Tahtawi bemoans what he characterizes as an epic erosion of Muslim greatness brought on by the *Reconquista* on the one hand, and the weight of Ottoman stagnation on the other. Such decay left Muslims weak and foundering while

the power of the Franks multiplied on account of their skills, organization, their knowledge of and adaptability and inventiveness in warfare. If Islam had not been protected by the might of God— praise be to Him the Almighty—it would be nothing compared to their [the Franks] prowess, population, wealth, skills ... mastery in the science of navigation, their knowledge of astronomy and geography, their appetite for business and trade, and their love of travel.[51]

Entranced, like his mentor, by these "wonders of travel," Tahtawi is nevertheless alarmed by the gap in power and prosperity thereby disclosed, and he fairly erupts in protest: "by God Almighty, during my entire sojourn in this land, I grieved that it so enjoyed that [knowledge] the Islamic kingdoms lacked."[52]

Having portrayed the knowledge found in Europe as a necessity, akin to a remedy for a sick patient, al-Tahtawi then justifies his travel to obtain them by reference to the authority of autopsy, in the sense not only of "seeing for oneself" but also of witnessing, as the verb he uses is *shahida*, which means simultaneously to see with one's own eyes, witness, certify, and confirm.[53] Just as the French *spectacle* is such an "extraordinary thing that it is impossible to understand just by describing it; it must be seen with one's own eyes," Tahtawi insists that the attempt to "arouse from their heedless slumber all Islamic communities, both

Arab and non-Arab" by way of knowledge from Europe similarly requires firsthand exposure to it. The many wondrous achievements of
France—the workshops and the factories, the schools and extraordinary army discipline—cannot be appreciated except "by those who
have seen the land of the Franks or have witnessed" these developments firsthand.[54]

Yet Tahtawi does not simply state a connection among travel, autopsy, and knowledge as if it is self-evident. Seeking a religious, literary, and political imprimatur to his *theôria*, he goes on to justify his
own pursuit of knowledge by reference to love of homeland (*hubb al-
watan*), the wisdom of the poets, and the example of the Prophet Muhammad himself. Indeed, Tahtawi portrays the Prophet as The Model
Traveler, suggesting that Muhammad's legendary peregrinations to
Syria and Medina and miraculous "night journey" (Qur'an 17:1) from
Mecca to Jerusalem in the company of the angel Gabriel endow not
only these specific excursions but travel itself with *baraka*.[55] As evidence, Tahtawi invokes both the Qur'an and the report in which Muhammad is said to tell his followers to seek knowledge as far as China,
as well as a hadith stipulating that "wisdom is the ultimate goal of
the believer; he should seek it even among polytheists. . . . In general,
whenever man is faithful to his religion, there is no harm in travel,
especially for as beneficial a purpose" as travel in search of knowledge.[56] Tahtawi then weighs in with the wisdom of the Arab poets,
drawing from one unattributed poem the suggestion that there is
"glory in travel," and from another the encouragement to

> spur your mount towards open country
> Take leave of beautiful women and palaces
> If not for separation from one's native country
> Pearls from the sea would never ascend to reach necks.[57]

Finally, the purpose of Tahtawi's travels are grounded in the specific
needs of his native land, for the primary audience and ultimate stage
for his efforts are not Parisians or their country—the ostensible subject
matter of the *Rihla*—but rather his "homeland" (*watan*), which Tahtawi
here defines both in terms of national allegiance to Egypt and religious
loyalty to the *Dar al-Islam*. Thus he counters the many poetic warnings
against the loss and loneliness of travel with the insistence that "travel
to acquire knowledge or a livelihood" does not preclude deep devotion
to one's "homeland and birthplace, which is innate."[58] Indeed, al-Tahtawi suggests that travel both serves and reinforces love of one's homeland because acquisition of new knowledge, whether it comes from
afar or from within, is essential not only to the greatness of the *watan*
but also to inspiring loyalty to it. The French love of travel is thus ad-

mirable largely because of the service it ultimately renders to France: Tahtawi marvels that they sometimes "spend many years and an extended period of time roving between east and west, to the point where they think little of putting themselves in danger if it benefits their homeland."[59]

As Tocqueville traveled throughout his life, he exemplifies what Tahtawi had in mind here, although in contrast to Tahtawi's lengthy stay in France, Tocqueville's time in America was quite brief: after a bruising thirty-eight-day voyage from Le Havre to New York, Beaumont and Tocqueville stayed only nine months in the New World.[60] Indeed, Tocqueville's visit can be characterized as whirlwind, alternating fairly rapid journeys to the Northwest, the South, and Canada, with more extended stays in the major cities of the East, including greater New York, Philadelphia, Boston, and Baltimore. Compared to al-Tahtawi's largely stationary sojourn in Paris, Tocqueville's itinerary was fairly wide-ranging but, ultimately, equally lopsided. André Jardin puts Tocqueville's exposure to the American South at a maximum of 50 days (40 days if Baltimore is not included) out of a total of 271 days spent in the United States, and half of the entire visit was spent settled in Eastern cities at the expense of other regions and rural environments.[61]

The uneven itinerary is matched by an imbalance of sources: scholars have argued that Tocqueville attended more to "the Yankee" than "the Virginian," and was particularly apt to lend his ear to New Englanders, American Catholics, federalists, and elites.[62] As Beaumont wrote to his family in May 1831, to "acquire information about institutions and public establishments, etc., etc., we really have to see people, and the most enlightened are in the best society."[63] Thus Pierson writes that "while in the U.S., Tocqueville clearly looked harder for Federalist arguments than for Jacksonian justifications. He even seemed to feel that there was more to be learned in Boston than in Ohio."[64] Just as a French reader of the *Rihla* accused Tahtawi of generalizing his observations about Parisians to all of France, Tocqueville is similarly inclined to derive rather sprawling generalizations from fairly limited firsthand experience, proffering sweeping claims about the character and future of rural, frontier, and southern America as well as broad characterizations about the relationship between the history of the New World and the nature of its inhabitants.

Although Tocqueville is often "puffed as prophet or seer,"[65] it is nevertheless the case that the origins and purposes of his journey to America can be understood in less grandiose terms. Tocqueville was, like al-Tahtawi, a mid-level bureaucrat at the time of his departure, and it was in the name of a bureaucratic mission that he and his friend obtained leave from the Ministry of Justice to travel to the United States. Widespread concern about the disorder and ineffectiveness of the French prison system necessitated firsthand observation of American penitentiaries, which had proven effective against recidivism. Or so Tocqueville and Beaumont successfully argued to the French Minister of the Interior, who assigned them the mission to the New World. In a later letter Tocqueville makes clear that the "penitentiary system was an excuse; I used it as a passport that would allow me to go everywhere in the United States."[66] Indeed, in a letter from August 1830, Tocqueville wrote of his determination to take up the "turbulent life of the traveler. For a long time now, I have had a very strong desire to visit North America. I will go there and see what a great republic is."[67] Yet other letters suggest that Tocqueville's pursuit of intellectual edification was itself a pretext of sorts: his burst of curiosity about America coincided with serious concerns about his career in a France unsteadily governed by Louis-Philippe, whom scholars have portrayed as a fragile "rampart . . . against revolutionary anarchy " in the wake of the 1830 Revolution that had removed Charles X from power.[68] Thus, while Tocqueville claims that he "didn't go there with the idea of writing a book at all . . . the idea of the book came to me," Jardin makes clear that the seeds for *Democracy in America* originated earlier and in connection with the author's preoccupation with his own professional advancement. In a letter dated well before his departure, the young aristocrat envisions a book on America as a way to "alert the public to your existence and turn the attention of the parties to you."[69]

In *Tocqueville and Beaumont in America*, George Wilson Pierson suggests that the three most powerful motivations for Tocqueville's cross-Atlantic trip were an increasing discomfort with the political situation in France, an ambition to make a name for himself, and finally a desire to be of service to his country.[70] As with al-Tahtawi, then, it is from the nexus of patriotism, curiosity, professional ambition, and political imperatives that the purposes of Tocqueville's pedagogical *theôria* are carved, and which guide the course and content of the resulting inquiry. This context does not diminish the theoretical significance or political prescience of some of his conclusions, but it does place front and center the comparative method in which France—her past, present, and future, as well as Tocqueville's place in it—serves always as an implicit or explicit point of reference. This comparative context has often been occluded by what Jean-Claude Lamberti characterizes as a national division of labor among Tocqueville scholars: preoccupied with his most explicitly "French" writings such as *The Ancien Régime*, French scholarship on *Democracy in America* was for a long time quite scant, while American scholarship on the two volumes proliferated at the expense of his other works.[71] As Lamberti points out, such an "artificial cleavage" had significant methodological as well as substantive implications:

> Severed from knowledge of the suffering and failure of revolution in Europe, reflection upon American democracy is likely to degenerate into utopian mythmaking, singing the praises of the "blessed republic" ... encourag[ing] belief in American exceptionalism while discouraging the use of comparative methods in political science.[72]

This outsized preoccupation with *Democracy* among Americans has sustained an assumption that the preoccupation must be requited. "One would think," one scholar comments, that Tocqueville "wrote in English, that his intended primary audience was American, that he never sailed back to France, and did not write *Democracy in America* in order to take part in a French debate."[73] It may well be, as Tocqueville writes in *Democracy*, that "only strangers or experience may be able to bring certain truths to the Americans' attention,"[74] but in the end it is not Americans' attention he seeks, nor is fidelity to his subjects' own point of view his measure of merit. This is, after all, a man who would write from America that in "the midst of all the theories with which I am amusing my imagination here, the memory of France is becoming like a worm that is consuming me. It manages to surprise me by day in the midst of our work, by night when I wake up."[75] So central was France to his observation of the New World that he actually wrote home from America seeking updates on French opinion to guide his comparisons:

> On a multitude of points we do not know what to ask because we do not know what exists in France and because, without comparison to make, the mind does not know how to proceed. It is therefore absolutely necessary that our friends in France furnish us part of what we need, if we are to gather some useful ideas here.[76]

In terms more than slightly reminiscent of Tahtawi, then, Tocqueville exhorts his countrymen to look to America, not "in order slavishly to copy the institutions she has fashioned for herself, but in order that we may better understand what suits us; let us look there for instruction rather than models."[77] Tocqueville's wish to discern "what a vast republic is, why it is practicable in one place, impracticable in another"[78] is guided neither by a desire to inventory America for American consumption nor primarily to contribute to the common stockpile of human knowledge: "I did not study America just to satisfy curiosity, however legitimate," he avers, "I sought there lessons from which we might profit."[79] Even more specifically, the book is designed as an intervention in the political dilemma he confronted at home, and which he recognized with uncommon clarity: given that the seemingly inexorable march of equality in France and all other "civilized Christian nations" could so readily come at the cost of liberty, uniting all in equal servitude rather than common freedom, by what means and under what circumstances might both proceed apace?

It is out of this specific context and in these terms that Tocqueville's pursuit of ultimately practical wisdom grows, a pursuit in which the great deeds and magical marvels so central to the narratives of Herodotus and Ibn Battuta are transfigured into the "land of wonders" that is America, an "admirable spectacle" where everything "is in constant movement and every movement seems an advance."[80] In Tocqueville's inquiry, however, the purpose of purveying such wonders is the urgent need to differentiate what is useful from what is dangerous in democracy, what is inevitable from what is susceptible to human will, what is universal and necessary from what is local and relative. In this endeavor, balance and comprehensiveness often take a back seat to an intuitive approach in which "engendering facts" serve "mother ideas,"[81] many of which Tocqueville formed before he ever set foot in the New World.[82] So, for example, Tocqueville's grand generalizations about a land of which he had seen but a small part derives from the "mother idea" that "societies, like other organized bodies, are shaped according to certain fixed rules from which they cannot escape. They are made up of certain elements which are found at all times and in all places." Thus he argues elsewhere that in

> America all laws originate more or less from the same idea. The whole of society, so to say, is based on just one fact: everything follows from one underlying principle. One could compare America to a great forest cut through by a large number of roads which all end in the same place. Once you have found the central point, you can see the whole plan in one glance. But in England the roads cross, and you have to follow along each one of them to get a clear idea of the whole.[83]

Setting aside scholarly debates about why and how Tocqueville appears to alternate or combine an inductive and deductive method at various moments in *Democracy*, I want to suggest that what Tocqueville misses in and about America derives less from willful ignorance or misguided method than from the purposes of a pedagogical *theôria* which, like the sharply circumscribed range of a powerful microscope, delimits both the scope of the inquiry and the itinerary required to pursue it. Thus Tocqueville writes that in my work on America ... [t]hough I seldom mentioned France, I did not write a page without thinking of her, and placing her as it were before me. And what I especially tried to draw out, and to explain in the United States, was not the whole condition of that foreign society, but the points in which it differs from our own, or resembles us. It is always by noticing likenesses or contrasts that I succeeded in giving an interesting and accurate description.[84]

Indeed, like al-Tahtawi, Tocqueville is less concerned with empirical breadth or exhaustive coverage than in facilitating a shift of perspective among those for whose sake he has undertaken his *theôria*. In this way, *Democracy in America* and *Takhlis* may each be understood as both a text and an *act*, a means of simultaneously reflecting and enacting lessons disclosed by comparative observation. In these cases,

the persuasiveness of the theory does not require the defeat of rival arguments or empirical proof. Rather, the account turns on the skill of the traveler-theorist to depict a state of affairs that, though fanciful, nonetheless appeals to the experience of his readers—their beliefs, longings, fears and grievances—so that they will not simply be charmed by his tale, or indulged in their fantasies, but conceive of themselves living differently.[85]

Importantly, for Tocqueville as for Tahtawi, the capacity for such discernment rests with autopsy and, concomitantly, travel abroad to "see for oneself." Likening a theorist to a "traveler who has gone out beyond the walls of some vast city and gone up a neighboring hill," Tocqueville famously writes that from this vantage "the city's outline is [now] easier to see, and for the first time he grasps its shape."[86] At once in but not of America, Tocqueville's claims to authority, like those of Tahtawi, derive from this location at the boundary of two cultures, two histories, two different societies and political systems that overlap sufficiently to illuminate one another. At the same time, his perspective from the heights makes possible a second kind of mediation, this one between overwhelming detail and generalizable patterns, "engendering facts" and "mother ideas," practices and theories. Such an elevated location at the boundary of two worlds may well account for what he misses in his observations, as well as for the rather scanty evidence he adduces in support of even warranted conclusions, as John Stuart Mill points out in his 1840 review of *Democracy in America*.[87] But it is also from this vantage that he claims "to see not differently but further than any party" in France and the reason for which his "book is not precisely suited to anybody's taste."[88] Thus he suggests at the end of volume 2 that it is precisely the constant mobility and exposure to different peoples characteristic of the democratic epoch rather than, for example, the increasing acquisition of detailed knowledge of the entire world and all its peoples, that makes possible the perspective from which patterns common to the human condition are visible:

> In ages of democracy, men are always on the move from place to place . . . and peoples of different countries mix, see one another, hear one another, and borrow from one another. . . . Thus for the first time all mankind can be seen together in broad daylight. . . . Just when every man, raising his eyes above his country, begins at last to see mankind at large, God shows himself more clearly to human perception in full and entire majesty. . . . Seeing the human race as one great whole, [men] easily conceive that its destinies are regulated by the same design and are led to recognize in the actions of each individual a trace of the universal and consistent plan by which God guides mankind.[89]

Travels across Time and Space

As is already evident, there are several valences to "travel" in these two texts and journeys. There is, of course, travel in the literal sense of physical movement from Egypt to Paris, France to America. There is also the travel from one culture to another such physical movement entails. Yet alongside these more obvious meanings of travel is movement of another kind: for each *theôros*, physical travel across space and history is mirrored by an inner journey through which each traveler is himself subtly transformed. This is not simply a reflection of the highly personal stakes of each voyage, although it is hardly irrelevant that, as Jardin puts it, the "drama of public life tended to become identified, for Tocqueville, with his own inner drama," or that Tahtawi sought in France solutions to an intellectual stasis that was simultaneously national in nature and personally immediate.[90] Yet "inner journey" here signals the extent to which these pursuits inaugurated within each traveler a kind of psychic movement from alienation to apprehension, an internal dialectic reflective of their *external* location at the intersection of two worlds, and indicative of those constant mediations between the new terrain through which they moved and the native land they carried with them wherever they went.

Attending to this often overlooked "internal movement" discloses sharp differences in the extent and nature of the alienation each traveler experienced, as well as in the kinds of mediations in which each had to engage: while Tahtawi negotiated between radically different cultures, languages, and political customs, Tocqueville's alienation was at least partially aesthetic, reflective of an aristocratic sensibility in tension with his emerging sympathy for the practices, institutions, and people that were somewhat familiar to him. Perhaps nowhere is this internal movement from alienation to recognition more vividly illustrated than in Tahtawi's initially disorienting encounter with a wall of mirrors in a French café:

> When I entered this café and lingered, I was under the impression that it was an enormous place, because of the seemingly large amount of people there. Then it became clear, as many people entered and left the café, that it was just their images reflected in the mirrors on all sides, and these appeared to multiply them as they were walking, sitting and standing. In fact, I thought the café was [open to] a street, and I realized it was enclosed only because I saw our own reflections in the mirror. Then I knew that this was all because of the property of glass.[91]

In an inversion of Plato's argument in *The Republic* that the order of the just soul may be viewed more clearly on the larger canvas of the ideal city, I want to suggest that this inner movement illuminates and anticipates the transformation of home both *theôroi* ultimately seek. Here, then, their own experiences of initiation—jagged and nonlinear as they may be—are at once an enactment of and argument for the kind of enlargement of understanding from which Tocqueville and Tahtawi thought their compatriots would most profit. For the country served by "those few persevering people" of whom Tocqueville writes, knowledge thus becomes a journey of apprehension, culminating in its last stage in "that deliberate and self-justified type of conviction born of knowledge and springing up in the midst of doubt."[92]

There is, finally, one other sense of "travel" embedded in these complexly overlapping journeys across physical, cultural, and psychic terrain. Not only does travel to a distant land serve as a source of instruction that must be sifted and vetted for an audience back home, but in both the *Rihla* and *Democracy*, it is also a kind of time travel to a potential future in which France and America serve as contrasting exemplars with utopian and dystopian features. The sense in which travel to other cultures comes to signify a temporal journey back to an earlier stage of human development is, of course, a trope characteristic of much of early European social contract theory in which the state of nature was said to still exist among "savage peoples" defined by innocence or barbarism, or both.[93] In the *Rihla* and *Democracy*, however, the convergence of spatial and temporal travel mark the coordinates of a constant mediation between past and future that reduces, orders, and

domesticates the unfamiliar yet, at the same time, attunes each *theôros*
to the losses and dangers represented by the very "wonders and marvels" they survey.

As is well known, the inquiry at the heart of *Democracy in America*
is framed by and articulated through the contrast between the age of
aristocracy and democracy. For a Frenchman who has always in mind
the passing of the *ancien régime* and the advance of "equality of conditions," the future of which was still uncertain, such a juxtaposition
is simultaneously a contrast between the past, present, and future of
France. While this sense of being located at a temporal crossroads is
perhaps most closely associated with Tocqueville, as Jardin points out,
it is evident in many of the debates within France's political class at
the time:

> . . . the new monarchy, set in place through a piece of hocus-pocus,
> seemed to have an uncertain future, and there was still the danger
> of another republican revolution. This idea of a republic, at the
> forefront of everyone's worries, evoked confused and contradic-
> tory images: ancient cities cemented by the civic virtues, Swiss
> cantons conforming to the eighteenth-century dogma which held
> that democracy was possible only in small states—but also the
> great upheaval of 1793, dictatorship and political clubs, the Reign
> of Terror and the guillotine, all of this finally degenerating into
> anarchy. Yet these concerns also brought renewed attention to bear
> on the great republic across the Atlantic, to which the French had
> long been warmly disposed. The legitimists felt none of the bitter-
> ness toward the United States of the old British leaders . . . and
> they contented themselves with ascribing the country's stability to
> unusual circumstances and prophesying that such stability
> wouldn't last forever. The liberals felt that this unusual democratic
> regime was well suited to a country that had remained rather
> primitive. It was the political expression of a rustic golden age al-
> ready past in Europe. . . . The revolution of 1830 thus presented a
> dilemma: did life in America portray scenes from the future or
> pictures of the past?[94]

In America, then, spatial and temporal travel converge, prompting
Tocqueville to seek in the New World an answer to the question,
"Whither, then, are we going?" Tocqueville's explicit answer is quite
clear—as America makes visible the complete shape of democracy, the
French may "see further into human history than could the generations
before" them, discerning the future contours of an epoch characterized
by the inexorable advance of equality.[95] What he seeks to derive from
this vision of the future, then, is "instruction" regarding those arenas

in which the intelligent exercise of human will and creativity may curtail the worst while realizing the best of the democratic epoch.

While Tocqueville's conviction that he could discern in America the outlines of a democratic future is well-known, less appreciated is the extent to which he saw the contours of Europe's feudal past in the dying cultures of Native Americans. Tocqueville admits that the "social state of these tribes was . . . different in many respects from anything known in the Old World."[96] Yet at the same time he sees in their manners a "sort of aristocratic courtesy," a warrior culture productive of a native nobility soon to be swept away by colonization, commercialism, and the centralization of an expanding state: "gentle and hospitable in peace, in war merciless even beyond the known limits of human ferocity. . . . the Indian knew how to live without wants, to suffer without complaint, and to die singing."[97] The point here, of course, is not that Tocqueville was correct but rather that his background, experiences, purposes, and interests led to the *perception* of affinities, for example, between medieval nobility and Native Americans. As Harry Liebersohn argues, along with other post-1789 aristocratic travelers, Tocqueville's "discovery" of an indigenous nobility "registered an odd moment of recognition in which the fate of exotic elites seemed to mirror the endangerment of nobility in Europe."[98] In this vein, Tocqueville writes that the

> Indian in the miserable depths of his forests cherishes the same ideas and opinions as the medieval noble in his castle, and he only needs to become a conqueror to complete the resemblance. How odd it is that the ancient prejudices of Europe should reappear, not among the European population along the coast, but in the forests of the New World.[99]

Tocqueville's elegiac lament for the passing of a warrior class "whose languages are forgotten and [whose] glory has vanished like a sound without an echo" thus serves as a dirge for the death of nobility itself, a far cry from Rousseau's valorization of the native savage as a "naturally virtuous democrat."[100]

In his analysis of the "three races" in America, moreover, Tocqueville goes on to embed such "native nobility" within a larger civilizational taxonomy that elaborates the coordinates of a particular temporal, political, and racial order. He writes that the "Negro has reached the ultimate limits of slavery, whereas the Indian lives at the extreme edge of freedom," civilization having no hold on the Native American whilst the African-American ever seeks membership in a civilization barred against him.[101] In *The Histories*, Herodotus establishes the nature of non-Greek civilizations in terms of extremities defined by gra-

dations of distance from all things Greek: Scythians are savage nomads existing in a cultural and geographical wilderness, Persians are
barbarians whose civilization represents the despotic inversion of
Greek democracy, Egypt and Scythia represent opposite extremes
from the Greek vantage.[102] Tocqueville's analysis works similarly: here
African-Americans are the inverse of Native Americans, and both represent two extremes along a spectrum in which Euro-American civilization—represented as civilization as such—is both cultural and historical epicenter.

Tocqueville goes on to read this civilizational taxonomy through the
behaviors of two women he observes on his travels, one Creek and the
other African-American. In the quick snapshot he sketches in words,
Tocqueville describes how each woman's clothing, bearing, and actions work to embody a larger set of contrasts between servility and
nobility, fear and freedom, fading pasts and potential futures, while
the white little girl in their care becomes the axis around which the
others move like satellites. Noting the relationship of each woman to
the child, he writes that

> there was a sort of barbarous luxury in the Indian woman's dress
> . . . the Negro was dressed in European clothes almost in
> shreds. . . . Crouched down in front of her mistress, anticipating
> her every desire, the Negro woman seemed equally divided be-
> tween almost maternal affection and servile fear, whereas even in
> the effusions of her tenderness, the savage woman looked free,
> proud, and almost fierce.[103]

Like the white girl, white women are located at the center of this civilizational spectrum, their behavior an index of "good morals in
America" (the section heading under which Tocqueville takes up the
topic of women), their "superiority" the linchpin "of the extraordinary
prosperity and growing power of this nation."[104]

Despite the sheer size of *Democracy in America*, Tocqueville only registers women in rare moments, whereas Tahtawi, as will become clear,
is all but fixated on them. Yet much as Ibn Battuta transforms gender
to the "legend" by which larger civilizational tendencies can be decoded or verified, here women serve as indices by which to measure
and affirm the characteristics of the races they represent, and the three
races more generally occupy three distinct points along a civilizational
spectrum that is at once cultural, moral, and temporal. Setting aside
Tocqueville's complex and highly contested views of slavery, what I
want to emphasize here are the ways in which the spatial journey to
America also becomes a form of time travel, not only to the future, but
also to a European past characterized by socially and legally codified

hierarchy and great nobility, a past for which Tocqueville felt some affinity yet also knew was doomed.

In a very different way, Tahtawi's journey to Paris is also a kind of time travel wherein a teleological view of history is grafted onto a narrative of decay. According to Tahtawi, as France possesses the requisite scientific knowledge for the perfection of civilization, it contains the seeds of Egypt's future. But as Egypt was once the greatest and most advanced of civilizations, teacher of the Greeks and of Solon himself, French knowledge is but a means of recuperating a lost greatness which is her destiny, a way Egypt may progress into a future that is simultaneously a realization of her Golden past.[105] Tahtawi embeds these arguments in a classification of civilizations that simultaneously evokes Ibn Khaldûn's mapping of human development through the constant rise and fall of tribal and sedentary civilizations and Montesquieu's classification of civilizations in terms of their "modes of subsistence" in *The Spirit of the Laws* (Tahtawi in fact describes Montesquieu as "the Frankish Ibn Khaldûn" and Ibn Khaldûn as the "Montesquieu of the East, that is, the Montesquieu of Islam").[106] More specifically, al-Tahtawi categorizes civilizations along a scale of "human achievements" and "knowledge." Thus there are "wild savages"—such as the peoples of Sudan—who are closer to animals than to humans, "uncivilized barbarians" such as nomadic Bedouin, and finally those of sedentary and urbanized (*tamassur*) peoples who are the bearers of "culture" properly understood.[107] Like Khaldunian categories, these civilizations represent stages of human development rather than peoples defined by religion, geography, or ethnicity; thus, the most advanced peoples include "Egypt, Syria, Yemen, the lands of the Romans, Persia, the Franks, the Maghrib, Sennar [in eastern Sudan], most of the lands of America [which Tahtawi later refers to as one of the "marvels of creation"], and many of the islands of the Surrounding Ocean [Oceania]."[108]

However, in contrast to Ibn Khaldûn's cyclical view of history where nomadic cultures develop into sedentary civilizations whose eventual decrepitude makes way for new waves of nomads, al-Tahtawi's civilizational grouping is distinctively evolutionary:

> the more you go back in time, the more you see the backwardness of people in regard to human industry and the knowledges of civilization. And the farther forward in time we look, the more you can see their progress and advancement. And this progress can be measured in stages by calculating the distance from or proximity to this primitive condition—so all of humankind can be divided into several stages.[109]

Indeed, there is a teleology built into the very word that Tahtawi often uses for civilization, *tamaddun* (from the Arabic root meaning to become civilized), which signifies both a process and achievement.[110] He rejects the possibility of establishing a single scale to measure all human civilization, however, preferring to distinguish sharply between moral and material *tamaddun*, both of which, he insists, are necessary for survival and happiness.[111] As the "cradle of Islam," Tahtawi avers, Asia represents the pinnacle of moral/religious development.[112] Moreover, as Muslims were once responsible for disseminating the greatest achievements in science and philosophy, Asia is the ancestral home of the teachers of the world. Yet accidents of history and politics have decoupled the scales of religious and scientific development: bearers of the true religion, Muslims have nevertheless fallen behind in the acquisition of knowledge while the Franks, who are primarily "infidels" or religiously misguided Christians "are now the most proficient in and learned about practical knowledge."[113] Only by mastering the material achievements of Europe can the cradle of Islam marry spiritual and material progress and once again become a light unto nations far and wide.

Multiple Meditations

Tahtawi's Egypt and Tocqueville's France were in many ways radically different worlds: nineteenth-century Egypt was governed by an absolute ruler intent on acquiring European knowledge to enhance his own power while France was an unstable republic riven by deep divides among those loyal to the old order and those intent on birthing the new. Tocqueville's and Tahtawi's pedagogical *theôriai* frequently reflect and reinforce such differences: Tahtawi was sent on a mission clearly defined by the *wali*'s designs and heavily supervised, while Tocqueville voluntarily sought his travels, defined his own purposes, and apparently felt little compunction in veering far afield of the study of American prisons. As the preceding discussion shows, however, both narratives range well beyond any narrow bureaucratic assignment to evaluate entire societies comparatively, as well as the practices, peoples, and knowledge that comprise them. Each inquiry proceeds, of course, by way of a set of culturally and historically specific presuppositions and representative strategies designed to render their observations intelligible for their intended audiences back home. Thus it is not only the case that each seeks very different kinds of knowledge for their compatriots, but that the terms of translation governing what and how they see are quite different. Yet inasmuch as the explicit focus of each text is the spectacle of a nineteenth-century republic, these *theôriai* together provide a uniquely doubled view not only of theorizing but also of "republican politics."[114] It is "doubled" both in the sense of providing a view of a similar object from two different angles and because the perspective of each *theôros* is itself equivocal: neither evinces passionate commitment or summary rejection but rather an "appreciative ambivalence" toward the object of study, an equivocation born of great admiration for the achievements of a "democratic age" and anxieties about what is jeopardized by its appearance and advance.

Teasing out al-Tahtawi's own perspective in *Takhlis* is a challenge, however, in part because the text is multivocal and obviously hybrid. He describes his book several times as a *rihla*, a genre which, as I have suggested in the previous chapters, straddles geography, history, ethnography, and story-telling. In style and tone, *Takhlis* must also be located in the tradition of *adab* literature in which knowledge and entertainment converge. As *adab* literature seeks, in Anouar Louca's words, to bring "together the sum of knowledge necessary to the making of a knowledgeable gentleman," instances of the genre not only incorporate a wide array of sources but exhibit a style that "allows for associations, digressions, and therefore amalgamation."[115] From the perspective of social science in which consistency of style and parsimoniousness of purpose are indicative of serious scholarship, *adab* literature appears unwieldy and indirect. Yet as in Herodotus's *Histories* and Ibn Battuta's *Rihla*, in Tahtawi's *Takhlis*, Cicero's boundary between truth and pleasure is deliberately breached, and with a double objective. As al-Mawardi (974–1058) suggests in the introduction to his famous *Kitab Adab al-Dunya wa al-Din*, in *adab* literature such multiple authorities and sources serve as witnesses for what follows, in effect testifying to the veracity of the text, while appealing to the reader on several levels, literary, spiritual, and intellectual.[116]

Yet Tahtawi's *Takhlis* is not only an exemplar of *rihla* and *adab* literature; it also reflects the French education he received in Paris, including exposure to works by Montesquieu, Voltaire, Rousseau, Condorcet, Descartes, Racine, Condillac, Newton, and Conrad Malte-Brun. His *Rihla* is thus multiply hybrid, bearing the imprint of nineteenth-century French thought, the conventions of the *rihla* genre in which an emphasis on ʿajaʾib (things that are marvelous, strange, or unusual) is central, and an ecumenical *adab* style that, in the case of *Takhlis*, is expressed as a mélange of detailed cultural observations, classifications, fragmentary translations, letters, documents, poetry (French and Arabic, Tahtawi's own and others, only some with attribution), hadith, and Qurʾanic verses.[117] *Takhlis* is clearly organized, divided into six essays—covering Tahtawi's trip to Paris; a taxonomy of civilizations; a detailed account of the habits, manners, and sciences of the French; a lengthy description of activities of the students on the mission; and an account of French politics, including a record of the events of 1830—but the multiplicity of often unattributed sources and quotations produce in the narrative radical shifts in voice, tone, and perspective.

Indeed, the "extraction of gold" referred to in the title of the *Rihla* might well refer not only to Tahtawi's sifting through French manners, customs, politics, and ideas for valuable lessons but also to the way in which *Takhlis* must itself be read. For discerning Tahtawi's own views is greatly complicated not only by the style of the *Rihla* but also by his efforts to reassure pious—and skeptical—Muslim readers of the legitimacy of his efforts, as evinced by the repeated invocation of Islamic sources to frame or authorize his arguments. Such efforts are further revealed by what Tahtawi chose to delete from the published manuscript: one excised passage, apparently deemed too controversial, described a French scientist's attempt to render the sacred texts allegorically in order to render religious teaching consistent with heliocentricity.[118]

Unlike Tocqueville, whose purposes and constraints were in many ways self-imposed, Tahtawi's own position is further obscured by the many textual gestures designed to please or at least avoid offending his powerful patron, who not only sponsored the student mission to Paris but, as *Takhlis* attests, exercised a fair amount of control over what the visitors studied and how hard they worked from his perch in distant Cairo. At one point, Muhammad ʿAli even sent a missive to Paris threatening the students with punishment if they did not work hard enough.[119] Young as he was, Tahtawi already recognized that Muhammad ʿAli was not known to welcome opposition or independence of mind from his officials. As one scholar describes it:

> None of his subordinates dared to contradict the Pasha or show disapproval of any of his projects, for if one did he would be certain to be considered an enemy and sent away to some distant place or exiled from the country. Consequently, no one could tell him the truth. . . . The Egyptians whom he had sent to Europe on educational missions and who occupied government posts were equally reluctant to reveal their true opinions.[120]

This accounts, in part, for the intermittent eruptions of praise to Muhammad ʿAli's greatness in *Takhlis*, the carefully worded assessments of constitutional control on unlimited authority,[121] and the inclusion of various documents, from examination evaluations to letters from his teachers and French scholars, meant to testify to the intensity and success of his studies.

The disorienting multivocality of the text is somewhat offset by a consistent strategy that is best captured by the word *mizan*, derived from the Arabic root meaning to balance, compare, weigh, or draw parallels.[122] Tahtawi uses this term explicitly when describing Montesquieu, and in particular the mediations between "Eastern and Western *adab*" in the *Persian Letters* (which he unaccountably attributes to Rousseau) and the comparison between "legal and political doctrines" in *The Spirit of the Laws*.[123] Tahtawi engages throughout *Takhlis* in the practice of *mizan* in which Parisians, the French, Europeans, and Christians are classified, described, and evaluated, but always by way of comparison, either explicit or implicit, to Egyptians, Arabs, and Muslims. Just as France haunts Tocqueville's reflections on America even when it all but disappears from the surface of the narrative, it is the constant preoccupation with the *watan* (homeland) driving Tahtawi's inquiry, organizing his observations, delimiting his vision, framing his mediations, and bringing into sharpest relief those instances of greatest cultural rupture and commonality.

Describing Tahtawi's endeavor as "comparative," however, requires dispensing with an understanding of comparative work as "rel[ying] on the clear separation of the entities to be compared, before serious comparison can begin."[124] Given that Tahtawi was singled out for training in translation while in Paris, somewhere along the way French literature and language ceased to be simply an object of study and became part of the frame through which he viewed the world. What appear on the surface to be a series of simple comparisons between two discrete worlds, Egypt and France, turns out to be embedded in an inquiry that is already culturally syncretic. A case in point: inasmuch as Tahtawi's observations of French manners and practices are largely organized around ʿajaʾib, his classifications reflect primarily what appear most unusual or strange from the perspective of his intended audience back home. Thus, refrigeration, the plumbing system, the prevalence of mirrors, indoor heating, the use of eating utensils, the volatility of Parisian weather (reflecting, he concludes, the capriciousness of its inhabitants), the preference for sitting on chairs rather than rugs, and the craftsmanship of a French man-of-war strike Tahtawi as particularly worthy of notice or comment.[125] Yet at the same time, parts of *Takhlis* are closely modeled on Georges-Bernard Depping's history of the food, clothing, women, trade, dance, and manners of various nations, a book which Tahtawi was in the process of translating into Arabic, and from which he quotes at length in the *Rihla*.[126]

Indeed, *Takhlis* can be understood, in part, as an elaborate linguistic mediation, for unlike Tocqueville, Tahtawi did not have a language ready-made to represent the new world he encountered; he was com-

pelled to coin Arabic neologisms, deploy classical Arabic terminology
in unorthodox ways, or directly borrow from other languages simply
to describe unfamiliar phenomena to his readers.[127] Thus alongside
various observations about French politics and culture, Tahtawi engages in a running commentary on the challenges of such linguistic
mediation. He argues, on the one hand, that "when one masters one
language, one knows all others potentially," but cautions, on the other,
that beauty and elegance are inevitably lost in the effort to render the
poetry of one language into another in which the principles and structure are radically different, and notes the particular problems of attempting to translate scientific books without adequate terminology.[128]
He occasionally seems to throw up his hands at the absence of linguistic equivalences, as in his exasperated admission that he cannot find
an Arabic noun adequate to convey the French *théater/spectacle*, and his
flat acknowledgment that there simply are many things in the world
for which there are no Arabic words.[129] Even when there are Arabic
terms available to him, Tahtawi at times finds them woefully outdated,
as with *bilad al-Ifranj* (literally "lands of the Franks"), at that time a
widely recognized way to refer to Europeans that had originated in
Arabic descriptions of the inhabitants of Charlemagne's empire. Tahtawi uses *Ifranj* for the convenience of his readers, but simultaneously
attempts to instruct his audience on its obvious inadequacies given
that the historic "lands of the Franks" included what became territories
of the Ottoman Empire.[130]

As *mizan* involves not only simple juxtaposition but an act of equili-
bration suggestive of evaluation and mediation, much of Tahtawi's
analysis entails a survey of those aspects of French culture and politics that are "strange," "admirable," and even occasionally—although
with clearly specified qualifications—worthy of imitation. These include advances in science, technology, and nonreligious knowledge
more generally, subjects which Muhammad ʿAli had charged the student mission to master. But Tahtawi also singles out as "remarkable"
very particular aspects of "French character," including a restless curiosity, ingenuity, love of travel, desire for knowledge, cleanliness,
warmth to strangers, freedom from enslavement to tradition, and
dedication to hard work.[131] Particularly worthy of his respect are character traits Tahtawi associates with Arabs, including a strong sense of
gratitude, antipathy toward homosexuality, love of freedom, justice,
honor, and pride.[132] His regard extends to the practice of French medi-
cine (he translates a doctor's guidebook in its entirety) as well as to
many aspects of French government, a system which, he carefully
writes, can serve as "a lesson to those who can learn from it."[133] In
this connection, Tahtawi expresses particular appreciation for the ef-

ficiency of the French system of taxation and financial management, freedom of a raucous press which checks oppression and corruption, and an "amazing" and "remarkable" justice system particularly evident in the aftermath of the 1830 Revolution. He is so taken with what he characterizes as the "precious" French Constitutional Charter of 1814—its embrace of meritocracy, commitment to equality before the law, and the preservation of private property—that he includes an Arabic translation of it in its entirety in the Third Essay of *Takhlis*.[134] In a revealing passage, however, Tahtawi makes clear that this choice requires explanation and justification:

> In it are many things the justice of which no one endowed with rationality could deny. . . .We will reproduce it here, even though much of it is not in the Book of God Almighty, nor in the *sunna* of His Prophet—peace be upon him—so that you may discover how their intellect determined that justice and equity are the foundations for the preservation of kingdoms and the flourishing of subjects. When rulers and their subjects were guided by this, their lands thrived, their knowledge multiplied, their wealth accumulated, and their hearts were content. For you do not ever hear any of them complain of tyranny; justice is indeed the basis of civilization.[135]

As Khaldun al-Husry aptly argues in regard to Tahtawi's view of France, we "need to bear in mind that in less than forty years the Paris in which no one complained of injustice was due for the Paris Commune, which was to inspire Marx to write 'The Civil War in France.'"[136] Yet what is of interest here is not accuracy but representation, for like Tocqueville, Tahtawi's objective is not exhaustive documentation but rather the extrapolation of instructive knowledge from (very eclectic) firsthand observation. This Tahtawi makes abundantly clear in his summary dismissal of French Orientalist Sylvestre de Sacy's objection that *Takhlis* inappropriately generalized to all France the behavior of Parisians and urban French.[137] The significance of observing Paris firsthand is like that of seeing Rome in its heyday, Tahtawi avers, and thus the part can be taken to represent the whole: "he who has not seen Rome or its people does not know anything of this world, or of humankind."[138]

Crucial to such extrapolation is the doubled view of France through the lenses of the two kinds of progress (*tamaddun*), material and religious. Unsurprisingly, Tahtawi regards Europe as the locus of material *tamaddun*, and praises and selectively advocates the adoption of particular French technological, scientific, and intellectual achievements as tools necessary for the prosperity of any nation:

It is well known that the level of civilization a country or city at-
tains depends upon its learning, and its distance from a state of
primitivism and savagery ... [and] the lands of the Franks are
filled with a variety of knowledge, arts, and fine customs which,
no one can deny, bring about sociability and the adornments of
civilization. It is well established that of the many Frankish countries, the French nation is the most excellent by virtue of their commitment to the sciences and knowledge, and is the greatest of all
in terms of culture and civilization.[139]

But when measured on a moral scale a quite different picture emerges:
here France embodies not only a kind of spiritual impoverishment but
a threat to the moral integrity of those exposed to its corruption.

In the first instance, the French are, regrettably, either infidels or
Christians, and as such they embrace many "dreadful" and "abominable" practices such as seeking forgiveness from the (merely human)
clergy, sacrilegious rituals such as the procession at Corpus Christi,
and heresies by men of the cloth that "cannot be counted"—including
the imposition of celibacy, a practice that only serves to "increase their
moral depravity."[140] Even more appalling, the French are ultimately religious "in name only," disregarding their own revealed scripture
when it is inconvenient or runs counter to their almost irrational faith
in rationalism.[141] They cultivate more respect for philosophers than
prophets, disregarding all that is not accessible to human reason. Inasmuch as religion operates as a restraint on human behavior, the French
see it as useful rather than true, and thus imagine that inevitable advances in knowledge conducive to mastering nature and human nature will soon render it obsolete.[142] The cost to French character and
mores is evident everywhere, Tahtawi insists, from the excessive
"money they spend on personal pleasures, satanic lusts, and on amuse-
ments and diversions," to their unrestrained greed, love of profit, commercialism, avariciousness, vanity, lack of individual generosity, and
untrammeled pursuit of reputation and glory.[143]

But nowhere is this moral turpitude more in evidence than in the
behavior of French women, whose relative sexual freedom, appearance, and manners at once rivet and revolt him in ways that echo earlier Muslim travelers who portrayed "Europe as an eroticized 'heaven
on earth' and European women and men respectively as nymphomani-
acs and effeminates."[144] Like Ibn Battuta and Tocqueville, Tahtawi takes
women as a moral index of the entire culture in which they are located,
and their behavior is measured always by gradations of distance from
the virtuous "Arab/Muslim woman" who, he writes elsewhere, is
veiled when among strangers, largely exists for men's pleasure, works

in the home, and does not govern either publicly or privately.[145] With a sniff of disdain, he takes note of where Parisian men and women mix—in schools, at balls, dance-halls, public parks. And while he praises the passion for knowledge and love of travel evident even among women, at one point admitting that there are some Frenchwomen of great virtue, he concludes rather summarily that most are not as the French in general are "seized by the art of love . . . their passion is an end in itself, because they don't regard it as having any other aim."[146] Thus Frenchwomen—particularly the aristocracy and the lower classes—are largely unchaste, while their men view such infidelity with equanimity because "among them, adultery is but a flaw or vice, and not a primary sin, especially in the case of unmarried people."[147] On this basis, Tahtawi decides that among the French, "men are slaves to the women and under their power, regardless of whether or not they are beautiful . . . they make the mistake of surrendering authority to their women."[148]

Yet like Ibn Battuta, Tahtawi also goes to great lengths to describe in precise detail exactly what parts of women's bodies are exposed and covered and with what effects, claiming that "Frenchwomen are extraordinarily beautiful, charming and eager to please," describing the relative beauty and superior "purity of the bodies" of women who live in cities versus towns, condemning in one breath the immodesty of women who "tie a thin girdle over their clothes in order to make their waists looks slender and their haunches full," but going on to note rather lasciviously that "what is remarkable is that, once the girdle is on, it is possible for a man to enclose this small waist between his two hands . . . they have many such wiles."[149] While fascinated by Frenchwomen's visual—and therefore presumably sexual—availability, like other visitors before him, Tahtawi often takes this very visibility as an "indication of the collapse of cultural distinctions between the moral and the immoral, and the decent and the indecent."[150] Tahtawi thus concludes that "it behooves a man to be wary of women."[151]

Yet the risk of sexual corruption from unchaste females is just emblematic of the many dangers of immersion in French life. "From this treatise, you will understand that learning the disciplines is not simple, and it is necessary for a seeker of knowledge to overcome dangers to reach his aims in these lands," Tahtawi writes.[152] There is, of course, the ever-present danger of "going native" as evinced by several Egyptians Tahtawi meets who have adopted French dress and customs, not to mention the Muslims who have converted to Christianity—"God save us from that."[153] But there are also the larger risks of being seduced and unmoored by the spiritual regress in evidence everywhere, from rampant materialism to an indifference to poverty—the moral price for the remarkable material achievements on display.[154] The risk to the traveler as well as the homeland to which he returns bearing instruction is thus that European knowledge itself may exercise a corrupting influence, undermining certainty and destabilizing truth: French "books of philosophy are completely filled with innovations/heresies [*bidaʿ*] . . . it is thus necessary that one who desires to delve into the French language—which contains within it some elements of philosophy—be firmly grounded in the Book and Sunna, so that he will not be seduced by this, nor his faith weaken."[155]

Like *Democracy in America*, the *Rihla* has been particularly susceptible to partisan and partial appropriations, and Tahtawi himself has been characterized alternately as religious and secular, conservative and progressive, a narrow nationalist and a cosmopolitan man of the world, an anti-Ottomanist reformer and a quintessentially Ottomanist bureaucrat.[156] Some scholars, for example, argue that *Takhlis* is essentially a brief for constitutionalism, freedom, and democracy, and thus represents a "conscious transition from a religious conception of nature and society and its goals to another which is 'civil' or 'secular.' "[157] Others argue that Tahtawi is ultimately a traditional and conservative thinker, an advocate of a system of rule in which subjects owe a single man "perfect obedience; for obedience to the ruler is a corollary to obedience to God and to His prophet. If the ruler is oppressive, the subjects should bear this patiently until God opens for them the gate of guiding him to the good and directing his state to justice."[158] Still others have insisted on the primacy of the bureaucratic context in which Tahtawi worked for understanding the development of his thought and the overlapping personal, political, and national commitments his entire body of work expresses.[159]

I have suggested that determining Tahtawi's own political and intellectual commitments in the *Rihla* is greatly complicated by the *adab* style of *Takhlis*, as well as its cautious and strategic mediations, many of which gestured to the authority of the Egyptian ʿulama back home, others of which reveal the extent to which Tahtawi felt constrained to justify or, at the very least, acknowledge the policies of the *wali* in which he may have believed but with which he most certainly could not have openly disagreed. Given that Tahtawi's emphases not only shifted over time but from book to book, moreover, it becomes quite difficult to pinpoint, once and for all, his final views about legitimate rule, the role of science, and the authority of religion.[160] It would be an injustice, however, to portray Tahtawi as an ambitious lower-level bureaucrat driven primarily by the desire to strengthen his position vis-à-vis the Turco-Circassian elites in Egypt on the one hand and the native ʿulama on the other. Nor is it warranted to characterize his

entire corpus as an "elaborate legitimation" for Muhammad ʿAli's policies, casting Tahtawi as little more than a writer in the "Mirror for
Princes" tradition[161] eager to justify, rationalize, and solidify absolutist
rule, administrative centralization, and Egyptian autonomy.[162] Neither a
simple reflection of bureaucratic imperatives nor philosophical influence, the *Rihla* is a convergence of both; Tahtawi's writing bears the
mark of the tension between them, however, and many of the contradictions and inconsistencies of his oeuvre are best read in these terms.[163]

In *Takhlis* such tensions issue in the kind of "appreciative ambivalence" toward postrevolutionary France that characterizes Tocqueville's view of American democracy. Despite arguments to the contrary,
Tahtawi was quite clearly impressed by the restless and relentless pursuit of new worldly knowledge characteristic of the French and the
remarkable administrative, technological, and scientific marvels that
were the result. The *Rihla* contains, moreover, a lively, detailed, and
fairly sympathetic account of the 1830 challenge to the French monarchy, which Tahtawi witnessed firsthand. Here Tahtawi's antipathies to
the Bourbons, dislike of Charles X who "dishonored the laws," admiration for the French love of freedom, and respect for a vibrant press are
quite clear.[164] And while he notes the obvious differences between the
divine and mundane sources of Muslim and French law respectively,
he suggests that much of what is valuable about the French exemplar
can either be located in or legitimized by Islamic traditions and texts,
thus rendering the innovative traditional, and the traditional as "modern."[165] For instance, he advocates adopting the French system of taxation as a useful innovation that can be justified by some opinions in
the Hanafi school of Islamic law—this despite the fact that Tahtawi
was himself of the Shafiʿi legal school.[166] He further argues that the
French understanding of freedom is equivalent to the emphasis on justice (*ʿadl*) and equity (*insaf*) in classical Muslim political thought, as
both are meant to check arbitrary power by invoking a ruler's responsibilities to adhere to universal law and attend to the welfare of his
subjects.[167] Perhaps for these reasons, a later edition of the *Rihla* omitted
Tahtawi's description of the French as *kafara* (infidels or unbelievers).[168]

Yet in contrast to other depictions of Tahtawi as a secular Franco-
phile, he quite clearly harbors substantial reservations about France
that extend well beyond his initial anxiety about the contagion of
"Frankish" moral corruption. For Tahtawi sees in the embrace of science and the rationalist epistemology crucial to its emergence a deeper
threat to the authority of revealed truth, drawing a connection between
the profoundly this-worldly philosophical underpinnings of science
and a morally bankrupt cosmology in which mortal sins are transfigured into natural urges, avaricious materialism is said to be rooted in

human nature, and the divine plan for the universe and all things in it are reduced to a system of physical causality just waiting to be mastered by way of human ingenuity. Ultimately, Tahtawi's preferences, anxieties, enthusiasms, and strategic negotiations suggest less a reflexive parochialism than a concern—political, intellectual, moral and pragmatic all at once—to adapt European achievements to Egyptian needs and imperatives. Toward this end, Tahtawi not only seeks to detach modern knowledge from Europe, but also to decouple the intellectual and technological fruits of modern science from the larger epistemological and philosophical framework in which they are embedded, much as generations of Muslim "reformists" would do after him. This enables him to transform science from a worldview requiring fealty to certain methodological and rationalist presuppositions into an instrument whose practice need not transgress either the domain of revealed truth or the authority of the ʿulama who serve as its gatekeepers.

Determining Tocqueville's view of American democracy does not present the same challenges as does discerning Tahtawi's view of republican France. This is in part because almost every aspect of Tocqueville's life and work, including his private letters, has been exceedingly, perhaps even excessively, well documented. It is also because *Democracy in America*, while intellectually and stylistically complex, is univocal rather than multivocal, drawing together observations and ideas from many directions into intersecting lines of inquiry over which Tocqueville claims complete sovereignty (despite his—often unattributed—debt to others, such as Guizot and Montesquieu).[169] Rather than review its well-known arguments, the following foregrounds those intra- and intertextual comparisons made possible by reading *Democracy in America* through the lens of travel.

To begin with, *Democracy*, like *Takhlis*, is intended as a political and intellectual intervention in the life of a nation-state. Indeed, the very understanding of "democracy" Tocqueville brings to the United States is inherently comparative: defined as the absence of the kind of social and political hierarchies that had characterized prerevolutionary France, it already contains within it the French experience, which serves as the implicit point of reference throughout.[170] The comparative dimension to "democracy" is, moreover, both spatial and temporal, for it refers to both an historical condition and a process. While in Europe the "democratic age" has superseded the age of aristocracy once and for all, the relentless equalization of conditions that defines it is ongoing, inescapable, and crucial to Tocqueville's argument, irreversible.

Like Tahtawi's doubled assessment of French political and cultural life, Tocqueville's attitude toward this development is, to put it mildly, mixed. While much ink has been spilled debating whether and to what extent Tocqueville is a conservative aristocrat at heart, an ambivalent democrat, or a full-blown liberal, his doubled awareness of a French republic in which feudal hierarchies have largely been swept away and a New World that never really knew them (despite the deep fissure of racial inequality) yields both sympathy for the characteristics of the democratic age and what he describes as a "kind of religious dread" toward its constant and inexorable advance. Like an orphan bereft of parental guidance, democracy in France "has been left to its wild instincts" while those who might have cultivated its benefits or "mitigated its vices" sat stolidly contemplating the receding ruins of the past.[171] Much as Tahtawi seeks to disentangle the necessary from the contingent, Tocqueville casts the challenge confronting Christian nations not in terms of how human beings may halt this inevitable leveling, but rather how they might ascertain through comparison across history and culture what about the dangers it poses and the opportunities it presents are susceptible to the exercise of human will.

In an effort to meet this challenge, *Democracy* entails a comparison across time, an imaginative journey back to beginnings, because for a nation as for a human being, the circumstances of birth—or what Tocqueville refers to as "the point of departure"—are crucial for discerning the trajectory and features of future development.[172] As the American republic is new, its "point of departure" is still visible, and as democracy in the New World emerged without the tumult of revolution, an inquiry into its passion for equality is a particularly illuminating and instructive contrast for France. Unlike Europe, where the continuing legacy of divisive passions make it difficult to discern the "true character and permanent instincts of democracy . . . in America democracy follows its own inclinations. Its features are natural and its movements free. It is there that it must be judged. And such a study should be interesting and profitable for nobody more than ourselves, for we are being daily carried along by an irresistible movement, walking like blind men toward—what?"[173]

To answer this question, Tocqueville draws a distinction between a democratic society where equalization of conditions proceeds with the force of gravity and those institutions that, if designed democratically, may temper the worst tendencies contained within it. This enables him to not only capture what is distinctive about American society but also to classify many others. Thus in contrast to the best that the American example offers, it is also possible to have in one place a "sort of equality in the world of politics without any political freedom. A man may be the equal of all his fellows save one, who is the master of all without distinctions."[174] Much as Montesquieu does in *The Persian Letters*, Tocqueville looks to a predominantly Muslim society for the perfect embodiment of "equality in servitude," describing Muhammad ʿAli's Egypt as a place where centralized despotism is "helped by the ignorance and democratic weakness of his subjects . . . the pasha has made the country his factory and the people his workmen."[175] Somewhere in between Egypt and America lies France, whose future is uncertain but whose history demonstrates the easy affinity between democratic revolution and anarchy, encroachment on private property, assault on individual freedoms, and a new and possibly more dangerous centralization of power, one that sweeps away both aristocratic and intermediate associations in the name of "the people."[176]

American stability, prosperity, security of property, and freedom represent a rebuke to French failures, but even the spectacle of democracy in the United States is not entirely reassuring. Tocqueville is famously dismayed by what he argues is the growing omnipotence of majority opinion, the pressures toward conformity, the mediocrity of mind and leadership, and the various conditions conducive to administrative despotism.[177] From a comparative perspective, it is also striking that, like Tahtawi, Tocqueville is particularly aghast at the rampant materialism on view. For in a society in which inequalities of wealth are not viewed as inevitable, god-given, or natural, Tocqueville argues, the relentless pursuit of material pleasures by all is seen as the ultimate expression of the exercise of freedom and the principle of equality.[178] Unlike France, then, American democracy demonstrates not the dangers of revolution but the specter of "universal uniformity" and political, intellectual, and civilizational stasis.[179]

It is precisely with these multiple vistas in view that Tocqueville searches for lessons conducive to "educating democracy" in France, an urgent endeavor critical to the future not only of his homeland but also of Christian nations and "civilization" itself; no less than the "fate of the world" hinges on it.[180] It requires in the first instance disentangling those circumstances unique to the flourishing of democracy in the United States—including its relative geographic isolation in the New World and the absence of an hereditary aristocracy—from characteristics that might yield instruction applicable to Europe. This he does by way of an additional series of spatial comparisons. Throughout the discussion he turns to England, Russia, Canada, and South America to bring what is distinctive about America and France into clearer view. Thus the failures of South American countries to replicate the features of American democracy suggest to Tocqueville that physical location in the New World is not as crucial to the American experiment as some would have it.[181] Canadians, on the other hand, demonstrate the folly of reproducing ancient virtues in a new context.[182] Formidable by virtue of sheer population and military might, Russian strength is built on an inversion of American principles, a nation comprised of subjects servile to one man and at war with civilization.[183] As English culture overlaps with but remains distinct from that of the United States, it becomes yet another vehicle to bring American (and by implication, French) features into sharp relief: the residue of aristocratic distinctions of wealth and status breeds in England an "unspoken warfare among all the citizens" as well as a "strange unsociability and reserved and taciturn disposition" in stark contrast to the triumph of patriotism over class in America.[184] Indeed, even his travels in England become an extension of his reflections on America, as when he claims that "it is infinitely easier to form clear ideas and precise conceptions about America than about Great Britain"[185] and contrasts the "vast chaos" of England to the coherence of the United States: "[t]his is certainly a different sort of difficulty to overcome than in the study of America. Here, there is not that single principle which tranquilly awaits the working out of its consequences, but instead lines that cross one another in every direction, a labyrinth in which we are utterly lost."[186]

Drawing on all these contrasts and observations, Tocqueville's famous conclusion, of course, is that the greatness of American democracy rests on its laws and mores, the latter defined quite broadly to include practical experience, beliefs, habits, and commitments. In addition to federalist institutional arrangements and an independent jury system, Tocqueville, like Tahtawi, singles out religion and the press as crucial to mitigating the preoccupation with material pleasures and the temptation to turn over matters of public interest to "an immense protective power."[187] While the subject of Tocqueville's own faith is a matter of great debate among scholars,[188] it is nevertheless the case that religion is central to *Democracy*, just as it is to Tahtawi's *Takhlis*. Indeed, much as Tahtawi regarded religion as at once true and necessary to progress, Tocqueville declares (Christian) religion to be both "useful and natural" to human beings,[189] arguing that it "is by a sort of intellectual aberration, and in a way, by doing moral violence to their own nature, that men detach themselves from religious beliefs; an invincible inclination draws them back. Incredulity is an accident; faith is the only permanent state of mankind."[190] Collapsing utility and truth, Tocqueville argues that religious dogmas are necessary because men require certain fixed answers to "primordial questions" that simultaneously serve as a bulwark against existential and moral anarchy and the foundation for effective action.[191] This is particularly necessary in a democracy where all other fixed truths and ideas have been called into question or swept away. And in America it is clear that religion has additional salutary effects: the separation of church and state preserves the independent religious influence necessary to combat the materialism and individualism of democracy by reminding people of their obligations to each other and to things beyond the body and this life.

While Tahtawi largely regards justice as the responsibility of the sovereign, and defines it in particular in terms of the ruler's obligation to protect the freedom of his subjects, Tocqueville locates the well-spring of freedom in participation in self-rule. More specifically, he argues that liberty is perhaps best protected through participation in self-governing free institutions, particularly those at the local level, where each citizen receives his initial training in the use of freedom, learns to care for and cooperate in matters within his own purview but also experiences an enlargement of vision conducive to a love of liberty, a commitment to public responsibility, and an appreciation of the need for individual restraint. By way of political action, then, the "debased taste for equality" that so jeopardizes human freedom is transfigured into "that manly and legitimate passion for equality which rouses in all men a desire to be strong and respected."[192] Central to this transformation is the vitality of the press which, he argues in a vein similar to Tahtawi, is crucial not only for communication but also for militating against the encroachments of centralized power: "equality isolates and weakens men, but the press puts each man in reach of a very powerful weapon which can be used even by the weakest and most isolated of men . . . to call to his aid all his fellow citizens and all mankind."[193]

Thus American democracy contains within itself the seeds of the solution to the dangers the passion for equality presents, and it is in these seeds that Tocqueville finds for France "new remedies for new ills."[194] American laws and mores are not the only ones suited to democratic societies, and indeed, may not be even the most appealing, Tocqueville acknowledges, but at a minimum they reveal that "we need not despair of regulating democracy by means of laws and mores," that there is within the "providential" march of equality an arena for the exercise of human will to "educate democracy" toward its better nature.[195] Importantly, he remains far from convinced that, "even in the most favorable circumstances . . . the government of the multitude is an excellent thing," and writes in a letter to a friend that "what I want is not a republic, but a hereditary monarchy" centralized and strong enough to resist majority opinion but sufficiently liberal to preserve a substantial sphere for provincial liberties and personal initiative.[196] The task at hand is determined not by desire but by Providence; as Mill writes in his review of *Democracy in America*, "man cannot turn back the rivers to their source; but it rests with himself whether they shall fertilize or lay waste to his fields."[197] What is necessary is to acquire the lessons that enable peoples of the democratic age to strive for that "form of greatness and of happiness which is proper to ourselves."[198]

By casting *Democracy* as a critical intervention in this endeavor, in large measure by identifying the mechanisms by which the most dangerous tendencies of equality might be contained, Tocqueville here evokes Tahtawi's insistence that the *Rihla* is the means by which to distinguish between what is culturally specific from what is (in his terms) universal, what is anomalous from what is necessary or inevitable. For Tahtawi it is science that is necessary and unavoidable, and for Tocqueville it is the equalization of conditions that is inescapable and inexorable. Yet within the realm of existence susceptible to human will, there is much both view with a jaundiced eye and see themselves as charged with charting, carefully negotiating the risks and rewards on view for the benefit of their compatriots back home. As with Tocqueville's claim that the fate of the world depends on efforts to "educate democracy," for Tahtawi, the stakes of his endeavor could not be higher: no less than the material prosperity and civilizational renewal of the *watan* hang in the balance, and thus only those "devoid of justice and experience" will deny the opportunity European "expertise" presents.[199]

Despite radical differences in the kind of instruction they seek abroad, Tahtawi's and Tocqueville's assessments of nineteenth-century France and America thus converge around admiration for the rule of law, the vibrancy of the press, the integrity of the justice system, and with serious caveats, the restlessness of a people constantly curious and on the move. At the same time, such admiration is tempered by revulsion at what both see as the crass materialism of a people too quick to jettison much of what gives life meaning, whether it is the capacity for greatness and individuality (Tocqueville), or the moral equilibrium necessary for ultimate happiness (Tahtawi). Finally, just as Tocqueville confessed in a letter his preference for a hereditary monarchy over a republic, much of *Takhlis* is an affirmation of the power of a single sovereign to usher in an age of regeneration despite Tahtawi's obvious attraction for constitutional principles; his analysis of the 1830 French uprising is less an argument for popular sovereignty than a veiled exhortation to Muhammad ʿAli to wield his absolute power justly.[200]

Yet I want to suggest that these ambivalences and preferences are due less to Tahtawi's "traditional conservatism" or Tocqueville's "nostalgic monarchism" than to a combination of perspective and pragmatism. Guided by the purposes of a pedagogical *theôria*, both seek practical instruction that requires tempering political, intellectual, and moral commitments with considerations of utility, applicability, and context. I also want to argue that both are ultimately drawn to these purposes because they are particularly well situated to be at once appreciative and skeptical of what they see, alert to both the promise and dangers of knowledge from afar, and in Tahtawi's case, to the risks of taking such knowledge home. Tahtawi, for instance, brings to his assessments of postrevolutionary France the memory of the four years of instability out of which Muhammad ʿAli's leadership emerged. Moreover, given the deprivations Tahtawi's family suffered as a result of Muhammad ʿAli's policies—his mother reportedly had to sell some of her jewelry and remaining property to support Tahtawi's studies—by the time he wrote the *Rihla*, he had experienced firsthand the despotism of the *wali* as well as the benefits of his favor.[201] Like Tocqueville, whose appreciation for American democracy was sharpened by acute awareness of the alternatives to it, Tahtawi was in this way well placed to appreciate the demands for political freedom he saw in France while attending always to the dangers invited by the vacuum of authority and the promise of order. And it is, finally, precisely Tahtawi's location at the intersection of the Islamic sciences in which he was trained and the European sciences in which he immersed himself in Paris that makes him so adept at registering the pull and limits of both.

Tocqueville is similarly situated to be appreciative of and ambivalent about what he sees. He was born into an aristocratic family with close ties to the Bourbon monarchy and, as his great-grandfather was executed during "the Terror" and his parents barely escaped the same fate, he had a quite personal understanding of the tyranny of which a radical democracy is capable. Yet as a member of the nobility, Tocqueville was also a close observer of its failings past and present, and it is from this doubled vantage that he views democracy in all its complexity. On the one hand, then, Tocqueville expresses contempt for members of his own class, accusing the nobility in France of having withdrawn from all its duties and responsibilities for public affairs, clinging instead to the residual benefits of its status. Yet at the same time, he remains appreciative of the aristocratic tendencies democracy has swept away, including a certain elevation of mind and scorn of worldly advantages; strong convictions and honorable devotedness; refined habits and embellished manners; the cultivation of the arts and of theoretical sciences; a love of poetry, beauty, and glory; and the capacity to carry on great enterprises of enduring worth.[202]

Tocqueville's appreciation of these aristocratic tendencies intrudes on his assessment of democracy throughout the argument; at moments, it becomes the standard by which he measures French democracy and calls it to account. "In abandoning our ancestors' social state and throwing their institutions, ideas, and mores pell-mell behind us, what have we put in its place?" he asks. His answer: "we have abandoned whatever good things the old order of society could provide but have not profited from what our present state can offer; we have destroyed an aristocratic society, and settling down complacently among the ruins of the old building, we seem to want to stay there like that forever."[203] His cautious appreciation of democracy derives not only from the dangers latent in the passion for equality but an aesthetic antipathy for what he characterizes as a kind of middle-class "coarseness," writing in a note that "I have an intellectual taste for democratic institutions, but I am an aristocrat by instinct, that is, I fear and scorn the mob."[204] He writes elsewhere that

> this country illustrates the most complete external development of the middle classes, or rather that the whole of society seems to have turned into one middle class. No one seems to have the elegant manners and refined politeness of the upper classes in Europe. On the contrary one is at once struck by something vulgar, and a disagreeable casualness of behavior."[205]

Indeed, throughout *Democracy in America*, he notes the particular "vulgarity" of corrupt democratic leaders as opposed to the "depravity of great noblemen" whose aristocratic refinement sustains an "air of grandeur," the vulgar tastes that accompany democratic materialism, and ultimately the dull monotony of a democratic society in constant movement, inhabited by a collection of hopelessly mediocre petty money grubbers more interested in wealth than greatness.[206]

An ambivalent believer in God, an aristocrat by taste and lineage who eventually evinced republican sympathies and political ambitions, Tocqueville's paradoxical commitments and equivocations can be seen both as a mirror of his time and a reaction to its penchant for extremes:

> Belonging to the old aristocracy of my homeland, I had neither hatred nor natural jealousy against the aristocracy, and that aristocracy being destroyed, I did not have any natural love for it either, since one only attaches oneself strongly to what is living. I was near enough to it to know it well, far enough away to judge it without passion. I would say as much about the democratic element. No family memory, no personal interest gave me a natural and necessary bent toward democracy. But for my part I had not received any injury from it; I had no particular motive for either loving it or hating it, independent of those that my reason furnished me. In a word, I was so thoroughly in equilibrium between the past and the future that I felt naturally and instinctively attracted toward neither the one nor the other, and I did not need to make great efforts to cast calm glances on both sides.[207]

Similarly, *Takhlis* registers the paradoxical perspective of a trained Azharite dedicated to recasting the foreign as indigenous and the innovative as traditional, a devoted servant of an absolute ruler profoundly sympathetic to the French uprising against arbitrary power. Thus situated by birth and experience to see, in a sense, contrapuntally, Tocqueville's and Tahtawi's intellectual, religious, political, and aesthetic distance from America and France—a remove reinforced by the literal distance of outside observers—makes possible a doubled perspective from which an appreciative ambivalence emerges. Neither committed democrats nor proponents of absolutism, both bring to their assessments a consciousness of the achievements of what was for them the modern age, as well as of the losses and dangers its appearance and advance represents.

Conclusion

As I have shown by example and argument, Tahtawi and Tocqueville self-consciously regard themselves as mediators between what is familiar and unfamiliar, past and future, translators and purveyors of instruction for their countrymen selectively gleaned from alternative political and cultural worlds. Much like Herodotus and Ibn Battuta, both explicitly establish their credibility and authority in terms of the status of mediator, observers who share but importantly stand apart from the perspectives of their compatriots. The presumption at work here is that such a broadened perspective cannot be reached solely by way of imagination, solitary reflection, or to paraphrase James Mill, reading quite a lot about India in an English closet. On the contrary, Tocqueville and Tahtawi ground their claims in the contrapuntal vision made possible by travel abroad, and rest their own authority on autopsy rather than, for example, the favor of God or innate ability. Tocqueville wrote that his travel plans reflected his "intention of examining, in detail and as scientifically as possible, all the mechanisms of that vast American society which every one talks of and no one knows," and like his claims that the American penal system requires firsthand observation, it is autopsy that helps him see not differently but more deeply and widely.[208] Al-Tahtawi similarly cautions his audience that

> If you find that my descriptions contradict your customs and are thus hard for you to believe, beware of regarding them merely as idle talk or fables, or dismissing them as exaggerations and hyperbole. In a word, "some suspicion is a sin," and a "witness to an event knows what a mere hearer does not"; and "if you don't see

the half-moon, rely on people who have seen it with their own eyes." I call on God Almighty to witness that I will never diverge from the path of truth in all that I say.[209]

While I have argued that Tocqueville and Tahtawi are in many ways well situated to be at once skeptical and appreciative of what they see, neither bring such skepticism to bear on the authority of autopsy itself. Much like Herodotus and Ibn Battuta, both prefer to certify rather than trouble the presumption that travel to observe other places and peoples firsthand produces a privileged vantage from which there is an unconstrained view of past and future, familiar and unfamiliar, home and abroad. Yet, among other things, *Takhlis* and *Democracy* vividly demonstrate that "seeing for oneself" emancipates neither those who travel nor those traveled to from distortion, myopia, and mistranslation. Indeed, it is precisely this shared confidence in the authority of such a doubled vantage that makes them blind to the limits of their own vision, unable to see the ways in which such physical and intellectual dislocation is insufficient to disrupt those deeply held systems of representation that refract and sift experience, and through which particular closures are sustained and reproduced. Just as analysis of the *Histories* and Ibn Battuta's *Rihla* in the previous chapter showed how mediations are both produced and enframed by shifting categories of contrast, examination of Tahtawi and Tocqueville through the lens of travel simultaneously provides a window onto those cross-cultural mediations conducive to an increasingly capacious understanding of the world and draws attention to the constraints, investments, political projects, and unconscious predilections that enact sharp closures to knowledge of others and the limits of their own vision.

Chapter 5

GENDER, GENRE, AND TRAVEL

Montesquieu and Sayyida Salme

Odysseus may be the hero "who has traveled a great deal . . . see[ing] the cities of men and learn[ing] their minds,"[1] but it is the immobility and fidelity of his wife Penelope that frame his voyage. And it is Penelope who, literally and figuratively, reproduces this masculine journey when, in Fénelon's *Telemachus,* her son departs in search of Odysseus, leaving her behind once again to endlessly reenact her virtue by refusing a phalanx of suitors. So thoroughly is travel materially and symbolically masculinized that Eric Leed terms it the "spermatic journey," opposing it to the feminization of "sessility," a botanical term connoting complete fixity and unrelieved rootedness; "there is no free and mobile male without the unfree and sessile female, no knight without the lady, no father without the mother."[2]

Despite the prevalence of such masculine metaphors, literary tropes, and the very real pressures for female immobility they reflect and reinforce, women have, in fact, traveled, both willingly and unwillingly, in a remarkable range of times and places. This raises the question, if "traveling, being on the road, makes a man a man—and makes masculinity and its power visible . . . [w]hat does it mean for a particular woman to gain access to this defining area of agency in the West?"[3] And if, as I have argued, peoples of the so-called non-West are often those to whom Western men travel rather than travelers themselves, objects rather than agents of "discovery," what does it mean for Muslim women in particular to become agents as well as subjects, travelers instead of mere exotics, speakers and writers rather than just Ibn Battuta's sexualized bodies or the veiled inhabitants of the "seraglio" so popular in the European imaginary?[4]

I have argued in chapter 2 that the explicit link between travel and the pursuit of knowledge is itself mobile, transcending cultural and historical boundaries to evoke resonances and anxieties across language and time. I suggested that exposures to the unfamiliar in particular are a "form of dystopic transgression,"[5] provoking a riot of fantasy about the grave dangers for and of those who travel, those traveled to, and those left behind. I further argued that such shared fears are testimony to the potentially transformative and irreducibly unpredictable character of literal or imaginative travel. Nowhere are these transcultural anxieties more pronounced, however, than in male contemplation of women's exposure to the culturally alien, either by way of female mobility or men who bring what is foreign home. Given the frequency with which the specter of sexual violence has been invoked to secure the gates of female domesticity, such anxieties might seem to reflect a concern for the physical vulnerabilities of women travelers.[6] Yet it turns out that most of the perils envisioned by men have little to do with actual physical harm, and instead revolve around fears of moral corruption and cultural corrosion. Railing against Iranians traveling to Europe in 1856, for example, Muhammad Karim Khan ties such travel to the "infection" of Iranian women with the aspiration to move and dress as they please, a development he sees as a signal of the decay of civilization itself:

> Can any Muslim allow the incompetent women to have the affairs in their hands so that they could go wherever they choose, sit with whomever they desire, leave the house whenever they wish? They [Europeans] have not yet gained control of Iran but they are already ordering our women not to cover themselves from men. Would any Muslim consent to women wearing makeup, sitting in the squares and at shops, and going to theaters? Can any Muslim consent to the independence and beautification of his wife and allow her to go to the bazar and buy wine and drink it and get intoxicated . . . and sit with rogues and ruffians and do whatever she chooses? God forbid! Would anyone consent to allowing freedom and losing charge of one's daughter, wife, slave, and housekeeper? And allow them to go wherever they please and do whatever they like and sit with whomever they choose and have available in their gatherings any kind of wine they desire and mingle with rogues, and not be able to protest because an unbeliever has ordered the establishment of a land of freedom?[7]

Khan here envisions a cascade of disasters inaugurated by women's mobility, and in so doing illuminates the deep stakes in female immobility: women who move and speak freely, either by virtue of their own travel or as a result of exposure to "subversive knowledge from afar," transgress and confound the domains of exterior and interior around which gender roles are largely organized. Like a house of cards that topples when just one is out of place, any instance of such transgressive mobility threatens the entire order on which civilization itself is said to rest, from the sexual division of labor to the social reproduction of culture to the meaning and integrity of family. Such anxieties, in other words, can only be understood in the context of a broader gender ideology that, as many scholars have shown, positions women as both the vessel of cultural integrity and its weakest link: "natural" caretakers and bearers of progeny, here women simultaneously become the repositories of moral purity and those whose proximity to nature perpetually jeopardizes virtue. Characterized by sensuality, emotion, and irrationality, woman, like nature, must be controlled, for she is both the danger from within and vulnerable to male predations from without.

In recent years, Islamist investments in guiding, guarding, and covering women have paradoxically transformed Muslim women's bodies into the most visible terrain over which these battles for control are fought, yet this gender ideology is hardly the monopoly of any particular culture, religious tradition, or historical period.[8] Consider, for example, the Arabic root *fa-ta-nun*, from which are derived both the verb meaning to seduce, entice, infatuate (*fatana*/فتن) and the word for civil strife or sedition (*fitna*/فتنة), which Malti-Douglas characterizes as the crucial concept for "defining the dangers that woman, and specifically woman's body, evokes in the medieval Arabo-Islamic mental universe."[9] Such associations and the gender ideology in which they are embedded are evident, moreover, in contemporary American Christian fundamentalism as well as in strains of Orthodox Judaism, and have been articulated in particular historical moments such as the "cult of true womanhood" in nineteenth-century America and the paradoxical position of women in the social imagination of the ancient Athenian polis.[10] Even travel in the name of religious devotion has failed to inoculate women's mobility from such charges of corruption and subversion: uncloistered Christian women in medieval Europe "who traveled around making claims ceaselessly in the name of the Lord were commonly condemned as heretics and delegitimized as bearers of God's word or interpreters of his purpose," and Nancy Tapper's study of a contemporary Muslim Turkish community suggests that those ceremonies and religious practices that involve the exclusive travel of women continue to be regarded by men as either trivial or verging on the heretical.[11]

As Janet Wolff has argued, the "gendering of travel (as male) both impedes female travel and renders problematic the self-definition of (and response to) women who *do* travel."[12] Put slightly differently, the gendering of travel has a disciplinary effect: the coding of travel as male and sessility female not only renders women who actually do travel somehow suspect, but often erases their movement altogether. Like the gender ideology just detailed, such erasures are transcultural and transhistorical: despite voluminous evidence to the contrary, for example, one European writer could suggest that "very few women broke out of the domestic circle in the nineteenth century to venture into the wider world as self-acknowledged travellers," and while lengthy discussions from and about male Persian travelers to Europe are recorded as early as 1599, the very names of Persian women who traveled to England in the eighteenth century have been lost to history.[13]

It is crucial, of course, to differentiate between the disciplinary effect at work in the way travel as a *category* is gendered and the experiences of men and women travelers. Indeed, a sharp distinction between "male travel" and "female travel" misses the complex overlap of actual experiences that rarely group themselves into neat binaries (not to mention the ways in which the gendering of mobility has occasionally produced a feminization of *men* who do not travel). For example, the voluntary voyages of wealthy white European women have more in common with their male counterparts than with the "Middle Passage," the slave trade that entailed the brutal transport of African men and women across the Atlantic for white profit, or with the experience of female Chinese immigrants to America who ran away from parents to avoid being sold, or who started out not as adventurers or scholars but as captives and mail-order brides.[14] Yet at the same time, Wolff's argument suggests that there is a close connection between the gendering of the category as male and the constraints governing women's actual travel experiences. It is thus not accidental that for most of history women of any class and race were not the officers, *theôroi, qadis* (judges), geographers, gentlemen, and diplomats commissioned to gather information from abroad. Rather they were often (although not exclusively) the wives, concubines, nurses, missionaries, slaves, maids, pilgrims, "spinsters," or "eccentrics" who traveled under duress, whose roles as travelers were severely circumscribed, or whose very mobility rendered them suspect or even outcasts from social convention by gender as well as by race or class.[15]

This suggests that women often departed, traveled, returned, wrote (if they were literate), and published (if they were able) under different circumstances than men.[16] Even the most privileged among them could rarely take for granted the freedom of movement, institutional support, and cultural imprimatur for "heroic quests" to seek knowledge that male travel writers so often enjoyed and that established a certain set of narrative conventions as the genre's standard.[17] Without presupposing some essentialist difference between masculine and feminine discourses, then, it is not surprising that the conditions of women's journeying, not to mention the gender conventions governing their mobility, informs and constrains the resulting travel narratives.[18] The issue thus becomes one of genre as well as gender, as the disciplinary effect governing women's movement extends to women's travel writing. Indeed, the invisibility or illegitimacy of female travel and the marginal status of women's travel writing appear to be mutually constitutive. For example, Paul Fussell's study of British travel writing between the wars in *Abroad* turns out to be exclusively a study of male travel writing, a lapse he addresses only parenthetically in his dismissal of Freya Stark as, essentially, a bad writer.[19] Similarly, Sayyida Salme, whose memoirs were published in three languages in eight different editions in just over a twenty-year period, according to one commentator, "had not a very facile pen."[20]

If the genre of travel writing is not only constituted by a set of rules and strategies derived primarily from male experiences but also depends, literally and figuratively, on female immobility and silence, women's very movement and voice—from the domestic to the potentially public, from object to agent, from written about to writer—entails multiple disruptions, political, social, cultural, and generic. Efforts to police the established conventions of the genre, then, to erase and efface interlopers of the wrong gender and their at times inconvenient detours, may not be just an attempt to maintain high standards of writing and observation but a precondition of the genre. Here I draw on Andrea Nightingale's helpful understanding of genres as not merely "artistic forms but *forms of thought*" each one of which, in Gian Biago Conte's words,

> must be thought of as a discursive form capable of constructing a coherent model of the world in its own image . . . a language, that is, a lexicon and a style, but . . . also a system of the imagination and a grammar of things. Genres are the expressive codification of a culture's models; indeed, they are those very models subjected to a process of stylization and a formalization which gives them a literary voice.[21]

In contrast to efforts to control women's bodies and actions, disagreements about genre hardly seem the stuff of politics, evoking instead the rarified discussions of literary journals and academic symposia. Once again, it is Plato's Athenian who, in book III of *The Laws*, spells out the implications of generic violations for political life:

> [After the Persian Wars,] in course of time, an unmusical license set in with the appearance of poets who were men of native genius, but ignorant of what is right and legitimate in the realm of the Muses. Possessed by a frantic and unhallowed lust for pleasure, they contaminated laments with hymns and paeans with dithyrambs, actually imitated the strains of the flute on the harp,

and created a universal confusion of forms. Thus their folly led them unintentionally to slander their profession by the assumption that in music there is no such thing as a right and a wrong, the right standard of judgment being the pleasure given to the hearer, be he high or low. By compositions of such a kind and discourse to the same effect, they naturally inspired the multitude with contempt of musical law, and a conceit of their own competence as judges. . . . Fear was cast out by confidence in supposed knowledge, and the loss of it gave birth to impudence. . . . So the next stage of the journey toward liberty will be refusal to submit to the magistrates, and on this will follow emancipation from the authority and correction of parents and elders; then . . . comes the effort to escape obedience to the law, and, when that goal is all but reached, contempt for oaths, the plighted word, and all religion. The spectacle of the Titanic nature of which our old legends speak is re-enacted; man returns to the old condition of a hell of unending misery.[22]

In this passage the Athenian argues that the mixing of genres not only undermines the standards appropriate to each artistic expression but also the capacity for judgment, and therefore of Law itself, aesthetic, political, and moral. It is not at all clear, of course, that Plato himself endorses the position he impersonates so well in this passage, especially given the extent to which his own work violates the very boundaries the Athenian seeks to police. Yet he here gives powerful voice to the anxieties often concealed in attempts to maintain inviolate the barrier between genres, genders, and cultures, even or especially when human experience bursts the bounds of such order.

As I argued in chapter 3, travel literature is particularly transgressive of such generic boundaries, promiscuously traversing the literary and historical, fantastic and ethnographic, quite independent of the stated motivations or intentions of the writer.[23] I am now suggesting not only that travel is gendered but that the gendering of mobility has epistemological, political, cultural, spatial, and generic valences not immediately evident in Leed's observation that masculine mobility requires female sessility to establish its definition and primacy. Inasmuch as mobility is tied to the multiplication of sight, insight, and the acquisition of wisdom, it also entails the mutual definition and privileging of what I call the domain of the exterior over the interior: abroad over home, public over domestic, open expanse over enclosure (such as house or harem), detachment over rootedness, impartiality over particular location, exteriority (in Said's sense) over indigenousness, scientific over subjective, *rihla* over memoir.

In this chapter, I want to argue that Montesquieu's *Persian Letters* and the *Memoirs* of Sayyida Salme, a nineteenth-century Arabian princess, can be read both with and against the grain of such binaries in ways that productively undermine an understanding of travel as that which is "heroic, educational, scientific, adventurous, ennobling," a challenge to Eric Leed's argument that

> in the west, travel produces a science [because it entails a] self-conscious stripping away of an enculturated self [which] succeeds in erecting a new edifice of knowledge. . . . Travel has long been valued, in both West and East, because it annihilates the ego of the traveler, reduces patriotism, acquaints travelers with a common nature, fate and identity that persist beneath the diversity of cultural types and careers.[24]

This particular vision of travel is subverted in part by way of genre. In the case of the *Persian Letters*, the multivocality of the epistolary genre subverts attempts to read the novel as a celebration of the masculine acquisition of objective knowledge by way of a heroic quest. Salme's *Memoirs* similarly subvert this vision of travel, but does so by opening a window onto the inner life of a "translated person"[25] negotiating multiple worlds, languages, and practices, a life that exemplifies not Said's "pleasures of exile" but rather its rough and jagged underbelly. More specifically, her writings are characterized by a homesickness which, "unlike the nostalgic, cannot be integrated or assimilated";[26] reveal her simultaneous resistance to and complicity in her place and privilege; and disclose both the reach and substantial limits of her capacity to theorize comparatively across racial, religious, class, cultural, and linguistic difference.

This vision of travel is also subverted by way of gender. In particular, I will argue that both texts make visible the extent to which the boundaries between the domains of exterior and interior so integral to "spermatic" travel are traversed, disrupted, and confounded by women—whether fictional or actual—from all cultures who most definitely do not know their place, or whose domestic space becomes the site of politics and comparative knowledge rather than their opposites. The point here is not to enact a simple inversion of the privileging of exterior over interior, male over female, mobility over immobility, but rather to bring into view the mutual implication of such ostensibly opposing terms within each text. Indeed, the analyses that follow suggest that such categories are not only cross-cutting but also profoundly unstable. They blur and invert in ways that render, for example, the equation of femininity, stasis, and subjectivity just as untenable as the presumption that women's mobility by definition produces greater insight into and empathy toward what is unfamiliar than masculine travel. Finally, although Montesquieu's *Persian Letters* and Salme's memoirs are themselves divided from one another by genre, gender, culture, and history, reading them both though the lenses of gender and genre not only undermines a series of binaries *within* each text but also those oppositions that sustain a sharp distinction *between* the two texts. A case in point: Montesquieu's novel establishes an opposition between masculine and feminine discourses only to then blur and invert its terms in a way that simultaneously undercuts the gender essentialism operating within the novel and demonstrates that "gender trouble" comes from male and female authors alike.

As always, the question raised by such an investigation is: why choose these travelers and texts as opposed to others, and why juxtapose these two particular accounts to explore the interplay of travel, gender, and genre? As in the previous chapters, both texts are an opportunity to shift the theoretical perspective, displacing the preoccupation with how the West constitutes the rest of the world in favor of an inquiry into the ways in which travelers of all kinds produce knowledge about themselves and others comparatively. More specifically, *The Persian Letters* is a novel that blurs fiction and fact in which travel in pursuit of knowledge, the comparative journeys from East to West, and the contrasts between male mobility and female sessility are central, but in ways that, I will argue, tend to confound rather than certify such oppositions. Much is also the case with Salme's writings, in which three different senses of travel overlap and intertwine. First, Salme literally travels, moving physically across countries and continents. Second, the *Memoirs*, to borrow from a description of Sara Suleri's *Meatless Days*, is itself a "densely patterned geographic circuit, traversing a variety of physical and cultural bodies"[27] including the harem, court life in Zanzibar, and the world of the German middle class, just to name a few. Third, as Salme's memoirs provide a window onto the dialectical process by which she compares and understands herself in terms of a shifting panoply of others, Western and non-Western, women and men, slaves and royalty, Muslim and Christian, her writings also trace

> the movements *within* the body as it acts upon, and is acted upon by, the various environments that surround it . . . it also records the movements *between* separate, related bodies as they interact with one another at different times or in a different space.[28]

Moveover, given "that still thinly covered era of Middle Eastern women's history, where primary, inside sources are so scarce,"[29] the *Memoirs* is an invaluable opportunity to hear the perspective of an Arab Muslim woman traveler.[30] It is particularly valuable given that the explosion of literature by and on women's travel writing within the last ten years has largely focused on the mobility and perspectives of European and American women, on their complex complicity in European imperialist endeavors, and on the mutually constitutive relationship between Western and non-Western women their writing often reveals.[31] In contrast to the paradoxical picture of colonial women traveling thousands of miles within the sprawling institutional circuitry emanating from the metropole, for example, Salme's work illuminates the disordered and disordering experience of having to negotiate multiple worlds, languages, and practices and, in so doing, discloses not only the multiple valences to travel and exile but also the complex and elusive ways in which they are inflected by gender and class. Finally, inasmuch as Salme's writings at once deploy and trouble particular kinds of literary conventions to reveal a discordant sense of plural selves, they illuminate the relationship between genre and gender in travel writing; here is an illustration of how, for example, a "genre that highlights vulnerability, silence, and adjustment is conceived as feminized and became dominated by female authors."[32]

These particular texts also serve to raise questions about the procedures and conventions by which some books as opposed to others achieve canonical status. In contrast to Tocqueville's *Democracy in America*, for example, *The Persian Letters* and the *Memoirs* have been cursed with a particularly pleasurable quality that, following Cicero's prediction, has continually jeopardized their standing as serious work. The *Memoirs'* evident popularity with readers—it was reprinted in multiple editions in several languages—has had an inverse relation to its scholarly status: there is virtually no secondary literature on the text, and a serious edited volume of Salme's collected works was only published in 1993.[33] Similarly, although political theorists have increasingly claimed *The Persian Letters* as their own, prior to its publication an observer famously quipped that *The Persian Letters* would "sell like bread."[34] Indeed, its very success as the Danielle Steele novel of its day, not to mention its humor and a plot centered on a harem, virtually guaranteed that critics would regard it as a largely frivolous work concerned with the exotic and erotic rather than the properly "political" for some time.[35]

The privileging of the *Spirit of the Laws* over *The Persian Letters* as Montesquieu's "real contribution" to the history of Western political thought (much like the privileging of Rousseau's *Social Contract* over his *Nouvelle Heloise*) suggests a parallel relationship between genre and political theory on the one hand and, on the other, the travel genre and gender: in both instances, the philosophical treatise is privileged over literary and narrative genres as an expression of the truly scientific, rationalist spirit appropriate to political inquiry. The policing of the generic boundary between them in this way becomes, à la Plato's Athenian, a matter of preserving the integrity of standards and the very capacity for judgment. Consequently, I single out such (once) noncanonical texts not to transform their scholarly standing, but rather to use such standing at the canonical margin to productively disrupt jurisdictions of genre that place them at the edge in the first place. The point is not that these books should be *reclassified* by genre, but rather that the genre in which they are placed depends in part on how they are read and for what purposes.

What is at stake here is not simply an effort to show that women from many cultures have traveled, that women's travel writing is worth reading, or that reading texts in which travel (fictional or so-called factual) is central through the lens of gender and genre troubles those easy oppositions on which the conventions of "spermatic" travel rests. As I have argued in chapter 1, what is at stake in travel as both a metaphor and practice is not just literal or imaginative mobility but also theorizing, a practice intimately and explicitly connected to the comparative insights firsthand observation often provides. For inasmuch as the association of travel, imagination, curiosity, knowledge, and reflexive self-understanding has implicitly linked immobility to stasis, inertia, narrowness, and complacency, the gendering of travel suggests that those who do not travel, whether they are the women tending the home or the "exotics" at the end of the journey, are incurious, unphilosophical, and unreflective. This justifies the transformation of political theory from a free-ranging inquiry into the conditions of living together into a parochial mapping of Western answers to fixed questions posed by a pantheon of male philosophers. To the extent that the capacity for critical thinking and reflection (whether or not it is exercised or exercised properly) has often served as the litmus test for citizenship, the "feminization of sessility" becomes one more tautology by which women—and others who are "discovered" rather than discoverers themselves—are properly excluded from the domain of the political as well. By contrast, finding in these texts the comparative mediation between worlds either temporally or spatially unfamiliar helps subvert the coding of travel as "scientific and heroic," a symptom and symbol of certain kinds of gender, racial, and cultural privilege. Inasmuch as this epistolary novel and personal memoir provide unique ways of illuminating the experience and dimensions of such mediation among cultural worlds, they also transgress the boundary between political theory and genres often considered beyond its jurisdiction.

MONTESQUIEU'S *PERSIAN LETTERS*

Printed anonymously in Amsterdam in 1721, *The Persian Letters* is a
novel in which Charles-Louis de Secondat, baron de la Brède et de
Montesquieu, masquerades as the unnamed translator who has rendered into French a collection of letters written to and from two "actual" Persian travelers to Paris.[36] Having departed Isfahan, Persia, in
"search of wisdom," Usbek and Rica's travels and letters—as well as
those written by a variety of other characters, sent to and from several
locales in Europe and Asia—serve as reflections on a variety of topics,
ranging from depopulation and the nature of true love to the relationship between monarchy and despotism, virtue and happiness, natural
law and cultural pluralism, fidelity and justice. The plot—to the extent
that there is one—essentially involves the contrast between the physical and philosophical journeys of the two men from Persia to Paris
with the increasingly disobedient and finally revolutionary events
among Usbek's wives trapped in his "seraglio" back home at Isfahan.

As a novel in epistolary form, there is no omniscient voice explicitly
orchestrating the narrative, and as a result, there are no instructions
to the reader on how to sift and interpret the polyvalent perspectives
gathered therein. The anonymous author claims only to be a "translator," despite the fact that translators are writers of a kind. Thus not
only the content and arrangement of the letters but also the authorial
voice "behind" them deliberately resists easy encapsulation and neat
resolution. This is, after all, a fabricated story published anonymously
by a real man who hatched up two fictitious Persian figures in part by
making rather creative use of actual European travelers' accounts to
Turkey and Persia.[37] Indeed, as if to release himself from fidelity to
some "real" Orient or "authentic" Islam, Montesquieu makes it clear
in an exchange between Usbek and a Muslim cleric early in the novel
that one of his central characters does not know much about Islam in
any case (XVIII).[38]

The engineered fog surrounding the novel's authorship and sources
perhaps explains why Montesquieu later felt the need to provide
some instructions on how to read the book in "Some Reflections on
the *Persian Letters*," attached to the novel thirty-three years after its
initial publication. Here Montesquieu suggests that lurking beneath
the digressions and apparent lack of "any preconceived design or
plan" in the epistolary form, the "author permits himself to join philosophy, politics, and ethics to the story, and to bind the whole with
a secret and, in some respects, hitherto unknown chain." Many scholars have taken Montesquieu's reference to a "secret chain" as license

to search for a single key to the novel, much like a hunt for buried treasure, thereby rendering the epistolary form a puzzle to be penetrated or transcended in pursuit of deeper philosophical coherence.[39] This simultaneously bypasses the possibility that the epistolary genre is itself a mode of inquiry and reinforces a tendency to read the *Persian Letters* as an incomplete exploration of what would become the fully developed philosophy of a mature man in *The Spirit of the Laws*: thus the novel "implies more than it tells; it shows the man working, not the completed work."[40] Seen as immature or somehow preliminary to his more consequential work, *The Persian Letters* has often been read through the lens of *The Spirit of the Laws* as an extension of the Enlightenment project rather than as a multivocal text that may satirize as much as certify Enlightenment presuppositions.[41] Authored by, in Isaiah Berlin words, "one of the fathers of the Enlightenment," *The Persian Letters* is thus taken to demonstrate rather than interrogate the connections between travel, impartiality, and the acquisition of rational knowledge in particular.[42]

Consider, for example, Jean Starobinski's claim that the hidden engine of the novel is actually Montesquieu's drive for the triumph of reason over dogma, unity over disunity, universality over contradiction, a reading in which the apparent cacophony of *The Persian Letters* dissolves into a mutually reinforcing structural and substantive order. Thus while the work is one of "plural consciousness," the reader "quickly comes to feel that these plural voices and subjects . . . are fronts for a hidden but omnipresent author who confronts passion with passion, dogma with critique of dogma, in such a way that the perception of *relations* leads imperceptibly to the triumph of reason."[43] The fictional form of the book is but a filter for classic principles and established truths that receive "an *electric charge* by attribution to the Persian letter-writer."[44] When inhabiting the role of the traveler in pursuit of wisdom who fled Persia for having spoken truth to power, the Janus-faced Usbek becomes the "enemy of masks" and the "reasoner" par excellence. Here he not only plays the leading role in the book but is no less than Montesquieu's "alter ego."[45] Through Usbek and, by extension, the author who speaks through the character at his best, travel is heroic and scientific, an embodiment of the Enlightenment spirit of curiosity, universalism, and cosmopolitanism:

> For Usbek the pursuit of knowledge implies mobility, openness to the outside world, and above all the refusal to submit solely to the authority of his native "culture" . . . Usbek renounces "Iranocentrism" in all its forms. . . . Confronted with the relativity of the absolute that people have revered in different times and different

places, the reader becomes aware of the need to rise to the level of the universal and experiences the awakening of a cosmopolitan concern for the happiness and prosperity of all peoples. The groundwork has been laid for the triumph of the universal concepts of Reason, Justice and Nature, in whose name local fanaticism and regional prejudice can be condemned.[46]

To the extent that Montesquieu has Usbek flee Isfahan in pursuit of knowledge—Usbek writes that "we were born in a flourishing realm, but we did not believe that its boundaries were those of our knowledge, nor that the light of the Orient should along illuminate us" (I) Usbek's mobility not only presupposes a connection between travel and knowledge but also partakes of the tropic features of "spermatic" travel. Travel is here an heroic adventure, an ennobling quest that, inasmuch as it begins to strip away those parochial prejudices that hinder perception of universal truths and a common human nature, in Leed's words, "produces a science." By contrast, immobility affirms a parochialism inimical to true knowledge, as with the Muscovites who "cannot leave their country even to travel; so, separated from other nations by their own laws, they have become even more attached to their old customs and cannot believe it possible for there to be others" (LI). The very power of mobility to distance the traveler from all that he once held dear is spelled out by the chief eunuch in a letter to the black eunuch forced to travel as part of Usbek's entourage: "You are about to travel through lands inhabited by Christians, who have never been believers; it is inevitable that you will be somewhat soiled" (XV). Such comments on the risks, virtues, and transformations of travel are in part borne out by the increasingly critical, reflective, and philosophical tone of Usbek's letters as his travels progress, on topics ranging from religion, monarchy, despotism, nature, custom, and depopulation. Such transformations are also and more ambiguously demonstrated by Rica's increasing ease in his new surroundings, to the point where he almost loses himself in French culture.

Yet the identification of Montesquieu with the Enlightenment, Usbek with Montesquieu, and Usbek with the cosmopolitan philosopher, unmasker of lies and hero of the novel, is seriously complicated by Usbek's counterveiling role as despot of his own household, sovereign of a tyranny that grows more extreme with the length of his absence from Isfahan. For scholars who see Usbek as both mouthpiece for Montesquieu and the novel's leading man, the two sides of Usbek illustrate a regrettable gap between theory and practice: inasmuch as Usbek, the "enemy of masks, a traveler enamored of rational knowledge" is also

a "true representative of Persian domestic customs," he and the domestic world he has left behind appear in jeopardy at the end of the
book because he has not freed himself sufficiently from the parochial
and (therefore) despotic.[47] "There are," Starobinski comments, "inherited certainties [Usbek] has not yet learned to question."[48]

Such an argument presupposes and reinforces a binary in which mobility, critical reflection, impartiality, and detachment is situated on one
side and rootedness, parochialism, and prejudice is on the other. From
this vantage, it becomes difficult to register the possibility that Usbek's
wives' supposed sessility—both physical and psychological—may
well be the precondition of his mobile sense of self as husband and
master. It also obscures the ways in which his travels and exposures
to the unfamiliar in the novel actually coincide with a hardening rather
than easing of his despotic tendencies. It further removes from consideration the possibility that Usbek's cultural and religious identity may
not be a residual parochialism to be transcended but constitutive of his
very desire to travel and learn, particularly given that Montesquieu's
phrase "search for wisdom" evokes the Muslim ethos of *talab al-ʿilm*
(see chapter 2). Finally, these binaries occlude from view the ways in
which Usbek's dislocation from a culture in which he is still inescapably rooted simultaneously enables his philosophical insights into the
nature of government, religion, and despotism and sustains his myopia about his own nature and the domestic hell he has created.

The *Persian Letters* is complex and multivocal, and it is far from implausible to read it as a precursor to—if not part of—the French Enlightenment, even given the extent to which what is commonly termed
"the Enlightenment" is itself characterized by deep fissures and multivocality. More specifically, it is quite possible to portray the novel as
an assertion of the connection between travel and the acquisition of
rational knowledge, and an argument for adherence to universal standards of justice in the face of almost ubiquitous injustice and narrow
parochialism. Yet given this very multivocality, the presumption that
Montesquieu's "secret chain" by definition entails progressive coherence rather than sustained paradoxes and unresolved skepticism simply erases textual evidence that does not tally. As one scholar rightly
suggests, there may in fact be no such secret chain despite Montesquieu's instructions, or at the very least, it may be misguided to interpret it to mean that there is some "hidden plan [to] be discovered
which will make everything fall into place."[49] Indeed, an interpretation
freed from the vise of such progressive coherence suggests that Usbek
is not only a vehicle for reflection on the nature of despotic regimes in
his philosophical letters but, in his exchanges with the harem, also an
embodiment of an increasingly absolutist temperament, his physical

movement inversely related to his capacity to move amongst and
imaginatively inhabit perspectives other than his own. As Suzanne
Gearhart argues:

> Once the impasse Usbek creates for himself in relation to his wives
> is analyzed, it becomes evident that Usbek's "failure" to resolve the
> contradiction between his philosophical ideals and his repressive
> politics is more than the result of some contingency of theory and
> practice. Indeed, Usbek's ideals are not "hollow" . . . it is precisely
> these ideals that order the disorder of Usbek's seraglio. Montes-
> quieu's novel is in fact a forceful critique of this central figure. For
> the *Lettres Persanes* shows that the universal values Usbek claims
> to embody in his opposition to Persian society and expects his voy-
> age to the West to confirm, when they are enforced on his seraglio
> in the form of "virtue," create disorder and repression.[50]

The mutual coexistence—indeed dependency—of blindness and insight, parochialism and cosmopolitanism, disorder and order does not,
it would seem, elude Montesquieu, who has Rica send Usbek a letter
in which a "Frenchman in Spain" writes of the Spanish that "they have
made enormous discoveries in the New World, and yet they do not
know their own country; their rivers are not yet entirely explored, and
their mountains hold nations unknown to them" (LXXVIII). Critics
who see Usbek as hero and mouthpiece for Montesquieu have often
regarded Rica, whose letters tend to be more satirical than philosophical, as a light distraction,[51] and as if to confirm the tone of the letters,
the name Rica is a play on the French verb "to laugh" at times "derisively." Yet Montesquieu may have had little intention of valorizing
Usbek to the exclusion of Rica, especially when one considers that the
name "Usbek" refers to the Tartar people, tyrants par excellence
(LXXXI).[52]

If Usbek is less the novel's center of gravity and just one among
several satellites, Rica's humor, his experiments with "going native"
in Paris, and his letter containing a Persian tale about a jealous husband that at once inverts the order of Usbek's harem and foreshadows
Roxana's suicide (CXLI), becomes absolutely crucial to the radical perspectivalism of the book. Indeed, Rica's letters often undermine not
only the view of travel as a linear progression from parochialism to
universal truth but also the very opposition on which such a view of
knowledge is built: "it seems to me Usbek," he writes, "that we judge
things only by applying them secretly to ourselves" (LIX). Here Montesquieu may well have wanted to emphasize, in Starobinski's words,
that "one must inevitably adopt a particular point of view even if one
aspires to transcend the particular . . . ," but this is not tantamount

to the lesson that "to transcend the relative we must begin with the relative."[53] Rather, Rica's suggestion may be that such commitments cannot be transcended because they are, in effect, both a feature of human identity and a prerequisite for cross-cultural understanding. Abandonment of the "particularistic" thus means abandonment of the very linguistic conditions of translation that make intelligibility across difference possible.

Just as Usbek's travel is in part premised on the psychic, physical, and metaphorical stasis of his wives, so is his mobility made possible by the eunuchs forced to travel in his entourage, as well as by those who stay home to guard his "seraglio."[54] Though largely silent or invisible in Ibn Battuta's *Rihla*, in the fictional *Persian Letters*, the slaves and wives speak—and loudly—about their fate and the relationship between immobility and enslavement. Indeed, they are in the end the agents who bring about the final events of the book. Thus the Chief Eunuch envies the slave traveling with Usbek, for he imagines that time passes quickly with each new sight; "it is not so with me, constrained as I am in a frightful prison, continually surrounded by the same objects, and consumed by the same regrets, I groan, crushed beneath fifty years of cares and anxieties; in the course of a long life I cannot remember one serene day or one tranquil moment" (IX). Usbek's wives, constantly guided, guarded, and covered in the harem, jockey for position and status with one another under the brutal rule of the eunuchs whom they torment in turn; a domestic despotism where all victims tyrannize one another, collectively reigned over by Usbek in absentia, who himself admits that his increasingly frenzied jealousy has more in common with a property owner than a lover (VI). "Far from being happy," writes Fatima, one of Usbek's wives, about her condition, a woman "must even forego the pleasure of serving another's happiness: a useless decoration of the seraglio, she is guarded for the honor, not the enjoyment of her husband!" (VII).

Despite the increasingly philosophical and reflective tone of many of Usbek's later letters, as the domestic tyranny of the harem begins to disintegrate, so does his stable identity as master and husband. E. J. Hundert persuasively argues that "as slaves, Usbek's wives fully exist only insofar as they are permitted to see and be seen by Usbek himself. . . . The veil thus becomes the most prominent, publicly displayed sign of Usbek's subordinating power; as it blocks the gaze of unauthorized eyes, it simultaneously conceals significant bodily parts that only Usbek's eyes may view."[55] As a consequence, Usbek's increasing despotism is enforced through ever rigorous enclosure, seclusion, and covering of his wives, and conversely, disclosure and exposure are signals of disorder and liberty. As men and messages circulate secretly about the harem and Zelis drops her veil on the way to the mosque, Usbek responds by shutting all the women in their own apartments and insisting they all be veiled even though they are alone (CLVI).[56]

While Persian women are in this way defined by physical and psychic enclosure, European women are made to signify the complete opposite, an embodiment of the absence of appropriate boundaries and limits. Thus, much like the tendency of Ibn Battuta, Tocqueville, and al-Tahtawi to decode entire cultures by way of women's bodies and behavior, for the Persian travelers, the moral character of the West is revealed by its women. European women *are* their sexual behavior, and such behavior is the opposite of what Usbek imagines the ideal Persian woman to be: covered, secluded, obedient, and accessible only to him. Thus Usbek sees Italian women's willingness to be seen by men not only as a signal of their freedom but as revealing the entire culture (XXIII), and describes Parisian women as exhibiting a "barbaric impudence" due to their having "lost all restraint. They present themselves barefaced to men, as if inviting conquest; they seek attention, and they accompany men to the mosques, on walks, even to their rooms" (XXVI).

Inasmuch as Usbek's relation to his wives is defined as much by possession as passion, his domination of the eunuchs in many ways serves as an extension of his identity as husband/master. Given that the chief eunuch describes the act that formed him as one "of separating me forever from myself" (IX), however, the eunuchs occupy an ambiguous place between genders, the symptom and symbol of a particularly "unnatural" barbarism whose intrusive "presence overshadows and undercuts Usbek's growing claim to tolerance, his inquiries into virtue . . . the eunuch's enraged and frustrated complaints spell out the degradation of his position which situates him at the pole opposite that of Western enlightenment."[57] The eunuch is a creature crafted entirely out of the despotic milieu, destined to both serve and reproduce it, his nature as well as his body completely remade into a slavery spelled out in no uncertain terms by Usbek:

> You exist only insofar as you know how to obey; you are in the world only to live under my rule, or to die as I may order; you breathe only because my happiness, my love, and even my jealously have need of your servility. In short, you can have no other recourse but submission, no soul apart from my will, and no hope except in my happiness. (XXI)

In a passage that seems to anticipate Hegel's master/slave dialectic, Montesquieu points out in *The Spirit of the Laws* that the despot, grown old and infirm, "is the first prisoner of the palace" (V, 14).[58] Just so, the problem for Usbek is that, much as his slaves depend on him for their lives, so does Usbek depend on them for his very sense of self. As the eunuchs and wives, each deprived of freedom of will, enact ever more tortuous tyrannies over one another, "Usbek slowly emerges as the singularly restricted subject of his own despotism. In order to literally preserve his self, he must continually watch and keep his wives in subjugation, the others whose recognition and obedience certify his identity."[59] Conversely, by the end of the novel, when his subjects exceed his capacities to impose control, Usbek himself becomes a kind of eunuch, impotent to effect his will, pledging to "return to shut myself behind walls more terrible to me than to the women they guard" (CLV).

While some have suggested that this despotic Persian husband and master represents a failure to overcome "Oriental prejudices about male honor," the polyvalent perspectives represented in the text suggest, on the contrary, that the overlapping relations of male and female, freedom and despotism, public and domestic, mobility and stasis are, like light and dark, mutually constitutive and could not be otherwise.[60] Thus Zelis, reflecting on the mutually defining nature of men and women, seems resigned that nature "has set us afire with passion, that men might be peaceful. She has destined us to restore to men the insensibility they sometimes lose, though it is never possible for us to enjoy that happy state into which we put them" (LXII). Yet Zelis seizes on this very interdependence to invert her relationship with Usbek:

> Yet do not suppose, Usbek, that your situation is happier than mine. I have tasted here a thousand pleasures you could not understand. My imagination has worked ceaselessly to make me realize their value, and I have lived while you have only languished. Even in this prison holding me I am freer than you. You can only redouble your efforts to guard me, that I may enjoy your uneasiness; your every suspicion, jealousy, and annoyance are so many marks of your dependence.

The wives' rebellion at the end of the novel—Zachi sleeps with a slave, Zelis drops her veil in public, Roxana has a secret lover—thus represents not only the freedom of the women but the disintegration of Usbek's identity, premised, as it has been, on his wives immobility, obedience, and seclusion, and on the eunuch's capacity to police them. Suddenly, Usbek begins to unravel, not only as a husband and master, but also as a traveler in search of knowledge, his heroic adventures having curdled into a "dreadful exile":

Happy is he who, knowing the value of a gentle and peaceful life, makes his family the center of his existence and knows no country other than that which gave him birth! I live in a barbarous country, surrounded by everything offensive to me, absent from all my interests. A somber sadness grips me; I am sinking into a frightening depression; it seems I am annihilating myself, and I recover only when dark jealousies come to kindle and nurture fear, suspicion, hate, and regrets in my soul. . . . Whatever the reason I had to leave my country, and even though I owe my life to my flight from it, yet . . . I can no longer endure this dreadful exile. Will I not die just the same, a victim to my grief? (CLV)

Read as fixed oppositions, the contrasts between men and women, freedom and despotism, master and slave, public and private, travel and immobility sustain a reading of the novel as valorizing male mobility and detachment over and against female sessility and parochialism. Yet the radical perspectivalism of the epistolary genre undercuts the heroic—if tragic—centrality of Usbek, foregrounding counterveiling valences that render these contrasts more a series of *relations* and tensions that sustain the text, rather than binaries that must resolve into the triumph of universal reason over particularism. As opposed to Starobinski's conclusion, then, that the novel is driven by "only one theme and pursues only one question" about the foundations of authority and the necessity of universal justice, it may well be that the polyphony of the epistolary genre was meant to delineate tensions and paradoxes that pose a series of questions to the reader without ever offering a clear or single resolution.[61] This reading may entail dispensing with the view that there is such a thing as a "secret chain" altogether, or rather just relinquishing the view that such a chain must be progressively coherent. For it may well be that the "secret chain," if there is one, is hidden in plain view, in the polyphony of an epistolary genre that here veils itself in the fiction of facticity while posing, examining, and re-posing from multiple perspectives a series of questions about everything from the nature of freedom to the meaning of happiness.

Nowhere is the epistolary genre's tendency to disrupt and confound expectations clearer than in attempts to see Montesquieu's *Persian Letters* as an exemplar of what Edward Said would call Orientalist fiction. As Said famously wrote, "Orientalism is premised upon exteriority, that is, on the fact that the Orientalist, poet or scholar, makes the Orient speak, describes the Orient, renders its mysteries plain for and to the West."[62] At first blush, *The Persian Letters* seems to epitomize Orientalism in its classic mode: the Iranian characters speak like Europeans and largely function as conduits for Montesquieu's satire of France, thereby disclosing as much if not more about eighteenth-century misconceptions and prejudices about Islam and Persia as they do about actual people and places.[63] Indeed, as Judith Shklar puts it, in the *Persian Letters*, the Orient is not "a geographic territory but a nightmare territory of the mind in which all the worst human impulses govern."[64] The very structure of the book, moreover, seems to set up a contrast between a Paris where "liberty and equality reign" (LXXXVIII) and the despotism of the Persian court from which Usbek flees because tyranny can only produce mendacity and servility.[65] Indeed, Montesquieu appears to affirm explicitly this essentialist position in the *Spirit of the Laws* when he argues that "power in Asia ought always to be despotic."[66]

Yet at least within the terms of the novel, Montesquieu's relentlessly satirical depiction of France denies any exemplary status to Europe or the West of which it is a part: no Parisian "type" is spared Montesquieu's sarcasm, from cuckolded men and their voracious wives, to those "infatuated with the sciences" who are nevertheless not very learned (LXVI), to wits who "render no useful service to their country" (XXXVI), to Parisians' general preoccupation with what is fashionable to the point where they "are willing to subordinate themselves to the laws of a foreign power if only French wigmakers are allowed to legislate on the shape of foreign wigs." (C). Moreover, the multiplicity of Persian perspectives in the novel—the two quite different main characters, the Persians who travel elsewhere in Europe, the wives (all very different) left behind, the eunuchs both black and white, and an occasional Muslim cleric—militate against Orientalist essentialism. Unlike the French satirized at length, for example, almost all the Persians have names. Furthermore, there is much about France that is *not* here despite the rendering of certain French customs and practices in minute detail, for Montesquieu narrows his imaginative play to that of his travelers' (supposed) interests and vision. Thus, while George Healy is surely wrong to suggest that the novel is about actual Persian lives, as Pucci writes, the "Persian model of difference and exoticism can be shown to erode in this text ... the 'oriental' functions as a bearer of disrupting differences and exteriority, which cannot be contained within the figure of exoticism: rather they operate textually, now as then, to constitute the Western notion of 'knowledge' and 'self.' "[67]

Finally, language itself becomes culturally unmoored in the course of the novel, as the strange and estranging representations of Montesquieu's foreign travelers render practices and people that would have been quite familiar to his French audiences bizarre or ludicrous. For example, Rica writes to a friend:

> The king is a great magician, for he exercises dominion even over
> the minds of his subjects and makes them think as he wishes. If
> he has only a million *écus* in his treasury, and has need of two
> million, he has only to persuade them that one *écu* is worth two,
> and they believe it. If he has a hard war to sustain and no money
> at all, he has only to put in their heads the notion that a piece of
> paper is money, and they are instantly convinced. So great is his
> power over their minds that he has even made them believe that
> he cures all kinds of disease, simply by touching them. You ought
> not to be astonished by what I say of this prince, for there is an
> even stronger magician than he, who is master of the king's mind
> even as the king is sovereign over his subjects. This magician is
> called the pope. Sometimes he makes the prince believe that three
> is only one, or that the bread he eats is not bread, or that the wine
> drunk is not wine, and a thousand similar things. (XXIV)

From the incestuous lovers Apheridon and Astarte, the siblings who
arguably have the most "normal" love in the novel (LXVII) to the Catholic casuist Usbek characterizes as a "dervish" who tells "his subjects
which [divine] laws they ought to obey and which they might violate"(LVII), here the familiar becomes exotic, the taboo conventional,
the sacred outlandish. In other words, the "epistolary form, in effect,
acts as a pivot to insure the potential reversibility of knowledge into
the exotic and vice versa."[68]

Such potential reversibility is also at work in the gendering of the
quest for knowledge established at the outset of the *Persian Letters*, for
the initial contrast between Usbek's heroic search for wisdom and his
supposedly imprisoned, servile wives has collapsed by the end of the
novel. In the first few letters of the book, Usbek's "thirst for wisdom"
is in sharp contrast to a clutch of letters from several of his wives com-
plaining of the sexual deprivation his departure means for them, all
written in the overheated, claustrophobic cadences of the harem, linguistically dissembling in ways appropriate to those who serve tyrants mind and body. For example, his wife Fatima claims that "even
though I might be allowed to leave this place where I am confined by
the necessity of my condition; even if I could escape my surrounding
guard; even if I were allowed to choose from all the men in this capital
of nations—Usbek, I swear I would choose only you" (VII). But, of
course, she has no choice but to choose Usbek, and later in this letter
she spells out how the sexual deprivation of the seraglio gives to the
husband that "which you could not dare to gain by your own merit."
Immediately after Usbek leaves, Zachi describes herself wandering
from apartment to apartment in the seraglio searching for him, while

Usbek wanders "in barbarian lands" (III), a contrast that suggests a sharp distinction between masculine heroic travel to the unknown and women's domestic quest for love. Yet it is not clear that his wives were ever completely servile or immobile, for in this same letter, Zachi makes it clear that no sooner has the Master of the house departed, than "we ordered the chief eunuch to take us to the country."[69] Indeed, Zachi contrasts the relative ease of the men's voyage with the enormous production women's travel must become in order to maintain their honor (i.e., seclusion and covering) even in the face of great physical danger, writing in an ironic letter to Usbek: "how difficult journeys are for women! Men are exposed only to threats against their lives, but we women are constantly fearful of losing either life or virtue" (XLVII).

There are more than a few nineteenth- and twentieth-century critics who dismissed the "harem plot" as a prurient digression, "a voluptuous and delirious conclusion, a 'fire and blood' end, that has nothing relating to us in it."[70] Yet as the novel progresses, Usbek's abstract philosophical reflections seem to lack the traction and immediacy of the increasingly intense politics of the harem which, as many scholars now note, is itself a metaphor for despotism.[71] Here, contrary to Fatima's protestations, his wives take advantage of any small opportunity for expression, action, or passion created by Usbek's absence and disorder in the eunuchs' chain of command. The disintegration of this domestic tyranny culminates in the grand final gesture of Roxana (not accidentally, the name of the Alexander the Great's Persian consort), the wife of whose fidelity Usbek was certain and who deceived him most completely with her lover. Although not the chronological end of the book, Montesquieu literally gives Roxana the last word in letter CLXI, where she seizes the language of transparency, making clear the extent of Usbek's ignorance and self-delusion: "How could you have imagined me credulous enough to believe that I existed only to adore your caprices, that in permitting yourself everything, you had the right to thwart my every desire? No: I have lived in slavery, but I have always been free." Roxana takes her own life, but inasmuch as the entire harem plot is inverted in the story of Anaïs told earlier by Rica (CXLI), there is a suggestion that Roxana's death, like that of Anaïs, is just the beginning of an immortal journey that will end in a heaven of physical pleasure as recompense for a life lived under the thumb of a brutal husband.

The preceding discussion suggests that the epistolary genre, rather than being incidental to the substance of the novel, a surface to be penetrated or a mess to be transcended, is absolutely integral to its argument. As Dena Goodman argues,

Each Persian letter presents not only a partial but an immediate vision of the world. . . . The first person style of the epistolary genre not only reveals the limitations of particular points of view but also creates what Bertil Romberg calls "a vibrant uncertainty" out of the simultaneity of experience and narration. The partiality and uncertainty that arise from the immediacy of first-person narration depend, furthermore, on the constantly recreated distinction between the limited visions and voices of the characters and the greater world that the reader is attempting to put together to make sense of what he reads. And that world is constantly compared with, and measured against, the world in which the reader lives.[72]

If the *Persian Letters* is an invitation to the reader to participate in the construction of the novel's meaning more than a lesson on a single theme or moral, the audience becomes a translator along with Montesquieu, moving among the characters and between his world and theirs to make a series of cultural comparisons. Indeed, Goodman argues that the *Persian Letters* enacts what she calls a "comparative critical method" that operates on three levels: first, and most obviously, through the comparisons the Persians make between Europe and their home country, second, through the comparisons the reader makes between the "prejudices" (in Gadamer's sense) the reader brings to the novel and what Paul Ricoeur calls the world of the text, a process which initiates, third, a comparison between cultural particularity and presumed universals that issues in a critical distance toward one's own world. Keeping in mind Nightengale's understanding of genres not only as artistic forms but forms of thought, the text, in short, invites the reader to participate in the practice of theorizing as I have defined it, a comparative mediation among worlds either temporally or spatially unfamiliar.

Sayyida Salme's *Memoirs*

The shift from Montesquieu's *Persian Letters* to the writings of Princess Sayyida Salme bint Saʿid ibn Sultan is not just a leap from France to Africa. Published more than 150 years apart, these two works are divided by genre as well as by culture and language: one is a work of fiction, the other a memoir, one is written by a Frenchman born Catholic, the other written by an Arab woman born Muslim. Indeed, Salme herself insists on distinguishing her *Memoirs* from such works of fiction:

It must be remembered that I have not been writing a novel or a tale of fiction, but the faithful recollection connected with the life of my native land in all its phases. If I have naturally felt tempted to exalt such of our customs and institutions which, in my opinion, are deserving of commendation, I have, on the other hand, never endeavored to excuse or disguise others which, in the eyes of more highly-cultured nations at least may justly be ridiculed or thought objectionable; and if, in drawing comparisons between foreign and Eastern customs, I have not shrunk from speaking my mind openly and candidly, and have sometimes sent home a shaft, I may aver, in justice to myself, that I have by no means spared myself, but have readily and frankly admitted the errors into which I fell.[73]

The genre of novel and memoir may be formally distinguished from one another by way of a set of aesthetic rules, yet such formalized rules are quite elastic in concrete cases, often shifting over time to make a text classified in one genre at one moment susceptible to different questions and new readings derived from another genre at some other moment. Much as Montesquieu's epistolary novel enacts a radical perspectivalism that blurs the distinctions between masculine and feminine discourses, political and domestic, mobility and stasis, West and East, the *Memoirs* often disrupts the very generic and epistemological conventions it is meant to reflect and reproduce. Salme's writings routinely and transparently traverse the distinction between the subjective and objective, offering her specific life experiences as a source of comparative knowledge and imposing in retrospect a coherent narrative for the consumption of a European audience. Indeed, to the extent that Salme not only translates her life but is herself a translated person, she can be seen as living at Montesquieu's blurred intersections, reminded of her permanent exile at every turn by the equivalent query posed so lightheartedly to Rica in *The Persian Letters*: "Indeed! He is Persian? [*Monsieur est Persan?*] How extraordinary! How can anyone be Persian?" (XXX).

Salme in fact led a life of profound psychic, linguistic, social, national, and religious homelessness, and her writings are haunted by precisely this unanswered—and perhaps unanswerable—question of identity. Described by the daughter of one of her English hostesses as "always an exile in spirit,"[74] Salme traveled thousands of miles in the course of her life, from East Africa to Hamburg to Dresden to London to Beirut and back. Such physical journeys often corresponded to dramatic and traumatic shifts in identity, from Muslim to Christian, "Sayyida Salme" to "Emily Reute," princess to middle-class housewife, wild child to devoted mother, Arab to European, "light skinned" to dark. Revisiting her childhood home of Zanzibar after a nineteen-year absence, Salme writes in her *Memoirs*: "I left my home a complete Arab woman and a good Muslim and what am I now?"[75] In a sentence she would delete from the published version, she sadly answers her own query: "A bad Christian, and somewhat more than half a German."[76]

The question can be only inadequately addressed by recourse to Salme's early life in Zanzibar that is the primary subject of *The Memoirs*. She was born in 1844 to the ruler of Oman and Zanzibar, Sultan Sa'id ibn Sultan al Bu-Sa'id, and Jilfidân, a Circassian slave captured in war who later became one of the sultan's secondary wives (*surias*), a status that entitled both wife and daughter to legal rights. As a light-skinned Arab princess in a royal family where domestic hierarchies rested not only on the women's legal status but also on skin tone and ethnic/racial origin, Salme enjoyed a charmed childhood—or so her *Memoirs* depict it in retrospect. Yet she lost both her parents in rapid succession: her father died on a return sea voyage from Oman in 1856 and, when she was only fifteen, her mother died in a cholera epidemic. Caught up in palace intrigues after her father's death, she followed the lead of a favorite sister in supporting a less-than-favorite brother, Barghash, in an abortive palace coup against the legitimate heir to the sultan's throne (the second palace rebellion led by women to appear in this chapter; that of Usbek's wives is the first). Young and impetuous, Salme was forgiven by the victor, Sultan Madjid, who happened to be one of Salme's favorite brothers, but her involvement would prove disastrous for her later attempts to reclaim her inheritance.

Around the time she was twenty-one, Salme fell in love with—and likely became pregnant by—Rudolph Heinrich Reute, a German merchant working in Zanzibar, and evidence suggests she fled her homeland and the family she had publicly dishonored not only to marry Reute but also for her safety.[77] In order to marry, move to Germany, and assume the life of a *Hausfrau*, however, she was first required to convert and take the new Christian name of Emily.[78] Only three years into their marriage, in 1870, Heinrich died after a grisly tram accident, the second loved one Salme lost to travel. This left twenty-six-year-old Salme with three small children and an inheritance that was quietly being embezzled by the trustee of their estate appointed, ironically, by a German law for the protection of widows and orphans. Reduced to the increasingly lower rungs of the middle class, Salme took up teaching Arabic and Swahili when possible. Yet it seems she put most of her energies into cultivating the sympathies of various European aristocrats and power brokers able to advance her claims to an inheritance from the Sultanate of Zanzibar, despite the fact that under Islamic law, her "apostasy" from Islam entailed its forfeiture. Haunted by the palace revolution in which she had participated as a teenager, alienated from her family as a "renegade from Islam," and caught up in the German and British maneuvering for influence in East Africa, Salme was forced to admit defeat in her endeavors by 1888. Thoroughly embittered by the experience, she abandoned both Germany and Zanzibar for the Syrian coast, where she lived for twenty-five years, leaving only at the outbreak of World War I to live alternately with her two daughters in Prussia, until her death in 1924. The tombstone of this woman who led a life of permanent exile read: "Faithful in his innermost heart is he, who loves his homeland like you."[79]

Salme's love of home largely intrudes in her writings as an inconsolable yearning, a homesickness that, Da Costa suggests, is by its nature inescapably tautological:

> The longing for mooring by which this loss is expressed (desire) is at once logical and futile, since the object (home, dwelling) is an irrecoverable for which only symbolic and imaginary reconstruction (the real) might offer compensation . . . to the person wracked by homesickness, language becomes the only legible figure to stand precariously between their solitary consciousness and/of the abyss of death.[80]

Living a life of permanent fragmentation and dislocation, then, Salme turned to writing, constructing a rosy past from the perspective of a painful present as consolation for a home she could never recover. To the extent that Salme actively sought and envisioned an audience for her *Memoirs*, however, the narrative is also organized to translate her life for readers located in different cultural and historical contexts. The terms of translation are revealed not only by the architecture of the *Memoirs* and what is included within it, but importantly by what is not included. For example, the *Memoirs* devote exactly three dispassionate pages to meeting Reute, the departure from Zanzibar, and the move to Germany and Beirut. By contrast, at least eight times that space are devoted to brief stories about several of her one hundred brothers and sisters, most of whom never reappear in the narrative.

Following Salme's death, however, her children discovered and subsequently published what would be titled *Letters Home*, a more than one-hundred-page uninterrupted and profoundly personal description of her life in Germany, including her experience of culture shock, an account of the death of her husband, depression, and increasing financial woes from 1867 to the mid 1880s. Addressed to an unidentified friend who may never have existed,[81] and written in a confessional tone in marked contrast to the measured and self-effacing style of the

Memoirs, *Letters Home* appear to be one of her few outlets for unedited self-expression, and in it the focus on her own inner life reaches what can only be described as a fever pitch. The difference, however, is not just one of tone and formality. The *Letters Home* bring into sharp relief all that was omitted from the published volume, and disclose the perspective from which Salme assessed the arc of her life at the very time of writing the *Memoirs* (she began them in 1875 and finished them in 1886, when they were first published).[82]

In *The Madwoman in the Attic*, Sandra Gilbert and Susan Gubar describe what they call an anxiety of authorship among women "built from complex and often only barely conscious fears of that authority which seems to the female artist to be by definition inappropriate to her sex."[83] For Euro-American middle-class women travel writers of the nineteenth century, such "anxiety of authorship" often played itself out in rhetorical strategies meant to negotiate the tension between the desire to travel and the prevailing ideal of femininity.[84] As Sidonie Smith argues, such strategies often legitimated female mobility by finding "cover" in the role of selfless ethnographers of domestic life:

> A bourgeois woman could not generously indulge herself in the autobiographical consciousness that was pervasive in men's writing during the nineteenth century and present herself as the hero of her own narrative. . . . To avoid the impropriety of self-preoccupation and self-promotion that were so much a part of travel narratives, women often masked their curiosity and their agency by muting their narrative "I." Some displaced any personal motivations for writing onto importunate friends and relatives who, the narrators hastened to tell their readers, pressed them to write. Others opened their chronicles with an apologia, gesturing to male travel narrators who had already covered the field, giving obeisance where it was dutifully due. Still others muted the pleasures of travel . . . by assuming the identity of dutiful wife or daughter. Certain motivations for travel were admissible to women—the search for improved health, for instance, or the devotion to a self-sacrificing mission—whereas others remained inadmissible. . . . Her attention could most properly be trained upon social arrangements, domestic relations, and the activities and lives of women.[85]

Among the inappropriate subjects for women's attention were the "exoticist narrative tropes" and fixation on sex and sexual mores so characteristic of male travel writing. Indeed, as Smith puts it, "a proper woman could neither confess to sexual desires nor describe sexually explicit behaviors if she wanted to maintain her social respectability."[86]

By contrast, the "domestic" haunts the narratives of women's travels, albeit in diverse ways. While Smith suggests that women of privilege were expected to reproduce a focus on the domestic even when abroad, for those less fortunate, "the domestic" is often a constant reminder of a place of violence or imprisonment from which they have escaped, as well as a refuge from the danger to which their mobility has exposed them. As Bonnie Frederick suggests, moreover, for fugitive slaves in South America, "home" represents an idyllic that they seek to recuperate literally and symbolically—a reversal of the itinerary often pursued by middle-class women fleeing the constraints of gilded domesticity.[87]

Salme's writings exemplify many of these rhetorical features, strategies, and tropes of women's mobility and travel writing, suggesting gendered patterns across culture I want to bring into relief by way of a triangulated contrast with Ibn Battuta's travels and his *Rihla*. Departing with the blessings of his family to complete the *hajj*, Ibn Battuta's extensive wanderings throughout the *Dar al-Islam* were motivated by a combination of curiosity, wanderlust, desire for spiritual fulfillment, power, women, and material gain. His *Rihla* was written at the behest of a sultan at the end of more than thirty years of relatively unconstrained traveling, and with the substantial assistance of a scribe. The purpose of Salme's travels, the stated reasons for her *Memoirs*, and the various interiors through which her narrative moves could not be farther from the adventures and *Rihla* of Ibn Battuta, nor more seemingly emblematic of the gendered nature of travel and the "spermatic" quest literature it authorizes. Salme fled her home in haste and under cover, not with the blessings of her family but in fear of them, seeking in Germany refuge from danger and a life with her lover, but not before having to forfeit her religion and her name. (Salme here might be imaginatively compared to the Princess Bayalun who, it will be recalled, had been forced to convert from Christianity to Islam when she was married off to a Mongol khan for strategic reasons, and in whose company Ibn Battuta had traveled to Constantinople.) Although Salme's *Memoirs* glosses over these developments, her *Letters Home* leave no doubt about the toll they took:

> That one voice only, which I believed to hear continuously . . . still rang in my soul: "And here you wish to pass the rest of your life?" It would have been easier to give my life than to be able to answer this dreadful question with an honest "Yes." In addition there was, externally, the Christian name, whereas internally I was as good a Muslim woman as you yourself are. I appeared to myself so utterly despicable for posing differently from what I in reality was. This I tell you quite frankly: beware of changing your religion

without true conviction. . . . Never in my whole life—neither before nor after—have I, morally speaking, felt so miserable and deprived of every support as immediately after my baptism. . . . It
cannot be questioned that it is thousandfold better to be a Muslim
than to be neither a Christian (at heart, that is) nor a Muslim.[88]

In contrast to a *rihla*, in the preface, Salme describes her published
work first as some "sketches of my life," then merely as a "personal
memoir" written after the fact, penned for the sake of "the dear children" rather than for public consumption, and protests that only "at the
urgent request of many" did she consent to have them published.[89] Indeed, Salme's life as represented in both her *Memoirs* and *Letters Home*
is at once defined and haunted by the "domestic." While Ibn Battuta
leaves "a girl in every port," in *Letters Home*, Salme explains that, despite her deepest desire to return to Zanzibar and Islam, she sees remaining as a Christian in Germany for her children as the final expression of love and loyalty to her dead husband. Doing so meant, however,
forfeiting her inheritance (a fact which she never seems to have completely absorbed) and the love of her Muslim family in Zanzibar at the
very moment she was apparently in dire financial and emotional straits.

The *Memoirs* itself can be characterized as an itinerary of the domestic: it opens with the journey of seven-year-old Salme from one of her
father's palaces to another, and proceeds to detail the daily life of an
Omani princess inside those walls (minus any reference to sexual mores
or desire which would have been as antithetical to Salme's respectability
as to a nineteenth-century Victorian woman), continuing to a move to
one of her plantations, then to the house in town where she met Reute.
In *Letters Home*, her declining financial fortunes are documented
through a series of moves into ever smaller abodes in Hamburg, Dresden, and Berlin, stripping "travel" of the romantic aura so often associated with exotic adventures and heroic quests. Even her return voyage
to Zanzibar after nineteen years was traumatic, as she almost lost her
life when the ship was hit by a monsoon.

Salme describes herself in retrospect as a "very wild, inexperienced
girl" and reflects with great regret about her impetuous participation
in the attempted palace coup that challenged the power of a brother
she had once cherished as a girl.[90] There is little wild impetuosity in the
Memoir's moments of evaluation, however, which tend to be cautious,
anxious not to overstate what she knows, or to assume the stature of
judge. Here perhaps we may speak not only of "anxiety of authorship"
but also of anxiety of judgment, an unease with asserting publicly the
kind of epistemological authority Ibn Battuta, Herodotus, Tahtawi, and
Tocqueville regarded as central to establishing their credibility. Speak-

ing about the comparative advantages of German and Arab education in the *Memoirs*, for example, she suggests that she may have "some advantage over the indigenous who, for being used to it, does not see many things which immediately catch the eye of an unbiased observer who grew up in different surroundings." But, she hastens to add, "I am by no means entitled to pose as a judge."[91]

There are many ways to approach Salme's complex life and writing. Indeed, they have served both as inspiration for an overheated American romance novel and as one of the primary sources for a serious ethnographic study of clothing, class, and gender in Zanzibar.[92] A triangulated contrast with Euro-American women's travel literature and Ibn Battuta's *Rihla* has suggested that Salme's *Memoirs* share many of the features of women's mobility and travel writing: an itinerary of the domestic, what I have called an anxiety of judgment, an emphasis on the role of wife and mother, and an experience of travel not as an unconstrained heroic quest, motivated by wanderlust, spiritual fulfillment, desire for knowledge, sex, or material acquisitions, but rather as a mode of survival in the face of less than optimal alternatives.

Yet to stop here would, both by commission and omission, violate the complexity of Salme's multilayered writings by organizing them in terms of a series of sharp oppositions between *rihla* and memoir, subjective and objective knowledge, domestic and political, interior and exterior, feminine and masculine discourses. Importantly, Salme's life and work can be read both in terms of and against the grain of these oppositions. Doing so, moreover, actually shows them to be unstable, discloses the political complexity of the various domestic worlds through which she moves, reveals her resistance to and complicity in her place and privilege, and illustrates quite vividly the conditions under which mobility can both occasion and disable the capacity to theorize comparatively across racial, religious, class, cultural, and linguistic difference.

In the first instance, Salme's location at the intersection of two cultures, and a life lived in consecutive interiors, many of which (she writes) had been "jealously guarded from the gaze of the outer world,"[93] discloses a picture, not of domestic peace, protected from the rough and tumble of public life, but rather of intense political rivalries, jealously guarded privileges, and minutely graded racial hierarchies. For example, the power of Salme's father's first wife, Azze bint Sêf bint Muza, over all other wives and their children was enacted in numerous ways large and small: she always remained seated while all others stood, the other wives kissed her hand as a sign of respect, and only she of all the wives sat at the sultan's table. Indeed, it is the substantial might of Azze bint Sêf, and not only over the entire household, that provides one of Salme's most detailed examples of women's substantial power in "the Orient": "she dominated my father completely, court and state not seldom depended upon her almighty mood."[94] Moreover, the secondary wives (*sarari*), those initially bought or enslaved, were themselves classified by color of skin: the Circassians[95] were of higher value than the darker-colored Abyssinian wives, each race ate at their own table, and the seating arrangements were a veritable map of social distinctions.[96] Although hierarchies of color were not meant to apply to children, according to Salme, the progeny of the Circassians were often resented by their darker-skinned siblings, especially as the sultan's favorite children were of Circassian descent. Salme herself was called a "white ape" by one of her darker sisters and the hostility was evidently mutual: in the *Memoirs*, Salme leaves no doubt but that she herself believed Circassians were of much greater beauty and elegance than Abyssinian women or their children.[97]

In Germany, however, Salme is transformed from "white" to "raced." As she tells it in *Letters Home*, at one of the less-expensive places to which she considers moving with her children as her financial woes in Germany worsen, she is met by a suspicious landlady "who certainly did not everyday meet people who, like my humble self, are born near the equator and do not have a completely white complexion. . . . Later too I often experienced this kind of mistrust towards those who are not pure-blooded Germans."[98] When first she moved to Germany, she was told that Arab women were "fat as a barrel," had the "hair and complexion of a negress," "feet as small as those of a Chinese woman," and encountered a woman who became "engrossed in my so-called negro-hair and took the peculiar freedom to even touch it."[99] Aware always that Germans believed Arabs lacked cultivation, education, and breeding, Salme felt she represented the entire "Arab race" with her every word and gesture, and was at times paralyzed with anxiety that her unfamiliarity with the language and customs of her new home would simply confirm Europeans prejudices.[100] Afflicted with this "double consciousness" of being in but not of Europe,[101] Salme's narrative often veers from essentialist generalizations about, for example, "the innate lust for power of Oriental princes and the passions of the Oriental in general" to sharp rebukes of European views of the so-called oppressed Arab woman.[102]

Salme's claim, moreover, to have recorded her life only for the sake of "the dear children" and without aspiration for public consumption is belied by the extended interregnum in the *Memoirs* on "Oriental life" for the benefit Europeans whose prejudices about, and ignorance of, Arabs and Muslims had become a daily part of her life in Germany. Indeed, by the time of the 1888 edition of the book, Salme articulates a new purpose for the *Memoirs*:

Even in this century of railroad and rapid communication, so much ignorance still exists among European nations of the customs and institutions of their own immediate neighbors, that one can hardly wonder how little is actually known about those races far removed. . . . Having been born and bred in the East, I am in a position to set down the unvarnished reflection of my oriental experiences—of its high life and its low life—to speak of many peculiarities, and lift the veil from things that are always hidden from profane eyes. This, I hope will constitute the main value of my book, and my object will have been fully gained if I have been able to contribute my share, and, above all, if I have succeeded in removing many misconceptions and distortions current about the East.[103]

In fact, whatever anxiety of judgment Salme betrays in the *Memoirs* is entirely absent in her *Letters Home* (which she apparently did not intend to publish) where she judges, and quite harshly, the hypocrisy of European claims to civilization. What is progress, she asks, when the weakest (here meaning widows such as herself, not the poor, for whom she exhibits little sympathy) are allowed to perish; when instead of veils, society requires elaborate masks of so-called civility; when "primitive" behaviors are replaced by "chilly calculation"; and where freedom means not the liberty to manifest one's individuality but to be watched, judged, and measured at every turn by society and a highly detailed schedule of laws and procedures that govern its citizens' every move?[104]

Even the *Memoirs'* at times lavish gestures of humility often precede some quite sharp judgments, many of which would have been unlikely to endear Salme to her German readers, suggesting that her anxiety of judgment may have been as much strategic as self-effacing. So, for example, at the start of a chapter picking apart, with fine-tuned logic, the self-serving prejudices of Europeans regarding the degradation of Muslim women, she claims that she "does not wish to write a learned book" and that, knowing the seductions of outward appearances when it comes to unfamiliar cultures, she "will try not so much to judge" as to report.[105] Yet if judging means only giving voice to one's prejudices, in this case a refusal to judge can itself be a kind of moral judgment. Thus, when she writes about education there is this double register to her claim of suspending judgment:

I have no desire to judge European education as a whole, for I am not able to do so; I only wished to express some of my observations, which convinced me that school and education here have many bad sides. At any event, it must seem understandable

after this, that for me it always is and will remain an open question, whether it is indeed justified for Europeans to deplore a
people as "unenlightened," and whether they are allowed to forcibly impart their enlightenment on such a people. Many will
sneer at this and shrug their shoulders; but nevertheless! In any
case I can state categorically that all those who believe that it is
in the interest of these peoples themselves to bring them education and enlightenment are very mistaken. Born and brought up
an Arab woman in an atmosphere which, according to European
ideas, is totally uncultivated, I know best with how little approval a general European education will meet with the Muslim
Orientals.[106]

Levi-Strauss has argued that inasmuch as writing entails the imposition of structure and narrative on human existence, it always involves
a corruption of experience.[107] If this is so, a sharp distinction between
a supposedly spontaneous travelogue and memoirs written at the end
of a journey is unwarranted. The distinction is particularly unpersua-
sive in the case of Salme's *Memoirs* and Ibn Battuta's *Rihla*, which, it
will be recalled, was written at the end of his voyages for the sultan's
pleasure with the substantial help of a scribe, and was characterized
by certain Arabic rhyming patterns and an emphasis on great wonders
and marvels (including a levitating yogi). To the extent that travel literature by definition blurs fiction and fantasy, ethnography and literature, history and epic, even the more general distinction between the
genre of the *rihla* and memoir may erode on closer examination. As I
have argued in previous chapters, a *rihla* is constrained by techniques
of representation derived from the world of the traveler; these techniques organize and delimit what the traveler sees and how he sees it,
and thus determine what is included and excluded from the narrative
and how it is translated for the audience quite independent of the
claims the traveler makes for the status of the knowledge conveyed
therein. So understood, the generic distinction between *rihla* and travel
memoir appears to be a matter of degree rather than kind: as a memoir
explicitly claims to represent only the perspective available to the author, it is just more transparent about the extent to which any traveler
carries her native city with her wherever she goes.
    Indeed, inasmuch as Salme largely remains trapped within domestic
circuits in both Africa and Europe, "home" is, in a literal sense, always
with her. Yet "home" also haunts Salme in a profoundly psychic sense
that has little to do with the abodes in which she lives and even less
in common with Ibn Battuta's brief bouts of homesickness. For Salme,
"home" is that magic place where she last recognized herself:

Thinking back on these beautiful days of my youth, when I knew the world only from its good, glorious sides and still had no idea of the numerous thorns which later would threaten to block my path through life everywhere, my heart turns heavy. But in the hours of distress, those holy remembrances of my youth, the remembrance of my parents, brothers and sisters, of my home country, again and again are a comfort to me and almost daily I bask in them.[108]

The paradox, however, is that while Salme carries Zanzibar with her wherever she goes, as her travels progress and she comes to see the "entire world as a foreign land," it is precisely this idealized image of "home" that is jeopardized. It is a truism that one can never go home again, not only because it is impossible to re-create what is past, but also because the meaning of "home" often emerges only after it is gone, built from memories, echoes and the sum of experience that fills the distance between past and present. In this way, the "temporalization of space effected by travel" means that the "very condition of orientation, the *oikos* [home] is paradoxically able to provoke the greatest disorientation."[109] Such disorientation is palpable when "Emily Reute" walks unveiled for the first time on her native soil after an absence of nineteen years, nearly overwhelmed with self-consciousness but equally bewildered that it should matter so much to her at after all that time.[110]

Just as Said points to the ways in which dislocation enables a contrapuntalism that can potentially "diminish orthodox judgment and elevate appreciative sympathy," Salme's disorientations are at times productive of a unique plurality of vision, one that illuminates, for example, the widespread human tendency to naturalize cultural conventions.[111] Much like Herodotus, she notes that the Arab no less than the European is afflicted with the same preferences for his own habits and customs: having "grown up with these views, he has not come to know any other ones so as to draw comparisons and he therefore considers them quite natural and correct. Everywhere the power of custom with its deeply penetrating influences!"[112] In the chapter on "Women's Position in the Orient," moreover, she seeks to explain to her European audience how misleading outward appearances can be, using as an illustration her own uncertain grasp of unfamiliar cultures and mores:

A tourist goes for a couple of weeks to Constantinople, to Syria, Egypt, Tunisia or Morocco, and then writes a bulky book on life, customs and habits in the Orient. He himself is never able to get an insight into real family life. He contents himself with writing down the stories which circulate—and thus gradually become more and more distorted—as he heard them told by a French or German waiter at his hotel, by sailors, or donkey drivers, and forms his opinion accordingly! . . . If his book is written in an amusing and interesting way, it certainly will be read more than those which in accordance with the truth offer less piquant stories, and it will control popular opinion . . . I too have for a long time judged things European by their outward appearance only. . . . Afterwards, however . . . I came into closer contact with the world and discovered more and more than I had misjudged people and situations, and had been dazzled by appearance far too much.[113]

There are moments when the *Memoirs* veers close to a hagiography of her family and friends, or when bitterness at her experiences in Germany threatens to overwhelm *Letters Home*. Yet more often than not Salme ably straddles multiple perspectives, acknowledging, for example, that only in Germany did she have the "pleasure to become acquainted" with "sciences such as history, geography, physics, mathematics," but also weighs carefully the advantages and disadvantages of Arab and European systems of education.[114] Watching her children overloaded with homework but recalling how little instruction she received (she secretly taught herself how to write on a slate made from the shoulder blade of a camel), she contends, "it seems to me that the Europeans demand too much from a school, and the Arabs demand too little."[115] She does not hesitate to write critically of Zanzibar's rituals of mourning, during which the wives of the deceased are confined to a darkened room for four months, as if temporarily buried alive. She also writes darkly of family feuds and heirs anxious always to grasp the reins of government, even by violence, "let[ting] law and justice retreat completely into the background." But she frequently shifts perspective, contending at another moment that it is not religious intolerance which causes Arabs to resist European impositions, but self-preservation: "the Arab is conservative by nature and adheres with the greatest tenacity to his traditions; innovations, which appear impossible and incomprehensible to him, should not be pressed upon him."[116]

She is able to be sharply critical of European ignorance and prejudices about Muslims and Arabs, yet takes apart such misrepresentations carefully, marshaling evidence and often Europeans' own history against them. Such is the case in the chapter on "Woman's Position in the Orient." After rendering in a single paragraph what is essentially Said's critique of Orientalism, she argues that based on her observations of both European and Arab marriages, it is not religion, not the prevailing customs and views which render marriages happier or unhappier: it depends upon the married couple's true understanding of each other. Where this is found happiness and peace will reign, there will develop that true harmony which makes a relationship into a real marriage.[117]

She acknowledges that the seclusion of Muslim women creates a measure of gender inequality and writes that, on occasion, such seclusion "can become really annoying and custom can carry things too far."[118] Yet she insists, first, that European rituals of courting simply degrade women differently and, second, that when Europeans see in Muslim societies female powerlessness rather than agency it is because they are looking in the wrong places. Thus she records with great relish the fact that, during a siege of the palace revolutionaries in Zanzibar, it was the women who conceived and executed a plan that kept defeat at bay "while the men were at a loss and indulged in empty talk."[119] She goes on to detail the enormous power women exercised in the royal household, adducing for evidence the career of her great-aunt, regent of Oman when her father was but a child, who sallied forth in men's clothing to fortify her soldiers against an armed invasion. Salme then defends polygamy as a brake on jealousy that is, in any case, rarely practiced, and after a strategically placed passing reference to Mormon polygamy, concludes:

But is marriage always looked upon as so sacred in Europe's moral society? The Christian may, of course, marry one wife only, and that is a prerogative of Christianity; Christian law wants the good and the just, Islamic law allows the evil; but existing usage and practical circumstances mitigate to a great extent the evil consequences of the law in the Orient—here, in spite of the law, sin very often has the upperhand. It would seem to me that the only difference in position between an oriental woman and a European one is, that the former knows the number and also the person and character of her female rivals, whereas the latter is kept in affectionate ignorance about this.[120]

While Said describes both exile and the plurality of vision made possible by "seeing the entire world as a foreign land" as a source of potential delight, Salme is often disoriented and unmoored by living at the crossroads of two radically different cultures. "It is only abroad," she writes," that one feels what one has lost with home."[121] While hardly seduced by so-called "civilization," she is unable to resist entirely the pull of "scientific sensibilities" in Germany and from this vantage she comes to view some of her own beliefs with skepticism,

unwilling to fully relinquish them yet also unable to take the same un-
questioned sustenance from them she once had. A case in point is the
faith in predestination, which Salme dismisses with as much contempt
as any good nineteenth-century European rationalist (she had received
scientific instruction from a Dresden professor in exchange for Arabic
lessons) when discussing attitudes toward disease in her home country: "It is well known how obstructive the belief in predestination is to
any progress, and how superfluous it makes appear the drawing of
cholera cordons or the setting of stricter watch over the large pilgrimages."[122] At the end of the ill-fated palace coup, she analyzes with cool
distance the intense prayers of the conspirators—including herself—
certain that their destiny is in the hands not of men but God: "in enlightened Europe, one may call this fanaticism, or whatever else, but
such a faith certainly brings indescribable peace to those who adhere
to it, saves them despair when in need, and makes even the most impracticable paths of our life appear less dangerous than they really
are."[123] Yet at other times, she describes the need to see her life as in
God's hands and attributes having survived the cholera epidemic that
took her mother to "the will of the All-good and the All-wise [to
which] I had to resign myself."[124]

Indeed, Salme is at times stationed at the intersection of no less than
three different cultural perspectives, German, African, and Omani-Arab.
Noting, for example, the prevalence of superstitious beliefs about the
embodied devil among Africans, Salme pointedly comments that Arabs
who have just arrived from Oman are particularly contemptuous of
such practices and "Africanized" Arabs who endorse them; after awhile,
she notes wryly, they grow convinced of a possession here or there. Of
course, Salme herself is a case in point: although she describes such su-
perstitions as "coarse practices," she also hesitatingly wonders if evil
spirits have captured the ruins of her childhood home when she finally
returns to Zanzibar, "but for nineteen years I have been remote from
this superstition and its adherents, so I may be mistaken."[125]

Such instances illustrate how Salme's often quite painful life of permanent and multiple exile at times amplifies her vision, disclosing to
her readers heretofore unavailable areas of comparative knowledge.
Yet her capacity to think across and through difference exists alongside
marked moments when her own prejudices deepen and congeal. Reduced in Germany to what were, to her, increasingly dire financial conditions, she never ceases to treat her hired servants—she was rarely
without one or two—with suspicion and contempt, sure that they are
slacking, stealing, or abusing freedoms to which they are not entitled.
Describing a system of voluntary charity in Zanzibar, Salme suggests
that, in both Europe and elsewhere, there are a "multitude of people

pretending to be poor. . . . begging is their trade, it has become second nature to them, and without begging they are no longer happy."[126] Salme feels she is a religious outcast in Germany; yet she does not hesitate to express an intense dislike of Jews—"Arabs in general despise the Jews and consider them as unclean"—despite her claim that, as a Semite herself, she cannot technically be an "anti-Semite" in the European sense.[127]

But perhaps nowhere is Salme's myopia more acute than when it comes to race, which must itself be situated in the context of her early life in Zanzibar. The Portuguese lost Zanzibar to Omani Arab rulers in 1698, and by the time of Salme's birth in the nineteenth century, the Arab Sultanate in Zanzibar had entered its golden days as the "dominant power and richest trade center from Arabia to the Cape."[128] She was thus raised as part of an Omani Arab colonial elite whose lives, identity, and privileges were built on African labor (she estimates her father alone owned six thousand to eight thousand slaves, although a scholar puts it at ten thousand)[129] and a deeply rooted belief in Arab ethnic and racial superiority.[130] In the chapter simply titled "Slavery" in the *Memoirs*, Salme marshals arguments about tradition, custom, European hypocrisy, and the abuses of foreign imperialism to proffer a full-throttled defense not only of slavery but of racial slavery in particular.[131] At the very moment in which the world in which she lived no longer counted her as "white," Salme repeatedly argues that black people are slow, lazy, childlike, forgetful, irreligious, in need of discipline and supervision, and are in any case inferior to lighter-colored slaves who are brighter and more alert.[132] The sympathies she so readily grants to those most like herself are noticeably absent in these repeated expressions of hostility to those who are darker-skinned; indifference to the lives of those who served her in Zanzibar and Germany; and blindness to the ways in which her mobility, daily life, and even her cherished childhood memories were built on the labor and pains of others whose very humanity is diminished in the course of the narrative.

CONCLUSION

It has often been claimed that women are more moral, empathic, and sensitive to human suffering than their male counterparts.[133] It is a credit to much of the literature on the complex relationship of Western women to imperialism that it rarely presupposes such gender essentialism, building arguments about complicity and resistance in terms of specific historical and political contexts rather than by reference to any innate qualities of women. The result is a nuanced picture of Western women living at an angle, as it were, to the colonial project in which they were inescapably implicated. For example, Sara Mills argues that the material,[134] physical, and psychological constraints on colonial women rendered them "at one and the same time part of the colonial enterprise, and yet marginalised within it."[135] She suggests that their travel writing is characterized by a "textual unease" in which their evident complicity in imperialist endeavors is tempered by a "stress on personal involvement" with the "natives" and a rendering of unfamiliar people as individuals, in "marked contrast to much Orientalist work, where the divide between 'us' and 'them' is carefully policed."[136] Mills elaborates:

> [British] women travel writers were unable to adopt the imperialist voice with the ease with which male writers did. The writing which they produced tended to be more tentative than male writing, less able to assert the "truths" of British rule without qualification. Because of their oppressive socialisation and marginal position in relation to imperialism, despite their generally privileged class position, women writers tended to concentrate on descriptions of people as individuals rather than on statements about the race as a whole. It is in their struggle with the discourses of imperialism and femininity, neither of which they could wholeheartedly adopt, and which pulled them in different textual directions, that their writing exposes the unsteady foundations on which it is based.[137]

Yet despite such careful formulations, the pervasive "hope that women, colonized themselves by gender, might recognize and oppose colonization based on race"[138] has often worked to overwhelm the distinction between women's lack of formal power in imperial endeavors and political innocence, thus contributing to what Indira Ghose has characterized as the "myth of women's non-involvement in colonialism."[139] In this way, the argument that living at an angle to the imperialist venture produces greater "personal involvement" with the "natives" subtly sustains the presumption of greater insight into and identification with the plight of the colonized. But as Salme reminds us, there is a substantial difference between gaining access to women's quarters about which European men could only fantasize and actual knowledge of the inhabitants therein; in fact, European women who visited the court harem in Zanzibar rarely succeeded in seeing anything more than the interior décor.[140]

Writing of European colonial women in particular, Susan Greenstein argues that "resistance and complicity cannot be seen as opposing categories; resistance, at least, is always colored by complicity."[141] The preceding discussion suggests that such a dynamic is also at work in Salme's writings, which detail not only the specific dimensions of her powerlessness but also her complicity and investment in elaborate racial hierarchies, in an Arab colonial enterprise in Africa, and in both the institution and rationale of slavery. Indeed, Salme demonstrates that the intersection of travel, exile, and gender, far from honing comparative sensibilities, may well deaden them. More specifically, she shows the ways in which narratives of unique anguish can be particularly tone deaf to perspectives and lives "not one's own," and blind to broader patterns of power and powerlessness that might link her experience to others. The constraints of gender have often served as the organizing ground on which coalitions across race, ethnicity, culture, and sexuality have been built. The complex relationship of women from various cultures to imperialist ventures of all kinds, however, challenges the expectation that simply being a "woman"—like any other identity constructed in part by way of constraint or marginalization—guarantees the imaginative capacity necessary to recognize common patterns of systematic and systemic powerlessness across difference.

Yet Salme's blindnesses are no more nor less egregious than those, say, of Ibn Battuta, whose practices of translation and mistranslation render entire classes of people all but invisible or radically refigured by his domesticating representations. And as travel is both a term and a practice of translation, and translation entails the "paradoxical duality of blindness and insight" which is, in turn, the "precondition of all knowledge,"[142] as in the previous chapters, here there is a simultaneous opening and closing built into the metaphor and practice. A translated person translating for others, Salme intentionally and inadvertently discloses to her readers an invaluable understanding of domains at once political and domestic; portrays vividly not the "pleasures" of permanent exile but how critical purchase on multiple worlds can unmoor a sense of self; and details how that unique plurality of vision offered by comparative knowledge can sharpen a sense of profound alienation both from the place in which she lives and a home that can never be recovered.

Chapter 6

COSMOPOLITANISMS PAST AND PRESENT,

ISLAMIC AND WESTERN

We created you from a male and female,
and formed you into nations and tribes
that you may recognize each other.
Verily, the most honored of you in the sight of God
is he who is the most righteous. (Qurʾan 49:13)

To each of you We have given a law
and a way and a pattern of life.
If God had pleased He could surely have made you
one people (professing one faith).
But He wished to try and test you
by that which He has given each of you.
So try to excel in good deeds.
To Him will you all return in the end;
it is He that will show you the truth
of the matters in which you dispute. (Qurʾan 5:48–49)

AN EXPLORATION of cross-cultural travels of the past from the perspective of the present is a comparison across history. As such, it offers a vantage from which to reflect critically on characterizations of the contemporary age in terms of mobilities and displacements said to be unprecedented both in scope and kind. We are all now said to live in a world in which "borders have stopped marking the limits where politics ends because the community ends," our identities not only shaped by particular places and spaces such as nation and domicile but subject to the multiple cross-currents and exposures created by rapid economic globalization and cultural hybridization.[1] The previous chapters serve as a timely reminder that the dynamics of fragmentation and unification, antagonism and mélange so closely associated with the whirl of contemporary life represent an extension, not a replacement, of the structural globalization of earlier epochs constituted by "long-distance cross-cultural trade, religious organizations and knowledge networks."[2] The fluidity of identities and attachments now associated with the postcolonial, increasingly globalized world thus has a long history and is not merely the product of the spread of Western cultural and economic power throughout the globe.

In a sense, then, "globalization is a very old story that is yet to be fully remembered."[3] This does not deny that technology and the globalization of capital have brought about mobilities and exposures that are most certainly new at least in terms of scope, scale, and speed.[4] What it does do is draw more sustained attention to historical precedents that, when they are not simply absent from scholarship on contemporary mobility, are largely invoked in passing as evidence for the radical break in space and time wrought by globalization. Continuities as well as discontinuities in the contexts, meanings, and practices of travel across history are more than matters of antiquarian interest, for they suggest that the past is as important a comparison for the present as contemporary cultural constellations are for one another. Indeed, I want to suggest that these narratives of past travel help restore a broader historical and cultural field for recognizing the mobility of theorizing and theorizing mobility across and within epochs and cultures. I would like to conclude by tracing some of the implications of this argument for contemporary politics, focusing in particular on how the previous chapters might illuminate both the reach and limits of current attempts to analyze the politics of displacement and the practices that do or can flow from them.

Political theory is often characterized as a field at once organized around canonical texts of Western thought and preoccupied with "the relations between sovereign and people, state and society," both of which supposedly render the discipline uniquely unable to contend with the deterritorialization of politics and culture.[5] Yet many political and social theorists are increasingly engaging precisely these developments under the rubric of the "new cosmopolitanism," a protean category that at the very least signals an attempt to rethink the scope and scale of moral and political obligations among human beings whose identities and loyalties are no longer coextensive with the modern nation-state. The "new" differentiates current expressions of cosmopolitanism from its somewhat jagged itinerary in Western history. As is often noted, the word itself comes from the ancient Greek for "citizen of the world," and its elaboration as a way of being is usually traced to the Stoics (although at least one scholar traces it to ancient Egypt).[6] Yet from the time of the Romans to that of Rousseau, cosmopolitanism has been construed quite differently in different epochs, serving at one moment to valorize the aspiration to love strangers as one's own, at another to vilify various undesirables as deracinated parasites, and at yet another to cloak in politically palatable garb a universalism tainted by association with Western imperialist ventures.

At once parasitic on and critical of this uneven past, the "new cosmopolitanism" is itself difficult to pin down, as it has been debated, restated, and endlessly qualified by a dizzying array of modifiers—discrepant, rooted, comparative, vernacular, critical, and actually existing, among others. As Pratap Mehta argues, these proliferating cosmopolitanisms have aesthetic, existential, moral, and legal valences, but minimally express a "suspicion of closed horizons . . . a willingness to engage with the 'Other' . . . [and] an aesthetic and intellectual openness to diverse strivings, cultures and forms of reasoning."[7] Animated by the conviction that cosmopolitanism is "the sensibility of our moment," most proponents seek not only to enact such a stance of openness in their own work but mobilize proliferating experiences of displacement for the kind of dialogue productive of genuine engagement with other cultural forms and critical purchase on one's own.[8] Despite—or perhaps because of—the ways in which increasing contact among peoples has produced as much hostility as hybridity, cosmopolitans also explicitly or implicitly nurture the hope that politics itself can be transformed by way of such engagements, "stretched" to meet the challenge of the times by being

> forced to include the variable power of sympathetic imagination to define collectivities of belonging and responsibility in the absence of that long history of face-to-face interaction that Dewey thought was necessary to community. . . . The opportunities for turning distant economic interdependence into conscious political cooperation have never been so promising. The time for cosmopolitics is now.[9]

My purpose here is not to track the shifting fortunes of cosmopolitanism over time, survey the various understandings of cosmopolitanism currently in vogue, nor finally, to adjudicate among the complex claims for and against it. Rather I approach the proliferating meanings of the "new cosmopolitanism" as symptomatic of a moment in which increasing awareness of contact among peoples, cultures, and ideas has engendered new attempts to take account of the import of mobility for political life. The "new cosmopolitanism" may be more usefully understood as signaling entry into a debate about the actual or desirable relationship between the local and global, rootedness and detachment, particularism and universalism, rather than denoting a consistent set of empirical or normative arguments. Nevertheless, its various articulations collectively represent an attempt to keep apace of the speed of current structural and cultural transformations, to develop conceptual tools capable not only of recognizing but theorizing new identities, interstitial public spaces, and deterritorialized cultures, and finally, to summon those ethical practices and precedents capable of countering "dramatic nostalgia politics" unleashed by globalization, ranging from ethnic cleansing to revanchist nationalism to violent strands of religio-political fundamentalism.[10]

The problem, however, is that while poised to meet the multiple challenges of what appears to be an unprecedented level of contact and exchange among peoples and information, current "analyses of cosmopolitanism are themselves rarely cosmopolitan," simultaneously enacting and disavowing a provincialism that is at once historical and cultural.[11] In the first place, the parameters of the current debate about cosmopolitanism are decidedly "presentist." This is so not only in the sense that those who write about it are animated by a concern with the world as it currently is, but also in the ways localism and globalism, particular and universal, vernacular and cosmopolitan are largely rendered coextensive with what happen to be their contemporary expressions. Discussions about the reach and limits of local and translocal attachments, for example, are almost entirely organized in terms of the nation-state, a distinctively modern invention however "modernity" is defined.[12] Some participants in these debates seek to shore up the centrality of the nation-state and the "societal culture" it is said to demarcate, others to document or facilitate its decline.[13] But in either case, politics, identities, allegiances, and communities under pressures conjured by the globalization of capital are invariably transnational, subnational, postnational, international, multinational. Whether conceptualized as a way of being in the contemporary world, a set of moral obligations to those beyond our (national) borders, a set of legal relationships among nation-states, or simply as a "domain of contested politics,"[14] cosmopolitanism in this way becomes a continual comment on the state of the nation-state. This suggests why, despite a variety of translocalisms and cosmopolitanisms of earlier epochs, one scholar would describe modernity, globalization, and cosmopolitanism as "concepts whose meanings and projects . . . largely overlap and coincide at the level of procedures and operational modes."[15]

Yet collective experience "has been in motion all along and the fixities of nation, community, ethnicity, and class have been grids superimposed upon experiences" too complex and subtle to be accommodated therein.[16] The ahistoricism characteristic of many analyses of cosmopolitanism thus may be related to what Norbert Elias once called the social science "retreat into the present."[17] But as political theory in particular prides itself on attending to ideas of the past, such ahistoricism seems less about privileging the present than about a selectively Eurocentric genealogy organized around cosmopolitanism as a particular idea about how to negotiate between the local and translocal, particular and universal. This is a genealogy in which the thread that begins with the Stoics, proceeds through the usual suspects such as Rousseau and Kant, and culminates in Nussbaum, Waldron, and others becomes the history of cosmopolitanism per se.[18]

As Sheldon Pollack points out, however, when cosmopolitanism is understood as an "action rather than idea, as something people do rather than something they declare, as practice rather than proposition (least of all, philosophical proposition)," a variety of ways of being and moving in the world come into view that are cosmopolitan without explicit justification or systematic articulation.[19] This shift in the understanding cosmopolitanism from "professions of moral commitment" to particular practices that transpire under specific circumstances make it possible to register not only the existence but also political import of a variety of cosmopolitanisms that can—and in many ways already do—serve as resources for the reworking of contemporary cultural imaginaries.[20]

As "religious communities are among the oldest of the transnationals,"[21] the networked nature of Muslim travel throughout history provides a particularly instructive area of inquiry into cosmopolitan precedents and practices. In the current political climate, of course, Islam has come to embody anticosmopolitanism par excellence, the antithesis of openness to diverse strivings and plural truths. Yet the Islamic ethos of travel in search of knowledge I have traced throughout this book illuminates the threads of a particularly rich countergenealogy of cosmopolitanism, one woven from a variety of doctrinal sources and historical practice. Such a genealogy might begin with the many exhortations to Muslims to seek wisdom wherever it resides adumbrated in the previous chapters. It might also include the Qurʾanic emphasis on the moral significance of the diversity of mankind evident in the epigraphs to this chapter, an ecumenism echoed in a hadith in which Muhammad characterizes difference of opinion (*ikhtilaf*) within the *umma* (community) as a source of mercy (*rahma*).[22] In Qurʾanic verse 5:48 in particular, Sohail Hashmi locates what he calls a "maximalist ethic of tolerance," one that entails not only respect for plural perspectives but a willingness to engage with them derived from the humility commanded by the reminder that "God knows, but/and you do not know" (3:66).[23] More than that, Hashmi contends, in the context of an integrated reading of the Qurʾan as a whole, this verse encourages Muslims to see in such plurality both God's creative hand and His inscrutable design:

Though each community advances along its own path toward a common goal, it is not the goal but the journey that is the real focus of this verse. The journey is the test, and this test is not only of conflict among rival and competing faiths struggling for hegemony. Nor is it a religious cold war, a journey of the deaf and mute. In this verse, the Qur'an affirms that the problem of religious and moral diversity is not a hindrance to be overcome, but an advantage to be embraced—a necessary facet of God's unknown plan for humanity. The journey can be meaningful only if there are a number of travellers, for just as human beings urge each other toward evil, so human beings urge each other toward the good.[24]

A countergenealogy of cosmopolitanism might weave together such doctrinal sources with all the disparate practices, moments, and ideas that punctuate the history of Muslim societies and continually shape collective memory. Such moments range from the cosmopolitan context of the ʿAbbasid Dynasty in which Islamic law can itself be understood as a response to a fluid, syncretic milieu, to the specific cultural, linguistic, and religious mélange of Umayyad Andalusia, to the interconnectivity of the transhemispheric *Oikoumene* of the Islamic Middle Periods, to the interchange among the multiethnic Ottoman, Safavid, and Mughal empires.[25] Such ideas and practices include the work of those Hellenized Muslim philosophers insistent that the Qur'an itself is a spur to philosophical reflection; the interest in and preservation of aspects of Stoic cosmopolitanism in Middle Period Arabo-Muslim thought; the emergence and dissemination of particularly ecumenical interpretations of Sufi theosophy; the import of an intensely cosmopolitan *hajj* past and present; and the immediacy of a virtual *umma* at once enacted and refigured electronically by Muslims across the world.[26]

The use of the term *genealogy* is deliberate here, for all genealogies are by definition selective; these contingent and eclectic precedents do not erase the conquest and bloodshed that often accompanied the expansionist ambitions of various Muslim states throughout history.[27] Even now, the potential of the internet to mobilize virtual communities of Muslims in the struggle against *jihadi* violence is continually offset by transnational cybernetworks committed to deeply xenophobic versions of political Islam. What this genealogy does do is foreground the *umma* as a cosmopolitan social imaginary captured more by the image of crisscrossing networks of mobile Muslims with multiple nodes serving plural purposes than, say, that of empire, either in the (older) sense of domination of the periphery by the center or in its more recent elaboration as a deterritorialized, impersonal, and homogenizing world market.[28] Here is a history in which extensive Muslim social networks largely flourished independently of territorially based state power, where institutions of the state constituted but one of "the dense knots where many network lines crossed."[29] Here is a civilization whose pre-eminence in the Middle Periods was secured less by the systematic consolidation of political power than by the extensive social and cultural mobility of Muslims bearing a moral code at once fixed and flexible enough to apply "wherever Muslims were to be found in sufficient numbers, being dependent upon no territorial establishment nor even on any official continuity of personnel, but only on the presence, among Muslims committed to it, of someone at least minimally versed in it to see to its application."[30] Here is a "global civil society" before the age of globalization, one constituted in part by a principle of free movement that simultaneously confounded state aspirations to total control and conferred legitimacy on those empires willing and able to safeguard routes of trade and pilgrimage.[31] And here is an organizing image of "networks" that actually corresponds to the "conceptual world of Islamic culture . . . [where] society is an ever living, never completed network of actions."[32]

Such touchstones and precedents are some of the terms in which the *umma* is continually reimagined as a moral, political, and even virtual *Oikoumene*, a cultural imaginary undimmed and in some ways even intensified (albeit in complex ways) by the advance of European colonialism, the rise of the nation-state, and now the march of globalization.[33] Yet these are just a few threads of one possible countergenealogy of cosmopolitanism to the one that currently prevails. One might "begin" earlier, later, or elsewhere. In his macrohistory of the dynamic of cosmopolitanism and vernacularism in South Asia, for example, Sheldon Pollack invokes another genealogy, and there are others still.[34] Just as there is more at stake in the investigation of travel narratives from all different directions than simple inclusion, the import of such countergenealogies is not reducible to the argument that, for example, "there are pre-modern cosmopolitanisms too." Recuperating these historical precedents reveals that the presentism of the current debate at once expresses and compounds a cultural provincialism that has several dimensions.

As scholars have pointed out, inasmuch as the new cosmopolitanism debate largely proceeds within "European analytical and temporal frameworks. . . . discussion typically takes place on a highly localized conceptual terrain and in a very vernacular idiom constituted by European culture."[35] Such a vernacular idiom both evinces and reinforces the valorization of a particular stance of skepticism toward certain modes of belonging and knowing that is itself the product of a specific genealogy rooted in a particular culture and religious tradition.[36] Moreover, it takes as central to emancipatory politics a cosmopolitan dialogue where "the dominant mode of that dialogue disowns or negates the substantive modes of self-definition of all cultures except the modern West and construes them as having never exercised the prerogatives of reflection."[37] The universalization of this skeptical stance as a way of being in the world particularly appropriate to our time thus entails a double move: it renders as a model to all a mode of self-understanding that emerged out of historically specific conditions and erases cosmopolitan precedents that transpire beyond the coordinates of Euro-American time and space.

With some notable exceptions, most advocates of the "new cosmopolitanism" ground openness to "diverse strivings" in a dialectic of local and attenuated attachments, and generally avoid the presumption that such ecumenicalism can or should be predicated on relinquishing all forms of belonging.[38] Yet cosmopolitanism as it is currently articulated embraces one particular form of "belonging" over others often without taking serious account of the inequalities of power that make a stance of ironic distance toward one's own community and commitments a luxury rarely enjoyed (or, depending on one's perspective, a depravity rightly avoided) by those whose place and identity is historically and politically marginal or continually jeopardized. The problem here is not the celebration of openness to others per se, for this often (although not always) expresses the aspiration to extend to all humans qua humans a certain imaginative generosity it would be churlish to impugn and distasteful to reject. Rather, the problem is insufficient attention to how history, culture, and power inflect the very meaning and value of "openness" in ways that render it politically suspect or untenable, even to those whose mobility is extensive and exposures to difference are multiple. Such is the clearly the case with those young, predominantly male, diasporic Muslims in Europe, whose intense embrace of religious identity within recent years has been forged under conditions of felt disenfranchisement and racial antagonism.[39]

The genealogy of Islamic cosmopolitanism I have traced not only suggests that the parameters of the current debate are unnecessarily narrow but that there are other contexts and precedents for thinking about cosmopolitan practice comparatively across history and culture. For example, broadening the temporal and analytic framework of cosmopolitanism makes visible the ways in which cultural imaginaries are continually forged not just by way of multiculturalism in general and through encounters with the West in particular, but also through an *intraculturalism* across time and space. The previous chapters suggest that diverse prenational histories, ones that disclose how attenuated memberships and local solidarities are articulated and reworked through movement across porous borders, are instructive points of comparison to what some are calling this current, "postnational" moment. This is particularly evident in Ibn Battuta's extensive travels throughout and beyond a transhemispheric Afro-Eurasian civilization in almost continuous intercommunication by way of an extraordinary fluidity of people and knowledge across political, cultural, and linguistic boundaries. This was a time, after all, in which the religious community was almost completely liberated from dependence on any territorial state, a development rooted in the mercantile, metropolitan, and cosmopolitan tendencies of an "Islamicate culture" in the process of expanding to become an "intercivilizational entity" encompassing both urban-based and pastoral nomadic communities.[40] In this world, cross-pollination is not solely the product of Muslim/non-Muslim exchange, but also of literal and imaginative interaction among Muslims located in different cultural milieus, encounters that at various moments articulate and occasion a reworking of racial, religious, and geographic frontiers.

Such an intracultural dynamic is also evident at later moments in Islamic history. Concentrating on the period up to the nineteenth century, for example, Frances Robinson points to the cosmopolitanism of a Sunni world in part constituted by itinerant scholars, individuals, and families whose mobility not only forged channels of interconnection but produced in communal institutions a shared body of knowledge across the Ottoman, Safavid, and Mughal empires.[41] These, then, are moments in which a continuous Islamic cosmopolitan imaginary is at once enacted and reworked by Muslims committed implicitly or explicitly to "the initial creative events and to the succeeding dialogue" about both the meaning of those events and the method of reworking them.[42] Such moments disclose ways of being, acting, and encountering others in a deterritorialized world in which engagement with others flows from deeply held local attachments and sodalities that travel and are themselves reworked by mobility, rather than requiring or producing a stance of ironic distance from too much—or the wrong kind of—"belonging."[43] As Bamyeh puts it, cosmopolitan culture here is "not a product of induction from the comforts of a sedentary hiding place but an outcome of conducting one's life on a route to a number of destinations."[44] Such a social imaginary informs a range of current practices and discourses, from those virtual communities constituted by Muslims from all over the world engaging in interpretive debates online (*e-ijtihad*), to working-class Pakistani cosmopolitans at home in transnational Sufi networks, to the recent judgment by Muslim jurists that migration to non-Islamic countries for the purposes of education and livelihood is not only permitted but obligatory, to the work of scholars such as °Abdolkarim Soroush, Muhammad Arkoun, Riffat Hassan, Amina Wadud, and Abdulaziz Sachedina, among others.[45]

The dynamic disclosed in these instances suggests, moreover, that the channels of such mobility, the paths by which such attachments are reworked, and the knowledge such itinerants carry, acquire, and rearticulate by way of human exchange are intimately related to the experience of cultural power or its perceived loss. In this connection, it is worth considering Tarif Khalidi's argument that an early confidence in the providential significance of the Islamic *umma* "gave medieval Muslim civilization an unparalleled capacity to learn from other cultures, an open and oft-expressed willingness to acknowledge its cultural debt to Indians, Persians and Greeks" at odds with the current tendency to read all of Islamic history through the juridical distinction between *Dar al-Islam* (Abode of Islam) and *Dar al-Harb* (Abode of War).[46] In many ways, Khalidi's observation about Muslim history picks up on what Hashmi characterizes as a central theme of the Qur°an, that is, contending with the "presence of moral and religious diversity among human beings."[47] Yet in the context of an ascendant and rapidly expanding Islamic civilization, such openness seems to derive less from a conscious moral commitment to toleration than from a vision of Islam as the culmination not only of all previous religious revelations but also as "the final heir of the world's cultures," a conviction that Khalidi argues produced a willingness to actively learn from rather than merely coexist with diverse cultural formations.[48]

This connection between knowledge and ascendant large-scale cultural imaginaries is further illustrated by Robinson's analysis of how shifts in political power contributed to the wax and wane of ecumenical forms of knowledge in the Ottoman, Safavid, and Mughal empires. He examines systems of formal learning and the path of mysticism in these Islamic states, tracking in particular the balance among the rational sciences (logic, philosophy, mathematics, many derived from ancient Greece), those "transmitted subjects" concerned with authenticating and interpreting the meaning and implications of the sacred texts, and finally, the resources for esoteric understanding (e.g., mysticism). Robinson is careful to note that "great scholarly traditions might have a life of their own regardless of the political context."[49] Nevertheless, he shows that when "Muslims were confidently in power" during the growth and consolidation of these empires, a Sufism conducive to discerning divinity even among non-Muslims flourished, as did the rational subjects, which at times served as a bulwark against a congealing orthodoxy grounded in the transmitted subjects.[50] By contrast, moments when Muslim power and ascendance were felt to be in jeopardy, either from within or without, coincided with the suppression of this ecumenical knowledge in favor of renewed emphasis on transmitted subjects seen as conducive to what Robinson calls "socio-moral reconstruction."[51]

I have argued that narratives of travel provide a window onto the ways in which ordinary people negotiate the disorienting ruptures often occasioned by exposures to the unfamiliar. Inasmuch as such narratives draw from a repertoire of culturally and historically specific "sense making devices" that are then reworked through various social encounters with others, they can also illuminate the ways in which macrohistorical patterns of power inform and constrain individual experiences of travel.[52] This is illustrated particularly well in the contrast between the nineteenth-century travels of al-Tahtawi and those of Sayyid Qutb, one of the most influential Islamist thinkers of the twentieth century. As I showed in chapter 4, Tahtawi's *Rihla* expresses a qualified "openness" to France enacted through complex and eclectic mediations between local and translocal knowledge, an engagement characteristic of a period in history when, as Hisham Sharabi aptly puts it, European ascendance appeared "less of a threat and more of a promise."[53] By the time of Qutb's twenty-one-month sojourn in America in the late 1940s, however, Western power had become inextricably associated with colonialism and ongoing cultural and economic imperialism. In contrast to Tahtawi, Qutb's experience in America is refracted entirely through a fixed opposition between a degenerate West and a virtuous Islam whose purity must be recuperated by excising the pernicious influence of foreign corruption.[54] While Qutb's own political thought was far more culturally syncretic than he would ultimately acknowledge, his written reflections on America explicitly enact a series of sharp closures not only to what is "foreign" but also to an entire body of "local knowledge," that is, those versions of Islam he deemed insufficiently pure and authentic.

There are, of course, many complicated reasons for any particular traveler's reaction to displacement, but these brief examples suggest a connection between propensities toward ecumenicalism and the experience of cultural ascendance or its loss—regardless of whether such a sense of loss or threat is corroborated by empirical indices. It is well established that empires and states at the height of power—Roman, Christian, and Muslim alike—frequently demonstrated an insular refusal to tolerate "diverse strivings" beyond or within their borders, at times inventing a sense of crisis for political purposes, just as in contemporary American politics an increasingly powerful religious right mobilizes followers with the specter of a Christianity imperiled from all directions. There is, moreover, a crucial difference between the ebb and flow of ecumenical *attitudes* on the one hand and, on the other, cosmopolitan *practices* that persist in spite of, and in some cases because of, shifts in political and cultural power. As Sami Zubaida points out, for example, particular aspects of the rise of European power and dominance in the nineteenth century actually produced rather than inhibited "the formation of social milieus and personalities which may be identified as cosmopolitan" in Ottoman societies.[55] Indeed, even in the current climate of what some characterize as neoimperialist globalization cosmopolitan practices—virtual and physical—proliferate under the radar or beyond the coercive control of often embattled Middle Eastern authoritarian regimes.

The connection I am suggesting between ecumenicalism and power is thus contingent, unpredictable, and can be discerned at a variety of historical moments in a range of cultural contexts. Yet it is particularly crucial given the current geopolitical landscape, one in which the legacy of specific historical asymmetries and current global inequalities continually reproduce a sense of Muslim powerlessness relative to the West. This is especially so because, until quite recently, awareness of the "Other" was quite unevenly distributed: while those who live in postcolonial societies have long contended with the universalization of "Occidental" culture, it is only recently and as a result of acts of horrific violence that Europeans and Americans have come alive to the dangers of their own insularity. Such inequalities form the context in which the inexorable forces of globalization are experienced, constrain the terms in which questions about openness—and to whom—can be asked and answered, and inflect how purportedly ecumenical calls for a "cosmopolitan sensibility" are received by those for whom hybridization looks more like a cultural invasion than a proliferation of restaurant options.

Indeed, as Sami Zubaida suggests, for many people, the connotation of cosmopolitanism is "not the fact of multi-cultural coexistence, but the development of ways of living and thinking, style of life which are deracinated from communities and cultures of origin, from conventional living, from family and home-centredness, and have developed into a culturally promiscuous life, drawing on diverse ideas, traditions and innovations."[56] The very language of "deracination" and "promiscuity" already suggests a view of cosmopolitanism and its multiple attachments less as an ecumenical way of being in the world than, in Jeremy Waldron's words, "a shallow and inauthentic way of living . . . [an embodiment of] all the worst aspects of classic liberalism—atomism, abstraction, alienation from one's roots, vacuity of commitment, indeterminacy of character, and ambivalence toward the good."[57] From this vantage, as Egyptian journalist Fahmi Huwaydi argues, Coca-Cola becomes just the most visible sign of a much more corrosive phenomenon:

> Is the goal Coca Cola-ization of the world, such that Coca-Cola becomes the pre-eminent drink among human beings, leading the roster [of what is] imposed on everyone, from hamburgers to jeans and the songs of Madonna and Michael Jackson? In other words, is this the meaning of globalization: that Western taste and its [entire] way of life be imposed on the world?![58]

In a post–September 11 world, such objections are easily assimilated into an ongoing narrative about an essential and timeless Muslim insularity and reflexive xenophobia. The previous discussion points to a different conclusion. It suggests that whether cosmopolitanism denotes imaginative generosity or inauthentic deracination depends less on the religion to which one belongs than on the range of available narrative scripts produced by the dialectical interplay between a discursive religious tradition conducive to diverse enactments and specific historical, political, and economic relations of power. In the contemporary geopolitical climate in particular, coerced and inescapable hybridization from the "outside" conjures new emphases on authenticities and purities that never were, rendering the costs of publicly advocating openness to aspects of Western culture in particular increasingly high—where "costs" are measured not in hard currency but in lost careers, liberties, and lives. This grants an outsized voice to those who seek to erase the ecumenical practices and precedents constitutive of Islamic cosmopolitanism in favor of an ahistorical "authentic" Islamic *umma* vigorously demarcated and vigilantly policed by highly mobile *mujahidin* moving with ease across and within national borders. Even attempts to reconcile the counterveiling pressures of global engagement and communal closure reveal how thoroughly anxieties about cultural corrosion have set the terms of the debate. Just as some Euro-American scholars argue that "the only way to be universal now is to be national," then, there are many Muslim thinkers for whom reclamation of certain kinds of Islamic authenticity is "not only a prerequisite for self-development, but also a precondition for dealing with the West on an equal footing . . . true contact can only be attained through authenticity."[59]

All of this suggests that much like the doubled-edged nature of travel itself, the path to and course of "reflective dialogue" dear to proponents of the new cosmopolitanism is ragged and contingent rather than linear and inevitable.[60] Indeed, attention to travels past and present, Muslim and non-Muslim, virtual and physical, fictional and factual underscores the irreducible unpredictability of the conditions, contexts, and outcomes of intensifying contact among different peoples. At the same time, it brings into sharp relief the extent to which such openings and closures past and present are endemic to practices of translation that are part of the human condition rather than characteristic of a particular culture or epoch.[61] It draws attention, however, to the specific ways in which history and power not only frame but in part constitute such openings and closures, albeit in ways that resist prediction or easy generalization.

Perhaps most significant from the vantage of contemporary politics, the previous discussion underscores the geopolitical asymmetries of power that currently render certain kinds of openness a prerogative enjoyed by only a select few, produce and reproduce the privilege of provincialism enacted in certain cosmopolitan claims, and strengthen the intellectual, religious, and political forces, emanating from all directions, that collude to erase from view the existence and import of non-European cosmopolitan genealogies.Under such conditions, the possibility of deriving "sympathetic imagination" from diverse experiences of displacement minimally requires attending to the complex nexus of power, history, and culture that differentially constrains potential participants to any "cosmopolitan dialogue" and establishes the grammar in terms of which such engagement at least initially proceeds. It also requires critical reflection on exclusions at once enacted and concealed by the current parameters of the cosmopolitan debate, an interrogation that enables recognition of other cosmopolitan genealogies continually reworked in and through contemporary political practice.

Recognizing a more capacious cosmopolitanism makes room for ecumenical practices and invocations of "openness" derived from diverse and specific cultural imaginaries, whether it is the revitalized Stoicism of Martha Nussbaum; the insistence by Tariq Ramadan that European Muslims inhabit not *Dar al-Harb* (Abode of War) but rather *Dar al-Shahada* (Abode of Testimony), a "space of responsibility" requiring "permanent involvement and an infinite self-sacrifice for social justice, the welfare of mankind, the environment . . . good and equity through *human brotherhood*"; or the argument by Hasan al-Turabi, perhaps the most prominent Sudanese Islamist leader and thinker, that global engagement and partnership between Muslims and non-Muslims is a duty not only sanctioned by Allah but presaged by a long Islamic history of "intercivilizational dialogue."[62] It is perilous to misread such imperatives as yet another demand to recognize and respect cultural differ-

ences. As Manichean discourses about "Islam versus the West" proliferate and congeal, pragmatism and politics together dictate that sustained
engagement among those who locate themselves on either side of this
"divide" requires terms each are willing or able to understand. The actual or potential commensurability of participants' understanding of
"openness" (and to what) and the conceptions of moral obligations (and
to whom) said to flow from such openness cannot be the starting premise of such efforts, for these are inescapably *political* questions, the answers to which can only be elaborated through sustained political engagement.[63]

At this point in the discussion, I want to return to poor James Mill,
whose robust defense of the superiority of reading about India in an
English closet over firsthand experience inaugurated these explorations of travel, theory, and knowledge across culture and history. In
contrast to Mill, I have suggested by argument and example that travel
occasions comparisons that, in turn, initiate an often (but not inevitably) transformative mediation between what is unfamiliar and familiar
and, by extension, between a condition of rootedness and a perspective
of critical distance. Yet given this brief discussion of cosmopolitanism,
the question arises: to what extent is travel and those firsthand exposures it makes possible necessary or sufficient to inaugurate such transformative mediations? I have argued that Mill's own knowledge of
India at once presupposes and conceals a dependence on the mobility
and firsthand observations of others. But even if his defense of immobility is logically inconsistent, is it still possible that "seeing with one's
own eyes" produces its own kinds of distortions of what is unfamiliar
and its own closures to critical reflection?[64] And what do the answers
to these questions suggest about the connection between multiplying
mobilities and the kind of evolutionary ecumenicalism cosmopolitans
understandably value?
    In these final pages, I want to argue that the pervasively double-
edged narratives of the previous chapters unintentionally trouble the
authority of autopsy by revealing the kinds of blindnesses at the heart
of sight and the insights made possible by imaginative vision. This is
a return to the discussion of travel, theory, and vision with which this
book began, although it is not in the service of the kind of final cumula-
tive synthesis characteristic of conventional concluding chapters. The
following does not propose, for instance, a model of mobility capable
of predicting what kinds of journeys and conditions will issue in critical reflection. As I have argued and illustrated throughout this book,
the motivations for travel as well as its consequences are various and
unpredictable, a complex and mercurial interaction of the personal,

cultural, historical, and institutional more suggestive of loose patterns than systematic paradigms. Nor does it proffer an empirical map of experiences of mobility or even a survey of all the valences of travel. In fact, rather than pointing to a kind of knowledge that can be fixed, mapped, possessed, and controlled, much of what is demonstrated here is the fluidity of knowledge itself, the constant transformation and contingency of what can be learned about human activity.

Throughout the previous chapters, numerous voices, speaking in different languages and times, have converged to posit the preeminence of autopsy (seeing for oneself), ʿiyan (direct observation), and *shahida* (to see with one's own eyes, witness, certify, and confirm) over any other route to knowledge. It is neither surprising nor conclusive that travelers, whose very claim to reliability rests on the capacity to witness firsthand what others cannot, would drape themselves in the authority of autopsy/ ʿiyan. Yet the status of "seeing for oneself" as a source of unmatched reliability is secured by the weight of several traditions, articulated by an impressive array of authorities. Aristotle argued that "we prefer seeing to everything else [because] this, most of all the senses, makes us know and brings to light many differences between things."[65] Heraclitus contended that "the eyes are more exact witnesses than the ears."[66] A hadith attributed to the Prophet Muhammad claims that information established by others is not the same as seeing with one's own eyes.[67] And Ibn Khaldûn argues that the "transmission of things one has observed with one's own eyes is something more comprehensive and complete than the transmission of information and things one has learned about. A habit that is the result of [personal observation] is more perfect and firmly rooted."[68]

Moreover, Deuteronomy 10:21 exhorts its readers to attend to the God "who performed for you those great and awesome wonders you saw with your own eyes" (Deuteronomy 10:21), and Exodus 19:11 states that on "the third day the Lord will come down in the sight of all the people upon mount Sinai." Some rabbinic interpretations have the people telling God, "Our wish is to see our King; one who hears is not comparable to one who sees," and one scholar argues that in Jewish mysticism "there is little question that the sense of sight assumes a certain epistemic priority, reflecting and building on those scriptural passages that affirm the visual nature of revelatory experience."[69] Thus Maimonides writes that a "man should never cast his reason behind him, for the eyes are set in front, not in back," and thirteenth-century Jewish writer Ibn Falaquera has the character of the scholar argue that seeing with one's own eyes is a crucial pillar of a strong faith.

There are many occasions in the previous narratives in which such confidence in firsthand observation seems warranted, where exposure to different practices and people yields an agonistic distance from the traveler's own commitments, inaugurating a journey to a broader field of vision. Such moments range from Herodotus's conclusion that all men deem their own *nomoi* superior to others to Tahtawi's synthesis of *hurriya* and French *liberté* to Salme's observation about the widespread human tendency to naturalize one's own cultural conventions and predilections. Such theoretical moments and flashes of insight are woven into narratives that work quite differently from one another. In the case of Ibn Battuta's *Rihla,* such moments remain discrete observations, part of a story designed to please a sultan; for Salme they are embedded in a larger effort to ground and make sense of her life. In the case of Tocqueville, they culminate in a full-blown theory of democracy and in Tahtawi's *Takhlis,* they serve a systematic argument for the acquisition of particular kinds of knowledge. Yet in all these cases, such theoretical moments occur cheek by jowl with a series of distortions, closures, misrepresentations, and moments of sheer blindness that, at the very least, trouble the assumption that direct observation emancipates both traveler and traveled to from the prejudices and prejudgments that presumably flourish like fungus in the dark safety of an English closet.

To take only the most striking example: consider the remarkably consistent schema governing the representation of women in the narratives of masculine travel that dominate the previous pages. These are men located in very different cultures and periods in history, their travels express plural purposes and their narratives represent diverse genres. And as I have argued, they negotiate the experience of dislocation by way of nested polarities particular to the worlds from which they come and through which they move—Greek versus barbarian, Sunni versus Shiʿite, Muslim versus Christian, European versus Arab, among others. Moreover, the attention each devotes to the opposite sex varies dramatically; while Ibn Battuta's narrative is fixated on women, for example, Herodotus barely registers them. Yet cutting across all these differences and distinctions is the transformation of women's bodies and behavior into a legend, as on a map, by which entire cultures can be decoded. Even the *Histories,* a book dominated by the epic deeds of men, largely figures women as the chaotic force against which all civilized political life must be secured, Greek and barbarian alike.

The iconization of women is in this way facilitated both by absence and presence: women loom large in the narratives of Herodotus, Ibn Battuta, Tocqueville, and Tahtawi, but assume a symbolic significance disproportionate to the fleeting moments when a woman flickers on the page. When female characters actually do materialize, they rarely speak and, with some noted exceptions, tend to act in ways that affirm the larger gender iconography governing the narratives. Even conditions of marital and sexual intimacy fail to jam this machinery: many of the women in Ibn Battuta's *Rihla* were his wives and lovers, often traveling with him for long stretches of time, yet their clothing, bodies, behavior, and sexual availability constitute an index around which an entire taxonomy of cultures is built. Paradoxically, then, although the appearance and behavior of women largely function to demarcate a "different order of politics and gender relations" from that of the traveler, by transforming women's bodies into a "terrain of political and cultural contestations and as an important metaphor for demarcating the self and the other," each of these narratives participate in a shared practice of representational power that cuts across history, culture, and genre.[70]

Montesquieu's fictional Persian travelers transform women from individuals to indices in much the same way: European women, for example, *become* their sexual behavior, and through them the entire moral character of the West is revealed. "Women here have lost all restraint," Usbek writes to Roxana, "they present themselves barefaced to men, as if inviting conquest . . . in place of the noble simplicity and charming modesty which is the rule among you, one finds here a barbaric impudence, to which one cannot grow accustomed" (XXVI).[71] The multivocality of the novel ultimately works to disrupt the iconization of women the male Persian characters enact, but not before demonstrating both the pervasiveness of such representations and violence they can sustain. This is nowhere clearer than in Usbek's letter to Roxana, in which he contrasts French womens' barbaric impudence with fond memories of the early days of their marriage:

> You would not satisfy my impatience but intensified it by the obstinate refusals of an alarmed modesty; for you confused me with all the other men from whom you must always hide yourself. Do you recall the day when I lost you among your slaves, who betrayed me by hiding you? Or that other time, when, finding your tears impotent to check the passion of my love, you employed your mother's authority? Do you remember how, when all such resources failed, you courageously found others? How you took a dagger and threatened to immolate the husband who loved you, if he persisted in demanding what you cherished even more than you did him? Two months passed in this combat of love and virtue, and you pushed your chaste scruples so far that you would not surrender even after being conquered. Defending your dying

virginity to the last, you saw me as an enemy who had outraged you, rather than as a husband who had loved you. For more than three months, you could not look at me without blushing . . . if you were here [in France] you would be incensed at the dreadful ignominy to which your sex has descended. You would run from these abominable places and yearn for that gentle retreat of inno-cence, where you are secure and afraid of no peril, where, in short, you can love me without fear of ever losing the love you dutifully owe me. (XXVI)

In these romantic recollections, physical and representational violence fairly seeps through Usbek's purple-prose: the relentless refiguring of Roxana's fear and desperation as enticing modesty, rape as passionate seduction, and a prison of sexual enslavement as a secure haven for the Virtue daily imperiled by the freedoms of foreign women.

One might well expect relief from such mechanisms of representa-tion in Salme's work, for in contrast to all of these texts, in these writ-ings a woman traveler does speak, and quite clearly. Salme writes, moreover, from the vantage of someone particularly fluent in various domains of the domestic, a perspective from which she is simultane-ously critical of the confinements women experienced in Zanzibar, the misrepresentations of Muslim women in European literature, and the prejudices of nineteenth-century Germans about "the Arab race." Sim-ply by conveying the texture of Salme's life, the foibles, strengths, and idiosyncrasies that make her an individual rather than an icon, these writings implicitly disrupt the mechanisms that have reduced Arab and Muslim women in particular to cultural and moral indices. They make clear, for example, Salme's complicity in both an Arab colonial enterprise and the institution of slavery, and further suggest that her own painful firsthand experiences of financial instability, racism, and political and social powerlessness in Europe do little to disrupt her deep commitment to the racial, ethnic, and class hierarchies that help ground her way of being in the world. Although inevitably susceptible to many kinds of appropriations, Salme's *Memoirs* and *Letters* never-theless militate against the mechanisms that so often transform women into indices of cultural authenticity while simultaneously resisting any attempt to replace this iconography with another in which the experi-ence of marginality produces a kind of political innocence.

Like the narratives of masculine travel, then, Salme's writings ulti-mately trouble the presumptive power of autopsy precisely because they allow the complex texture of her experiences and observations to emerge in full (albeit mediated through language and editing). The point here is not that because Salme is a woman she should be held to higher standards than Tocqueville or Ibn Battuta. Rather the point is that experiences of marginality do not guarantee the imaginative capacity necessary to recognize common patterns of systematic and systemic powerlessness across difference any more than seeing with one's own eyes assures clarity of vision. This suggests that Mill is right to challenge the privileging of firsthand observation over other routes to knowledge, but for the wrong reasons: it is not so much that autopsy/ʿiyan automatically distorts understanding, but rather that firsthand experience alone is insufficient to disrupt those deeply held systems of representation that refract and sift experience, and through which particular closures are sustained and reproduced. As the discussion in the introductory chapter suggests, systems of representation can be impervious to mechanisms of verification and argumentation because they are not only a way of making sense of the world but are also the basis on which we judge and act in it. Authorities ranging from Aristotle to Ibn Khaldûn may well rest the stature of sight on the presumption that, unlike perusing data or hearing arguments, witnessing firsthand has an unmatched disruptive power, one capable of shifting the tectonic plates undergirding even the most passionately held systems of representation. Yet these narratives suggest that just as travel itself is unpredictable in course and consequence, autopsy/ʿiyan alone cannot bear the weight of these epistemological claims.

As the only explicitly fictional journey in these pages, Montesquieu's *Persian Letters* does not stand or fall on the authority of autopsy. Thus it is unsurprising that it alone among these texts has the luxury and critical distance to register the insights of immobility and blindness of travel. For despite the ways in which Usbek has been read as exemplifying the connection between travel and philosophical reflectiveness, as I argued in chapter 4, his physical movement is actually inversely related to his capacity to move amongst and imaginatively inhabit perspectives other than his own. Indeed, Usbek's travels and exposures to the unfamiliar in the novel coincide with a hardening rather than easing of his despotic tendencies, and his increasingly philosophical insights into the nature of government, religion, and tyranny do nothing to enlighten him about his own character and the domestic hell he has created in Isfahan. Where Usbek is mobile, free, and autocratic, his wives are imprisoned in the seraglio, unable to move without surveillance or love without permission. Yet Montesquieu has Usbek's wife, Zelis, insist in a letter to him that "I have tasted here a thousand pleasures you could not understand. My imagination has worked ceaselessly to make me realize their value, and I have lived while you have only languished. Even in this prison holding me I am freer than you."

Furthermore, Montesquieu makes Roxana's actions the pivot of the plot and gives her the last word in which she, like Zelis, refuses to be determined by the conditions of bondage. "I have lived in slavery," she tells Usbek, "but I have always been free."

Zelis's and Roxana's letters admit the reader to a world from which Usbek is symbolically barred by his own cruel blindness, and it is a world in which mobility and freedom are not matters of the body but of the mind and soul. While evocative of Stoicism, this emphasis on imaginative travel is also central to another fictional novel, Naguib Mahfouz's *Rihlat Ibn Fattuma*, a tale of a traveler whose search for wisdom is at once modeled on and a parody of Ibn Battuta's *Rihla* ("Fattuma" has the same consonant-vowel pattern as "Battuta").[72] The book ostensibly follows its lead character, Qindil, through an array of political systems representing different stages of civilizational and moral development, but it is largely a "journey of the mind despite its spatial apparel."[73] After many trials and losses, the journey culminates in a voyage that is a beginning rather than ending: the novel leaves Qindil in the company of other pilgrims, still in pursuit of the elusive land of Gebel (literally, "mountain," from the Arabic root meaning to shape, fashion, create, to be born for), place of absolute justice and "incomparable perfection" which gleams atop a mountain perpetually beyond reach.[74] Qindil had thought that all his adventures and travels enabled him to see "matters with greater clarity than before," but he now learns that the inhabitants of Gebel are distinguished by their capacity to recognize that vision and knowledge are matters not of physical sight but of "latent powers within themselves."[75] Longing for "life far from observers; observers who are outwardly corporeal but who vibrate within," Qindil forsakes his home for a homecoming that is, like the Greek root of *utopia*, at once no place and every place: "decision and destiny, vision and action, beginning and end."[76]

The journey of Qindil and the characters Zelis and Roxana all suggest that there are specific kinds of knowledge available to those who do not or cannot travel, just as the character of Usbek suggests there are particular blindnesses characteristic of those who do travel. Here Montesquieu echoes the paradoxical relationship among travel, vision, and knowledge captured so vividly in Sophocles' *Oedipus the King*. Like Usbek, Oedipus's travel gives him access to the theoretical knowledge necessary to solve the riddle of the Sphinx yet blinds him to his own identity. In Jonathan Lear's description, Oedipus "cannot recognize any dimension of meaning other than the one he already knows . . . [his] confidence in his powers of practical reason shields him from recognition of another realm of meaning."[77] By contrast, Tieresias is aged and blind, and must rely on others even to walk. Yet the old man sees more fully and completely into nature and human nature than Oedipus, whose own self-inflicted blindness is both cause and consequence of seeing the truth, as well as a dramatization that, in J. Peter Euben's words, "blindness lies at the heart of sight."[78] In this way, Oedipus is "helmsman, path finder, puzzle solver, knower, guide, and liberator and so a wanderer, pursuing false trails, confused himself and confusing others, without shelter or home at the very hearth where he belongs. It is as if uncertainty of place yields a mind able to discern hidden abstract truths at the cost of understanding immediate and intimate realities."[79]

While the actual travelers of the previous chapters remain mostly blinded to the limits of their own vision, these explicitly fictional texts make possible a critical assessment of autopsy/°iyan itself by bringing into view the counterintuitive relationship between travel and myopia on the one hand and, on the other, immobility and imaginative insight. In so doing, they at once illuminate and themselves exemplify the ways in which imaginative travel can make available a level of reflective knowledge the very emphasis on and practice of autopsy can preclude. This is an apt reminder of the double meaning of vision, both in the physical sense of seeing the world as it is with one's own eyes and the imaginative capacity to envision potentialities not yet present. Unlike the physical act of seeing, however, this imaginative capacity may be enacted in diverse ways, including those mystical visions in which the "eye of the soul" permits apprehension of what is usually veiled from ordinary human sight. Such an understanding of vision is usually linked to mystical communion with the divine, yet Plato's *Republic* suggests that it is precisely this contrapuntal contrast between the ideal and actual that is crucial to political life, a prerequisite not only of wisdom but of what Wolin calls the architectonic impulse central to political theorizing.[80] Indeed, as Shaul Shaked suggests, even the most mystical of religious visions can have social dimensions, for the "recounting of these visions institutionalizes the process of personal transformation . . . listening to these stories of transformation or reading about them communicates some of the experience, and enables others to partake of this experience indirectly, if not at first hand."[81]

The dialectical relationship between embodied sight fixed on things that are and imaginative visions released from fidelity to facts suggests why it is that, throughout the previous chapters, the distinction between sacred and profane journeys, imaginative and literal travel, the divide between the genres they supposedly represent, and the bright line between one as a repository of fantasy and the other as a source of factual knowledge are blurred at every turn, often by those most deeply invested in maintaining them. Indeed, these narratives suggest that what is crucial to the "journey" is not the mobility of the body but rather the dislocating character of the encounter. Particularly instructive in this regard is Wolin's characterization of the work of historically minded theorists as facilitating a kind of "political initiation," that is,

> of introducing new generations of students to the complexities of politics and to the efforts of theorists to confront its predicaments; of developing the capacity for discriminating judgments . . . and of cultivating that sense of "significance" which, as Weber understood so well, is vital to scientific inquiry but cannot be furnished by scientific methods; and of exploring the ways in which new theoretical vistas are opened.[82]

Crucial to such political initiation, however, is engagement with theories that are strange and estranging rather than familiar or confirmative: the capacity for imagination, reflection, and judgment is cultivated not by reading to affirm what one already knows but by exposure to what disturbs, provokes, and dislocates. Just as travel can serve to confirm or challenge inherited certainties and shibboleths, here it is a matter both of *what* and *how* one reads. Texts that themselves reflect and enact such dislocation and, in particular, those that bring alive for a reader the experiences, press of events, fear, wonder, and sense of loss, at work in the jagged mediation between the familiar and unfamiliar can serve as an invaluable resource for those who do not or cannot travel, in part by enabling imagination of and reflection on modes of life other than their own.

Descartes once wrote that "to hold converse with those of other ages and to travel, are almost the same thing."[83] The "almost" here is crucial, of course, for the immediate, physical exposure to what is strange and estranging is quite different from reading about or imagining it, perhaps most importantly because the "armchair traveler" incurs none of the bodily dangers or risks so evident in the itineraries detailed in these pages. Yet imaginative exposures are not therefore without risk; after all, imagined "doesn't mean unreal: nothing could be more powerful than the human imagination."[84] In both cases, there can be moments when the friction between what people think they know and what they do not yet know produces the kind of dislocation in which the deep certainties that ground our everyday judgments and actions are suddenly and violently put into play. This is quite different from the kinds of exposures that domesticate cultures into lifestyle options organized around eclectic patterns of consumption—or what could be called hybridization lite. In such a case, cultural openness thrives because, as Mehta argues, it extends "only to those activities that dance at the surface of our lives . . . the restaurants we visit, the movies we see, the carpets we drape our floors with." By contrast, encounters that put at risk the "deepest issues that give our lives the purposes" we think they have enact a dislocation that unsettles, disturbs, and even frightens.[85] As Paul Ricoeur writes:

> When we discover that there are several cultures instead of just one and consequently at the time when we acknowledge the end of a sort of cultural monopoly, be it illusory or real, we are threatened with destruction by our own discovery. Suddenly it becomes possible that there are just *others*, that we ourselves are an "other" among others.[86]

The everyday political implications of how, when, and in what ways people negotiate such unsettling dislocation is precisely why Said's "traveling theory," with its emphasis on the circulation of big ideas through the work of extraordinary thinkers at epoch-making junctures, is inadequate to my purposes. Many of the travelers in these pages are in some way privileged—or at the very least, come to attain a certain stature, either as a direct result of their travels or by way of posthumous "canonization." Yet narratives even of privileged travelers whose sense of self, knowledge, time, and space emerges and is transfigured by the doubled mediation between rootedness and distance, home and abroad enact and bring alive for others what I have called those theoretical moments that erupt erratically in ordinary lives. As I have argued throughout this book, such exposures and mediations, physical or otherwise, that put deep certainties at risk are radically unpredictable in course and consequence. Yet it is precisely at these moments of flux that a window opens onto the ways in which social imaginaries are incrementally articulated and transfigured, not exclusively by intellectuals, but by a diverse array of people who find themselves negotiating the destabilization of what they do know through exposure to what they do not. Such negotiations can and do culminate in reflexive closure but on other occasions make room for the sense of wonder to which both Aristotle and Plato traced the origin of reflection and philosophy, "that peculiarly thoughtful response to awe."[87] These openings are thus more than quaint exercises in fantasy or private epiphanies; they are crucial instances of the "everyday cultural practice through which the work of imagination is transformed."[88] If Wittgenstein is right that the deepest certainties are embedded in a passionate system of reference that defies mechanisms of intellectual persuasion and verification because it is "really a way of living, or of assessing one's life," here are those rare moments in which the capacity for wonder about those who do live differently makes it possible to conceive of oneself living differently.[89]

NOTES

CHAPTER 1: FRONTIERS

1. Janet Wolff, "On the Road Again: Metaphors of Travel in Cultural Criticism," *Cultural Studies* 7 (1993): p. 228. *The Nation*'s special issue on "The Politics of Travel" (October 6, 1997) is just one case in point.

2. This use of "contact zones" here draws from two sources. Mary Louise Pratt uses contact zones to refer to the "space of colonial encounters, the space in which peoples geographically and historically separated come into contact with each other and establish ongoing relations, usually involving conditions of coercion, radical inequality, and intractable conflict." *Imperial Eyes: Travel Writing and Transculturation* (New York: Routledge, 1992), p. 6. Yet Patrick Holland and Graham Huggan argue that the complex intersection of historical, political, anthropological, cultural, mythical, and experiential knowledge produced by Western travelers create "complex textual zones" that are only "incidentally geographical." Patrick Holland and Graham Huggan, *Tourists with Typewriters: Critical Reflections on Contemporary Travel Writing* (Ann Arbor: University of Michigan Press, 2002) p. 67.

3. Michel Foucault, *Discipline and Punish: The Birth of the Prison*, Alan Sheridan, trans. (New York: Pantheon, 1977), p. 31. Norbert Elias, "The Retreat of Sociologists into the Present," in *Modern German Sociology*, ed. Volker Meja, Dieter Misgeld, and Nico Stehr (New York: Columbia University Press, 1987), pp. 150–72.

4. Paul Rabinow, *Reflections on Fieldwork in Morocco* (Berkeley: University of California Press, 1977), p. 5, quoting from Paul Ricoeur, "Existence et hermeneutique," in *Le Conflit des Interprétations: Essais d'herméneutique* (Paris: Editions Du Seuil, 1969), p. 20. The English edition is *The Conflict of Interpretations* (Evanston, IL: Northwestern University Press, 1974), p. 17; Pratt, *Imperial Eyes*, p. 5, emphasis in the original.

5. Karl Marx, *Capital* (New York: The Modern Library, 1936), pp. 12–13.

6. Adonis (ʿAli Ahmad Saʿid), "Beyond the East/West: Towards a Culture of the Future," public address delivered at Dartmouth College, May 9, 2001.

7. The phrase is from Kishore Mahbubani, "The West and the Rest," *The National Interest* (summer 1992): 3–13.

8. Zillah Eisenstein, *Against Empire: Feminisms, Racism, and 'the' West* (London: Zed, 2004).

9. For example, Steven Runciman's research on the Crusades demonstrates a "long sequence of interaction and fusion between Orient and Occident out of which our civilization has grown." Runciman, *A History of the Crusades*, vol. 3 (Cambridge: Cambridge University Press, 1954), p. 480.

10. William Dalrymple, "The Truth about Muslims," *New York Review of Books* 51 (17), November 4, 2004. See also Richard Fletcher, *The Cross and the Crescent: Christianity and Islam from Muhammad to the Reformation* (New York:

Viking, 2004). Marshall Hodgson makes a similar claim, arguing that the Latin Occident "played almost no role in building up the Hellenic scientific corpus even at the height of Roman power, and the Occidentals can less properly be called its heir than can the Muslims in whose lands much of the scientific corpus originated." Hodgson, *The Venture of Islam: Conscience and History in a World Civilization* (Chicago: University of Chicago Press, 1974), vol.2, p. 366.

11. John Gaventa, *Power and Powerlessness: Quiescence and Rebellion in an Appalachian Valley* (Urbana: University of Illinois Press, 1980).

12. See, for example, Nicholas B. Dirks, ed., *Colonialism and Culture* (Ann Arbor: University of Michigan Press, 1992), pp. 22–23.

13. For example, Charles C. Mann argues that American democracy owes much to the great Iroquois confederation established a full 200 years before Columbus arrived in the New World. Mann, "The Founding Sachems," *The New York Times*, July 4, 2005, p. A17 (for a more extensive re-reading of Native American cultures before Columbus, see Mann's *1491: New Revelations of the Americas before Columbus* [New York: Knopf, 2005]). And Eisenstein argues that "expressions of eighteenth century democratic theory derive as much from the slave revolts in Haiti as from Europe, as much from the demands of the slaves' humanity as from Western ideas of freedom." Eisenstein, *Against Empire*, p. 32.

14. Jan Nederveen Pieterse, "Globalization as Hybridization," in *Global Modernities*, ed. Mike Featherstone, Scott Lash, and Roland Robertson (London: Sage, 1995), p. 53.

15. See, for example, Aziz al-Azmeh, *Islams and Modernities* (London: Verso, 1996).

16. Mandaville, *Transnational Muslim Politics: Reimagining the Umma* (New York: Routledge, 2001), p. 56.

17. Indeed, the distinction between juridical and mystical Islam is often overstated. As Francis Robinson points out, for example, by the sixteenth and seventeenth centuries, "most learned men . . . were also Sufis," although the receptivity of orthodox Muslims towards mysticism would vary dramatically in the following centuries. Robinson, "Ottomans-Safavids—Mughals: Shared Knowledge and Connective Systems," *Journal of Islamic Studies* 8 (1997): p. 164. The supposed opposition between Islamic orthodoxy and Sufism in the Maghrib is further challenged by Vincent Cornell in *Realm of the Saint: Power and Authority in Moroccan Sufism* (Austin: University of Texas Press, 1998). For a discussion of the pervasive and problematic construction of an opposition between "popular rural" Islam and "scripturalist urban" Islam, see Talal Asad, "The Idea of an Anthropology of Islam," Center for Contemporary Arab Studies, Georgetown University (1986), pp. 6ff.

18. Khaled Abou El Fadl, *Speaking in God's Name: Islamic Law, Authority, and Women* (Oxford: OneWorld, 2001), p. 32.

19. David Waines, *An Introduction to Islam* (Cambridge: Cambridge University Press, 1998), p. 101.

20. There is a fair amount of diversity of views about the relationship between and content of "Islam" and "the West" among Islamists. As opposed to those who at once presuppose and advocate a fundamental antagonism among "civilizations," for example, Hasan al-Turabi of the Sudan insists that "inter-

civilizational dialogue" and even global partnership is not only necessary but "a God sanctioned duty upon Muslims." Larbi Sadiki, *The Arab Search for Democracy: Discourses and Counter-Discourses* (New York: Columbia University Press, 2004), p. 362.

21. There is an increasing amount of literature on the intellectual lineage of American neoconservativism, and in particular on the influence of a distinctively American version of Straussianism (which may or may not have much to do with Leo Strauss himself) on many of the architects of the Bush administration's foreign policy. See, for example, Anne Norton's *Leo Strauss and the Politics of American Empire* (New Haven: Yale University Press, 2004); Seymour Hersh, "Selective Intelligence," *The New Yorker*, May 12, 2003, 79.11; "The Closing of the Straussian Mind," by Mark Lilla, *The New York Review of Books*, 51(17), November 4, 2004; "Leo-Cons; A Classicist's Legacy: New Empire Builders," by James Atlas, *New York Times*, May 4, 2003; "The Power of Nightmares: Part 1—Baby it's Cold Outside," *BBC Documentary*, by Adam Curtis. For a discussion of this view of the world among Islamists, see Roxanne Euben, "The New Manichaeans," *Theory & Event* 5, no.4 (2002).

22. Bamyeh, "Global Order and the Historical Structures of *Dar al-Islam*," in *Rethinking Globalism*, ed. Manfred Steger (Lanham, MD: Rowman and Littlefield, 2004), p. 223.

23. Asad, *Genealogies of Religion* (Baltimore: Johns Hopkins University Press, 1993), pp. 16–17.

24. Gooding-Williams, "Race, Multiculturalism, and Democracy," *Constellations* 5, no.1 (1998): p. 23.

25. Zerilli, "Doing without Knowing: Feminism's Politics of the Ordinary," *Political Theory* 26, no. 4 (August 1998): p. 447, 451.

26. Ludwig Wittgenstein, *On Certainty*, trans. Denis Paul and G.E.M. Anscombe (New York: J & J Harper, 1969), §144.

27. Zerilli, "Doing without Knowing," pp. 443–44, emphasis in the original.

28. Ibid., p. 442.

29. Wittgenstein, *Culture and Value*, trans. Peter Winch (Chicago: University of Chicago Press, 1980), 64e; Zerilli, "Doing without Knowing," p. 449.

30. Romond Coles, personal exchange, February 1, 2005.

31. Again, this draws from Zerilli's discussion of how feminists have sought to finesse the persistence of the category of woman ("Doing without Knowing," p. 437).

32. Talal Asad usefully defines tradition as consisting of "discourses that seek to instruct practitioners regarding the correct form and purpose of a given practice that, precisely because it is established, has a history . . . an Islamic discursive tradition is simply a tradition of Muslim discourse that addresses itself to conceptions of the Islamic past and future with reference to particular Islamic practice in the present." Asad, "The Idea of an Anthropology of Islam," p. 14.

33. Michael Gillespie argues that the re-reading of history, geography, and culture through the prism of "the West"—understood in its current sense, as both a cultural and historical category—began no earlier than the nineteenth century. "Liberal Education and the Idea of the West," in *America, The West,*

and Liberal Education, ed. Ralph C. Hancock (Lanham, MD: Rowman and Littlefield, 1999), pp. 7–10. The extent to which the divide between East and West is a recent product read back into history is evident, moreover, in Jeremy Brotton's study of the geographical, diplomatic, and intellectual exchanges between Europe and the Ottoman Empire in the early modern period. The range and amity of these exchanges, not to mention persistent uncertainty at the time about where, precisely, Europe ended and Asia "began," undermines the idea of a timeless and bright line between West and East. It also challenges histories that continue to define the emergence the European Renaissance and "its love of learning and commitment to a civilizing process in direct opposition to the menacing threat of the Islamic Ottoman Empire, persistently represented as a dark despotic threat looking over the forces of enlightenment and disinterested intellectual inquiry which supposedly characterized late fifteenth- and early sixteenth-century Europe." Brotton, *Trading Territories: Mapping the Early Modern World* (New York: Cornell University Press, 1998), pp. 96–97, 90.

34. Thomas Asbridge, *The First Crusade: A New History* (Great Britain: The Free Press, 2004), pp. 334–39; and R. I. Moore, "First Froth," *The Times Literary Supplement*, October 1, 2004.

35. Sayyid, *A Fundamental Fear: Eurocentrism and the Emergence of Islamism* (London: Zed, 1997), p. 47; Mandaville, *Transnational Muslim Politics*, p. 55.

36. Glyne A. Griffith, "Travel Narrative as Cultural Critique: V. S. Naipaul's Travelling Theory," *Journal of Commonwealth Literature* 29, no. 2 (1993): p. 87, 88.

37. Although recent re-examinations of the range and content of such Western journeys abroad have also served to complicate this emphasis on the connection between Euro-American travel accounts and imperialist power. See, for example, Rana Kabbani's discussion of Wilifrid Scawen Blunt in *Imperial Fictions: Europe's Myth of Orient* (London: HarperCollins, 1986), pp. 95–103; and Ali Behdad's explorations of the "discursive ambivalences" of late Orientalism in *Belated Travelers: Orientalism in the Age of Colonial Dissolution* (Durham, NC: Duke University Press, 1994).

38. Arjun Appadurai, "Disjuncture and Difference in the Global Cultural Economy," *Public Culture* 2, no. 2 (1990): p. 6; Sanjay Subrahmanyam, "Connected Histories: Notes towards a Reconfiguration of Early Modern Eurasia," *Modern Asian Studies* 31, no. 3 (1997): pp. 761–62.

39. Mary M. Gergen, "Narrative Structures in Social Explanation," in *Analysing Everyday Explanation*, ed. Charles Antaki (London: Sage, 1988), p. 96.

40. Fred R. Dallmayr, *Alternative Visions: Paths in the Global Village* (Lanham, MD: Rowman and Littlefield, 1998), p. 186.

41. See Roxanne Euben, *Enemy in the Mirror: Islamic Fundamentalism and the Limits of Modern Rationalism* (Princeton, NJ: Princeton University Press, 1999). The "comparative" here does not preclude, and indeed enjoins, attending to the radically different historical contexts in which such work takes place, an endeavor which, as Arjun Appadurai points out, today requires particular attention to the question: if comparative work "relies on the clear separation of the entities to be compared, before serious comparison can begin . . . how are we to compare fractally shaped cultural forms which are also polythetically

overlapping in their coverage of terrestrial space?" Appadurai, "Disjuncture and Difference in the Global Cultural Economy," p. 20. On comparative political theory also see Stephen Salkever and Michael Nylan, "Comparative Political Philosophy and Liberal Education: "Looking for Friends in History," *Political Science and Politics* 26 (June 1994): pp. 238–47; Anthony Parel and Ronald C. Keith, eds. *Comparative Political Philosophy: Studies under the Upas Tree* (New Delhi: Sage, 1992); and *Border Crossings: Toward a Comparative Political Theory,* ed. Fred R. Dallmayr (Lexington, 1999).

42. Nietzsche, *Thus Spake Zarathustra,* trans. Thomas Common (Buffalo, NY: Prometheus, 1993), Prologue, Part IV.

43. Said, "Traveling Theory," *The World, The Text, and the Critic* (Cambridge, MA: Harvard University Press, 1983), p. 226.

44. Bruce Robbins, "The East Is a Career: Edward Said and the Logics of Professionalism," in *Edward Said: A Critical Reader,* ed. Michael Sprinker (Oxford: Blackwell, 1992), pp. 64–65. Mandaville, *Transnational Muslim Politics,* p. 89. In a later essay, Said revisits his argument, suggesting that there are occasions where theory, "instead of becoming domesticated . . . flames out, so to speak, restates and reaffirms its own inherent tensions by moving to another site," becoming in this way transgressive rather than a new orthodoxy. "Traveling Theory Reconsidered," in *Reflections on Exile and Other Essays* (Cambridge, MA: Harvard University Press, 2000), pp. 438–49, 452. The debates occasioned by Said's essay are extensive. See for example Abdul R. JanMohamed, "Worldliness-without-World, Homelessness-as-Home: Toward a Definition of the Specular Border Intellectual," in *Edward Said: A Critical Reader,* 96–120; and James Clifford, "Notes on Travel and Theory," *Inscriptions* 5 (1989): 177–88.

45. "Traveling Theory," p. 242.

46. Ibid., p. 241; Robbins, "The East is a Career," p. 66.

47. Sheldon Wolin, *Politics and Vision: Expanded Edition* (Princeton, NJ: Princeton University Press, 2004), p. 17.

48. Said is often faulted for insisting in the essay that "relocation *in itself* precipitates the transformation" of theories, thus failing to fully "elaborate the mechanisms through which meanings shift as theory travels." JanMohamed, "Worldliness-Without-World," p. 100, emphasis in the original; Mandaville, *Transnational Muslim Politics,* p. 89.

49. Taylor, *Modern Social Imaginaries* (Durham: Duke University Press, 2004), p. 23.

50. Ibid., pp. 23–25.

51. Appadurai, *Modernity at Large: Cultural Dimensions of Globalization* (Minneapolis: University of Minnesota Press, 1996), p. 9.

52. Zerilli, "Doing without Knowing," p. 449; Sheldon Wolin, *Tocqueville Between Two Worlds: The Making of a Political and Theoretical Life* (Princeton, NJ: Princeton University Press, 2001), pp. 35–36.

53. Leslie Poles Hartley, *The Go-Between* (New York: Knopf, 1954), prologue.

54. Tim Youngs has sought to bring into relief the economics of travel often overlooked in the focus on travel writing in "Where Are We Going? Cross-Border Approaches to Travel Writing," *Perspectives on Travel Writing,* ed. Glenn Hooper and Tim Youngs (England: Ashgate, 2004).

55. This builds on argument of those feminist theorists, critical race theorists, and theorists of postcoloniality, among others, who stress the importance of recognizing theory in a variety of settings, practiced by a variety of people, in a variety of genres. See, for example, bell hooks, *Talking Back: thinking feminist, thinking black* (Boston, MA: South End Press, 1989), pp. 36–37.

56. *Travellers' Tales: Narratives of Home and Displacement*, eds. George Robertson, Melinda Mash, Lisa Tickner, Jon Bird, Barry Curtis, and Tim Putnam (New York: Routledge, 1994), p. 2; James Redfield, "Herodotus the Tourist," *Classical Philology* 80 (1985): p. 123.

57. See Hala Fattah, "Representations of Self and the Other in Two Iraqi Travelogues of the Ottoman Period," *International Journal of Middle East Studies* 30, no. 1 (February 1998): 51–76; Husain Muʾnis, *Ibn Battuta wa-Rihlatuhu: Tahqiq wa-dirasa wa-tahlil* (Cairo: Dar al-Maʿarif, 1980); Sam I. Gellens, "The Search for Knowledge in Medieval Muslim Societies: A Comparative Approach," pp. 50–65, and Abderrahmane El Moudden, "The Ambivalence of *Rihla*: Community Integration and Self-Definition in Moroccan Travel Accounts, 1300–1800," pp. 69–84, both in *Muslim Travellers: Pilgrimage, Migration and the Religious Imagination*, ed. Dale F. Eickelman and James Piscatori (Berkeley: University of California Press, 1990); and Ian Richard Netton, "Basic Structures and Signs of Alienation in the *rihla* of Ibn Jubayr," in *Golden Roads: Migration, Pilgrimage, and Travel in Mediaeval and Modern Islam*, ed. Ian Richard Netton (United Kingdom: Curzon, 1993), 57–74.

58. Marshall Hodgson, "Hemispheric Inter-regional History as an Approach to World History," *Journal of World History* 1 (1954): 715–23, and *The Venture of Islam*. See also William H. McNeill, *The Rise of the West: A History of the Human Community* (Chicago: Chicago University Press, 1963); and Philip D. Curtin, *Cross-Cultural Trade in World History* (Cambridge: Cambridge University Press, 1984).

59. Here I borrow from James Clifford's "Traveling Cultures," in *Cultural Studies*, ed. Lawrence Grossberg, Cary Nelson, and Paula A. Treichler (New York: Routledge, 1992), p. 110.

60. Robertson et al., eds, *Travellers' Tales*, p. 3.

61. *Oikoumene* in Greek originally referred to the inhabited as opposed to the uninhabited world, an opposition that corresponded roughly to the distinction between the Hellenic world and the world of barbarians. But the term became significantly more inclusive over time, evolving first to include in the "inhabited world" both Greeks and some non-Greeks, and later to denote an even more expansive understanding of "the whole." It is the etymological precursor to "ecumenical," meaning "belonging to the whole world."

62. See, for example, Nabil Matar, "Confronting Decline in Early Modern Arabic Thought," *Journal of Early Modern History* 9, no.1–2 (2005): 51–78; Christopher Tyerman, *Fighting for Christendom: Holy War and the Crusades* (Oxford: Oxford University Press, 2004), p.13

63. Sheldon Wolin, "Political Theory as a Vocation," *The American Political Science Review* 63, no. 4 (December 1969): p. 1077.

64. María Lugones and Elizabeth V. Spelman, "Have We Got a Theory for You! Feminist Theory, Cultural Imperialism, and the Demand for 'the Woman's Voice,'" *Women's Studies International Forum* 6, no. 6 (1983): p. 577.

CHAPTER 2: TRAVELING THEORISTS AND TRANSLATING PRACTICES

1. Mill, *The History of British India*, 3rd ed. (London: Baldwin, Cradock and Joy, 1826), p. xii.

2. It is worth distinguishing between the perfectly reasonable presumption that one can learn something about others secondhand or by way of a reflective distance that may be physical, temporal, and imaginative on the one hand and, on the other, Mill's privileging of such solitary distance over the "distortions" of actual travel. I will return to Mill's argument and this point in the concluding chapter.

3. Contemporary Islamist examples of this are legion, but a lesser-known warning against travel to the non-Islamic world is the pronunciation by Abu ʿAbdallah Malik b. Anas (d. 795), the Muslim jurist, that Islam "permits non-Muslims to enter dar al-Islam and trade with Muslims but does not approve of Muslims going to dar al-harb for this purpose." Majid Khadduri, *War and Peace in the Law of Islam* (Baltimore: The Johns Hopkins Press, 1955), p. 224.

4. *The Epic of Gilgamesh*, trans. N. K. Sandars (New York: Penguin, 1972), p. 61. Scholars have argued that aspects of what is called the Western tradition may well have originated in the ancient Near East, including Sumeria. For a discussion of the connections between the Near East and early ancient Greek literature, see M. L. West, *The East Face of Helicon: West Asiatic Elements in Greek Poetry and Myth* (New York: Oxford University Press, 1997).

5. Homer's *Odyssey*, trans. Carol Dougherty, *The Raft of Odysseus: The Ethnographic Imagination of Homer's Odyssey* (Oxford: Oxford University Press, 2001), p. 4. There are many available English translations of this passage, but I prefer Dougherty's.

6. This evident, for example, in al-Tahtawi's nineteenth-century journey that is the subject of chapter 4, as well as in recent arguments by scholars of Islamic law that travel to non-Muslim societies in pursuit of knowledge and livelihood is not only permissible but obligatory. See Muhammad Khalid Masud in "The Obligation to Migrate: The Doctrine of *hijra* in Islamic Law," *Muslim Travellers*, pp. 42–43. See also Susan Miller's *Disorienting Encounters: Travels of a Moroccan Scholar in France in 1845–1846* (Berkeley: University of California Press, 1992), p. 76.

7. Leed, *The Mind of the Traveler: From Gilgamesh to Global Tourism* (New York: Harper-Collins, 1991), pp. 5–6.

8. Herodotus, *The Histories*, trans. George Rawlinson (New York: Alfred A. Knopf, 1997), 1.30; Clarence P. Bill, "Notes on the Greek Θεωρός and Θεωρία," *Transactions and Proceedings of the American Philological Association* 32 (1901), pp. 196–97.

9. James Ker, "Solon's Theôria and the End of the City," *Classical Antiquity* 19, no. 2 (October 2000): 308–9.

10. Translated by Ker, in "Solon's Theôria and the End of the City," pp. 314.

11. *The Laws*, trans. A. E. Taylor, in *Plato: The Collected Dialogues*, ed. Edith Hamilton and Huntington Cairns, 13th ed. (Princeton, NJ: Princeton University Press, 1987).

12. Ian Rutherford, "Theoric Crisis: The Dangers of Pilgrimage in Greek Religion and Society," *Studi e materiali di storia delle religioni* 61 (1995): p. 283.

13. Ibid., pp. 282–83.

14. Ibid., p. 282.

15. Ker, "Solon's Theôria and the End of the City," pp. 309–10, 326–27.

16. It is well known that Aristotle, even more than Plato, defined the study of politics in comparative terms. Yet Plato in particular illuminates what I call the double-edged nature of travel (see below). For a detailed discussion of Aristotle's reconfiguration of *theôria* and its implications, see Andrea Wilson Nightingale, *Spectacles of Truth in Classical Greek Philosophy: Theoria in its Cultural Context* (Cambridge: Cambridge University Press, 2004), esp. pp. 187–252.

17. Arendt, *The Human Condition* (Chicago: University of Chicago Press, 1958), p. 20.

18. Ian Rutherford, "*Theoria and Darśan*: Pilgrimage and Vision in Greece and India," *Classical Quarterly* 50, no. 1 (2000): p. 141; J. Peter Euben, "Plato's *Republic*: the Justice of Tragedy," in *The Tragedy of Political Theory*, pp. 235–77.

19. Such "semantic imbrication" is also evident in Plato's *Symposium* (210d–e).

20. Nietzsche, *Thus Spake Zarathustra*, Prologue, part 4.

21. Dallmayr, *Alternative Visions*. Many scholars have implicated the ethnographic enterprise central to modern anthropology in imperialist ventures and disciplinary purposes. Carol Dougherty points out such connections in the ancient world as well when she asks: "Is it an accident that the *Odyssey* is especially interested in the worlds beyond Greek shores, interested in exploring the nature of relationships (commercial and colonial) between Greeks and peoples overseas, at exactly the moment when its audience is settling those shores and establishing trade contacts throughout the Mediterranean?" Dougherty, *The Raft of Odysseus*, p. 11.

22. Dougherty, *The Raft of Odysseus*, p. 6.

23. Redfield, "Herodotus the Tourist," p. 98.

24. Bacon, *New Atlantis and the Great Instauration*, ed. Jerry Weinberger (Arlington Heights, IL: Harlan Davidson, 1989), p. 81; *The Persian Letters* (Indianapolis: Hackett, 1999), translated by George R. Healy, p. 9; Nietzsche, *Human All-Too-Human*, trans. Paul V. Cohn (New York: Macmillan, 1924), pp. 117–18. There are too many examples of this theme to be exhaustive here, but it is perhaps worth adding that it appears in some unexpected places and texts, from Karl Popper's argument that "perhaps the most powerful cause of the breakdown of the closed society was the development of sea-communications and commerce" to the description of St. Paul "bringing certain strange things" to the ears of the Athenians and disputing in the market and synagogues with devout Jews, Epicureans and Stoics (Acts 17:16–34). Popper, *The Open Society and Its Enemies*, vol. 1 (London: Routledge & Kegan Paul, 1957), p. 177. I am grateful to Jeremy Waldron for pointing this out to me.

25. For a useful overview of medieval European travel practices, see Marjorie Nice Boyer, "Travel and Transport, Western European," in *Dictionary of the Middle Ages*, ed. Joseph R. Strayer (New York: Charles Scribner's Sons, 1989), vol. 12, pp. 148–62.

26. *The Prince and Discourses*, trans. Luigi Ricci (New York: Random House, 1950), p. 4.

27. Although little is known about Herodotus's life, John L. Myres refers to Herodotus having to "take refuge in Samos" fairly early in his life, the beginning of an extensive phase of "wandering." Myres, *Herodotus: Father of History* (Oxford: Clarendon Press, 1953), p. 2, 4, 14. See also Susanna Stambler, "Herodotus," in *Ancient Writers: Greece and Rome*, vol. 1, ed. T. James Luce (New York: Charles Scribner's Sons, 1982), pp. 225–27.

28. Thucydides, *The Peloponnesian War*, trans. Steven Lattimore (Indianapolis: Hackett, 1998), 5:26, 1:22.

29. Montaigne, *The Essays of Michel de Montaigne*, trans. Charles Cotton (London: G. Bell, 1913), 185, 213; *Complete Works: Essays, Travel Journal, Letters*, trans. Donald M. Frame (Stanford, CA: Stanford University Press, 1957); *The Diary of Montaigne's Journey to Italy in 1580 and 1581*, trans. by E. J. Trechmann (New York, Harcourt, Brace, 1929).

30. Tocqueville, *Democracy in America* (New York: Anchor Books, 1969), trans. George Lawrence, "Author's Preface to the 12th Edition"; vol. 1, conclusion, p. 408.

31. *Alfarabi, The Political Writings: "Selected Aphorisms" and Other Texts*, trans. Charles E. Butterworth (Ithaca: Cornell University Press, 2001), pp. ix–x. On al-Ghazali, see Ebrahim Moosa's *Ghazālī and the Poetics of Imagination* (Chapel Hill: University of North Carolina Press, 2005); Ibn Rushd (Averroës) also traveled extensively. Averroës, *Decisive Treatise and Epistle Dedicatory*, trans. Charles E. Butterworth (Utah: Brigham Young University Press, 2001), p. xiv.

32. Just as Plato had sought in vain to transform the young Dionysius of Syracuse into a Philosopher-King and Aristotle sought to train the young Alexander the Great, the event that occasioned Ibn Khaldûn's departure in this instance was his failed attempt to instruct the young new ruler of Muslim Spain, Muhammad V, in the principles of good governance and Islamic philosophy. Ibn Khaldûn was banished from Granada by a powerful advisor to Muhammad V, Ibn al-Khatib, who was suspicious of Khaldûn and was convinced the young ruler was unable take good advantage of the knowledge, an assessment that was to prove prescient.

33. Afghani intentionally hid his origins as a Shi'ite Iranian, preferring to be thought of as a Sunni Afghan. Al-Afghani left Iran voluntarily and over the years travelled to India, France, Russia, and England, as well as to Afghanistan, Turkey, and Egypt, countries from which he was ignominiously expelled for his political and intellectual activities.

34. Instead of becoming "Americanized," however, on his return to Egypt, Qutb joined the Muslim Brotherhood and published a series of damning articles later gathered together under the title *The America I Have Seen*. As Qutb's experience of exile only intensified his dislike of the foreign influence on Islam, he serves as one example of the double-edged nature of travel that emerges in the following chapters, that is, the extent to which exposures to the unfamiliar can occasion "closings" as well as "openings." Qutb, of course, did not associate his sojourn with a narrowing of vision; in his view, it made it possible to see clearly for the first time. Qutb, *Amrika min al-dakhil bi minzar Sayyid Qutb*,

[America From Within as seen by Sayyid Qutb], ed. Salah ʿAbd al-Fattah al-Khalidi (Jeddah: Dar al-Manara, 1986).

35. The list of prominent contemporary Muslims figures who have traveled is extensive and includes Tariq al-Bishri, Amin Huwaydi, Muhsin Kadivar, (Ayat Allah) Mihdi Haʾiri Yazdi, ʿAbdolkarim Soroush, Muhammad Khatami, and Hasan al-Turabi, among others.

36. JanMohamed, "Worldliness-Without-World, Homelessness-as-Home," pp. 96–120.

37. Said, "The Mind of Winter: Reflections on Life in Exile" *Harper's*, vol. 269 (September 1984), p. 49; "Edward Said: The Voice of a Palestinian Exile," *Third Text* 3, no. 4 (spring/summer 1998), p. 48.

38. Said, "The Mind of Winter," p. 55, emphasis in the original.

39. Said, *The World, the Text and the Critic*, p. 8.

40. Leed, *The Mind of the Traveler*, p. 219.

41. Haraway, "Situated Knowledges: The Science Question in Feminism and the Privilege of Partial Perspective," in *Simians, Cyborg, and Women: The Reinvention of Nature* (New York: Routledge, 1991), p. 188.

42. Walzer, *Interpretation and Social Criticism* (Cambridge, MA: Harvard University Press, 1987), pp. 36–37.

43. Bloch, *The Principle of Hope*, Part 4, "Outlines of a Better World," trans. Neville Plaice, Stephen Plaice, and Paul Knight (Cambridge, MA: MIT Press, 1986), p. 479, 480.

44. Thomas More, *Utopia*, trans. David Wooten (Indianapolis: Hackett, 1999); Naguib Mahfouz, *Rihlat Ibn Fattuma* (Cairo: Maktabat Misr, 1983).

45. Sheldon Wolin, *Politics and Vision: Continuity and Innovation in Western Political Thought* (Boston: Little, Brown, 1960), p. 21, 19.

46. Ibid., p. 19.

47. Bloch, *The Principle of Hope*, pp. 480–81.

48. See, for example, Paul Gilroy's *The Black Atlantic: Modernity and Double Consciousness* (New York: Verso, 1993), and James Clifford, "Diasporas," *Cultural Anthropology* 9, no. 3 (1994): 302–38;

49. Dallmayr, *Alternative Visions*; Mandaville, *Transnational Muslim Politics*, p. 84, 103.

50. Wolff, "On the Road Again: Metaphors of Travel in Cultural Criticism." See also Sara Mills, *Discourses of Difference: An Analysis of Women's Travel Writing and Colonialism* (New York: Routledge, 1991); Caren Kaplan, *Questions of Travel: Postmodern Discourses of Displacement* (Durham, NC: Duke University Press, 1996); and Pratt, *Imperial Eyes*.

51. Montaigne, *The Essays of Michel de Montaigne*, pp. 214–15.

52. Clifford, "Traveling Cultures," p. 105. Although Clifford, along with Said, has been criticized for failing to acknowledge fully how travel is itself a gendered category.

53. See, for example, Nancy Tapper, "*Ziyarat*: Gender, Movement, and Exchange in a Turkish Community," in *Muslim Travellers*, pp. 236–55.

54. Holland and Huggan, *Tourists with Typewriters*, p. 111; Wolff, "On the Road Again," p. 234, emphasis in the original.

55. Stephen Melville, "Division of the Gaze, or, Remarks on the Color and Tenor of Contemporary "Theory," in *Vision in Context: Historical and Contemporary Perspectives on Sight*, ed. Teresa Brennan and Martin Jay (New York: Routledge, 1996), p. 103. Martin Jay surveys both the privileging and denigration of vision in Western thought in his *Downcast Eyes: The Denigration of Vision in Twentieth-Century French Thought* (Berkeley: University of California Press, 1994). See also Haraway, *Simians, Cyborgs and Women*; Michel Foucault, *Discipline and Punish*; Laura Mulvey, "Visual Pleasure and Narrative Cinema," in *Visual and Other Pleasures* (Bloomington: Indiana University Press, 1989); and Norman Bryson, *Vision and Painting: The Logic of the Gaze* (New Haven: Yale University Press, 1983).

56. Pierre Loti, *Japan: Madame Chrysanthemum*, trans. Laura Ensor (London: KPI, 1985), p. 13. For a discussion about the feminization of Japan in travel literature, see *Tourists with Typewriters*, pp. 81–90. For an exploration of such motifs in American expansionism, see Annette Kolodny, *The Lay of the Land: Metaphor and History in American Life and Letters* (Chapel Hill: University of North Carolina Press, 1975).

57. "Remarks on Legitimation through Human Rights," *Philosophy and Social Criticism* 24, no. 2–3 (1998): p. 162. For a discussion of this aspect of Habermas's thought in particular, see Gerard Delanty, "Habermas and Occidental Rationalism: The Politics of Identity, Social Learning, and the Cultural Limits of Moral Universalism," *Sociological Theory* 15, no. 1 (March 1997): pp. 30–59.

58. Mehta, "Cosmopolitanism and the Circle of Reason," *Political Theory* 28, no. 5 (October 2000): p. 681, emphasis in the original.

59. Mahbubani, "The West and the Rest"; Samuel Huntington, "The Clash of Civilizations?" *Foreign Affairs* 72 (summer 1993): 22–49. See also Huntington, *The Clash of Civilizations and the Remaking of World Order* (New York: Simon & Schuster, 1996).

60. Richard Rorty and Gianni Vattimo, *The Future of Religion*, ed. Santiago Zabala (New York: Columbia University Press, 2005), p. 72.

61. Renan, *L'Islamisme et la Science: Conférence faite a la Sorbonne le 20 mars 1883* (Paris: Calmann Lévy, 1883), p. 3.

62. Hodgson, *The Venture of Islam*, vol. 2, p. 438. Eickelman, "The Art of Memory: Islamic Education and its Social Reproduction," *Comparative Studies in Society and History* 20 (1978), pp. 489–90. One might suppose that such assertions are part of a bygone era, yet Mohammad Arkoun has written fairly recently that the "Muslim cognitive system is essentially mythical." *Rethinking Islam: Common Questions, Uncommon Answers*, trans. Robert D. Lee (Boulder, CO: Westview Press, 1994), p. 99.

63. Lewis, *The Muslim Discovery of Europe* (New York: W. W. Norton, 1982), p. 80. Lewis reiterates versions of this thesis in many different places, including essays in his recent *From Babel to Dragomans: Interpreting the Middle East* (Oxford: Oxford University Press, 2004).

64. *The Muslim Discovery of Europe*, p. 280.

65. Ibid., p. 301.

66. Ibid., p. 87.

67. Ibid., p. 75.

68. Said, among others, has taken aim at Lewis's repeated insistence that "the western quest for knowledge about other societies is unique, that it is motivated by pure curiosity, and that in contrast Muslims neither were able nor interested in acquiring knowledge about Europe, as if knowledge about Europe was the only acceptable criterion for truth knowledge." Said, "Orientalism Reconsidered," in *Orientalism: A Reader*, ed. A. L. Macfie (New York: New York University Press, 2000), p. 351.

69. Hodgson, *The Venture of Islam*, vol. 2, p. 362.

70. Lewis, "Europe and Islam," in *From Babel to Dragomans* (Oxford University Press, 2004), p. 132.

71. Khalidi, "Islamic Views of the West in the Middle Ages," *Studies in Interreligious Dialogue* 5 (1995), p. 42.

72. Matar, *In the Lands of the Christians: Arabic Travel Writing in the Seventeenth Century* (London: Routledge, 2003), p. xxxvi–xxxvi. See also Matar's *Turks, Moors and Englishmen in the Age of Discovery* (New York: Columbia University Press, 1999), and "Early Modern Europe Through Islamic Eyes," unpublished manuscript.

73. Matar further suggests that misunderstandings about the extent of Muslim knowledge about Christians derives, in part, from where such knowledge was located: at least before the "diffusion of mass-produced books," Matar argues that much of Maghribi knowledge about Europeans, for example, resided in those "allusions, anecdotes, recollections, images, and news that appear at unexpected moments," as well as in informal oral anecdotes that constituted "popular culture and memory." Nabil Matar, "Early Modern Europe Through Islamic Eyes," pp. 37–39; ʿAbd al-Majid Qadduri, *Sufaraʾ Maghariba fi Urubba, 1610–1922: fi al-waʿy bi al-tafawut* (Rabat, Morocco: al-Mamlaka al-Maghribiyya, Jamiʿat Muhammad al-Khamis, Kulliyyat al-Adab wa al-ʿUlum al-Insaniyya bi al-Rabat, 1995). Along with Matar, other scholars have suggested a greater awareness of the diversity of languages and cultures within the category of "European" than Lewis suggests. For example, E. M. Sartain discerns in 12th–15th century Muslim officialdom an understanding of Europe less as a coherent entity and more as a conglomeration of warring and culturally and linguistically distinct kingdoms. Sartain, "Medieval Muslim-European Relations: Islamic Juristic Theory and Chancery Practice," *Images of the Other: Europe and the Muslim World before 1700*, ed. David Blanks, *Cairo Papers in Social Science*, vol. 19, Monograph 2 (Egypt: American University in Cairo Press, 1996), pp. 81–95. This complicates Lewis's assertion that as "Islam was conceived as a single entity, it was natural to think of the House of War in the same terms. The subdivisions among the infidels, particularly those of them who lived beyond the Islamic frontier, were of no interest or significance." *The Muslim Discovery of Europe*, p. 202.

74. *In the Lands of Christians*, pp. xxv–xxviii.

75. Helms, *Ulysses Sail: An Ethnographic Odyssey of Power, Knowledge, and Geographical Distance* (Princeton, NJ: Princeton University Press, 1988), see chapters 1 and 3 in particular.

76. Subrahmanyam, "Connected Histories: Notes towards a Reconfiguration of Early Modern Eurasia," p. 737.

77. As Nigel Leask shows, there are multiple valences to "curiosity" within the West, and travel in the name of curiosity occasioned a diversity of responses, not all of them celebratory. Leask, *Curiosity and the Aesthetics of Travel Writing, 1770–1840* (Oxford: Oxford University Press, 2004), p. 4 and chap. 1. For the doubled ways in which Western political thought and culture has conceptualized what is foreign as a problem and a resource, see Bonnie Honig, *Democracy and the Foreigner* (Princeton, NJ: Princeton University Press, 2001). For the complexity of Western attitudes toward the foreign over time, also see "Elizabethans and Foreigners," by G. K. Hunter in *Shakespeare in His Own Age*, ed. Allardyce Nicoll (Cambridge: Cambridge University Press, 1964), pp. 37–52.

78. Cicero, *De Legibus* [*The Laws*], trans. Clinton Walker Keyes (London: William Heinemann, 1928), I. I. 5, p. 301.

79. Importantly, Lewis does not attribute any inherent superiority to Europeans, yet he goes on to note that while Europe had "shared the general lack of curiosity concerning strange peoples," the combined impact of the discovery of the New World, the Renaissance, and the Reformation produced a spirit of "intellectual curiosity and scientific inquiry" in direct contrast to the Muslim world. *The Muslim Discovery of Europe*, pp. 300–301.

80. Wolin, *Politics and Vision: Expanded Edition* (Princeton, NJ: Princeton University Press, 2004), p. 19; Suzanne Gearhart, *The Open Boundary of History and Fiction: A Critical Approach to the French Enlightenment* (Princeton, NJ: Princeton University Press, 1984), p. 3.

81. Thomas A. McCarthy, *The Critical Theory of Jürgen Habermas* (Cambridge, MA: MIT Press, 1991), p. 302.

82. In addition to Matar's work see, for example, the work of Abdenbi Daker, as well as *Muslim Travellers: Pilgrimage, Migration, and the Religious Imagination*, ed. Dale F. Eickelman and James Piscatori (Berkeley: University of California Press, 1990); André Miquel, *La géographie humaine du monde musulman jusqu'au milieu du 11ᵉ siècle*, 2 vols (Paris: La Haye, Mouton, 1967); Anwar G. Chejne's "Travel Books in Modern Arabic Literature, *Muslim World* 52, no. 3 (1962), pp. 207–15; Abderrahmane El-Moudden, *Al-Badawi al-Maghribiyya qabla al-istiʿmar: qabaʾil inawan wa al-Makhzan bayna al-qarn al-sadis ʿashar wa al-tasi ʿashar* (Rabat, Morocco: Jamiʿ at Muhammad al-Khamis, Kuliyyat al-Adab wa al-ʿUlum al-Insaniyya bi al-Rabat, 1995); *Al-Rihla bayna al-Sharq wa al-Gharb*, ed. Mohammed Hammam (Rabat, Morocco: Kulliyyat al-Adab wa al-ʿUlum al-Insaniyya bi al-Rabat, 2003); *Golden Roads: Migration, Pilgrimage, and Travel in Mediaeval and Modern Islam*; Subrahmanyam, "Connected Histories," pp. 735–62; Mohamad Tavakoli-Targhi's "Modernity Heterotopia and Homeless Texts," *Comparative Studies of South Asia, Africa, and the Middle East*," 18, no. 2 (1998), pp. 2–13, and *Refashioning Iran: Orientalism, Occidentalism and Historiography* (New York: Palgrave, 2001); a forthcoming series on Muslim and Arab voyagers called *Irtiyad al-Afaq*, jointly published by Dar Suwaydi li-l-nashr and Al-Muʾassasa al-Arabiyya li-l-dirasat wa al-nashr; and Mustapha al-Ghashi's 2003 Ph.D. dissertation, "Al-Rihla Al-Maghribiyya wa al-Sharq al-ʿUthmani, Muhawala fi bina al-sura," University Muhammad V, Faculty of Arts, Rabat, Morocco.

83. Rosenthal, "The Stranger in Medieval Islam," *Arabica* 44 (1997), p. 54; *The Glorious Qur'an*, translated by Mohammed Marmaduke Pickthall (NY: Tahrike Tarsile *Qur'an*, 2000). See also verses 2:156, 50:43; 42:53.

84. Rosenthal, "The Stranger in Medieval Islam," p. 42, 54, 58. See, for example, Yusuf Ibish, "Ibn ʿArabi's Theory of Journeying," in *Traditional Modes of Contemplation and Action*, ed. Y. Ibish and P.L. Wilson (Tehran, Iran: Imperial Iranian Academy of Philosophy, 1977), pp. 441–49. For the particular significance of networks of Sufi *turuq* to the practice of travel and the emergence of Muslim interregional unity in the wake of the ʿAbbasid Caliphate, see John Voll, "Islam as a Special World-System," *Journal of World History* 5, no. 2 (1994): pp. 221–22. See also Stefan Reichmuth, "The Interplay of Local Developments and Transnational Relations in the Islamic World: Perceptions and Perspectives." in *Muslim Culture in Russia and Central Asia from the 18th to the Early 20th Centuries*, vol. 2, *Inter-Regional and Inter-Ethnic Relations*, eds. Anke von Kügelgen, Michael Kemper and Allen J. Frank (Berlin: Klaus Schwarz Verlag, 1998), pp. 13–21.

85. *Al-Qur'an*, trans. Ahmed Ali (Princeton, NJ: Princeton University Press, 1984). The verb used in all eight verses is *sāra*/ سار.

86. Jamal al-Din al-Suyuti, *Jamiʿ al-ahadith li-l-Jamiʿ al-saghir wa-zawaʾidihi wa al-Jamiʿ al-Kabir* (Damascus: Matbaʿat Muhammad Hashim al-Kutubi, 1979–81), vol. 1, 3207, 3208, p. 618; Muhammad al-Tirmidhi, *Sunan al-Tirmidhi wa-huwa al-Jamiʿ al-Sahih* (al-Medina al-Munawwara: al-Maktaba al-Salafiyya, 1965), Vol. 4, 2:2785, p. 137; 2:2786, p. 138, my translations.

87. Muhammad Ibn Yazid al-Qazwini Ibn Majah, *Sunan* (Cairo: ʿIsa al-Babi al-Halabi, 1972), vol. 1, hadith no. 223, p. 81, my translation.

88. Even among political theorists in the West, the divide between the religious and secular is increasingly permeable, from William Connolly's *Why I am Not a Secularist* (Minneapolis: University of Minnesota Press, 1999) to the rediscovery of Benjamin's interest in the Kabbalah to the Old Testament sources of Levinas's work.

89. Franz Rosenthal, *Knowledge Triumphant: The Concept of Knowledge in Medieval Islam* (Leiden: Brill, 1970), pp. 28–32. Rosenthal goes as far as arguing that "there is no other concept that has been operative as a determinant of Muslim civilization in all its aspects to the same extent as ʿilm," which is "something of supreme value for Muslim being." p. 2.

90. As Carlo Ginzburg shows, there was a similar tendency to read the Pauline warning against moral arrogance in his Epistle to the Romans (xi. 20) as a condemnation of intellectual curiosity. Ginzburg, "High and Low: The Theme of Forbidden Knowledge in the Sixteenth and Seventeenth Centuries," *Past and Present* 73 (November 1976), pp. 28–30.

91. *Encyclopedia of Islam*, CD-ROM Edition v. 1.0 (Leiden, The Netherlands: Koninklijke Brill NV, 1999), "ʿilm." According to Rosenthal, the etymological connection derives from the fact that in pre-Islamic Arabia, such signposts were "characteristic marks in the desert, which guided [the Bedouin] on his travels and in the execution of his daily tasks" and that constituted "the kind of knowledge on which his life and well-being principally depended." *Knowledge Triumphant*, p. 10.

92. Lenker, "The Importance of the Rihla for the Islamization of Spain," Ph.D. Diss., University of Pennsylvania, 1982, p. 195, 194, 189, 224. Lenker's study is particularly useful in challenging Ignaz Goldziher's restriction of ʿilm to the study of hadith and *sunna*. Goldziher, *Muslim Studies* (London: George Allen & Unwin, 1971), trans. C. R. Barber and S. M. Stern, vol. 2, pp. 164–80. Goldziher himself seems to recognize the wider scope of ʿilm when he notes that an *ijaza* (authorization or license) was often given no matter "whether the book concerned belonged to the class of religious or profane literature." Goldziher, pp. 178–79.

93. Simon Coleman and John Elsner, *Pilgrimage: Past and Present in World Religions* (Cambridge, MA: Harvard University Press, 1995), p. 206.

94. "Pilgrimages as Social Processes," in Victor Turner's *Dramas, Fields, and Metaphors: Symbolic Action in Human Society* (Ithaca: Cornell University Press, 1974); Coleman and Elsner, *Pilgrimage Past and Present in the World Religions*; Juan Eduardo Campo, "The Mecca Pilgrimage in the Formation of Islam in Modern Egypt," in *Sacred Places and Profane Spaces: Essay in the Geographics of Judaism, Christianity, and Islam*, ed. Jamie S. Scott and Paul Simpson-Housley (New York: Greenwood Press, 1991); Barbara D. Metcalf, "The Pilgrimage Remembered: South Asian Accounts of the *Hajj*," and Mary Byrne McDonnell, "Patterns of Muslim Pilgrimage from Malaysia: 1885–1985," both in *Muslim Travellers*, pp. 85–107, 111–30; Robert R. Bianchi, *Guests of God: Pilgrimage and Politics in the Islamic World* (Oxford: Oxford University Press, 2004); Noël Q. King, "Egeria, Fa Hsien, and Ibn Battuta: Search for Identity through Pilgrimage?" *Identity Issues and World Religions* (Australia: Wakefield Press, 1986), pp.42–46; Rutherford, "Theoric Crisis," and "*Theoria and Darśan*: Pilgrimage and Vision in Greece and India."

95. See Rutherford, "Theoric Crisis" and "*Theoria and Darśan*." Such continuities in the practice and meaning of pilgrimage across cultures have also been discerned across time. A case in point is Nelson Graburn's provocative suggestion that tourism is "the modern equivalent for secular societies to the annual and lifelong sequences of festivals for more traditional, God-fearing societies." While the rewards of pilgrimage tend to be "accumulated grace and moral leadership in the home community . . . the rewards of modern tourism are phrased in terms of values we now hold up for worship: mental and physical health, social status, and diverse, exotic experiences." Nelson H. H. Graburn, "Tourism: The Sacred Journey," in *Hosts and Guests: The Anthropology of Tourism*, ed. Valene Smith (Philadelphia: University of Pennsylvania Press, 1977), pp. 21, 24.

96. J. Peter Euben, "Creatures of a Day: Thought and Action in Thucydides," in *Political Theory and Praxis*, ed. Terence Ball (Minneapolis: University of Minnesota Press, 1977), pp. 33–35. The association of theory with the divine is even closer in the figure of Apollo who, because he "travels great distances to see his people he is called a *theorios* and *thearios*." Ibid., p. 241, n.17.

97. Ibid. p. 35; Sam Gellens, "The Search for Knowledge in Medieval Muslim Societies: A Comparative Approach," in *Muslim Travellers*, ed. Eickelman and Piscatori, p. 53.

98. Eickelman and Piscatori, *Muslim Travellers*, p. xii.

99. Ibid., p. 18.

100. Rosenthal, "The Stranger in Medieval Islam," p. 41.

101. *Muslim Networks: From Hajj to Hiphop*, ed. Miriam Cooke and Bruce B. Lawrence (Chapel Hill: University of North Carolina Press, 2005), p. 5.

102. Muslim Ibn al-Hajjaj al-Qushayri al-Nisaburi, *Sahih Muslim bi Sharh al-Nawawi*, ed. ʿIsam al-Sababiti, Hazim Muhammad, and ʿImad ʿAmir (Cairo: Dar al-Hadith, 1994), vol. 1, p. 453; "Idjara," by W. Montgomery Watt, *Encyclopedia of Islam*. Indeed, drawing on the *Sunna*, Qadi al-Nuʿman (d. 974) distinguishes between two kinds of etiquette (*muruʾa*), one that governs "settled habitation," the other that governs travel. The latter consists in "generosity in spending provisions, abstaining from discord with fellow travellers and transmitting reports from them" when they part ways. *The Pillars of Islam: Laws Pertaining to Human Intercourse/Daʿaʾim al-Islam of al-Qadi al-Nuʿman*, trans. Asaf A. A. Fyzee (New Delhi: Oxford University Press, 2002), vol. 1, pp. 431–32. I am grateful to Ali Aslam for pointing this out to me.

103. *Muslim Networks*, pp. 1–8. For the usefulness of a "network model" of Islamic societies, see Ira M. Lapidus, "Hierarchies and Networks: A Comparison of Chinese and Islamic Societies," in *Conflict and Control in Late Imperial China*, ed. Frederic Wakeman, Jr., and Carolyn Grant (Berkeley: University of California Press, 1975), pp. 26–42; Nehemia Levtzion and Gideon Weigert, "The Muslim Holy Cities and Foci of Islamic Revivalism in the Eighteenth Century," in *Sacred Space: Shrine, City, Land*, ed. Benjamin Z. Kedar and R. J. Zwi Werblowsky (New York: New York University Press, 1998), pp. 259–77; Voll, "Islam as a Special World-System," pp. 213–26; Stefan Reichmuth, "Murtadā al-Zabīdī (1732–91) and the Africans: Islamic Discourse and Scholarly Networks in the Late Eighteenth Century," *The Transmission of Learning in Islamic Africa*, ed. Scott R. Reese (Leiden: Brill, 2004), pp. 121–53, and "The Interplay of Local Developments and Transnational Relations in the Islamic World: Perceptions and Perspectives." in *Muslim Culture in Russia and Central Asia from the 18th to the Early 20th Centuries*, vol. 2, *Inter-Regional and Inter-Ethnic Relations*, ed. Anke von Kügelgen, Michael Kemper and Allen J. Frank (Berlin: Klaus Schwarz Verlag, 1998), pp. 5–38.

104. Muhammad Qasim Zaman, "The Scope and Limits of Islamic Cosmopolitanism and the 'Discursive Language' of the ʿUlama," in *Muslim Networks*, p. 84.

105. *Muslim Networks*, p. 3.

106. Gellens, "The Search for Knowledge in Medieval Muslim Societies," p. 51. *Baraka* is a complex term with multiple valences as will become clear in the following chapter. In connection with Ibn Battuta, for example, Charles Beckingham describes it as "the blessings both in this world and the next which would come from visiting holy places and obtaining the blessings of saintly men." Beckingham, "In Search of Ibn Battuta," *Royal Society for Asian Affairs* 8 (1977), p. 267.

107. Importantly, as Piscatori and Eickelman note, "Muslims share more explicit doctrinal tenets enjoining movement than do the followers of other major religious traditions . . . [but] such phenomena need not be seen as unique to the Muslim world in order for their significance to be affirmed," p. xvii, p. 5.

108. Clifford, "Traveling Cultures," p. 110.

109. Colin Thubron, "Both Seer and Seen," *The Times Literary Supplement,* July 30, 1999. As will become clear in chapter 5, virtually every aspect of travel is gendered, including the perception and reality of physical vulnerability. Thus, for example, Mary Morris argues, "the fear of rape, for example, whether crossing the Sahara or. . . . just crossing a city street at night, most dramatically affects the ways women move through the world." Morris, *Maiden Voyages: Writings of Women Travelers* (New York: Vintage, 1993), p. xvii.

110. Helms, *Ulysses Sail,* p. 17.

111. Herodotus, *Histories,* I:52–54, 9–92. This in part suggests why, from Thucydides to Plato, the "political function of *theôria,* as in conceptions of theory now, was not always viewed as positive." James Ker, "Solon's *Theôria* and the End of the City," pp. 304–5.

112. *Information for Pilgrims unto the Holy Land,* ed. E. Gordon Duff (London: Lawrence & Bullen, 1893), attributed to John Moreson and originally printed ca. 1498. See also Donald R. Howard, *Writers and Pilgrims: Medieval Pilgrimage Narratives and their Posterity* (Berkeley: University of California Press, 1980), pp. 20–22.

113. Al-Jahiz, *Rasaʾil al-Jahiz,* ed. ʿAbd al-Salam Muhammad Harun (Cairo: Maktabat al-Khanji, 1964), 2:385. See also Rosenthal, "The Stranger in Medieval Islam," pp. 42–49. This is echoed in an inscription on the tomb of ʿAli ibn Abi Bakr al-Harawi (d. 1215), who authored a pilgrimage guide based on his extensive travels throughout medieval Byzantium, North Africa, and the Middle East: "I roamed the lands east and west; to many a wanderer and hermit was I a companion / I saw every strange and marvellous wonder; and experienced terror in comfort and misery." Al-Harawi, *A Lonely Wayfarer's Guide to Pilgrimage: ʿAli ibn Abi Bakr al-Harawi's* Kitab al-Isharat ila Maʿrifat al-Ziyarat, trans. Josef W. Meri (Princeton, NJ: Darwin Press, 2004), p. xxv.

114. René Descartes, *Discourse on Method for Reasoning Well and for Seeking Truth in the Sciences* (1637), part 1.

115. There is a difference between the lexical etymology of *bidʿa,* and its theological connotation as that which is not based on the customs established in Muslim traditions. Vardit Rispler shows, for example, that despite the negative theological connotations of the term in early Islamic history, over time Muslim scholars transformed the various classifications of *bidʿa* into system to "evaluate new ideas and practices." "Toward a New Understanding of the Term *bidʿa,*" *Der Islam* 68 (1991), p. 321. This use of the term as a mode of classification is evident, for example, in the *Rihla* of al-Tahtawi, discussed in chapter 4.

116. Franz Rosenthal, *The Technique and Approach of Muslim Scholarship* (Rome: Pontificium Institum Biblicum, 1947), p. 57.

117. *Imitation of Christ,* ed. Ernest Rhys (London: J. M. Dent & Sons, 1910), part 4, chapter 1, pp. 233–34.

118. *The Confessions of St. Augustine,* trans. Rex Warner (New York: New American Library, 1963), Book 10, chap. 35. Augustine's characterization of curiosity as a kind of vice is echoed by later Christian thinkers increasingly worried about the temptations of pilgrimages motivated by curiosity. See

Christian K. Zacher, *Curiosity and Pilgrimage: The Literature of Discovery in Four-teenth-Century England* (Baltimore: Johns Hopkins University Press, 1976).

119. Howard, *Writers and Pilgrims*, p. 24. The substantial ambivalence to-ward curiosity about worldly knowledge in European and Christian political thought is well documented. See, for example, Ginzburg, "High and Low: The Theme of Forbidden Knowledge in the Sixteenth and Seventeenth Centuries"; G. K. Hunter, "Elizabethans and Foreigners," pp. 37–53; Samuel Chew, *The Crescent and the Rose* (New York: Oxford University Press, 1937), p. 29.

120. *The Workes of that Famous and Worthy Minister of Christ, In the Universitie of Cambridge, M. W. Perkins* (London: John Haviland, 1631), 3:539.

121. Daniel Caner, *Wandering, Begging Monks: Spiritual Authority and the Promotion of Monasticism in Late Antiquity* (Berkeley: University of California Press, 2002).

122. Rosenthal, "The Stranger in Medieval Islam," p. 54.

123. Shahrough Akhavi, "Sunni Modernist Theories of Social Contract in Contemporary Egypt," *International Journal of Middle East Studies* 35 (2003), p. 31.

124. The term, *gharbzadigi*, was actually coined by Sayyid Jalal Al-i Ahmad.

125. Pagden," The Effacement of Difference: Colonialism and the Origins of Nationalism in Diderot and Herder," in *After Colonialism: Imperial Histories and Postcolonial Displacements*, ed. Gyan Prakash (Princeton, NJ: Princeton Univer-sity Press, 1995), p. 134.

126. Diderot, in *Histoire philosophique et politique des etablissemens et du com-merce des Européens dans les deux Indes* (Geneva, 1781), 10, 297 (XIX, 1), in Pag-den, "The Effacement of Difference," 134.

127. Michel de Certeau, *The Writing of History*, trans. Tom Conley (New York: Columbia University Press, 1988), p. 232. In a similar vein, Leask docu-ments the decidedly less-than-high-minded conjunction of curiosity, acquisi-tive desire, and pursuit of the exotic for commercial profits in European his-tory. *Curiosity and the Aesthetics of Travel Writing, 1770–1840*, see esp. p. 4 and chap. 1.

128. Diderot in Pagden, "The Effacement of Difference," p. 133, and Pagden, p. 132, 133.

129. *Tourists with Typewriters*, p. 70.

130. The historical continuities in these features and anxieties challenge Eric Leed's sharp distinction between the meanings of ancient and modern travel. While the "ancients valued travel as an explication of human fate and neces-sity," he writes, "for moderns, it is an expression of freedom and an escape from necessity and purpose." *The Mind of the Traveler*, p. 7. This argument begs the question of what constitutes "modernity" and, as Simon Goldhill argues in connection with the history of classical vision, treating the "classical period" as an "unbroken tradition ignores fundamental paradigm shifts in the culture and philosophy of viewing over what is a more than seven-hundred-year span." "Refracting Classical Vision: Changing Cultures of Viewing," in *Vision in Context: Historical and Contemporary Perspectives on Sight*, ed. Teresa Brennan and Martin Jay (New York: Routledge, 1996), pp. 17–18.

131. Clifford, "Traveling Cultures," p. 110.

132. Hartog, *The Mirror of Herodotus: The Representation of the Other in the Writing of History,* trans. Janet Lloyd (Berkeley: University of California Press, 1988).

133. Maghrib, which means "the west," is usually taken to refer to North Africa, and in particular to the region occupied by what is now Libya, Tunisia, Algeria, and Morocco (although over the centuries, writers have disagreed about the precise boundaries of the region).

134. Redfield, "Herodotus the Tourist," p. 102.

135. I am grateful to Anne Norton for this formulation of the point.

136. Hartog, *The Mirror of Herodotus,* p. 214.

137. I am grateful to Pratap Mehta for these examples.

138. Margaret Leslie, "In Defense of Anachronism," *Political Studies* 18, no. 4 (1970), p. 435.

139. *In a Different Voice* (Cambridge, MA: Harvard University Press, 1993), p. 173.

140. Catherine Gimelli Martin, "Orientalism and the Ethnographer: Said, Herodotus, and the Discourse of Alterity," *Criticism* 32, no. 4 (fall 1990): p. 521.

141. Ibid., p. 527.

142. Benjamin, "The Task of the Translator," *Illuminations*, ed. Hannah Arendt (New York: Schocken, 1988), pp. 76.

143. Hocquard, "Faire quelque chose avec ça," *Ma Haie* (Paris: P.O.L., 2001), p. 525. I am grateful for James M. Petterson for this.

144. Benjamin, of course, does not here enter the wood, but he effectively displaces the "valorization of transparency" which, in other models of translation, have tended to efface the preconditions and effects of translating practices, Lawrence Venuti, ed., *Rethinking Translation: Discourse, Subjectivity, Ideology* (New York: Routledge, 1992), pp. 4–5.

145. Importantly, that which is to be translated is already, in some sense, a translation. As Lawrence Venuti argues, "the original is itself a translation, an incomplete process of translating a signifying chain into a univocal signified, and this process is both displayed and further complicated when it is translated by another signifying chain in a different language," Venuti, *Rethinking Translation,* p. 7. See also Dipesh Chakrabarty, *Provincializing Europe: Postcolonial Thought and Historical Difference* (Princeton, NJ: Princeton University Press, 2000); Tejaswini Niranjana, *Siting Translation: History, Post-Structuralism, and the Colonial Context* (Berkeley: University of California Press, 1992); Gayatri Chakravorty Spivak, "Politics of Translation," *Outside in the Teaching Machine* (New York: Routledge, 1993); Ritva Leppihalme, *Culture Bumps: An Empirical Approach to the Translation of Allusions* (Clevedon, Great Britain: Multilingual Matters, 1997); Jenine Abboushi Dallal, "The Perils of Occidentalism: How Arab Novelists are Driven to Write for Western Readers," *The Times Literary Supplement* (April 24, 1998), 4960:9.

146. A version of such arguments is evident in scholarship on problems of translation in analytic philosophy, where it is now widely acknowledged that translation cannot proceed without the presumption of some potential connection between the vocabulary of the translator and that of the 'target-language culture.' In his critique of Donald Davidson, Charles Taylor argues, "I cannot

see how we can conceive or carry out this process without allowing into our ontology something like alternative horizons or conceptual schemes." Taylor, "Gadamer on the Human Sciences," in *The Cambridge Companion to Gadamer*, ed. Robert J. Dostal (Cambridge: Cambridge University Press, 2002), p. 139; Donald Davidson, "On the Very Idea of a Conceptual Scheme," *Inquiries into Truth and Interpretation* (Oxford: Clarendon Press, 1984), pp. 183–98.

147. Anna Lowenhaupt Tsing, "Transitions as Translations," in *Transitions, Environments, Translations. Feminisms in International Politics*, ed. Joan W. Scott, Cora Kaplan, and Debra Keates (London: Routledge, 1988), p. 253.

148. Venuti, p. 13. Thus translation not only reveals how, in Vincente L. Rafael's words, "language was . . . the companion of empire," but also the way "vernacularization" could deflect the exercise of colonial power. Rafael, *Contracting Colonialism: Translation and Christian Conversion in Tagalog Society under Early Spanish Rule* (Ithaca: Cornell University Press, 1988), p. 23, 21.

149. Martin, "Orientalism and the Ethnographer," p. 523.

150. J. Peter Euben, "Philosophy and Politics in Plato's *Crito*," *Political Theory* 6, no. 2 (May 1978): p. 165.

151. Martin Jay, "Vision in Context: Reflections and Refractions," in *Vision in Context: Historical and Contemporary Perspectives on Sight*, ed. Teresa Brennan and Martin Jay (New York: Routledge, 1996) (see Cathryn Vasseleu's essay in this volume for an analysis of Irigaray's increasing ambivalence to vision in her later work); Isabelle R. Gunning, "Arrogant Perception, World-Travelling, and Multicultural Feminism: The Case of Female Genital Surgeries," *Columbia Human Rights Law Review* 23 (1991–92): 189–248; María Lugones, "Playfulness, 'World'-Travelling, and Loving Perception," in *Making Face, Making Soul: Haciendo Caras*, ed. Gloria Anzaldúa (San Francisco: Aunt Lute Foundation, 1990), pp. 390–402.

CHAPTER 3: LIARS, TRAVELERS, THEORISTS

1. Given the quality and accessibility of Franz Rosenthal's translation, I have opted to use his rather than my own. Ibn Khaldûn, *The Mugaddiman: An Introduction to History*, trans. by Rosenthal (New York: Pantheon, 1958), vol. 1, pp. 370–371.

2. Although Thucydides does not directly mention Herodotus, scholars agree that Thucydides' statement (*Peloponnesian War*, book I, chapters 20–22) about the purpose of good history is a direct repudiation of Herodotus's "attempt to describe events he had not witnessed or to tell the story of men whose language he could not speak." J.A.S. Evans, "Father of History or Father of Lies; the Reputation of Herodotus," *The Classical Journal* 64, no. 1 (October 1968): p. 12; Arnaldo Momigliano, *Studies in Historiography* (New York: Harper and Row, 1966), pp. 130–32. See also Hartog, *The Mirror of Herodotus*, pp. xv–xxv; and Myres, "Herodotus and his Critics," in *Herodotus: Father of History*, pp.17–31.

3. Plutarch, *De Malignitate Herodoti* [*The Malice of Herodotus*], translated by Anthony Bowen (Warminster, England: Aris and Phillips, 1992), pp. 29–37 (857A–859A), 49–51 (861E–862C). The accusation that Herodotus relied much

too heavily on biased Athenian sources is not Plutarch's alone. See for example, Terry Buckley, *Aspects of Greek History, 750–332 BC* (New York: Routledge, 1996), pp. 13–14.

4. Gibbon, *The Decline and Fall of the Roman Empire* (New York: Harcourt, Brace, 1960), vol. 2, XXIV, footnote.

5. "Herodotus and Anthropology," in *Anthropology and the Classics*, ed. Arthur J. Evans, Andrew Lang, Gilbert Murray, F. B. Jevons, J. L. Myres, and W. Warde Fowler (Oxford: Clarendon Press, 1908), p. 125. Regarding Herodotus, ethnography, and Orientalism see, for example, Catherine Gimelli Martin, "Orientalism and the Ethnographer," p. 515 and Redfield, "Herodotus the Tourist."

6. Ibn Khatib, quoted by Ibn Hajar al-ʿAsqalani (d. 1448), in *Durar al-Kamina fi Aʿyan al-miʾah al-thaminah* (Hyderabad, al-Dakan, al-Hind: Matbaʿat Majlis Daʾirat al-Maʿarif al-ʿUthmaniyya, 1929), vol. 3, pp. 480–81; This is H.A.R. Gibb's rendering of the description. Gibb, *The Travels of Ibn Battuta* (London: Munshiram Manoharlal Publishers Ltd., 1999), vol. 1, pp. ix–x. ʿAsqalani reports that Ibn Battuta had also been accused of lying by al-Balfiqi, but that others defended him. For a discussion of some reactions to Ibn Battuta by his contemporaries, see also Ross E. Dunn, *The Adventures of Ibn Battuta* (Berkeley: University of California Press, 1986), pp. 314–15.

7. Lucille McDonald, *The Arab Marco Polo: Ibn Battuta* (New York: Thomas Nelson, 1975); Daniel P. Browne and Neal H. Schultz, "A Visit with Ibn Battuta: Prince of Travelers," *Social Science Record* 30, no. 2 (fall 1993): 29–31. A. G. Hopkins refers to Ibn Battuta as "the Marco Polo of the Tropics." A. G. Hopkins, *An Economic History of West Africa* (New York: Columbia University Press, 1973), p. 78.

8. With the exception of those passages in the *Rihla* where Ibn Juzayy explicitly identifies his contributions, it is difficult if not impossible to differentiate between his words and those of Ibn Battuta. Indeed, Ibn Juzayy's role in creating the *Rihla* was closer to that of ghostwriter than editor: Ibn Battuta dictated the *Rihla* to him, but in his introduction, Ibn Juzayy describes his own efforts as refining, revising, and pruning the stories. It seems well established that, at a minimum, Ibn Juzayy is responsible for the "re-arrangement of several itineraries at the sacrifice of the logical chronologies of the journeys, the poetical quotations and, above all, the use of an elaborate prose style." *Rihlat Ibn Battuta*, pp. 12–13; A. Miquel, "Ibn Battuta," *Encyclopedia of Islam*. Indeed, Husni Mahmud Husayn holds Ibn Jazayy responsible for much of what he regards as the *Rihla*'s stylistic flaws. *Adab al-Rihla ʿinda al-ʿArab* (Cairo: al-Hayʾa al-Misriyya al-ʿAmma li-l-Kitab, 1976), pp. 71–75. Further complicating efforts to fix final responsibility for the *Rihla* (and some of its problems) is the fact that Ibn Battuta refers to having lost some notes during his adventures, and H.A.R. Gibb's suggestion that Ibn Battuta "did not himself read the book at all, or if he did, read it negligently." Gibb, *Ibn Battuta: Travels in Asia and Africa, 1325–54* (London: Routledge and Kegan Paul, 1957), p. 12. See also, J. S. Mattock, "Ibn Battuta's Use of Ibn Jubayr's *Rihla*," *Proceedings of the Ninth Congress of the Union Européene des Arabisants et Islamisants*, ed. Rudolph Peters (Leiden: Brill,

1981), p. 217. Thus, there are in fact two authors of this text, although for the sake of clarity, I will hereafter refer to it as *Rihla* of Ibn Battuta.

9. Stephen Janicsek concludes that Ibn Battuta's description of his trip to Bulghar is sheer fabrication and Ivan Hrbek contends that the journey to Constantinople is similarly suspicious. Janicsek, "Ibn Battuta's Journey to Bulghar: Is it a Fabrication?" *Journal of the Royal Asiatic Society of Great Britain and Ireland* (October 1929): pp. 791–800; Hrbek, "The Chronology of Ibn Battuta's Travels," *Archiv Orientálni* 30 (1962): p. 473. See also Mu'nis, *Ibn Battuta wa-Rihlatuhu: Tahqiq wa-dirasa wa-tahlil.*

10. Adel Allouche contends that Ibn Battuta's well-known description of the famous Hanbali scholar Ibn Taymiyya as "having a screw loose" (translation George Makdisi, "Ibn Taymiya: A Sufi of the Qadiriya Order," *American Journal of Arabic Studies* 1 (1973): pp. 118–19) was based on an encounter that could never have happened. "A Study of Ibn Battuta's Account of His 726/1326 Journey through Syria and Arabia," *Journal of Semitic Studies* 35, no. 2 (autumn 1990): 283–99.

11. Ibn Battuta is most often accused of plagiarizing his predecessor, Ibn Jubayr, who undertook much more modest travels to Mecca in the twelfth century as expiation for drinking alcohol. See, for example, Mattock's "Ibn Battuta's Use of Ibn Jubayr's *Rihla,*" pp. 209–18, and "The Travel Writings of Ibn Jubair and Ibn Batuta," *Glasgow University Oriental Society* 21, no. 165–66: pp. 35–46. Scholars have identified other sources of plagiarism, however: Amikan Elad argues that much of Ibn Battuta's account of Palestine is copied from the *rihla* of Muhammad b. Muhammad al-ʿAbdar, who began his travels in 1289. Elad, "The Description of the Travels of Ibn Battuta in Palestine: Is it Original?" *Journal of the Royal Asiatic Society of Great Britain and Ireland* 2 (1987): pp. 256–72.

12. J. N. Mattock, "Ibn Battuta's Use of Ibn Jubayr's *Rihla,*" p. 214. Husayn concurs, suggesting that Ibn Battuta lacked the critical and analytical skills of Ibn Jubayr (*Adab al-Rihla ʿinda al-ʿArab*, pp. 70, 77.

13. Janice Radway has argued that embedded in the term *audience* is a conceptual legacy that conceives of a message as a "fixed, enduring entity that remains unchanged by the transmission process which delivers it in identical fashion to that aggregate group of receivers, the audience." This is not the notion of "audience" I have in mind here, but rather the linguistic and cultural world Ibn Battuta imagined he was addressing. Radway, "Reception Study: Ethnography and the Problems of Dispersed Audiences and Nomadic Subjects," *Cultural Studies* 2 no. 3 (1988): p. 360.

14. Letter from Joseph Spence, quoted in Percy G. Adams, *Travel Literature and the Evolution of the Novel* (Lexington: University Press of Kentucky, 1983), p. 82. As Percy Adams argues and demonstrates in *Travelers and Travel Liars*, the tradition of traveler as liar has a long and illustrious history; indeed, a character from George Farquhar's *The Beaux' Strategem* insults a priest by saying he "tells lies as if he had been a traveler from his cradle." Adams, *Travelers and Travel Liars: 1660–1800* (Berkeley: University of California Press, 1962); George Farquhar, *The Beaux Strategem* (Lincoln: University of Nebraska Press, 1977), act 3, Scene 3, p. 57. The suspicion of travelers tales is echoed in a French say-

ing, "A beau mentir celuí qui vient de loin." I am grateful to Abderrahmane El-Moudden for bringing this saying to my attention.

15. See, for example, Jonathan Cohn, "When Did Political Science Forget about Politics? Irrational Exuberance," *The New Republic*, October 25, 1999, pp. 25–31; Michael M. Weinstein, "Students Seek Some Reality Amid the Math Economics," *The New York Times*, September 18, 1999, pp. B9, B11; Rick Perlstein, "Getting Real: Homo Economicus Goes to the Lab," *Lingua Franca*, April/May 1997, pp. 59–65; D. W. Miller, "Storming the Palace in Political Science," *The Chronicle of Higher Education*, September 21, 2001, p. 16; Ian Blecher, "How Cult Internet Character Mr. Perestroika Divided N.Y.U.'s Political Science Department," *New York Observer*, January 7, 2002, p. 3.

16. Cicero, *De Legibus* [*The Laws*], I. I. 5, p. 301. Voltaire makes a similar distinction between Herodotus, the historian of the Persian Wars, and "another who is primarily the Herodotus of 'others,' of non-Greeks," the traveler and storyteller. Hartog, *Mirror of Herodotus*, pp. xx–xxi.

17. Herodotus, *The Histories*, Book I, Clio.

18. J.A.S. Evans, "Father of History or Father of Lies," p. 16

19. Hartog, *Mirror of Herodotus*, p. 232.

20. One scholar terms such wanderlust the *"rahhala* impulse." Ian Richard Netton, "Arabia and the Pilgrim Paradigm of Ibn Battūta: A Braudelian Approach," *Arabia and the Gulf: From Traditional Society to Modern States*, ed. by Ian Richard Netton (Totowa, NJ: Barnes and Noble, 1986), p. 37.

21. Ibn Battuta, *Rihlat Ibn Battuta* (Beirut: Dar Sadir, 1964), pp. 14, 190, my translations. This is the Arabic text based on what is regarded as the best edition of *Rihla* edited by C. Defrémery and B. R. Sanguinetti. See Miquel, "Ibn Battuta," *Encyclopedia of Islam*.

22. *Rihlat Ibn Battuta*, from the introduction by Ibn Juzayy, p. 12 (hereafter referred to as *Rihla*).

23. Husain Muʾnis, for example, takes Ibn Battuta's *Rihla* as a window onto the political authority wielded by holy men in the medieval Islamic world, S. Maqbul Ahmad describes it as the "most important mediaeval travel account in Arabic for the lands of India, South-East Asia and other countries of Asia and North Africa," and Mahdi Husain characterizes it as a "mine of history" in the introduction to his translation of parts of the *Rihla*. Muʾnis, "Rahhalat al-Islam Ibn Battuta," *al-Tarikh wa al-Mustaqbal* 3, no. 1 (1989): pp. 141–43; "Djughrafiya," by Maqbul Ahmad, *Encyclopedia of Islam*; *The Rehla of Ibn Battuta (India, Maldive Islands and Ceylon)*, trans. Mahdi Husain (Baroda: Oriental Institute, 1976), p. xviii.

24. Miquel, "Ibn Battuta," *Encyclopedia of Islam*.

25. *Adab* is itself a complex Arabic term that at one time referred primarily to habits, customs, and norms of conduct, but has more recently been used as a synonym for literature or the tradition of belles-lettres. The newer, narrower connotation of "literature" occludes its ethical and social as well as intellectual dimensions, however. In many contexts, *adab* is meant to "imply the sum of knowledge which makes a man courteous and 'urbane,' profane culture . . . based in the first place on poetry, the art of oratory, the historical and tribal traditions of the ancient Arabs, and also on the corresponding sciences:

rhetoric, grammar, lexicography, metrics." "Adab," *Encyclopedia of Islam*, by F. Gabrieli. On Ibn Battuta and *adab*, see Ian Richard Netton, "Tourist *Adab* and Cairene Architecture: The Medieval Paradigm of Ibn Jubayr and Ibn Battutah," *The Literary Heritage of Classical Islam: Arabic and Islamic Studies in Honor of James A. Bellamy* (Princeton: Darwin Press, 1993), pp. 275–84.

26. Gibb, *Ibn Battuta: Travels in Asia and Africa*, p. 2.

27. Roger Allen, *The Arabic Novel: An Historical and Critical Introduction* (Syracuse, NY: Syracuse University Press, 1982), p. 12.

28. "ʿAdjaʾib," by C. E. Dubler, *Encyclopedia of Islam*, and Khalidi," Islamic Views of the West in the Middle Ages," p. 38. The literature on this subject is extensive; what is crucial here is that *ʿajaʾib* is already a fusion of the Qurʾanic emphasis on God's marvels and the ancient Greek appreciation of great monuments and deeds.

29. *De Legibus*, p. 301.

30. Hartog, *The Mirror of Herodotus*, pp. xxiii–xxiv.

31. Henry R. Immerwahr, *Form and Thought in Herodotus* (Cleveland, OH: Press of Western Reserve University, 1966), p. 4.

32. Dougherty, *The Raft of Odysseus*," p. 11. For a comparison between Herodotus and Homer in particular, see Stambler, "Herodotus," pp. 210–12.

33. Marshall G. S. Hodgson characterizes the Islamic world of the Middle Periods as a "trans-regional Oikoumene" in his *Venture of Islam*, vol. 2, *The Expansion of Islam in the Middle Periods*.

34. *The New Century Handbook of Classical Geography*, ed. by Catherine B. Avery (New York: Appleton-Century-Crofts, 1972), pp. 155–56. Biographical details are drawn from the following: Buckley, *Aspects of Greek History*, pp. 10–16; Stambler, "Herodotus," pp. 225–27; K. H. Waters, *Herodotus the Historian* (Oklahoma: University of Oklahoma Press, 1985); Myres, *Herotodus: Father of History*; Hartog, *The Mirror of Herodotus*; and Rosalind Thomas, introduction to Herodotus's *Histories*.

35. Waters, *Herodotus the Historian*, "'Life' of Herodotus."

36. Immerwahr, *Form and Thought in Herodotus*, p. 8, Thomas, introduction to Herodotus's *Histories*, p. xxix; Waters, *Herodotus the Historian*, p. 7.

37. Hartog, *Mirror of Herodotus*, p. xvii.

38. Waters, *Herodotus the Historian*, p. 3; Thomas, introduction to Herodotus's *Histories*, p. xxiii.

39. Approaches to these questions include those of the "unitarians," "geneticists," and "separatists." For an overview of such positions and arguments, see Charles W. Fornara, *Herodotus: An Interpretative Essay* (Oxford: Clarendon Press, 1971), pp 1–23.

40. John Marincola, "Herodotean Narrative and the Narrator's Presence," *Arethusa* 20, no. 1/2 (spring/fall 1987): p. 121; Myres, "Herodotus and His Critics," in *Herodotus: Father of History*, p. 9; Stambler, "Herodotus," pp. 211–12.

41. Stambler, "Herodotus," p. 212.

42. Marincola, "Herodotean Narrative," p. 126.

43. For a detailed description of Herodotus's source materials, see Buckley, *Aspects of Greek History*, pp. 12ff. See also Oswyn Murray, "Herodotus and Oral History," *Achaemenid History* 2 (1987): 93–115.

44. *The Mirror of Herodotus*, p. 4.

45. Ibid., p. 5.

46. Hartog, *Mirror of Herodotus*, pp. xxiii–xxiv.

47. In this way, Hartog is able to avoid the "cult of the text" where the only legitimate questions are those posed within the terms of the text, the answers to which are thereby tautological.

48. Hartog, *Mirror of Herodotus*, p. 7.

49. Stambler, "Herodotus," p. 213.

50. Hartog, *Mirror of Herodotus*, p. 319.

51. Stambler, "Herodotus," p. 215.

52. *Histories*, II, pp. 35–37.

53. Rosalind Thomas, introduction to the *Histories*, p. xxxiii.

54. Hartog, *Mirror of Herodotus*, pp. 94–96, 319.

55. Ibid., p. 36. Hartog's approach is not without critics. See for example, B. M. Lavelle's review of *The Mirror of Herodotus* in *The Classical World*, 84 (March/April 1991): 313; and David Grene's review in *The Journal of Religion* 70 (January 1990): 136.

56. Hartog, *Mirror of Herodotus*, p. 258.

57. Ibid., p. 225. For a reading of the ancients that complicates the presumption that the Greeks ordered the world by way of polarities, see J. Peter Euben, "Antigone and the Languages of Politics," in *Corrupting Youth: Political Education, Democratic Culture, and Political Theory* (Princeton, NJ: Princeton University Press, 1997).

58. Marincola, "Herodotean Narrative," p. 124.

59. Aristotle, *Metaphysics*, 980a25; Heraclitus in *Ancilla to the Pre-Socratic Philosophers*, trans. Kathleen Freeman (Cambridge, MA: Harvard University Press, 1978), p. 31, 101a.; *Histories* I: 8.

60. Hartog, *Mirror of Herodotus*, p. 61.

61. Ibid., pp. 322–25.

62. Gray, "Herodotus and the Rhetoric of Otherness," *American Journal of Philology* 116 (1995): 185–211.

63. An important part of Gray's analysis is that the paradigm of the "vengeful queen" is more a marker of barbarism than it is of gender, for her specific traits are also exhibited by royal men. This is then complicated by the distinction made between barbarian royals—whether male or female—and their subjects, who are depicted as "more humane than royals, less concerned with power than with living," p. 205.

64. Roger Just, *Women in Athenian Law and Life* (New York: Routledge, 1989), p. 152, 192, 193. As David Cohen argues, the actual practices of Athenian women often diverged significantly from this picture, suggesting that they had a much greater role in public life than is often assumed. *Law, Sexuality, and Society: The Enforcement of Morals in Classical Athens* (Cambridge: Cambridge University Press, 1991).

65. Just, *Women in Athenian Law*, p. 217.

66. On the portrayal of Persian queens by Herodotus and the Greeks in general, see Heleen Sancisi-Weerdenburg, "Exit Atossa: Images of Women in Greek Historiography on Persia," *Images of Women in Antiquity*, ed. Averil

Cameron and Amélie Kuhrt (Detroit: Wayne State University Press, 1983), pp. 20–33.

67. *Histories*, IV: 46; Herodotus notes, however, Scythians' admirable ability to repel invaders.

68. Hartog, *Mirror of Herodotus*, pp. 14–19, 232–35; *Histories*, II:35.

69. Ibid, p. 322, 320.

70. Martin, "Orientalism and the Ethnographer," p. 520.

71. Redfield, "Herodotus the Tourist," p. 107, 110–11. For a detailed analysis of Herodotus's construction of Scythia and Egypt in terms of one another, see also Redfield, "Herodotus the Tourist," pp. 106–10.

72. Rosalind Thomas's introduction to the *Histories*, p. xxvi.

73. Ibid., p. xxxv.

74. Plato, *Republic*, Book V, 469D–470C; Aristotle, *Politics*, Book I. 2.

75. Gray, "Herodotus and the Rhetoric of Otherness," p. 201. Edith Hall argues that in Greek tragedy, and in the tragedians' characterization of the Persians in particular, the "three main flaws in the barbarian psychology selected for repeated emphasis are its hierarchalism, its immoderate luxuriousness, and its unrestrained emotionalism." Hall, *Inventing the Barbarian: Greek Self-Definition through Tragedy* (Oxford, England: Clarendon Press, 1989), p. 80.

76. Redfield, "Herodotus the Tourist," p. 117, 102.

77. Ibid., p. 100. Susan O. Shapiro argues that the character of Solon expresses Herodotus's views, but Redfield suggests that Solon represents Herodotus's "alter ego." Shapiro, "Herodotus and Solon," *Classical Antiquity* 15, no. 2 (October 1996): 348–64; Redfield, "Herodotus the Tourist," p. 102. Here I intentionally set aside thorny questions about the relationship, if any, between Herodotus's Solon and the historical Solon, and about whether or not Solon in some sense 'speaks for' the author Herodotus.

78. Martin, "Orientalism and the Ethnographer," p. 520.

79. Redfield, "Herodotus the Tourist," p. 97; Hartog, *Mirror of Herodotus*, p. 235.

80. Hartog, *Mirror of Herodotus*, p. 214.

81. As the fourteenth-century Middle East will be less familiar to scholars of the English speaking world, there is of necessity a certain imbalance between the length of the previous analysis and the one that follows. On the assumption that such scholars are more familiar with Herodotus than Ibn Battuta, it made sense to start with the *Histories*, keeping in mind, of course, that it is equally important not to privilege what is familiar beyond the moment.

82. Lenker, "The Importance of the Rihla for the Islamization of Spain," p. 34. Ibn Jubayr, *Rihlat Ibn Jubayr*, ed. William Wright (Leiden: Brill, 1907). For a discussion of the development and features of travel writing in the eras preceding Ibn Battuta, see André Miquel, *La géographie humaine du monde musulman jusqu'au milieu du 11ᵉ siècle*, chap. 4, "Les gens du voyage."

83. Dunn, *The Adventures of Ibn Battuta*, p. 3. Ch. Pellat describes Ibn Jubayr's *rihla* as "one of the first and best works of this kind," but as Ian Netton argues, while Ibn Battuta's journey is rightly characterized as *talab al-ᶜilm*, one can only apply this to Jubayr's *rihla* in a limited way. Ch. Pellat, "Ibn Djubayr," *Encyclopedia of Islam*; Netton, "Basic Structures and Signs of Alienation in the

Rihla of Ibn Jubayr," pp. 57–58, and "Myth, Miracle, and Magic in the *Rihla* of Ibn Battuta," *Journal of Semitic Studies* 29, no. 1 (1984): pp. 132–33. A sharp distinction between the *rihlatayn* (two *rihlas*) should not be overstated, however, as either Ibn Battuta or his editor simply lifted entire passages from Ibn Jubayr's account, at times without attribution. See note 12 above.

84. Al-Manuni provides a typology of the kind of journeys from Morocco that prevailed between the 16th and 18th centuries in particular. It includes *rihla hijaziyya*, *rihla* in the land of Morocco, and *rihla sifariyya*, those journeys undertaken for largely diplomatic reasons. Muhammad al-Manuni, *Al-Masadir al-ʿArabiyya li-Tarikh al-Maghrib* (Rabat, Morocco: al-Mamlaka al-Maghribiyya, Jamiʿat Muhammad al-Khamis, Kulliyyat al-Adab wa al-ʿUlum al-Insaniyya, 1983), pp. 186–92. Netton identifies in the *rihla* a general "pilgrim paradigm" constituted by a pattern of overlapping intentions much broader than pilgrimage: the visit to shrines, the search for knowledge, the pursuit of recognition or power, and fulfillment of wanderlust. "Arabia and the Pilgrim Paradigm of Ibn Battūta: A Braudelian Approach."

85. *Rihla*, p. 191, 190.

86. Beyond the *Rihla* and Ibn Khaldûn's comments, H.A.R. Gibb reprints the one biographical notice about Ibn Battuta that appears in a 15th-century dictionary of eminent persons. Gibb, *The Travels of Ibn Battuta*, vol. 1, p. ix. The *Rihla*, Gibb's introduction to *Ibn Battuta: Travels in Asia and Africa*, and Dunn's *The Adventures of Ibn Battuta* are the primary sources for the following details.

87. *Rihla*, p. 14. The *Rihla* gives his age as twenty-two, but scholars put him at twenty-one.

88. Ibid., p. 14. For a detailed discussion of Ibn Battuta's wives, slaves, and children, see Remke Kruk, "Ibn Battuta: Travel, Family Life, and Chronology— How Seriously Do We Take a Father?" *Al-Qantara* 16 (1995): 369–84.

89. These are the dates on which both Dunn and Gibb rely. Mahdi Husain unaccountably gives the dates of Ibn Battuta's death as either 1377 or 1378. Husain, *The Rehla of Ibn Battuta*, p. lix.

90. On the appropriateness and advantages of the phrase "Muslim societies" over either "Islamic world" or "Islamic/Muslim society" in the singular, see Asef Bayat, "The Use and Abuse of 'Muslim Societies,'" *International Institute for the Study of Islam in the Modern World Newsletter* 13 (December 2003), p. 5.

91. Dunn, *The Adventures of Ibn Battuta*, p. 317.

92. Ibid., p. 317; Gibb notes the tenor of early European commentators but seems to admit of similar reactions when he writes that the preoccupation with religion is "apt to make heavy demands on the patience and knowledge of modern readers." Gibb, *Ibn Battuta: Travels in Asia and Africa*, p. 35, 27.

93. Samuel Lee, *The Travels of Ibn Batuta*, (London: Oriental Translation Committee, 1829), p. xii. A similar effort to vindicate the accuracy of the *Rihla* is found is Mirza M. Wahid's "Khusrau and Ibn Battuta: A Comparative Study," in *Professor Muhammad Shafī Presentation Volume*, ed. S. M. Abdullah (Lahore, Pakistan: The Majlis-e-Armughān-e-ʿIlmi, 1955).

94. In addition to many of the citations that follow, examples of this approach include M. R. Haig, "Ibn Battuta in Sindh," *Journal of the Royal Asiatic*

Society of Great Britain and Ireland 19 (1887): 393–412; and Joseph Chelhod, "Ibn Battuta, Ethnologue," *Revue de l'Occident Musulman et de la Méditerranée* 25 (1978): 5–24. Examples of very different approaches to Ibn Battuta's *rihla* (and travel literature· more generally) include the work of Ian Richard Netton, Ross E. Dunn, Husain Mu²nis, and the editors and authors of *Muslim Travellers*.

95. For an argument against, see Gabriel Ferrand, *Relations de voyages et textes géographiques Arabes, Persans et Turks relatifs a l'Extrême-Orient du VIII au XVIII siècles*, vol. 2 (Paris: Ernest Leroux, 1913–14), pp. 429, 432–33. But Tatsuro Yamamoto concludes Ibn Battuta did make it to China, as does Gibb. Yamamoto, "On Tawālisī Described by Ibn Batuta," *Memoirs of the Research Department of the Toyo Bunko* (Tokyo: The Toyo Bunko, 1936), p. 103; Gibb, *Ibn Battuta: Travels in Asia and Africa*, p. 14. Mu²nis is the most judicious in this regard, suggesting that whether or not Ibn Battuta actually made it to China is almost as difficult to verify as the rest of what he claimed to have seen in the *Rihla*, as much of the narration was supplemented by hearsay. "Rahhalat al-Islam Ibn Battuta," p. 147.

96. Abdel Majed Khan, "The Historicity of Ibn Batuta re: Shamsuddin Firuz Shah, the so-called Balbani King of Bengal," *The Indian Historical Quarterly* 18 (March 1942): pp. 65–70; Umesh Kumar Singh, "Ibn Battutah's Rehlah," *The Quarterly Review of Historical Studies* 18, no. 3 (1978–79): pp. 192–96; Mahdi Husain, *The Rehla of Ibn Battuta*, pp. vii–lxxvii.

97. Hrbek, "The Chronology of Ibn Battuta's Travels; H. T. Norris, "Ibn Battuta's Journey in the North-Eastern Balkans," *Journal of Islamic Studies* 5, no. 2 (1994): pp. 209–20.

98. Janicsek, "Ibn Battuta's Journey to Bulghar: Is it a Fabrication?"; Elad, "The Description of the Travels of Ibn Battuta in Palestine: Is it Original?"; Allouche, "A Study of Ibn Battutah's Account of his 726/1326 Journey through Syria and Arabia."

99. Beckingham, "In Search of Ibn Battuta," p. 267.

100. Agha Mahdi Husain, "Ibn Battuta and his Rehla in New Light," *Sind University Research Journal* 6(1967): 25–32.

101. H. G. Rawlinson, "The Traveller of Islam," *Islamic Culture* 5 (1931): p. 86

102. Yamamoto, "On Tawālisī Described by Ibn Batuta," p. 133; C. Edmund Bosworth, Review of Ross E. Dunn's *The Adventures of Ibn Battuta: A Muslim Traveller of the 14ᵗʰ Century, Journal of Islamic Studies* 4 (1993): p. 110.

103. Gibb, *Ibn Battuta: Travels in Asia and Africa*, p. 36; Netton, "Myth, Miracle and Magic in the *Rihla* of Ibn Battūta," pp. 138–39.

104. Min Byung Wha, "*Baraka*, as Motif and Motive, in the *Rihla* of Ibn Battuta," Ph.D. Diss., University of Utah, 1991.

105. Aga Mahdi Husain, "Studies in the *Tuhfatunnuzzar* of Ibn Battuta and Ibn Juzayy," *Journal of the Asiatic Society of Bangladesh* 23 (1978): 18–49.

106. Netton, "Arabia and the Pilgrim Paradigm of Ibn Battūta."

107. Beckingham, "In Search of Ibn Battuta," pp. 267–68; Herman F. Jannsens, *Ibn Batoutah: Le Voyageu de l'Islam* (Brussels: Office de Publicité, 1948), p. 89.

108. Mahdi Husain, "Ibn Battuta: His Life and Work," *Indo-Iranica* 7 (1954): p. 13, n. 3; Henry Yule, *Cathay and the Way Thither*, vol. 4 (London: Hakluyt Society, 1913–16).

109. Madhi Husain argues that Ibn Battuta "aspired at an advanced stage of his experience to write out the story of his travels" ("Ibn Battuta and his Rehla in New Light," p. 25). See also Mahdi Husain, "Ibn Battuta: His Life and Work," p. 13, n. 1. But Gibb contends that he "was not himself a man of letters who was likely to regard his experiences as material for a book; on the contrary, he seems to have entertained no idea of writing them down." *Ibn Battuta: Travels in Asia and Africa*, p. 11.

110. Madhi Husain states that "it is evident that he used to take copious notes during his travels." Husain, "Ibn Battuta: His Life and Work," p. 13; Mahdi Husain's introduction to *The Rehla of Ibn Battuta*, pp. lxxiv–lxxvii. Adel Allouche and Joseph Chelhod concur. Allouche, "A Study of Ibn Battutah's Account of his 726/1326 Journey through Syria and Arabia," p. 297; Chelhod, "Ibn Battuta, Ethnologue," p. 11. Elad, Gibb, and Dunn all argue that he either never took notes or at the very least did not have them at the conclusion of his journey. Elad, "The Description of the Travels of Ibn Battuta in Palestine: Is it Original?" p. 256; Gibb, *Ibn Battuta: Travels in Asia and Africa*, p. 10; Dunn, *The Adventures of Ibn Battuta*, p. 313.

111. Miquel, *La géographie humaine du monde musulman jusqu'au milieu du 11e siècle*, p. 148.

112. Dunn, *The Adventures of Ibn Battuta*, p. 13.

113. *Rihlat Ibn Battuta*, p. 9; Dunn, *The Adventures of Ibn Battuta*, p. 19 and *Ibn Battuta in Black Africa*, ed and trans. Said Hamdum and Noël King (Princeton, NJ: Markus Wiener, 1994), p. 5

114. *Rihla*, pp. 257.

115. Ibid., p. 17.

116. Beckingham, "In Search of Ibn Battuta," p. 269

117. Bamyeh, "Global Order and the Historical Structures of *Dar al-Islam*," pp. 218–19.

118. Mahdi Husain, "Ibn Battuta: His Life and Work," p. 6. Late in his travels, Ibn Battuta relates that a *shaikh* identifies him as "the traveler from the Maghrib," p. 870. He is also explicitly identified in this way in the *Rihla* on pp. 743 and 871.

119. Lenker, "The Importance of the Rihla for the Islamization of Spain," pp. 195–96; Gellens, "The Search for Knowledge in Medieval Muslim Societies: A Comparative Approach," p. 59. For a discussion of the purpose and problems with the terminology of an Islamic east versus west, see Hogdson, *The Venture of Islam*, vol. 1, pp. 308–13, esp. note 6.

120. El Moudden, "The Ambivalence of *Rihla*," p. 29; Dunn, "International Migrations of Literate Muslims in the Later Middle Period: The Case of Ibn Battuta," in *Golden Roads*, p. 76; see also Dominique Urvoy, "Effets Pervers du Hajj, d'après le Cas d'al-Andalus," in *Golden Roads*, pp. 43–53; and Miller, *Disorienting Encounters*, p. 52.

121. Gellens, "The Search for Knowledge in Medieval Muslim Societies," *Muslim Travellers*, pp. 50–65; Dunn, *The Adventures of Ibn Battuta*, p. 30. J. Hey-

worth-Dunne suggests that there are similar regional patterns in the modern period as well. "Rifaʿah Badawī Rafiʿ al-Tahtāwī: The Egyptian Revivalist," *Bulletin of the School of Oriental and African Studies* 9 (1940–42), p. 401.

122. El Moudden, "The Ambivalence of *Rihla*," pp. 69–84.

123. Gibb, *Travels of Ibn Battuta*, vol. 1, p. 189, n7; *Rihla*, p. 131.

124. *Rihla*, pp. 367–68.

125. Ibid., p. 188.

126. Ibid., p. 615.

127. Ibid., p. 261

128. Ibid., p. 659.

129. Cornell, *Realm of the Saint*, pp. 129–30.

130. *Rihla*, p. 40. For an analysis of Ibn Battuta's attitude toward each legal school, see André Miquel, "L'Islam d'Ibn Battuta," *Bulletin d'âetudes orientales* 30 (1978), pp. 75–83. As Miquel notes, Ibn Battuta exhibits the "spirit of the sect but not the sectarianism of it," and even Malikites come in for an occasional criticism by the traveler (p. 75).

131. This aspect of Ibn Battuta's character has provoked at least one scholar to refer to him as a "Maghribi Savonarola" and "Malikite Calvin." G. H. Bousquet, "Ibn Battuta et les institutions musulmanes," *Studia Islamica* 24 (1966): p. 105.

132. N. Cottart, "Malikism," *Encyclopedia of Islam*; Dunn, *The Adventures of Ibn Battuta*, pp. 90–91.

133. *Rihla*, p. 220.

134. Ibid., p. 67.

135. Miquel rightly argues that Ibn Battuta's division between Sunnism and all other Muslims and non-Muslims is not as absolute as it initially appears. However, he goes on to suggest that Ibn Battuta's antipathies have less to do with particular practices or peoples and more to do with his dislike of excess or of extremes. But this begs the question of the standard by which "extreme" is measured; in fact, deviance and excess in the *Rihla* are determined by gradations of distance from his own Islam, universalized as Islam as such. *L'Islam d'Ibn Battuta*, p. 78.

136. *Rihla*, pp. 244, 572, 264, 442.

137. *La géographie humaine*, p. 149.

138. For a detailed examination of the *rihla* through the trope of *baraka*, see Wha, "*Baraka*, as Motif and Motive, in the *Rihla* of Ibn Battuta." For an ethnographic approach to *baraka* see, for example, Abdellah Hammoudi, *Master and Disciple: The Cultural Foundations of Moroccan Authoritarianism* (Chicago: University of Chicago Press, 1997). See also Edward Westermarck, *Ritual and Belief in Morocco* (London: Macmillan, 1926), vol. 1, pp. 35–261.

139. *Rihla*, p. 544.

140. Ibid., pp. 24–25, 30, 51, 420.

141. Cousin and son-in-law of the Prophet Muhammad, ʿAli was the fourth caliph and was assassinated in ah 40 / 661 ce. Revered by both Sunnis and Shiʿa, Ali is of particular significance to the latter (Shiʿa refers to partisans of ʿAli), who regards him as their first Imam.

142. *Rihla*, p. 178.

143. Ibid., p. 25, 35.

144. Lenker, "The Importance of the Rihla for the Islamization of Spain," p. 207, 202.

145. T. H. Weir and A. Zysow, "Sadaka," *Encyclopedia of Islam*

146. "Hiba," by F. Rosenthal and G.S. Colin, *Encyclopedia of Islam*. For a rich ethnographic reading of the overlapping political, religious, and social elements enacted through ceremonial exchanges between a Sultan and his subjects in nineteenth-century Morocco, see Rahma Bourqia, "Don et théâtralité: Réflexion sur le rituel du don (Hadiyya) offert au sultan au XIXe siècle," *Hesperis* 31 (1993): pp. 61–75. See also Franz Rosenthal "Gifts and Bribes: The Muslim View," *Proceedings of the American Philosophical Society* 108, no. 2, (April 1964): pp. 135–44; and Marcel Mauss, *The Gift: The Form and Reason for Exchange in Archaic Societies*, trans. W. D. Halls (London: Routledge, 1990).

147. Dunn's Foreward in Hamdun and King's *Ibn Battuta in Black Africa*, p. xviii. Mu'nis argues that the acquisition of wealth, slaves, and other such symbols of status ultimately corrupted the simple *Maghribi*. By the time Ibn Battuta actually came to wield some power in the Maldives, Mu'nis suggests, he had turned into a "tyrant" [*tughiyya*]. "Rahhalat al-Islam Ibn Battuta," p. 146.

148. *Rihla*, pp. 149, 291.

149. Ibid., pp. 461; 462.

150. Ibn Battuta repeatedly uses the term ʿata (gift, present, alms); by contrast, here the sultan's servant describes the gift toward which Battuta is so disdainful as *hadiyya*, defined by the *Encyclopedia of Islam* as an "effort on the part of a person on a lower level of society to get into the good graces of a recipient of a higher social status." "Hiba," *Encyclopedia of Islam*. Bourqia (p. 72) further defines *hadiyya* by distinguishing it from *hiba*, arguing that while *hiba* was used either to designate gifts of God to a man or from a sultan to an inferior without expectation of reciprocity, *hadiyya* does not connote such a hierarchy and implicitly suggests the expectation of a gift in return. The very word used, then, expresses the intent of the gift, despite Ibn Battuta's contempt for it. *Rihla*, p. 682.

151. *Rihla*, p. 682.

152. Ibid., p. 683.

153. Ibid., p. 577.

154. Ibid., p. 566.

155. Ibid., p. 523.

156. Ibid., p. 130.

157. Ibid., p. 420.

158. Ibid., p. 529.

159. Ibid., p. 592; 420; 191.

160. Miquel, *La géographie humaine*, chap. 4; Ibn Khaldûn, *Muqaddimah*, vol. 2, p. 346.

161. *Rihla*, pp. 441–42.

162. "Early Modern Europe through Islamic Eyes," pp. 50–51.

163. Miller, *Disorienting Encounters*, p. 57; Rosenthal, "The Technique and Approach of Muslim Scholarship," p. 6; *Alberuni's India*, edited by Edward C.

Sachau (London: Trübner, 1881), vol. I, chap. 16, p. 81, my translation. Commonly known in Arabic as *Kitab al-Hind*, it first appeared in ce 1030.

164. *Rihla*, pp. 108–9, 201–2.

165. Ibid., p. 55.

166. Ibid., pp. 264, 543, 600.

167. Ibid., p. 391.

168. Ibid., p. 374.

169. *The Muqaddimah*, 3:306; I, foreword, also note 16.

170. Gibb states that for Ibn Battuta as for other Moroccans at the time, the title of caliph, legitimate ruler of the *umma*, was reserved for the Marinid king Abu 'Inan. By contrast, "for all other temporal rulers, great and small alike, Muslim and also non-Muslim, Ibn Battuta used the non-committal term 'sultan,' which implied only *de facto* possession of temporal authority." Gibb, *Travels of Ibn Battuta*, vol. 1, p. 3, n. 9.

171. *Rihla*, p. 385.

172. Ibn Khaldûn, *The Muqaddimah*. The nomads of the *Rihla* are primarily Arab, Berber, Mongol, and Turkish, and largely appear in the text without the weighty cultural apparatus Herodotus attaches to the Scythian nomads. Ibn Battuta does occasionally describe certain nomads as a threat to the safety of travelers, refers in one instance to the "rudeness of the desert folk" (p. 689) and, despite his family's Berber origins, details the habits of life of Berber nomads with the care of an anthropologist in exotic territory (p. 972).

173. *Rihla*, pp. 595, 622.

174. Ibid., p. 613.

175. Ibid., p. 635.

176. Netton, "Basic Structures and Signs of Alienation in the *Rihla* of Ibn Jubayr," *Seek Knowledge: Thought and Travel in the House of Islam* (Great Britain: Curzon Press, 1996), p. 130, emphasis in the original.

177. *Rihla*, p. 59, 88.

178. Ibid., p. 344.

179. Ibid., pp. 27, 57, 283, 353, 355.

180. Ibid., pp. 329, 302.

181. Beckingham, "In Search of Ibn Battuta," p. 272. While Ibn Battuta does on occasion refer to Hindus, more often he refers to undifferentiated "infidels" in India, see for example, *Rihla*, pp. 385; 410; 507.

182. *Rihla*, p. 343.

183. Ibid., p. 345. In its earliest uses, *rum* referred to the Romans but over time came to mean Byzantines as well. C. E. Bosworth, "Rūm," *Encyclopedia of Islam*; Gibb, *Travels of Ibn Battuta*, vol. 1, p. 115, n. 171.

184. *Rihla*, p. 346.

185. Ibid., pp. 350, 349, 355. Gibb notes that "Muslims held the ringing of bells in the greatest abhorrence" and cites a hadith which says that the "angels will not enter any house in which bells are ringing," *Travels of Ibn Battuta*, vol. 2, p. 470, n. 214.

186. For the dates of his African voyages, I have followed the chronology provided in Hamdun and King, *Ibn Battuta in Black Africa* and that of Noël

King in "Reading between the Lines of Ibn Battuta for the History of Religions in Black Africa," *Milla wa-milla* 19 (1979): pp. 26–33.

187. Hamdun and King, *Ibn Battuta in Black Africa*, p. xxv.

188. In Arabic, *Sudan* designates both a geographic area—a particular region of Africa—and a skin color. When speaking of the former, Ibn Battuta uses *bilad al-Sudan* (lands of black people), and when referring to the latter, he simply uses *al-Sudan*. On the complexity of Arabic terms for Africa and Africans, see John Wansbrough, "Africa and the Arab Geographers," *Language and History in Africa*, ed. David Dalby (New York: Africana, 1970), esp. pp. 97, 99.

189. *Rihla*, p. 182; pp. 695–96.

190. Ibid., p. 681.

191. Ibid., p. 677.

192. Ibid., p. 689.

193. Ibid., p. 690.

194. Eve M. Troutt Powell, "From Odyssey to Empire: Mapping Sudan through Egyptian Literature in the mid-19th Century," *International Journal of Middle East Studies* 31 (1999): p. 404.

195. *Rihla*, pp. 677, 690, 685.

196. Hamdun and King, *Ibn Battuta in Black Africa*, p. xxx; King, "Reading between the Lines of Ibn Battuta for the History of Religions in Black Africa," pp. 26ff. Such disapproval often presupposes a link between climate, skin color, and behavior similar to that of Ibn Khaldûn. See *The Muqaddimah*, I, 169, 170, 174, 301; and Akbar Muhammad, "The Image of Africans in Arabic Literature: Some Unpublished Manuscripts," *Slaves and Slavery in Muslim Africa*, vol. 1, ed. John Ralph Willis (Totowa, NJ: Frank Cass, 1985), pp. 47–74.

197. In this the *Rihla* provides a small window onto African Islam, which flourished particularly in the Western Sudan from the time of the 11th century, the "great century of the initiation into Islam of the royal courts situated at the termini of the trans-Saharan routes." "Bilad al-Sudan," by J. L. Triaud, *Encyclopedia of Islam*. See John Hunwick, "Ahmad Bābā and the Moroccan Invasion of the Sudan (1591)," *Journal of the Historical Society of Nigeria* 2, no. 3 (December 1962): pp. 312–13.

198. Fedwa Malti-Douglas goes as far as suggesting that in medieval Arabo-Islamic literature, religious partisanship and cultural differences were often "largely occulted in favor of the gender politics." Malti-Douglas, *Woman's Body, Woman's Word: Gender and Discourse in Arabo-Islamic Writing* (Princeton, NJ: Princeton University Press, 1991), p. 62.

199. Kruk, "Ibn Battuta: Travel, Family Life, and Chronology," p. 370.

200. Ibid., pp. 370–71; *Rihla*, p. 588.

201. Emma Ben Miled, "Vie de Femmes a Travers La Rihla d'Ibn Battutah," *Revue tunisienne de sciences sociales: publication du Centre d'âetudes et de recherches âeconomiques et sociales* 104/105 (1991): p. 111.

202. *Rihla*, p. 381.

203. Ibid., p. 203, 696.

204. Ibid., p. 264, 548.

205. Ibid., p. 541. Bousquet argues that Ibn Battuta "adopts the system of 'a girl in every port,' and when I say 'a,' that is a euphemism." Bousquet, "Ibn Battuta et les Institutions Musulmans," p. 97.

206. *Rihla*, p. 149, 248.

207. Ibid., p. 334.

208. Ibid., p. 330.

209. Ibid., p. 647, 691, 233, 678.

210. *Woman's Body, Woman's Word*, pp. 58–59. Malti-Douglas goes on to suggest that the "problematic nature of woman, her voice, her body" is a consistent feature of medieval Arabo-Islamic philosophy, a trope that helped secure the dominance of utopian homosocial narrative scripts in which women tend to be absent, silent or transfigured (p. 67).

211. *Rihla*, pp. 121, 230–31, 423.

212. Kruk, "Ibn Battuta: Travel, Family Life, and Chronology," pp. 373, 375.

213. *Rihla*, pp. 467, 239, 412.

214. This must be distinguished from the complaint about those aspects of fourteenth-century life that fall outside of Ibn Battuta's interests—it is true but not terribly revealing, for example, that the *Rihla* is a "disappointing record of fourteenth-century shipbuilding and seamanship." Dunn, *The Adventures of Ibn Battuta*, p. 121.

215. King, "Reading between the Lines of Ibn Battuta for the History of Religion in Black Africa," p. 28.

216. *Rihla*, p. 638.

217. Ibid., p. 287.

218. Ibid., p.283.

219. Jacqueline Sublet, "Les Frontières chez Ibn Batuta," *La signification du Bas Moyen Age dans l'histoire et la culture du monde musulman: actes du gme Congrès de l'Union Européene des Arabisants et Islamisants* (Aix-en-Provence: Edisud, 1978), p. 306.

220. *Rihla*, pp. 625–27, 677.

221. See Marina A. Tolmacheva, "Ibn Battuta on Women's Travel in the Dar al-Islam," in *Women and the Journey: The Female Travel Experience*, ed. Bonnie Frederick and Susan H. McLeod (Pullman: Washington State University Press, 1993), pp. 119–40, which contains a detailed discussion of which women do and do not travel in the *rihla*.

222. *Rihla*, p.248.

223. Ibid., p. 110.

224. Ibid. p. 353.

225. Ibid. p. 336.

226. Ibid. p. 100.

227. Ibid. p. 186.

228. Ibid. p. 635.

229. See, for example, D. O. Morgan, "Ibn Battuta and the Mongols," *Royal Asiatic Society of Great Britain and Ireland* 11, no. 1 (2001): p. 3.

230. A. Abel, "Dar al-Islam," *Encyclopedia of Islam*; Dunn, *The Adventures of Ibn Battuta*, pp. 6–7. There are other reasons Ibn Battuta is always ranked second to Marco Polo, among them the fact that it was largely 19th-century European scholars who were responsible for igniting a scholarly interest in Ibn Bat-

tuta, long after Marco Polo's reputation as "the" preeminent traveler was well established. Dunn, *The Adventures of Ibn Battuta*, p. 317.

231. Rutherford, "Theoric Crisis: The Dangers of Pilgrimage in Greek Religion and Society," and "*Theoria and Darśan*: Pilgrimage and Vision in Greece and India"; Dunn, *The Adventures of Ibn Battuta*, p. 11. For an example of this kind of argument, see Muhammad Menouni and M'hammad Benaboud, "A Moroccan Account of Constantinople," in *Les provinces arabes à l'époque ottomane: études*, ed. A. Tememi (Zagwan: Centre d'études et de recherches ottomanes et morisco-andalouses, 1987), pp. 39–76.

232. Marshall G. S. Hodgson, "The Unity of Later Islamic History," *Journal of World History* 5 (1960): 879–914. This was the second great expansion; the first was the flow of Arabs from Arabia in the 7th and 8th centuries ce.

233. Hodgson, "The Unity of Later Islamic History," p. 883; Dunn, *The Adventures of Ibn Battuta*, pp. 9–11.

234. As Voll notes, this view represents a substantial revision of the gloomy historical narrative in which the abolition of the ʿAbbasid caliphate by Mongol forces is portrayed as the beginning of a long process of civilizational decay and stagnation. John Voll, "Islam as a Special World-System," pp. 215–17. Hodgson, "Hemispheric Inter-regional History as an Approach to World History" and *The Venture of Islam*. See also McNeill, *The Rise of the West*; Curtin, *Cross-Cultural Trade in World History*; and Janet L. Abu-Lughod, *Before European Hegemony: The World System A.D. 1250–1350* (New York: Oxford University Press, 1989).

235. Hodgson, "The Unity of Later Islamic History," 884.

236. Ibid., p. 891.

237. Dunn, forward to Hamdun and King, *Ibn Battuta in Black Africa*, pp. xv–xvi; Miquel, *La géographie humaine*, p. 126. In fact, Bamyeh argues that *Pax Mongolica* should be understood as a "*transhistorically recurrent linkage system* of safe roads [that] secured multicultural passage." Bamyeh, *The Ends of Globalization* (Minneapolis: University of Minnesota Press, 2000), p. 104, emphasis in the original.

238. Bamyeh, "Global Order and the Historical Structures of *Dar al-Islam*," p. 223.

239. *Muslim Travellers*, p. xv

240. For a discussion of notions of "center" and "periphery" in the context of a networked Islamic 'world-system,' see Reichmuth, "The Interplay of Local Developments and Transnational Relations in the Islamic World: Perceptions and Perspectives," pp. 12ff. For a quite specific example, see Harry Norris's account of how Ibn Battuta provides a window onto inter- and intracultural exchanges on the Crimean Peninsula. Norris, "Ibn Battuta on Muslims and Christians in the Crimean Peninsula," *Iran and the Caucasus* 8, no. 1 (2004): 7–14.

241. "Le géographe malgré lui," Gibb, *Ibn Battuta: Travels in Asia and Africa*, p. 12

242. Susan Gilson Miller, *Disorienting Encounters*, p. 60.

243. El Moudden, "The Ambivalence of *Rihla*," pp. 69–84. Netton similarly argues that Ibn Jubayr's journey to Mecca, the embodiment of Islamic unity, at times provided an experience of Islam at its most disunited. "Basic Structures and Signs of Alienation in the *rihla* of Ibn Jubayr," *Golden Roads*, p. 63.

Chapter 4: Travel in Search of Practical Wisdom

1. This and much of the following biographical information on al-Tahtawi is drawn from al-Sayyid Salih Majdi, *Hilyat al-Zaman bi-Manaqib Khadim al-Watan: Sirat Rifaʿa Rafiʿ al-Tahtawi*, ed. Jamal al-Din al-Shayyal (Cairo: Maktabat Mustafa al-Babi al-Halabi, 1958); Ahmad Ahmad Badawi, *Rifaʿa Rafiʿ al-Tahtawi* (Cairo: Lajnat al-Bayan al-ʿArabi, 1959); Mahmud Fahmi al-Hijazi, *Usul al-Fikr al-ʿArabi al-hadith ʿinda al-Tahtawi, maʿa al-nass al-kamil li-kitabihi "Takhlis al-Ibriz"* (Cairo: al-Hayʾa al-Misriyya al-ʿAmma li-l-Kitab, 1974); Jamal al-Din al-Shayyal, *Tarikh al-tarjama wa al-haraka al-thaqafiyya fi ʿasr Muhammad ʿAli* (Cairo: Dar al-Fikr al-ʿArabi, 1951); Israel Altman, "The Political Thought of Rifaʿah Rafiʿ at-Tahtawi: A Nineteenth Century Egyptian Reformer," Ph.D. Diss., UCLA, 1976; and Daniel Newman's introduction in *An Imam in Paris: Al-Tahtawi's Visit to France (1826–1831)* (London: Saqi Press, 2004).

2. Most of the members of the mission were Muslims, but a few were Christians. Counting al-Tahtawi, only eighteen of the students were native-born Egyptians; the rest were Circassians, Greeks, Turks, Georgians, and Armenians, in part a reflection of the nonnative makeup of the elites in Muhammad ʿAli's Egypt.

3. Of course, the language of "awareness," like that of the "Arab awakening" so often used in this connection, presupposes a prior state of oblivious slumber that is highly problematic in ways discussed by Timothy Mitchell in *Colonising Egypt* (Berkeley: University of California Press, 1991), p. 119. J. Heyworth-Dunne, *An Introduction to the History of Education in Modern Egypt* (London: Frank Cass, 1968), p. 167; Anouar Louca, "Présentation: Le Voyage d'un orpailleur," in *L'Or de Paris: Relation de Voyage, 1826–1831* (Paris: Sindbad, 1988), p. 11, 15; Ibrahim abu-Lughod, *Arab Rediscovery of Europe* (Princeton: Princeton University Press, 1963), p. 46; Raouf Abbas Hamed, *The Japanese and Egyptian Enlightenment: A Comparative Study of Fukuwaza Yukichi and Rifaʿah al-Tahtawi* (Tokyo: Institute for the Study of Languages and Cultures of Asia and Africa, 1990), p. 149. There had been a school of translation created in the 1820s as part of the Royal School of Administration, but in 1836, a separate school of translation called Dar al-Aslun opened, and Tahtawi was placed in charge of it in 1837. A Translation Bureau was later established under al-Tahtawi's guidance, which was to prove enormously important in the transmission of non-Arabic works to Egypt. See Heyworth-Dunne, *An Introduction to the History of Education in Modern Egypt*, p. 150, 264–66; Lisa Pollard, "The Habits and Customs of Modernity: Egyptians in Europe and the Geography of Nineteenth-Century Nationalism," *Arab Studies Journal* 7–8 (fall 1999/spring 2000): p. 55; Hamed, *The Japanese and Egyptian Enlightenment*, pp. 42–43; Abu-Lughod, *The Arab Discovery of Europe* p. 46ff; and Altman, "The Political Thought of Rifaʿah Rafiʿ at-Tahtawi," p. 26ff.

4. *Du système pénitentiaire aux Etats-Unis et de son application en France* (Paris, 1832).

5. Donald Pease, "After the Tocqueville Revival; or, The Return of the Political," *Boundary* 2, no. 26.3 (1999), p. 97; see also Klaus J. Hansen, "Tocqueville:

Frenchman for all Seasons?" *Canadian Journal of History* 38 (August 2003): pp. 295–305.

6. Harvey C. Mansfield and Delba Winthrop's introduction to their translation of *Democracy in America* (Chicago: University of Chicago Press, 2000), p. xvii. Tocqueville has been invoked approvingly by everyone from Newt Gingrich to Muhammad Khatami, former president of the Islamic Republic of Iran. Nader Hashemi, "Islam, Democracy, and Alexis de Tocqueville," *Queen's Quarterly* 110, no. 1 (spring, 2003): 21–29; Khatami's interview with CNN, January 7, 1998; Pease, "After the Tocqueville Revival."

7. In fact, it seems that linguistic barriers contributed substantially to such misreadings. For example Renan's interpretation was based on selections from the unpublished manuscript translated from Arabic to French by Orientalist A. Caussin de Perceval, with whom al-Tahtawi had developed a friendship during his stay in Paris. It was published as "Relation d'un voyage en France, par le cheikh Réfaa," in *Nouveau Journal Asiatique*, Tome 11, Vol. 11 (Paris, 1833): 222–51. The extracts de Perceval translated and that excited Renan's anti-Muslim passions contained two passages Tahtawi eventually omitted from the published version that Renan did not read. The first related the prophetic dream of one of Tahtawi's fellow students, and the second makes clear Tahtawi's caution (probably strategic, given the ʿulama who would read it) regarding modern scientific arguments about how the solar system works (Louca, "Présentation: Le Voyage d'un orpailleur," pp. 24–25, 30–31, and Newman, *An Imam in Paris*, p. 85). Renan claims on the bases of these extracts that al-Tahtawi regarded science as heretical. Ernest Renan, *L'Islamisme et la Science: Conférence faite a la Sorbonne le 20 mars 1883*, (Paris: Calmann Lévy, 1883). French scholars who actually read the text in its original language tended to view it less as a valuable analysis of French culture and politics, and more as a novel window onto the mind of a somewhat parochial 19th-century Egyptian: as de Perceval writes, while the *Takhlis* will be crucial in undermining Egyptian prejudices about Europe and encouraging Tahtawi's countrymen to travel west for the "knowledge they lack . . . for us, in truth, it will be much less important, for it adds nothing to our knowledge . . . [although] it shows us a completely new phenomenon, that of an Arab painting a portrait of Paris." Perceval, "Relation d'un voyage en France, par le cheikh Réfaa," p. 222.

8. Yet as Timothy Mitchell argues, it was al-Tahtawi who, in his later writings, would help transform "politics" (*siyasa*) from "being one of several words for governing . . . [to] a definite field of knowledge, debate and practice." *Colonising Egypt*, p. 103.

9. *Democracy in America*, p. 12. According to George Wilson Pierson, despite the fact that Tocqueville himself "personally believed that he was using a scientific method, and the most rigorous accuracy," *Democracy* was "scientific neither in method nor in result." Pierson, *Tocqueville and Beaumont in America* (New York: Oxford University Press, 1938), p. 758.

10. For an overview of this tradition, see André Jardin, *Tocqueville: A Biography*, translated by Lydia Davis with Robert Hemenway (New York: Farrar Straus Giroux, 1989), pp. 101–5.

11. It is in many ways paradoxical that Tocqueville has been dubbed the father of contemporary political science. As will become clear in the following discussion, the economic vocabulary and presuppositions that currently dominate many parts of the discipline would have been anathema to him.

12. See, for example, Chejne, "Travel Books in Modern Arabic Literature," and Boyer, "Travel and Transport, Western European."

13. Redfield, "Herodotus the Tourist," p. 98.

14. Said, "The Mind of Winter," p. 55, emphasis in the original.

15. Al-Tahtawi (and his students) is often credited with developing the Arabic equivalent of "nation" in his concept of *watan* (literally "homeland"), and pioneering a variety of patriotic poems (*qasayid wataniyya*) that expressed what might be called a nationalist sensibility. See for example Jack A. Crabbs, Jr., *The Writing of History in Nineteenth-Century Egypt: A Study in National Transformation* (Cairo: The American University in Cairo Press, 1984), p. 78. In this connection, see also Jamal Hamdan, *Shakhsiyyat Misr dirasa fi ʿabqariyyat al-makan* (Cairo: Maktabat al-Nahda al-Misriyya, 1970); Khaldun S. al-Husry, *Three Reformers: A Study in Modern Arab Political Thought* (Beirut: Khayats, 1966), pp. 29–30; Heyworth-Dunne, "Rifaʿah Badawī Rafiʿ al-Tahtāwī: The Egyptian Revivalist," p. 399; Ezzat Orany, " 'Nation,' 'Patrie,' 'Citoyen,' chez Rifaʿa al-Tahtāwi et Khayr-al-Dīn Al-Tounsi," *Mélanges de l'Institut Dominicain d'Etudes Orientales du Caire* (156), 1983: pp. 179–81. As Altman points out, Tahtawi tended to situate Egypt within the larger context of the Islamic *umma* in the 1830s, but by the 1860s and 1870s, his primary emphasis was on the position of Egypt vis-à-vis Europe ("The Political Thought of Rifaʿah Rafiʿ at-Tahtawi"). Consequently, it is in his later writings that the definition and relationship between his national and religious allegiances are spelled out most explicitly (for example, in *Manahij al-Albab al-Misriyya fi Mabahij al-Adab al-ʿAsriyya* [Cairo: Matbaʿat Shirkat al-Rajaʾib, 1912] and *Kitab al-Murshid al-Amin li-l-Banat wa al-Banin* [Egypt: Matbaʿat al-Madaris al-Malakiyya, 1872]). See Orany, " 'Nation,' 'Patrie,' 'Citoyen,'" pp. 174, 177; Anouar Abdel-Malek, *Idéologie et Renaissance National, l'Egypte Moderne* (Paris: Editions Anthropos, 1969), p. 227; and Albert Hourani, *Arabic Thought in the Liberal Age: 1798–1939* (Cambridge: Cambridge University Press, 1983), pp. 78–79. Given the scholarly debate on this topic and the fact that Tahtawi's arguments in the later *Manahij* in many ways are different from those of the *Rihla*, I will conduct this analysis primarily in terms of *Takhlis*.

16. Anderson, *Imagined Communities* (London: Verso, 1992), pp. 53–65.

17. As Melvin Richter argues, it is only in light of the "practicing statesman . . . [whose] ideas were oriented to choice and actions, rather than to careful definition and systematic consistency" that Tocqueville's arguments about Algeria on the one hand and America on the other, can be rendered intelligible. Richter, "Tocqueville on Algeria," *The Review of Politics* 25 (1963), pp. 363–65. Olivier Zunz points out that "Tocqueville was genuinely torn between theory and action and, in fact, valued the latter more than the former. . . . He worked hard, albeit unsuccessfully, at being an effective politician. He was upset when excluded from political life, even in self-inflicted retirement." Zunz, "Holy Theory," *Reviews in American History* 30, no. 4 (2002): p. 566.

18. Richter, "Tocqueville on Algeria," p. 366.

19. For an account of Tahtawi's role in the mapping of Sudan for Egyptian nationalist and colonialist purposes, see Troutt Powell's excellent "From Odyssey to Empire: Mapping Sudan through Egyptian Literature in the Mid-19th Century," and *A Different Shade of Colonialism: Egypt, Great Britain, and the Mastery of the Sudan* (Berkeley: University of California Press, 2003).

20. Tahtawi himself provides only one vague reason for the exile, namely "slander on the part of a personage," (*Manahij*, p. 265) who may well have been his rival for power in the translation bureaucracy, ʿAli Mubarak, a reason also suggested by Heyworth-Dunne and Newman (pp. 54–55). Among those who endorse the idea that the publication of the second edition of the *Rihla* and its detailing of the French parliamentary system provoked the enmity of ʿAbbas are Newman (*An Imam in Paris*, pp. 52–53) and Louca, in his introduction to *L'Or de Paris* (pp. 31–32). Heyworth-Dunne emphasizes the hostility of the ʿulama to al-Tahtawi in his *Introduction to the History of Education in Modern Egypt*, p. 297, and in his "Rifaʿah Badawī Rafiʿ al-Tahtāwī: The Egyptian Revivalist," p. 967.

21. Moosa, *The Origins of Modern Arabic Fiction* (Boulder, CO: Lynne Rienner, 1997), p. 6.

22. *Mawaqiʿ al-Aflak fi waqaʾiʿ Tilimak* (Beirut: al-Matbaʿa al-Suriya, 1867), p. 22.

23. *Takhlis*, p. 7.

24. *Manahij al-Albab al-Misriyya fi Mabahij al-Adab al-ʿAsriyya* [Program for Egyptian Minds in the Pleasures of the Modern Arts/Manners] , pp. 265ff.

25. Troutt Powell, *A Different Shade of Colonialism*, p. 30, and "From Odyssey to Empire," p. 424. See also Pollard, "The Habits and Customs of Modernity." One might well attribute this shift in attitude to the difference between voluntary travel and involuntary exile, yet the continuity of his arguments regarding *bilad al-Sudan* from the *Rihla* to this *qasida* suggest otherwise. Indeed, in the *Rihla*, Tahtawi includes a poem he wrote memorializing Muhammad ʿAli's greatness, and in it Tahtawi's celebrates how the *wali* "subjugated the insolent Sudanese." *Takhlis*, p. 57. For a discussion of Tahtawi's arguments about colonialism advanced in his *Manahij*, see Altman, "The Political Thought of Rifaʿah Rafiʿ at-Tahtawi," pp. 96ff, and Troutt Powell, pp. 47–55.

26. See Laura Franey, "Ethnographic Collecting and Travel: Blurring Boundaries, Forming a Discipline," *Victorian Literature and Culture* (2001): p. 219.

27. Troutt Powell, "From Odyssey to Empire: Mapping Sudan Through Egyptian Literature in the mid-19th Century," p. 404.

28. According to Jacob Landau, inasmuch as nineteenth-century Arab travel literature is still organized around ʿajaʾib, it is closer to medieval travel accounts than those of the twentieth-century, which tend to "stress factual information, usually presented attractively, with a clear starting point." This, however, misses the shift in character in the *kinds* of marvels emphasized in a nineteenth-century *rihla* such as *Takhlis*, thus positing the existence of a radical break between "modern" and "pre-modern" travel literature that is not quite evident. Landau, "Muhammad Thabit, a Modern Arab Traveler," *The Journal of Arabic Literature* 1 (1970): pp. 70, 74.

29. For a more detailed discussion of this, see Euben, *Enemy in the Mirror: Islamic Fundamentalism and the Limits of Modern Rationalism*, p. 21. What I am calling the "modernization narrative" here does not refer to outdated versions of modernization theory but rather refers to, in Ira Lapidus's words, "processes of centralization of state power and the development of commercialized or capitalist economies which entail the social and cultural changes we call modernity," Lapidus, "Islamic Revival and Modernity: The Contemporary Movements and the Historical Paradigms," *Journal of the Economic and Social History of the Orient* 40 (1997): p. 444, n. 1.

30. Although *entzauberung* is often translated as "disenchantment," Stephen Kalberg argues persuasively that Weber intended it to signify the religiously specific concept of "de-magification" rather than "disenchantment," which is a "far more general term that conjures up images of the romanticist's yearning for the *Gemeinschaft* and an earlier, simpler world." Kalberg, "Max Weber's Types of Rationality: Cornerstones for the Analysis of Rationalization Processes in History," *American Journal of Sociology* 81 (March 1980): p. 1146, n. 2.

31. The quotation marks here are meant to signal that what travels under the rubric of "modernity" is less a set of universal characteristics than historically specific European experiences universalized as modernity as such by way of the rise and spread of Euro-American power. Thus the modern period for the Islamic *umma* (community) is largely framed by the rise and spread of European power from the 18th century on, a development that also served as a transmission belt for the West's claim to embody a modernity that is, in essence, an expression of the ways in which Europe has ordered its past in relation to its present. More specifically, the West's self-defined modernity congealed in contrast to both the distant past of the ancient Greeks and the more immediate past of the European Middle Ages in which "a Great Chain of Being" issuing from God was said to hold sway.

32. Max Weber, *The Sociology of Religion*, trans. Ephraim Fischoff (Boston: Beacon Press, 1964), p. 166.

33. K. Anthony Appiah, foreword to Saskia Sassen's *Globalization and its Discontents* (New York: New Press, 1998), p. xi, emphasis in the original.

34. For instance, both Tahtawi and Tocqueville had exchanges with a leading French Orientalist, Sylvestre de Sacy, both were influenced by Montesquieu, Tocqueville used Muhammad ʿAli's Egypt as an illustration of absolute rule, and the *Rihla* contains a detailed account of the French Revolution of 1830.

35. The nature and controversial legacy of Muhammad ʿAli's rule is itself the subject of an enormous amount of scholarship. For an introduction to the man, see "Muhammad ʿAli Pasha," *Encyclopedia of Islam*, by E. R. Toledano, and for overviews of his role in the making of modern Egypt, see Afaf Lutfi Al-Sayyid Marsot, *A Short History of Modern Egypt* (Cambridge: Cambridge University Press, 1985), P. J. Vatikiotis, *The Modern History of Egypt* (London: Weidenfeld and Nicolson, 1969), and Helen Anne B. Rivlin, *The Agricultural Policy of Muhammad ʿAli in Egypt* (Cambridge, MA: Harvard University Press, 1961).

36. See *Encyclopedia of Islam*, "Mamluk," by D. Ayalon

37. Jamal Mohammed Ahmed, *The Intellectual Origins of Egyptian National-ism* (New York: Oxford University Press, 1960), pp. 6–7.

38. Newman, *An Imam in Paris*, p. 28.

39. Beginning in 1809, Muhammad ʿAli dispatched various students to Europe, and Italy in particular, to study engineering, military and naval sciences, the art of printing, and so on. For an overview of these missions as well as a discussion of the shift in destination from Italy to France, see Alain Silvera's "The First Egyptian Student Mission to France under Muhammad ʿAli," *Middle Eastern Studies* 16, no. 20 (1980): pp. 1–22, Pollard, "The Habits and Customs of Modernity," and Newman's introduction to *An Imam in Paris*.

40. Stanley Lane Poole, *Life of Edward William Lane* (London: Williams and Norgate, 1877), pp. 70–71.

41. Heyworth-Dunne, *History of Education in Modern Egypt*, p. 266 and Newman, *An Imam in Paris*, p. 44.

42. Japanese and Egyptian Enlightenment, pp. 38–39; Hasan al-ʿAttar, *Hashi-yat Abi al-Saʿada Hasan al-ʿAttar ʿala Sharh al-tahdhib li-ʿUbayd Allah ibn Fadl al-Khabisi* (Cairo: Matbaʿat Bulaq, 1879), p. 259.

43. Al-Tahtawi, *Takhlis al-Ibriz ila Talkhis Bariz; aw al-Diwan al-nafis bi-iwan Baris* (Egypt: Dar al-Taqaddum, 1905), p. 4. Hereafter referred to as *Takhlis*. Daniel L. Newman has recently translated the *Rihla* in its entirety into English under the title *An Imam in Paris: Al-Tahtawi's Visit to France (1826–1831)*, as has Tarek Shamma (unpublished manuscript). While both are excellent, I have opted to use my own translations.

44. Ibid., pp. 4, 5.

45. Such religious sciences include Qurʾanic exegesis, the Hadith (all the collected practices and sayings of the Prophet Muhammad), Islamic jurisprudence (*fiqh*), and all the various disciplines designed to facilitate understanding and elaboration of them.

46. Although Muhammad ʿAli was the driving force behind the student mission, as Altman points out, the intended audiences for *Takhlis* were primarily native Egyptians in Muhammad ʿAli's bureaucracy and in his government schools, as well as the "social and spiritual leadership of the native social groups" which was "comprised of the native ʿulama," ("The Political Thought of Rifaʿah Rafiʿ at-Tahtawi," p. 76).

47. *Takhlis*, p. 5.

48. John W. Livingston, "Western Science and Educational Reform in the Thought of Shaykh Rifaʿa al-Tahtawi," *International Journal of Middle East Studies* 28 (1996), pp. 544–45.

49. *Takhlis*, p. 4.

50. Ibid., p. 8.

51. Ibid., pp. 9, 20.

52. Ibid., pp. 25, 4.

53. Ibid., pp. 10, 25.

54. Ibid., pp. 43, 5, 10.

55. Ibid., p. 2. Regarding *baraka*, see chapter 2 of this book.

56. Ibid., pp. 10–11. Newman argues that this hadith was particularly popular among 19th-century Muslim reformers as a way to justify the acquisition of European knowledge.

57. Ibid., p. 20.

58. Ibid., p. 20.

59. Ibid., p. 61.

60. Tocqueville traveled to Italy, Switzerland, Germany, England, Ireland, and Algeria, sometimes visiting more than once.

61. Jardin, *Tocqueville: A Biography*, pp. 106–7. Scholars such as Jardin and others generally rely for their accounts of Tocqueville's itinerary on Pierson's *Tocqueville and Beaumont in America*. More recent accounts of the relationship between Tocqueville's itinerary and his ideas include James T. Schleifer's *The Making of Tocqueville's* Democracy in America (Chapel Hill: University of North Carolina Press, 1980) and Lamberti's *Tocqueville and the Two Democracies*, trans. Arthur Goldhammer (Cambridge, MA: Harvard University Press, 1989).

62. Jardin, *Tocqueville: A Biography*, p. 107. Virtually every aspect of Tocqueville's thought has cheerleaders and critics. Scholars who dispute Tocqueville's accuracy have not only suggested that there is much that Tocqueville simply missed—the experience of ordinary Americans, the material bases of American life, the impact of the steamboat and an emerging railroad system—but also that his method often entailed searching only for evidence that could corroborate his preformed ideas. Other scholars accuse him of making snap judgments without warrant or sufficient evidence, from his claim that Americans are "antipoetic" to his conclusion on the basis of his visit to one state capital, Albany, that in America there is an "absence of what we call government or the administration" (*Democracy*, p. 72). See Pierson, *Tocqueville and Beaumont in America*, pp. 755–67; Edward Pessen, *Jacksonian America: Society, Personality, and Politics* (Illinois: The Dorsey Press, 1969), p. 44ff; Garry Wills, "Did Tocqueville 'Get' America?" *The New York Review of Books*, April 29, 2004; and Klaus Hansen, "Tocqueville: Frenchman for All Seasons?" *Canadian Journal of History/Annales Canadiennes d'histoire* 38 (August 2003): 295–305.

63. Quoted in Pierson, *Tocqueville and Beaumont in America*, p. 86.

64. Ibid., p. 737.

65. Richter, "Tocqueville on Algeria," p. 362.

66. Quoted in Jardin, *Tocqueville: A Biography*, pp. 91–94.

67. Quoted in Ibid., p. 90.

68. Ibid., pp. 88–90.

69. From a letter dated October 4, 1830, quoted in Ibid., p. 90.

70. Pierson, *Tocqueville and Beaumont in America*, pp. 27–28.

71. *L'ancien régime et la Révolution* (Paris: Michel Lévy Frères, 1856). Cheryl Welch's overview of the wax and wane of American and French interest in Tocqueville's work is instructive here. She notes that while recent French scholarship reveals new interest in Tocqueville's entire oeuvre, "Americans have been appropriating him, as they have in the past, to reflect on the particular social and institutional underpinnings of their own exceptional democratic experiment. And, as always, they focus almost exclusively on the two volumes of *Democracy in America*." Welch, *De Tocqueville* (Oxford: Oxford University Press,

2001), p. 234 and p. 220ff. For an account of the changing fortunes of *Democracy in America* in the United States, see Robert Nisbet, "Many Tocquevilles," *American Scholar* 46 (winter 1976–77): pp. 59–75.

72. Lamberti, *Tocqueville and the Two Democracies*, p. 2.

73. Mark Hulliung, *Citizens and Citoyens: Republicans and Liberals in America and France* (Cambridge, MA: Harvard University Press, 2002), p. 17.

74. *Democracy in America*, p. 256.

75. Letter to Louis de Kergolay (1831), in *Selected Letters on Politics and Society*, trans. Roger Boesche and James Toupin (Berkeley: University of California Press, 1985), p. 58.

76. Letter to Ernest de Chabrol (1831), in Ibid., p. 59.

77. Tocqueville, *Democracy in America* (New York: Anchor, 1969), trans. George Lawrence, "Author's Preface to the 12th Edition." All subsequent references to *Democracy in America* refer to the 1969 Anchor Books, 12th edition.

78. Unpublished letter, quoted in Jardin, *Tocqueville: A Biography*, p. 90.

79. *Democracy*, p. 18.

80. Ibid., p. 404; Letter to Louis de Kergorlay (1831), in Olivier Zunz and Alan S. Kahan, eds., *The Tocqueville Reader: A Life in Letters and Politics* (Oxford: Blackwell, 2002), p. 48.

81. Letter to Eugène Stoffels (February 21, 1835) in *Selected Letters on Politics and Society*, p. 99. Thus Tocqueville writes during a journey to England that "it is the manner in which the smallest of affairs are managed that leads to a comprehension of what is happening in the great ones." Letter to Louis de Kergorlay (August 4, 1857), *Selected Letters on Politics and Society*, p. 356.

82. Lamberti, *Tocqueville and the Two Democracies*, p. 10. Scholars have traced the origin of many of Tocqueville's ideas about America to a series of lectures François Guizot delivered on the history of civilization in Europe (1828–29) that both Tocqueville and Beaumont attended before the trip to the United States, and which Tocqueville did not acknowledge in the final version of *Democracy in America*. Pierson, *Tocqueville and Beaumont in America*, p. 23, 33, and Melvin Richter, "Tocqueville and Guizot on Democracy: From a Type of Society to a Political Regime," *History of European Ideas* 30 (2004): pp. 61–82. It is this tendency that prompted one of his contemporaries, Sainte-Beuve, to say of Tocqueville that "he began to think before having learned anything."

83. *Democracy in America*, p. 209; Tocqueville, *Journeys to England and Ireland*, trans. George Lawrence and J. P. Mayer (New Brunswick, NJ: Transaction, 1988), p. 18.

84. Alexis de Tocqueville, *Memoir, Letters and Remains*, vol. 1, translated by the translator of *Napoleon's Correspondence with King Joseph* (London: Macmillan, 1861), p. 359.

85. Wolin, *Tocqueville between Two Worlds*, pp. 35–36.

86. Tocqueville, *Democracy in America*, vol. 1, conclusion, p. 408.

87. *The Edinburgh Review* 145 (October 1840): p. 7ff. J. S. Mill points out, for example, that Tocqueville "devotes but little space to the elucidation" of his presumption that increasing equality of conditions represents the recent past and entire future of Europe, but then proceeds to substantiate a modified version of precisely this claim in regard to English history. Similarly, Mill argues

that the "greatest defect" of Tocqueville's book is the "scarcity of his examples," particularly in regard to the supposed dangers of the "tyranny of the majority." But Mill again goes on to substantiate with examples what Tocqueville does not (p. 22ff).

88. Tocqueville, *Democracy in America*, p. 20.

89. Ibid., pp. 485–86.

90. Jardin, *Tocqueville: A Biography*, p. 483.

91. *Takhlis*, pp. 40–41. For an excellent discussion of this passage and the function of mirrors in the *Rihla*, see Sandra Naddaf, "Mirrored Images: Rifaʿah al-Tahtawi and the West," *Alif: Journal of Comparative Poetics* 6 (spring 1986): pp. 74–45.

92. *Democracy in America*, p. 187.

93. For an analysis of the convergence of spatial and temporal travel in tourism, for example, see Barry Curtis and Claire Pajaczkowska, " 'Getting There': Travel, Time, and Narrative," in *Travellers' Tales*, pp. 199–215.

94. Jardin, *Tocqueville: A Biography*, pp. 92–93.

95. *Democracy*, p. 12, 19, 32.

96. Ibid., p. 28.

97. Ibid., pp. 28–29. The discourse of "noble savagery" has a long history in European thought, although the antinomies it tends to presuppose and reify change sharply in response to political and historical changes. As Harry Liebersohn argues, after 1789, when civilization appeared to signify the advance of equality against the hierarchy of the past, and "nobility was losing legal force, it underwent a paradoxical revival in the imagination of observers of exotic cultures." Liebersohn, "Discovering Indigenous Nobility: Tocqueville, Chasmisso, and Romantic Travel Writing," *The American Historical Review* 99, no. 3 (June 1994): pp. 747–48.

98. Liebersohn, "Discovering Indigenous Nobility," p. 749.

99. *Democracy*, p. 328.

100. Ibid., p. 30; Liebersohn, "Discovering Indigenous Nobility," p. 755.

101. *Democracy*, p. 318.

102. This theme is developed at length by Hartog in *The Mirror of Herodotus*.

103. *Democracy*, p. 320.

104. Ibid., p. 603.

105. Tahtawi makes these arguments in much more detail in later works, such as *Manahij*. For an overview of these arguments, see Livingston, "Western Science and Educational Reform in the Thought of Shaykh Rifaʿa al-Tahtawi."

106. Melvin Richter, "Montesquieu's Theory and Practice of the Comparative Method," *History of the Human Sciences* 15, no. 2 (2002): p. 24. *Takhlis*, p. 188.

107. *Takhlis*, p. 7.

108. Ibid., pp. 7, 16.

109. Ibid., pp. 7, 96.

110. Altman, "The Political Thought of Rifaʿah Rafiʿ at-Tahtawi," pp. 68–69. Tahtawi defines *tamaddun* in *al-Murshid al-Amin li-l-Banat wa al-Banin* in the following terms: "the *tamaddun* of the homeland [*watan*] consists in the attainment of what is indispensable to a cultured people, namely the means critical

to improving their circumstances, their development in morals and customs and perfection in education, [what] stimulates them to cultivate praiseworthy characteristics, the accumulation of urban luxuries and the development of comforts." Tahtawi, *Kitab al-Murshid*, p. 124.

111. *Takhlis*, p. 8. See also Altman, "The Political Thought of Rifaʿah Rafiʿ at-Tahtawi," p. 69. Despite the Qurʾanic emphasis on Islam as a way of life encompassing both religion and this world (*din wa dunya*), the attempt to distinguish between two scales of achievement, that of religion (*din*) and of the world (*dunya*), is common to many Arab and Muslim writers, travelers and thinkers contending with the rise of European political and technological power. Matar, "Confronting Decline in Early Modern Arabic Thought."

112. *Takhlis*, p. 18.

113. Ibid., pp. 6, 22.

114. The France that Tahtawi visited was a republic and not a democracy, of course, yet in the various challenges to monarchical prerogatives—issuing in the popular uprising of 1830 which Tahtawi saw firsthand—he witnessed democratic *politics* in action, even if the events ultimately solidified a constitutional monarchy.

115. Louca, "Présentation: Le Voyage d'un orpailleur," pp. 20, 28.

116. Abu al-Hasan ʿAli b. Muhammad b. Habib al-Mawardi, *Adab al-Dunya wa al-Din*, ed. Mustafa al-Saqqa (Egypt: Mustafa al-Babi al-Halabi, 1973), pp. 17–18. For a discussion of al-Mawardi's influence on Tahtawi's later work, *Manahij*, and for an understanding of both books as part of a tradition of practical philosophy, see Juan R. Cole, "Rifaʿa al-Tahtawi and the Revival of Practical Philosophy," *Muslim World* 70 (1980): pp. 29–46.

117. Miquel suggests that ʿajaʾib is one of the crucial elements of travel *adab* literature in particular. *La géographie humaine du monde musulman jusqu'au milieu du 11e siècle*, p. 121.

118. This and other excised passages were included in Perceval's published translation of excerpts from the unpublished *Rihla*. Perceval, ""Relation d'un voyage en France, par le cheikh Réfaa."

119. *Takhlis*, pp. 176–77.

120. Rivlin, *The Agricultural Policy of Muhammad ʿAli in Egypt*, p. 106.

121. For example, *Takhlis*, p. 82.

122. Louca, "Présentation: Le Voyage d'un orpailleur," p. 21.

123. *Takhlis*, pp. 187, 188.

124. Appadurai, "Disjuncture and Difference in the Global Cultural Economy," p. 20.

125. *Takhlis*, pp. 30, 38, 51–52, 58, 105.

126. Ibid., p. 31. Louca, "Présentation: Le Voyage d'un orpailleur," p. 16, and Pollard, p. 64ff. Among the works Tahtawi studied while in Paris are Voltaire's *Dictionary of Philosophy*, Montesquieu's *Esprit de Laws* and *Lettres Persanes*, Depping's *Aperçu historique sur les moeurs et coutumes des nations* (Paris, 1826), which al-Tahtawi translated and appeared in Arabic in 1829, Etienne Bonnot de Condillac's *La Logique* (to which al-Tahtawi refers in his *rihla* as having studied while in Paris, *Takhlis*, p. 187), Malte-Brun's multivolume *Précis de la Géographie Universelle: ou description de toutes les parties du monde, sur un plan nouveau* (Brus-

sels, 1829) [the complete title in English is *System of Universal Geography, Containing a Description of all the Empires, Kingdoms, States and Provinces of the Known World, Being a System of Universal Geography or a Description of All the Parts of the World on a Known Plan, According to the Great Natural Divisions of the Globe, Accompanied with Analytical, Synoptical, and Elementary Tables*], which al-Tahtawi also refers to having read in the *Rihla* (p. 187), and the first volume of which al-Tahtawi eventually translated (it was published in 1838–39).

127. Muhammed Sawaie, "Rifaʿa Rafiʿ al-Tahtawi and his Contribution to the Lexical Development of Modern Literary Arabic," *The International Journal of Middle East Studies* 32 (2000): 395–410. A case in point is Tahtawi's rendering of civil rights as *huquq baladiyya*, literally "country rights" (*Takhlis*, p. 94), which as Newman suggests, would no doubt have had his Arabic-speaking audience scratching their heads. An example of Tahtawi's redeployment of an already existing Arabic term is his rendering of French liberté as *hurriya* (*Takhlis*, p. 83), which the *Encyclopedia of Islam* suggests had historically designated those of "noble character," that is, the opposite of slavery, much as the Indo-European word for freedom and the Latin and Greek words for liberty all referred to the opposite of slavery. (David Hackett Fischer, "Freedom's Not Just Another Word," *New York Times*, February 7, 2005). In this view, Tahtawi's equation of freedom with liberté, and his definition of *hurriya* in terms of the classical Islamic emphasis on justice and equity represents a crucial step in transforming "freedom" from its older meanings into a right to which all subjects have a claim. "Hurriyya," by F. Rosenthal and B. Lewis, *Encyclopedia of Islam*. See also Newman, *An Imam in Paris*, p. 196. See discussion below.

128. *Takhlis*, pp. 70, 78–79, 232, 113.

129. Ibid., pp. 111, 158.

130. Ibid., p. 15; "Ifrandj," *Encyclopedia of Islam*, by J.F.P. Hopkins.

131. *Takhlis*, pp. 62, 54, 154, 170, 62, 143, 60. Running alongside the primary contrast between France and Egypt is a comparison *among* Christians, more specifically between those in France and the Egyptian (Coptic) Christians, whom he portrays as filthy, ignorant, and stupid throughout the *Rihla*. *Takhlis*, pp. 31, 60, 102.

132. Ibid., pp. 63, 64, 249ff.

133. Ibid., pp. 120–38, 79.

134. Ibid., pp. 91, 148, 146, 214, 90.

135. Ibid., pp. 81–82.

136. al-Husry, *Three Reformers: A Study in Modern Arab Political Thought*, p. 17.

137. *Takhlis*, pp. 149–50, 180. This is the same de Sacy who, in 1840, would publish a largely unfavorable review of Tocqueville's *Democracy in America*, and to whom Tocqueville would later write concerning the possibility of learning Arabic for his study of colonial Algeria. Jardin, *Tocqueville: A Biography*, pp. 272, 320.

138. *Takhlis*, p. 25.

139. Ibid., p. 96.

140. Ibid., pp. 18, 150, 151.

141. Ibid., 22, 149

142. Ibid., pp. 65, 149.

143. Ibid., pp. 63, 143, 147, 60, 139–40, 142.

144. Tavakoli-Targhi, "Imagining Western Women: Occidentalism and Euro-Centrism," *Radical America* 24, no. 3 (1993): p. 76.

145. Tahtawi, *Kitab al-Murshid*, pp. 37, 54–55, 66.

146. *Takhlis*, p. 102.

147. Ibid., pp. 65, 251–52.

148. Ibid., pp. 63, 67, 250.

149. Ibid., pp. 107, 66, 44, 107.

150. Tavakoli-Targhi, "Imagining Western Women," p. 76.

151. Ibid., p. 63.

152. Ibid., p. 170.

153. *Takhlis*, pp. 41, 42.

154. Ibid., p. 139.

155. Ibid., pp. 152–53. *Bid'a* has the double connotation of innovation and heresy, in the sense that what is innovative is also a departure from precedent: the "innovator is one who introduces something on an arbitrary principle without having any basis in the recognised foundations of Islam." "Bid'a", by J. Robson, *Encyclopedia of Islam*. Yet much of Tahtawi's project here is to render innovation traditional, or at least to allow for the possibility of what he refers to as "useful innovations" (p. 155).

156. For example, Albert Hourani argues that Tahtawi blamed Muslim stagnation on Ottoman and Mamluke domination. Hourani, *Arabic Thought in the Liberal Age*, p. 82. In this connection, see also Louis ʿAwad, *Tarikh al-Fikr al-Misri al-Hadith: min al-hamla al-Faransiyya ila ʿasr Ismaʿil* (Cairo: Maktabat Madbouli, 1987). By contrast, Juan Cole insists this reading of Tahtawi "cannot be sustained," and that he had "nothing but reverence for the Ottoman sultans." Cole, *Colonialism and Revolution in the Middle East: Social and Cultural Origins of Egypt's ʿUrabi Movement* (Princeton, NJ: Princeton University Press, 1993), p. 39.

157. ʿAbd al-Rahman al-Rafiʿi, *ʿAsr Muhammad ʿAli* (Cairo: Maktabat al-Nahda al-Misriyya, 1951), pp. 510–11; Orany, "'Nation,' 'Patrie,' 'Citoyen,'" p. 177.

158. Zolandek, "Al-Tahtawi and Political Freedom," *Muslim World* 54 (1964): pp. 91–92. Crucially, Zolandek bases this interpretation of Tahtawi on his later work, *Manahij*, not the *Rihla*.

159. Altman, "The Political Thought of Rifaʿah Rafiʿ at-Tahtawi: A Nineteenth Century Egyptian Reformer." For the view of Tahtawi as largely a traditional Muslim thinker, see Vatikiotis, *The Modern History of Egypt*, pp. 118–19; Zolandek, "Al-Tahtawi and Political Freedom," pp. 90–97. For an emphasis on Tahtawi as a transitional thinker, see al-Husry, *Three Reformers: A Study in Modern Arab and Political Thought*, pp. 11–31; Hourani, *Arabic Thought in the Liberal Age*, pp. 69–84. For a reading of Tahtawi as the father of a revolutionary sociopolitical philosophy see Louis ʿAwad, *al-Muʾaththirat al-Ajnabiyya fi al-Adab al-ʿArabi al-Hadith*, vol. 2 (Cairo: Jamiʿat al-Duwal al-ʿArabiyya, Maʿhad al-Dirasat al-ʿArabiyyah al-ʿAliah, 1962), pp. 122–95, and Khayri ʿAziz, *Udaba ʿala Tariq al-Nidal al-Siyasi: Rifaʿa al-Tahtawi, Salamah Musa, ʿAbbs al-ʿAqqad, Muhammad*

Mandur (Cairo: Al-Hayʾa al-Misriyya al-ʿAmma li-l-Taʾlif wa al-Nashr, 1970), pp. 10–65. Nazik Saba Yared provides a (rather implausible) account of Tahtawi's work as expressing "nothing but admiration for the West." Yared, *Arab Travellers and Western Civilization*, trans. Sumayya Damluji Shahbandar (London: Saqi, 1996), p. 203.

160. Livingston, "Western Science and Educational Reform in the Thought of Shaykh Rifaʿa al-Tahtawi," p. 547. As Livingston suggests, for example, there is substantial disagreement about the extent to which Tahtawi's work should be seen as a pioneering synthesis of Muslim and European knowledge or as a superficial and inconsistent gloss on science adjusted to national imperatives and conventional convictions. Tahtawi's views on political rule are clearest in his later writings, in particular in *Manahij al-Albab al-Misriyya fi Mabahij al-adab al-ʿAsriyya* (1869) and *Kitab al-Murshid al-amin li-l-Banat wa al-Banin* (1872).

161. Euro-American political theorists will readily recognize the "Mirror of Princes" as referring to a medieval European genre of advice literature of which Machiavelli is perhaps the most famous (although unorthodox) example. But there is also an extensive "Mirror of Princes" genre in Islamic history. See, for example, Muhammad ibn Zafar al-Siqilli, *Sulwan al-Mutaʿ fi ʿUdwan al-Atbaʿ* [*Consolation for the Ruler during the Hostility of Subjects*], written in the 12th century. Available in translation in Joseph A. Kechichian and R. Hrair Dekmejian's *The Just Prince: A Manual of Leadership* (London: Saqi Books, 2003). See also Louise Marlow, "Kings, Prophets, and the ʿUlama in Medieval Islamic Advice Literature," *Studia Islamica* 81 (1995): 101–20.

162. Altman, "The Political Thought of Rifaʿah Rafiʿ at-Tahtawi," pp. 14, 203.

163. Livingston, "Western Science and Educational Reform in the Thought of Shaykh Rifaʿa al-Tahtawi," p. 552.

164. *Takhlis*, p. 198.

165. Ibid., p. 96.

166. Ibid., p. 91.

167. Ibid., p. 90.

168. Ibid., p. 18; Newman, *An Imam in Paris*, p. 119, n. 5.

169. For an account of the influence of Montesquieu on Tocqueville, see Melvin Richter, "The Uses of Theory: Tocqueville's Adaptation of Montesquieu," in his *Essays in Theory and History: An Approach to the Social Sciences* (Cambridge, MA: Harvard University Press, 1970), pp. 74–102.

170. In Tocqueville's work as a whole, "democracy" often seems to be a moving target, prompting Pierson to comment, "how he ever allowed himself to use *démocratie* in seven or eight different senses is still something of a mystery." Pierson, *Tocqueville and Beaumont in America*, p. 757. In a similar vein, Lamberti argues that in Tocqueville's oeuvre, democracy "can refer to political realities as different as France and the United States, and it can be used as both an antonym and synonym of revolution." Lamberti, *Tocqueville and the Two Democracies*, p. 5. Seymour Drescher suggests that notes for *Democracy in America* show Tocqueville recognizing and trying to sort out this very problem, but without any appreciable impact on the final manuscript. Drescher, *Tocqueville and England* (Cambridge, MA: Harvard University Press, 1964), p. 215. For a

discussion of the various "clusters" of meaning Tocqueville gave to democracy, see Schleifer, *The Making of Tocqueville's Democracy in America*, pp. 263–74.

171. *Democracy in America*, p. 13.

172. Ibid., vol. 1, chapter 2, and Tocqueville, *Journey to America*, edited by J. P. Mayer (London: Faber and Faber, 1959), p. 181. In his notes on Ohio, Tocqueville writes that "one cannot help but be astonished at the influence which the point of departure has on the good or ill destiny of peoples," Ibid., p. 263.

173. *Democracy*, p. 196.

174. Ibid., p. 503.

175. Ibid., p. 677. Despotism is also embodied by "the Turks" who are, Tocqueville writes, a people who "have never taken any part in the control of society's affairs" except for when religious inspiration has sparked participation in conquest (p. 94).

176. Ibid., p. 396.

177. Ibid., pp. 436, 540

178. Ibid., p. 462.

179. Ibid, pp. 707, 645.

180. Ibid, pp. 12, xiv.

181. Ibid., pp. 305–6.

182. Ibid, pp. 284–85.

183. Ibid, pp. 412–13, 659.

184. Ibid., pp. 566–67.

185. *Journeys to England and Ireland*, p. 18.

186. Unpublished letter to his father (1835) quoted by Jardin, *Tocqueville: A Biography*, p. 235.

187. *Democracy*, 692.

188. While Tocqueville was raised and educated as a practicing Catholic, identifies himself as such in *Democracy*, and defends Catholicism against its critics as the Christian doctrine "most favorable to equality of conditions," by his own account he suffered a crisis in faith in his youth from which it is unclear he ever completely recovered. *Democracy*, 295, 288, Letter to Mme. Swetchine (February 26, 1857) in Zunz and Kahan, *The Tocqueville Reader*, p. 336. For an analysis of the debate over the extent and consistency of Tocqueville's religious conviction and, in particular, whether Tocqueville experienced a kind of religious conversion at the end of his life, see Jardin, *Tocqueville: A Biography*, pp. 528–33.

189. *Democracy*, p. 291. In *Democracy* (p. 452), Tocqueville warns of the necessity to struggle against the particular appeal of pantheism in democratic ages, and his writings on colonialism in India and Algeria suggest he applied a double standard when it came to religions other than Christianity. As Richter writes, "whereas in almost all his other writings, religion is viewed as a potential source of strength for a free government, [in his treatment of Hinduism and Islam] it appears purely as a weak point in non-Christian societies apt to be invaded by European powers." Richter, "Tocqueville on Algeria," p. 365. See also Christopher Kelly, "Civil and Uncivil Religions: Tocqueville on Hinduism and Islam," *History of European Ideas* 20, no. 4–6 (1995): pp. 845–50, and

Tocqueville's *Writings on Empire and Slavery,* trans. by Jennifer Pitts (Baltimore: Johns Hopkins University Press, 2001).

190. *Democracy,* p. 297.

191. Ibid., pp. 442–43.

192. Ibid., p. 57.

193. Ibid., p. 697.

194. Ibid, p. 701.

195. Ibid., p. 311.

196. Letter to Louis de Kergorlay (June 29, 1891) and Letter to Eugène Stoffels (October 5, 1836) in Zunz and Kahan, *The Tocqueville Reader,* p. 46, 156–57.

197. Mill, *History of British India,* p. 5.

198. *Democracy,* pp. 705, 671.

199. *Takhlis,* p. 261.

200. Letter to Eugène Stoffels (October 5, 1836) in Zunz and Kahan, *The Tocqueville Reader,* p. 46, 156–57; *Takhlis,* pp. 9–10.

201. Heyworth-Dunne, *History of Education in Modern Egypt,* p. 265.

202. *Democracy,* pp. 232, 245.

203. Ibid., pp. 16–17.

204. Note for *Democracy,* quoted in Drescher, *Tocqueville and England,* p. 15.

205. *Journey to America,* ed. J. P. Mayer, p. 274.

206. *Democracy,* pp. 221, 631.

207. Letter to Henry Reeve (March 22, 1837) in Boesche, p. 116.

208. Letter from 1831, quoted in Pierson, *Tocqueville and Beaumont in America,* p. 32.

209. *Takhlis,* p. 4. At one point, Tocqueville also relates that he was accused of lying or of ignorance (p. 105).

CHAPTER 5: GENDER, GENRE, AND TRAVEL

1. Homer's *Odyssey,* trans. by Dougherty in *The Raft of Odysseus,* p. 4.

2. Leed, *The Mind of the Traveler,* pp. 114, 220, 221.

3. Sidonie Smith, *Moving Lives: 20th-Century Women's Travel Writing* (Minneapolis: University of Minnesota Press, 2001), p. x.

4. See, for example, Montesquieu's *Persian Letters;* Rana Kabbani's *Imperial Fictions: Europe's Myths of the Orient* (London: HarperCollins, 1986), esp. "The Salon's Seraglio"; Inderpal Grewal, *Home and Harem: Nation, Gender, Empire, and the Cultures of Travel* (Durham, NC: Duke University Press, 1996); Malek Alloula, *The Colonial Harem,* trans. Myrna and Wlad Godzich (Minneapolis: University of Minnesota Press, 1986); and Alain Grosrichard, *The Sultan's Court: European Fantasies of the East,* trans. Liz Heron (London: Verso, 1998).

5. Holland and Huggan, *Tourists with Typewriters,* p. 70.

6. Charlotte Perkins Gilman points out the irony of men insisting that women are only safe in the home where men can guard them. But, she asks, "guarded from what? From men." Gilman, *The Home: Its Work and Influence* (New York: Charlton, 1910), pp. 254–55.

7. Muhammad Khan Kirmani, *Risalah-i Nasiriyah*, quoted in Tavakoli-Targhi, "The Persian Gaze and Women of the Occident," *South Asia Bulletin* 11, nos. 1–2 (1991): p. 27.

8. The extent to which Muslim women's bodies have become the focal point of such battles was vividly illustrated in Afghanistan after American forces arrived in 2001: Taliban fixations on covering women's bodies and American preoccupations with uncovering them combined to produce an outsized focus on the burqa as well as a tendency to reduce Afghan women to objects rather than subjects. The fact that many Afghan women were and are much more concerned with feeding their children, becoming literate, having decent health care, and living free from violence all but disappeared from view. See James Meek, "Unveiled: The Secret Life of Women: The Female Victims of the Taliban's Brutal Five-year Regime Yearn for Greater Choice and Freedom," *The London Guardian*, November 16, 2001; and Laila al-Marayati and Semeen Issa, "Muslim Women: An Identity Reduced to a Burka," *Los Angeles Times*, January 20, 2002.

9. *Woman's Body, Woman's Word*, p. 106.

10. See, for example, Barbara Stowasser, "Religious Ideology, Women, and the Family: The Islamic Paradigm," in *The Islamic Impulse* (Washington D.C.: Center for Contemporary Arab Studies, 1987), pp. 262–96; Abu al-Ala Mawdudi, *Purdah and the Status of Woman in Islam* (1972; reprint Lahore, Pakistan: Islamic Publications, 1991); Rabbi Ezriel Tauber, *To Become One: The Torah Outlook on Marriage* (Monsey, NY: Shalheves, 1990), pp. 171, 173; Tzadok Shmuel Suchard, *Make Your Marriage Work* (New York: Suchard, 1981), p. 57; H. E. Yedidiah Ghatan, *The Invaluable Pearl: The Unique Status of Women in Judaism* (New York: Bloch, 1986), pp. 67, 70, 73–74 (I am grateful to Batya Swift Yasgur for these sources); Barbara Welter, "The Cult of True Womanhood: 1820–1860," *American Quarterly* 18, no. 2, part 1 (summer 1966): pp. 151–74; Ruth H. Bloch, "American Feminine Ideals in Transition: The Rise of the Moral Mother, 1785–1815, *Feminist Studies* 4, no. 2 (June 1978): pp. 101–26; Just, *Women in Athenian Law and Life*, esp. pp. 152, 192; and Cohen, *Law, Sexuality, and Society: The Enforcement of Morals in Classical Athens*.

11. Smith, *Moving Lives*, p. 11; Tapper, "*Ziyaret*: Gender, Movement and Exchange in a Turkish Community," pp. 241, 247.

12. Wolff, "On the Road Again," p. 234, emphasis in the original.

13. Linda Kraus Worley, "Through Others' Eyes: Narratives of German Women Travelling in Nineteenth-Century America," *Yearbook of German-American Studies* 21 (1986): p. 40; Tavakoli-Targhi, "The Persian Gaze and the Women of the Occident," p. 22.

14. The "shame" of such travel reflects and reinforces what one scholar has described as the presumption "that no 'decent' woman of the Chinese upper or middle class could travel even to a shop in the village without escort or covered face." Annette White-Parks, "Journey to the Golden Mountain: Chinese Immigrant Women," in *Women and the Journey: the Female Travel Experience*, ed. Bonnie Frederick and Susan H. McLeod (Washington: Washington State University Press, 1993), pp. 102, 103.

15. See, for example, *Western Women and Imperialism: Resistance and Complicity*, ed. Nupur Chaudhuri and Margaret Strobel (Bloomington: Indiana University Press, 1992), as well as previous citations.

16. Such divergent conditions suggest in part why it is that there have been several women who traveled disguised as men, from Isabelle Eberhardt and Hester Stanhope to what Cecily Mackworth describes as a "long tradition of female marabouts, several of whom had scoured the desert disguised as men" in "Arab mythology." Mackworth, *The Destiny of Isabelle Eberhardt* (New York: Ecco Press, 1975), p. 116. On Eberhardt, see also Ali Behdad's *Belated Travelers*, pp. 113–32.

17. As I suggested in chapter 2, the *rihla* has largely been a genre produced by Muslim men of a particular status and education. Similarly, one scholar has argued in regard to 19th-century Germans traveling to America that travel writers could be divided into "roughly four classes: professional authors whose customary writing was in the field of fiction; men of means—usually younger sons of noble families—who wrote semiscientific books; individuals commissioned by European governments at the state or local level to investigate and then describe conditions in America as they might affect potential emigrants; and four, persons urging settlement of a particular place, usually because of vested interests. Only one of the more than two hundred books under consideration was written by a woman." Raymon Jürgen Spahn, "German Accounts of Early Nineteenth-Century Life in Illinois," *Papers on Language and Literature* 14 (fall 1978): pp. 476–77.

18. It is a dangerous slide from analyzing, as Tim Youngs puts it, "ideological constructions of gendered discourses" to "an essentialist conviction of the differences between them," as Alison Blunt does in her discussion of Mary Kingsley's "adoption of both masculine and feminine voices and codes of conduct on her travels and in her writings" on West Africa. Youngs, "Buttons and Souls: Some Thoughts on Commodities and Identity in Women's Travel Writing," *Studies in Travel Writing: Papers from the Essex Symposium on 'Writing Travels'* (Nottingham, UK: Nottingham Trent University, 1997), p. 123; Blunt, *Travel, Gender, and Imperialism: Mary Kingsley and West Africa* (New York: Guilford Press, 1994), p. 110.

19. Fussell, *Abroad: British Literary Traveling Between the Wars* (New York: Oxford University Press, 1980), p. 197.

20. John Gray, "Memoirs of an Arabian Princess," *Tanganyika Notes and Records* 37 (1954): p. 66.

21. Andrea Wilson Nightingale, *Genres in Dialogue: Plato and the Construct of Philosophy* (Cambridge: Cambridge University Press, 1995), p. 3, emphasis in the original; Gian Biago Conte, *Genres and Readers*, trans. Glenn W. Most (Baltimore: The Johns Hopkins University Press, 1994), p. 132.

22. Plato, *The Laws*, 700d–701d.

23. Such transgressiveness and generic instability prompts one scholar to challenge the characterization of travel writing as a genre at all. As Jan Borm argues, travel writing is really a "collective term for a variety of texts, both predominantly fictional and nonfictional whose main theme is travel." Borm, "Defining Travel: On the Travel Book, Travel Writing, and Terminology," *Per-*

spectives on Travel Writing, ed. Glenn Hooper and Tim Youngs (United Kingdom: Ashgate, 2004), p. 13.

24. Clifford, "Traveling Cultures," p. 105; Leed, *The Mind of the Traveler*, p. 219. Clifford, along with Said, has been criticized for failing to acknowledge fully how travel is itself a gendered category.

25. Robertson et al., eds, *Travellers' Tales*, p. 3.

26. Suneeta Peres da Costa, "On Homesickness: Narratives of Longing and Loss in the Writings of Jamaica Kincaid," *Postcolonial Studies* 2, no. 1 (1999): p. 79.

27. Holland and Huggan, *Tourists with Typewriters*, p. 129.

28. Ibid., p. 129.

29. Billie Melman, review of "Sayyida Salme/Emily Reute, *An Arabian Princess between Two Worlds*," *The International Journal of Middle East Studies* 26, no. 3 (1994): p. 526.

30. Although there are many records of Arab and Muslim women traveling throughout history, narratives by or scholarship on such travelers in either Arabic or English are fewer than one would hope. Two examples of such scholarship in English are Tavakoli-Targhi's "Imagining Western Women: Occidentalism and Euro-Centrism," and Mervat Hatem's "Through Each Other's Eyes: The Impact on the Colonial Encounter of the Images of Egyptian, Levantine-Egyptian, and European Women, 1862–1920," in *Western Women and Imperialism*.

31. In addition to the many works already cited in this chapter see, for example, Marilyn C. Wesley, *Secret Journeys: The Trope of Women's Travel in American Literature* (Albany: State University of New York Press, 1999); Wulf Wülfing, "On Travel Literature by Women in the Nineteenth Century: Malwida von Meysenbug," *German Women in the Eighteenth and Nineteenth Centuries: A Social and Literary History*, eds. Ruth-Ellen B. Joeres and Mary Jo Maynes (Bloomington: Indiana University Press, 1986), pp. 289–304; Susan Morgan, *Place Matters* (New Brunswick, NJ: Rutgers University Press, 1996); Dea Birkett, *Spinsters Abroad: Victorian Lady Explorers* (Oxford: Basil Blackwell, 1989); Eva-Marie Kroller, "First Impressions: Rhetorical Strategies in Travel Writing by Victorian Women," *Ariel* 21 (1990): 87–99; Helen Callaway, *Gender, Culture, and Empire: European Women in Colonial Nigeria* (Urbana: University of Illinois Press, 1987); Ann Stoler, "Rethinking Colonial Categories: Communities and the Boundaries of Rule," *Comparative Studies in Society and History* 31, no. 1 (January 1989): 134–61; *Ladies on the Loose: Women Travellers of the 18th and 19th Centuries*, ed. Leo Hamalian (New York: Dodd, Mead, 1981); Indira Ghose, *Women Travellers in Colonial India: The Power of the Female Gaze* (Delhi: Oxford University Press, 1998).

32. Aneta Pavlenko, "Language Learning Memoirs as a Gendered Genre," *Applied Linguistics* 22, no. 2 (2001): p. 225.

33. Sayyida Salme/Emily Reute, *An Arabian Princess between Two Worlds*, ed. E. Van Donzel (Leiden: Brill, 1993). Aside from the book reviews of various editions of *An Arabian Princess*, the secondary literature is particularly scanty and consists largely of Sir John Gray's "Memoirs of an Arabian Princess," van Donzel's "Sayyida Salme, Rudolph und die deutsche Kolonialpolitik," in *Die*

Welt des Islams 27 (1987): pp. 13–22, and the text of a lecture, "Sayyida Salme/ Emily Reute: Between Zanzibar and Germany, Between Islam and Christianity," first delivered by Heinz Schneppen on June 23, 1999, at the Palace Museum in Zanzibar and published by the National Museums of Tanzania as Occasional Paper No. 12 (Dar es Salaam, 1999). There is, however, a foundation in London named after her devoted to promoting "cross-cultural understanding through the teaching of languages and . . . cultural exchange." The foundation's website is www.sayyidasalmefoundation.org/ssf/index.htm.

34. Pierre-Nicolas Desmolets, quoted in George Healy's introduction to *The Persian Letters*, p. vii.

35. Marshall Berman notes this imbalance, insisting against those who have written off the novel as "exoticism or pornography" that the work "is in fact one of the first *Bildunsromane*, a novel of education and self-discovery . . . [and] the first distinctively *political* novel written in the West. Its personal and political themes are thoroughly intertwined: Usbek's seraglio is at one a household, a society and a state." Berman, *The Politics of Authenticity: Radical Individualism and the Emergence of Modern Society* (New York: Atheneum, 1970), pp. 6, 7, emphasis in the original. Unfortunately, Berman advances this argument by way of a reading that subsumes the polyphony of the text into a "basic unity" through which "the emergence of a radically new form of individualism in European civilization" is announced, an interpretation that, as I will discuss below, problematically renders Usbek the sole philosophical pivot of the novel. Berman, pp. 5, 8.

36. I learned much about the *Persian Letters* from participants in the Liberty Fund Colloquium, "Liberty, Despotism, and Nature in Montesquieu's *Persian Letters*," held May 2002, in Emigrant, Montana, and I am indebted to them and to Stuart D. Warner in particular.

37. There is evidence suggesting that Montesquieu may also have been inspired by the journey of Iranian Muhammad Riza Bayk to France in 1714. See Tavakoli-Targhi's "Imagining Western Women: Occidentalism and Euro-Centrism," p. 74, and p. 85, n. 9.

38. Among the most important of the sources Montesquieu relied on are two he mentions in *The Persian Letters*, (LXXII): Jean-Baptiste Tavernier's *Les six voyages de Jean-Baptiste Tavernier . . . en Turquie, en Perse, et aux Indes* (The Hague, 1718), and Jean Chardin's *Voyages de Monsieur le Chevalier Chardin en Perse et autres lieux de l'Orient* (Amsterdam, 1711). Two others were Sir Paul Ricaut's *Histoire de l'État présent de l'Empire ottoman*, trans. M. Briot (Amsterdam, 1670) and Joseph Pitton de Tournefort, *Relation d'un voyage fait par ordre du Roy* (Lyon, 1717). For a discussion of Montesquieu's sources on Persia and Turkey, see David Young, "Montesquieu's View of Despotism and His Use of Travel Literature," *The Review of Politics* 40, no. 3 (July 1978): pp. 392–405.

39. Pauline Kra, for example, contends that "beneath the variety which gives an impression of disorder, he achieved a basic order" disclosed by juxtaposition with the arguments in *The Spirit of the Laws* of which "the moral, political and sociological ideas" of the *Persian Letters* are forerunners. From this vantage, the close reader can locate a series of subjects organized "in a logical sequence," which constitute the "invisible chain" of the novel. Kra, "The Invis-

ible Chain of the *Lettres Persanes*," *Studies in Voltaire and the 18th Century* 23 (1963): p. 11. Although Lucas Swaine suggests that "the mere fact that Montesquieu alludes to the existence of a secret chain does not go to show that one is actually present" in the novel, Swaine then proceeds to "reveal" that the secret chain is actually the literary techniques designed to disclose how "self-interest can overawe justice, emphasizing the need for fair and reasonable third party involvement in order to achieve justice in human affairs." Swaine, "The Secret Chain: Justice and Self-Interest in Montesquieu's *Persian Letters*," *History of Political Thought* 22, no. 1 (spring 2001): pp. 85, 84.

40. Healy, "Translator's Introduction," p. ix, *Persian Letters*. Others were even less generous, dismissing it simply as a "piece of frivolity and protracted joke"; a book bogged down with "logical inconsistency"; a chaotic "mass of ideas" that are "often confused, undeveloped and inconsistent"; or as a failed novel, a "rather unhappy experiment" the effect of which "was to retard the development of the epistolary novel." Werner Stark, *Montesquieu: Pioneer of the Sociology of Knowledge* (Toronto: University of Toronto Press, 1961), p. 7; Robert Shackleton, *Montesquieu: A Critical Biography* (Oxford: Oxford University Press, 1961), p. 45; F. C. Green, "Montesquieu the Novelist and Some Imitations of the 'Lettres Persanes,'" *The Modern Language Review* 20 (1925): p. 37.

41. Christopher J. Betts goes as far as claiming that the *Persian Letters* "inaugurated that eighteenth-century phenomenon known as the Enlightenment, a literary and intellectual movement which, in the name of freedom and humanity, attacked almost every traditional value in sight." Introduction to *The Persian Letters* (New York: Penguin, 1973), p. 18.

42. Berlin, *Against the Current: Essays in the History of Ideas* (London: Hogarth Press, 1979), p. 136.

43. Starobinski, *Blessings in Disguise; or, The Morality of Evil*, trans. Arthur Goldhammer (Cambridge, MA: Harvard University Press, 1993), p. 61, emphasis in the original.

44. Ibid., p. 63, emphasis in the original.

45. Ibid., pp. 68, 72. Starobinski even argues that the "'voluptuous' images are described with too much comaisance not to correspond to the imaginary lusts of Montesquieu." *Montesquieu par lui-meme* (Paris: Éditions du Seuil, 1953), p. 68, translated in Diana J. Schaub, *Erotic Liberalism: Women and Revolution in Montesquieu's* Persian Letters (London: Rowman and Littlefield, 1995), p. 6.

46. Starobinski, *Blessings in Disguise*, pp. 69–71.

47. Ibid., p. 74. See also Roger Laufer, *Style rococo, style des "lumières"* (Paris: J. Corti, 1963).

48. Starobinski, *Blessings in Disguise*, pp. 74–75.

49. Christopher J. Betts, *Montesqueiu: Lettres persanes* (London: Grant and Cutler, 1994), pp. 15–16. Even Berlin qualifies his characterization of Montesquieu as a "father of the Enlightenment" by suggesting that he "did not altogether share in this mood," (Berlin, p. 136), and Judith Shklar suggests that the polyphonic form of the epistolary genre "suited Montesquieu's skeptical purposes perfectly." Shklar, *Montesquieu* (Oxford: Oxford University Press, 1987), p. 30.

50. Gearhart, *The Open Boundary of History and Fiction*, p. 113;

51. According to Starobinski, for example, "Rica merely complements Usbek, who plays the leading role," *Blessings in Disguise*, p. 68.

52. I am grateful to Stuart Warner for pointing this out to me.

53. Starobinski, *Blessings in Disguise*, p. 68.

54. Montesquieu here uses the term *seraglio*, an Italian approximation of a Turkish word for royal palace, rather than using the correct Arabic term for the women's quarters—*harem*.

55. Hundert, "Sexual Politics and the Allegory of Identity in Montesquieu's *Persian Letters*," *The Eighteenth Century* 31, no. 2 (1990): p. 106.

56. The equation of the veil with despotism and disclosure with freedom is, of course, characteristic of much contemporary Euro-American commentary on women and Islam.

57. Pucci, "Orientalism and Representations of Exteriority in Montesquieu's *Lettres Persanes*," *The Eighteenth Century* 26 (1985): p. 264. Josué V. Harari's actually places the eunuch at the "center of the novel's system of meaning just as he is at the center of the seraglio's chain of command." *Scenarios of the Imaginary: Theorizing the French Enlightenment* (Ithaca: Cornell University Press, 1987), p. 70. On the particular place of the eunuch in the European imaginary and its highly racialized character, see Grosrichard, *The Sultan's Court*, esp. pp. 148–65.

58. Hegel, *The Phenomenology of Mind*, 5th ed., trans. J. B. Hallie (1807; reprint London: George Allen and Unwin, 1961), "Independence and Dependence of Self-Consciousness: Lordship and Bondage."

59. Hundert, "Sexual Politics and the Allegory of Identity," p. 109.

60. Starobinski, *Blessings in Disguise*, p. 75.

61. Ibid., pp. 82–83.

62. Said, *Orientalism* (New York: Pantheon, 1978), p. 20–21.

63. As Ahmad Gunny demonstrates, the Islam and Persia portrayed in the novel are full of inaccuracies and rife with classic Christian myths despite the fact that, in some cases, Montesquieu was clearly familiar with fairly accurate French sources on the subject. Gunny, "Montesquieu's View of Islam in the *Lettres persanes*," in *Studies on Voltaire and the Eighteenth Century*, ed. Haydn Mason (Oxford: Cheney and Sons, 1978), pp. 151–66. While it is perhaps an overstatement to attribute to Montesquieu a hostility to Islam commensurate with that of Voltaire (Gunny, p. 161), it is equally implausible to insist that Montesquieu's allusions are "never fictions, conjured up by the author's fertile imagination," that the author is "careful, even in matters of the smallest detail, to ensure that his story shall bear the stamp of verisimilitude," and that his work in general flows from the "pen of the scrupulous scholar who collected evidence in support of his theories from all parts of the world." Muriel Dodds, "The Persian Background of the *Lettres persanes*," *Durham University Journal* 29 (1935): pp. 88, 158, 167.

64. Shklar, *Montesquieu*, p. 46.

65. It is the need to preserve himself from enemies flourishing at a corrupt court that Usbek gives as the second motivation for his departure from Isfahan (VIII).

66. *The Spirit of the Laws*, trans. Anne M. Cohler, Basia Carolyn Miller, and Harold Samuel Stone (Cambridge: Cambridge University Press, 1989), book XVII, 6. Earlier, Montesquieu writes: "Hence it follows that the genius of the Getic or Tartarian nation has always resembled that of the empires of Asia. The people in these are governed by the cudgel; the inhabitants of Tartary by whips. The spirit of Europe has ever been contrary to these manners; and in all ages, what the people of Asia have called punishment those of Europe have deemed the most outrageous abuse" (book XVII, 5).

67. Healy, Introduction to *The Persian Letters*, p. x. Pucci, "Orientalism and Representations of Exteriority," pp. 264, 277. Hundert contrasts the detailed picture of French life, even refracted through the alien and deliberately alienating language of the "Persian foreigners," to the deployment of "signifiers as formal symbols" when it comes to the Persians (pp. 104–5).

68. Pucci, "Orientalism and Representations of Exteriority," p. 276.

69. I am grateful to Stuart Warner for pointing this out to me.

70. Schaub, *Erotic Liberalism*, p. 4; C. A. Sainte-Beuve, "Montesquieu," in *Portraits of the Eighteenth Century: Historic and Literary*, trans. Katharine P. Wormeley (New York: Frederick Ungar, 1964), 1:128. More recently, scholars have recognized the importance of the "harem plot" to establish, among other things, a critical perspective on Usbek's standing as "hero."

71. See for example, Berman, *The Politics of Authenticity*, p. 8.

72. Goodman, *Criticism in Action: Enlightenment Experiments in Political Writing* (Ithaca: Cornell University Press, 1989), p. 24.

73. *An Arabian Princess between Two Worlds*, p. 405.

74. Mrs. Charles E. B Russell, *General Rigby, Zanzibar and the Slave Trade, with Journals, Dispatches, Etc.* (London: George Allen and Unwin, 1935), p. 309.

75. *An Arabian Princess*, p. 389.

76. Ibid., Van Donzel's introduction, p. 32.

77. Salme denies that she was ever in any danger. Then again (see below), she deals with all these events in exactly three pages, and with hindsight clearly regrets her participation in the unsuccessful coup to usurp Madjid from the throne, and so is perhaps anxious to deny his complicity in any plot to kill her. Based on the extensive research completed by van Donzel, however, there is evidence to suggest that her pregnancy by Reute had, at the very least, put pressure on Sultan Madjid to execute her as a matter of honor. See van Donzel's introduction, pp. 15–16.

78. Although christened "Emily Reute," there is sufficient evidence in both the *Memoirs* and *Letters Home* that she never ceased to think of herself as "Salme," and so I have taken my cue from her. See *An Arabian Princess*, p. 457.

79. *An Arabian Princess between Two Worlds*, p. 107.

80. Da Costa, "On Homesickness," pp. 76, 80.

81. Schneppen, "Sayyida Salme/Emily Reute," p. 1.

82. Under the auspices of Brill Publishers, van Donzel has also included as part of *An Arabian Princess* the eleven page "Sequels to My Memoirs," which detail Salme's attempts to gain the help of the German government to obtain her inheritance from Zanzibar, as well as the brief "Syrian Customs and Us-

ages," Salme's observations on her time in Beirut, where she lived from 1892 to 1914.

83. *The Madwoman in the Attic: The Woman Writer and the Nineteenth-Century Literary Imagination* (New Haven: Yale University Press, 1979), p. 51.

84. Such negotiating strategies were at times much more than rhetorical: as Behdad's fascinating analysis of the travels of Wilfrid and Lady Anne Blunt suggests, their "orientalist journeys" reproduced a gendered division of labor within the marriage, one that not only mirrored 19th-century gender norms but "reaffirmed and deepened these in ways that made Lady Anne doubly dependent on Wilfrid's authority." Behdad, *Belated Travelers*, pp. 94–102. On the Blunt's journeys, see also Billie Melman, *Women's Orient: English Women and the Middle East, 1718–1918* (Ann Arbor: University of Michigan Press, 1992).

85. Smith, *Moving Lives*, pp. 18–19.

86. Ibid., p. 19.

87. Bonnie Frederick, "Fatal Journeys, Fatal Legends: The Journey of the Captive Woman in Argentina and Uruguay," in *Women and the Journey*, pp. 85–99. Aisha Ismat al-Taimuriya, a Turkish contemporary of Salme, characterizes the domestic solitude imposed on Muslim women in seclusion as an exile even "harder to bear than exile from home's homeland." Al-Taimuriya, "Introduction to the Results of Circumstances in Words and Deeds," (1887–88), trans. Marilyn Booth in *Opening the Gates: A Century of Arab Feminist Writing*, ed. Margot Badran and Miriam Cooke (Bloomington: Indiana University Press, 1988), p. 128.

88. *Letters Home*, pp. 411–12.

89. *An Arabian Princess*, p. 144. Here it is worth recalling that texts explicitly located within the *rihla* genre are, for a variety of reasons discussed in chapter 2, almost exclusively authored by men. The travel experiences of Arab and Muslim women, by contrast, tend to appear in the form of memoirs, autobiographies, or even fictionalized accounts of "female travel." Driven in part by the market created by Euro-American women's "harem literature," for example, 19th-century memoirs and travel accounts by Middle Eastern women (often written in English) proliferated. See, for example, Musbah Haidar, *Arabesque* (London: Sphere, 1968); Halidé Adivar Edib, *Memoirs of Halidé Edib* (New Jersey: Gorgias Press, 2004); Selma Ekrem, *Unveiled: The Autobiography of a Turkish Girl* (New York: Ives Washburn, 1930); Zeyneb Hanoum, *A Turkish Woman's European Impressions* (New Jersey: Gorgias Press, 2004). See also Reina Lewis's "Harem Literature and Women's Travel," *ISIM* [*International Institute for the Study of Islam in the Modern World Review*] 16 (autumn 2005): pp. 48–49, and *Rethinking Orientalism: Women, Travel, and the Ottoman Harem* (New Brunswick, NJ: Rutgers University Press, 2004). For more recent examples of women's memoirs, see Sattareh Farman Farmaian, *Daughter of Persia: A Woman's Journey from Her Father's Harem through the Islamic Revolution* (New York: Anchor, 1993), Fadhma A. M. Amrouche, *My Life Story: the Autobiography of a Berber Woman*, translated by Dorothy S. Blair (New Brunswick, N.J. : Rutgers University Press, 1989), Sara Suleri, *Meatless Days* (Chicago: University of Chicago Press, 1987), Leila Ahmed, *A Border Passage: From Cairo to America—A Woman's Journey* (New York: Penguin, 1999), and the fiction of such *Beur* (children born

in France of North African parents) women writers as Leila Sebbar and Ferrudja Kessas.

90. *An Arabian Princess*, p. 262.

91. Ibid., pp. 212–13. Salme makes a similar argument on p. 269.

92. Mary Margaret Kaye, *Trade Wind* (New York: Bantam, 1981); Laura Fair, "Dressing Up: Clothing, Class, and Gender in Post-Abolition Zanzibar," *The Journal of African History* 39, no. 1 (1998): pp. 63–94.

93. *An Arabian Princess*, p. 405, n. 98.

94. Ibid., p. 276.

95. From an area, then part of the Ottoman Empire, near the Russian border, Circassians were known to be pale and dark haired, and occasionally had blue eyes.

96. The extent to which gradations of skin color established the relative value of slaves, and the way this scale operated in particular to distinguish among Circassian, Abyssinian, and the darkest African slaves are elaborated in detail by Edward Lane in *The Manners and Customs of the Modern Egyptians* (1860; reprint London: Everyman's Library, 1966), pp. 136, 190–91, as well as by Arnold Kemball, British assistant resident in the Persian Gulf in an 1842 report on the African slave trade, quoted in Bernard Lewis, *Race and Color in Islam* (New York: Harper and Row, 1971), pp. 83–84.

97. *An Arabian Princess*, pp. 174, 176, 248.

98. Ibid., p. 470.

99. *Letters Home*, p. 422.

100. Ibid., pp. 428, 427.

101. Here I borrow from W.E.B. Du Bois's concept of double consciousness as elaborated by Gilroy in *The Black Atlantic*.

102. *An Arabian Princess*, pp. 267, 268–79.

103. Ibid., p. 405.

104. Ibid., pp. 405, 413, 446, 506

105. Ibid., pp. 268, 69.

106. Ibid., pp. 214–15.

107. Claude Levi-Strauss, *Tristes Tropiques* (New York: Penguin, 1992), pp. 298–99.

108. *An Arabian Princess*, p. 363.

109. Georges Van Den Abbeele, *Travel as Metaphor: From Montaigne to Rousseau* (Minneapolis: University of Minneapolis Press, 1992), p. xix.

110. *An Arabian Princess*, p. 390.

111. Said, "The Mind of Winter," p. 55.

112. *An Arabian Princess*, p. 290. She makes the same point on p. 305.

113. Ibid., pp. 268–69.

114. Ibid., p. 211.

115. Ibid, p. 213.

116. Ibid., pp. 239–40, 340, 330. There are places in *An Arabian Princess* where Salme's language appears to 21st-century sensibilities as a kind "false consciousness," as when she refers to "the innate lust for power of Oriental princes and the passions of the Oriental in general" (p. 267), and Arabs' "inborn hotbloodedness," (p. 368) or when she writes that "the Arab, once he

loves, hangs on the beloved with such tenacity and devotion that he uncondi-
tionally loses sight of every external consideration" (p. 369). Some of this is
related to the style of European disquisitions on "the Oriental" popular in the
19th century, the phraseology in German, and what Salme no doubt thought
was necessary to explain to Europeans about "Arab culture." Some passages
are clearly meant to entertain a European audience, as well as glorify the virtues of non-European culture in exoticizing terms familiar to them. Such is the
case, for example, in Salme's description of her participation, at fifteen, in a
sacrificial feast at a sacred spring that any 19th-century Victorian tourist might
have written: the women sat around, "shining with beauty, with gaily-col-
oured, glimmering attire and with costly jewellery in the wildly-romantic, rich
vegetation of a tropical forest, in front of a merrily bubbling spring, amidst the
richest virgin nature . . . completely in accordance with the fabulous descriptions of Thousand-and-one-Nights." Ibid., p. 316.

117. Ibid, p. 269.

118. Ibid., p. 270.

119. Ibid., p. 346.

120. Ibid., pp. 271–72.

121. Ibid., p. 507.

122. Ibid., p. 322.

123. Ibid., p. 353.

124. Ibid., p. 334.

125. Ibid., pp. 324, 326, 396

126. Ibid., pp. 310–11.

127. This comment is prompted by an experience with a Jewish couple,
whose behavior Salme describes as cheap and "sordid," *Letters Home*, p. 499.
Taken in tandem with Ibn Battuta's notable dislike of the Jews he encounters
on his travels, it is worth noting how consistently Jews are regarded with suspicion in these travel narratives.

128. Van Donzel's introduction, *An Arabian Princess*, p. 9; Jane Campbell,
"Multiracialism and Politics in Zanzibar," *Political Science Quarterly* 77, no. 1
(March 1962): p. 74.

129. *An Arabian Princess*, p. 308; A.M.H. Sheriff, "The Slave Mode of Production Along the East African Coast, 1810–1873," in *Slaves and Slavery in Muslim
Africa*, vol. 2, ed. John Ralph Willis (London: Frank Cass, 1985), p. 166.

130. The extent to which an Arab sense of ethnic superiority over non-Arab
peoples (both Muslim and non-Muslim) shaded into a sense of superiority
based on color is a matter of great controversy. The Qur'an is fairly unequivo-
cal in its commitment to racial equality, stating that "among other signs of His
is the creation of the heavens and the earth, and the variety of your tongues
and complexions. Surely there are signs in this for those who understand"
(30:22). There is also much evidence pointing to a longstanding tendency
among Arab Muslims to regard matters of religious piety as superseding all
other considerations, such as differences in skin color. This is evident, for example, in Ibn Battuta's *Rihla*. Yet Arab expansion into Asia and Africa, the particular historical circumstances surrounding the slave trade, and later the
emergence of the territorial nation-state contributed to growing social and po-

litical distinctions based on race. John Hunwick, "Islamic Law and Polemic over Race and Slavery in North and West Africa (16th–19th century)," in *Slavery in the Islamic Middle East*, ed. Shaun E. Marmon, (Princeton: Markus Wiener, 1999), pp. 43–68; Troutt Powell, *A Different Shade of Colonialism*; Lewis, *Race and Color in Islam*. Many of the derogatory characterizations of black Africans and of "Zanj" (sometimes used to refer to East Africans) in particular are the same Salme uses to describe the "Negroes" of Zanzibar.

131. The Moresby Treaty of 1822 curtailed the highly profitable slave trade out of East Africa but slavery was only legally abolished in Zanzibar 1897, several years after it officially became a British protectorate. "Bu Saʿid," by C. F. Beckingham, *Encyclopedia of Islam*. As a "merchant prince," Salme's father complained that the Moresby Treaty cost him $40,000 to $50,000 in lost revenue. Sheriff, "The Slave Mode of Production along the East African Coast, 1810–1873," p. 165.

132. Lewis argues that when black slaves became more common and came to be associated with menial labor, they were accorded lesser value than white slaves (*Race and Color in Islam*, pp. 64–81). Salme's argument that lighter-skinned slaves are thus of greater value may be based on firsthand observations, but also should be located in this historical and economic context.

133. There's a great deal of scholarship demonstrating that, in fact, women's attitudes toward the colonized and those less powerful in general vary widely. Thus one 19th-century traveler, Annie Hore, argues against the slave trade by infantalizing black Africans while Salme defends the Arab slave trade on the same grounds, that is, that "Negroes" are childlike, immature and in need of discipline. Annie B. Hore, *To Lake Tanganyika in a Bath Chair* (London: Sampson Low, Marston, Searle, and Rivington, 1886), pp. 167–68; Salme's *An Arabian Princess*, pp. 327–33. See also Susan L. Blake, "A Woman's Trek: What Difference Does Gender Make?" in *Western Women and Imperialism*, pp. 32, 30; Judy Wajcman, *Feminism Confronts Technology* (University Park: The Pennsylvania State University Press, 1991), p. 143; Smith, *Moving Lives*, p. 10.

134. Tim Youngs's "Buttons and Souls: Some Thoughts on Commodities and Identities in Women's Travel Writing" in particular looks at the "role of commodities as indicators of socially constructed gender roles" among female travellers (p. 117).

135. *Discourses of Difference*, p. 106. That such ambivalence might detract from the force of the argument about Orientalism perhaps explains, Mills suggests, the general absence of women's colonial writings from pioneering critiques of Orientalist scholarship, including that of Edward Said. *Discourses of Difference*, p. 61. Such an absence paradoxically reproduces the silencing of women, often referred to as the "internal Other," at the very moment the silencing of cultural Others is brought into sharp relief. At the same time, the omission ignores and reinforces the extent to which colonialist discourse not only cohered by virtue of the exercise of representational power *across* cultures but also *within* them, in part by delegitimizing or erasing the gendered fissures or contradictions behind the idea of a coherent West.

136. *Discourses of Difference*, pp. 106, 62. Patricia Romero makes similar claims about the personal and more empathic nature of women's traveling ex-

periences. Romero, ed., *Women's Voices on Africa: A Century of Travel Writings* (New York: Markus Wiener, 1992), p. 10.

137. Mills, *Discourses of Difference*, p. 3.

138. Blake, "A Woman's Trek: What Difference Does Gender Make?" p. 19.

139. Ghose, *Women Travellers in Colonial India*, p. 9.

140. *An Arabian Princess*, p. 275.

141. Greenstein, ""Ladies Bountiful," *Women's Review of Books*, September 1992, p. 20. See also Inderpal Grewal, *Home and Harem: Nation, Gender, Empire, and the Cultures of Travel* (Durham, NC: Duke University Press, 1996). The dynamic of resistance and complicity Greenstein identifies here parallels the complex relationship between agency and passivity scholars have studied extensively in connection with women. As Nancy Cott puts it in her study of gender in 18th- and 19th-century America, for example, "women were neither victims of social change—passive receivers of changing definitions of themselves—nor totally mistresses of their destinies." Nancy Cott, *The Bonds of Womanhood: "Woman's Sphere" in New England, 1780–1835* (New Haven: Yale University Press, 1977), p. 4.

142. Martin, "Orientalism and the Ethnographer," p. 523.

CHAPTER 6: COSMOPOLITANISMS PAST AND PRESENT

1. Etienne Balibar, "The Borders of Europe," in *Cosmopolitics: Thinking and Feeling Beyond the Nation*, ed. Pheng Cheah and Bruce Robbins (Minneapolis: University of Minnesota Press, 1998), p. 220. Roland Robertson points out that since the term *globalization* gained popularity in the second half of the 1980s, it has taken on a number of meanings, not all necessarily compatible or precise. Robertson, "Mapping the Global Condition: Globalization as the Central Concept," in Mike Featherstone, ed., *Global Culture: Nationalism, Globalization, and Modernity* (London: Sage, 1990), pp. 19–20. This is especially so because "globalization" groups together multiple processes approached quite differently in various disciplines, from economics to history to cultural studies. For a useful discussion, see Jan Nederveen Pieterse, "Globalization as Hybridization," in *Global Modernities*, ed. Mike Featherstone, Scott Lash, and Roland Robertson (London: Sage, 1995), p. 45ff.

2. Pieterse, "Globalization as Hybridization," p. 46.

3. Bamyeh, "Global Order and the Historical Structures of *Dar al-Islam*," p. 218. In this connection, see also Reichmuth, "The Interplay of Local Developments and Transnational Relations in the Islamic World," pp. 37–38.

4. Some go so far as to argue that the current conditions have produced the "death of distance." Peter van der Veer, "Transnational Religion," Working Paper 01-06h, July 2001, The Center for Migration and Development, Princeton University, p. 3.

5. Pieterse, "Globalization as Hybridization," p. 58.

6. Hugh Harris, "The Greek Origins of the Idea of Cosmopolitanism," *The International Journal of Ethics* 38, no. 1 (1927): pp. 1–2. Harris refers to inscriptions at Tell-el-Amarna that indicate that Akhnaton, pharaoh of Egypt from

1375–1358 bce, viewed "himself as owing the same duties to all men, irrespective of race or nationality." He quickly concludes, however, that "this was an isolated phenomenon, without any apparent influence on the subsequent history of human thought. . . . the ancient Greeks were the first of Europeans to promulgate this idea, and it is from them that Western civilization has directly inherited it."

7. Mehta, "Cosmopolitanism and the Circle of Reason," pp. 621–22.

8. Bruce Robbins, "Comparative Cosmopolitanisms, *Social Text* 31/32 (1992): p. 183.

9. Ibid., pp. 8–10.

10. Pieterse, "Globalization as Hybridization," p. 62.

11. Sheldon Pollack, "Cosmopolitanism and Vernacular in History," *Public Culture* 12, no. 3 (2000): p. 596.

12. There are various accounts of the precise "origins" of the nation which presuppose different national ontologies. Some scholars, for example, root "the nation" in emotive solidarities evident in antiquity, while others argue that the nation-state is both dependent on and produced by material, structural, ideological, and cultural developments constitutive of the European transition from feudalism. See, for example, Anthony Smith, *The Ethnic Origins of Nations* (Oxford: Basil Blackwell, 1988), and Ernest Gellner, *Nations and Nationalism* (Oxford: Blackwell, 1983). Here I rely on Benedict Anderson's account of nations as "imagined communities" consolidated in part by the emergence of print capitalism and the decline in belief in divine providence characteristic of a post-Enlightenment world. Anderson, *Imagined Communities*.

13. Will Kymlicka, *Multicultural Citizenship: A Liberal Theory of Minority Rights* (Oxford: Clarendon Press, 1995), esp. p. 76ff.

14. Bruce Robbins, "Introduction Part I: Actually Existing Cosmopolitanism," *Cosmopolitics*, p. 12.

15. Mamadou Diouf, "The Senegalese Murid Trade Diaspora and the Making of a Vernacular Cosmopolitanism," *Public Culture* 12, no. 3 (2000), p. 679.

16. Pieterse, "Globalization as Hybridization," p. 64.

17. Elias, "The Retreat of Sociologists into the Present," pp. 150–72.

18. As Uday Singh Mehta shows, within this European genealogy there are important differences between, for example, a "cosmopolitanism of reason" that tended to infantilize colonized others, and a "cosmopolitanism of sentiments" Mehta associates with Burke, which was characterized more by sympathy than paternalism. Mehta, *Liberalism and Empire: A Study in Nineteenth-Century British Liberal Thought* (Chicago: Chicago University Press, 1999), esp. pp. 20–23. Indeed, Pauline Kleingeld discerns at least six varieties of cosmopolitanism in late-18th-century Germany alone. Kleingeld, "Six Varieties of Cosmopolitanism in Late-Eighteenth-Century Germany," *The Journal of the History of Ideas* 60, no. 3 (1999): pp. 505–24.

19. Pollack, "Cosmopolitan and Vernacular in History," p. 593.

20. Ibid., p. 602. This is a point also made by the editors of *Cosmopolitanism*, Carol A. Breckenridge, Sheldon Pollack, Homi K. Bhabha, and Dipesh Chakrabarty (Durham, NC: Duke University Press, 2002), p. 10, and William Gallois, "Andalusi Cosmopolitanism in World History," *Cultural Contacts in Building a*

Universal Civilisation: Islamic Contributions, ed. Ekmeleddin Ihsanoğlu (Istanbul: Research Center for Islamic History, Art and Culture, 2005).

21. Susan Hoeber Rudolph, *Transnational Religion and Fading States*, ed. Suzanne Hoeber Rudolph and James Piscatori (Boulder, CO: Westview Press, 1997), p. 1.

22. Isma'il ibn Muhammad al-'Ajluni al-Jirahi, *Kashf al-Khafa wa Muzil al-Ilbas* (Beirut: Mu'assasat al-Risala, 1979), vol. 1, pp.66–68. Joseph Schacht traces this expression to Abu Hanifa, arguing that it was attributed to the prophet only later. "Ikhtilaf," J. Schacht, *Encyclopedia of Islam*. For a discussion of *ikhtilaf* and counterveiling impulses toward consensus, unity, and uniformity among Muslim scholars, see Khaled M. Abou El Fadl, *And God Knows the Soldiers: The Authoritative and the Authoritarian in Islamic Discourses* (Lanham, MD: University Press of America, 2001), esp. pp. 24–25.

23. Sohail H. Hashmi, "The Qur'an and Tolerance: An Interpretive Essay on Verse 5:48," *Journal of Human Rights* 2, no. 1 (March 2003): p. 82. Some scholars see in the order of the Qur'anic Revelations a move *from* toleration of others required when Muhammad is militarily weak (the Meccan period), *to* an increasingly eliminationist stance as the *umma* grows in strength (the Medinan period). Yet as Hashmi, Muqtedar Khan, and many others insist, the authority and meaning of any one verse cannot be understood in isolation from the larger ethical thrust of the Qur'anic message in which it is embedded. This message depends not only on the (contested) chronology of the revelations, but also on the complex relationship between a set of particular historical circumstances and thematic patterns suggestive of universalist principles. Hashmi, p. 96; M. A. Muqtedar Khan, "The Quran Recognizes Jews and Christians as the Spiritual Equals of Muslims," http://www.ijtihad.org/.

24. Hashmi, "The Qur'an and Tolerance," pp. 100–101.

25. On the distinctiveness of Andalusi cosmopolitanism, which Gallois dates from 711 to 1492, see his "Andalusi Cosmopolitanism in World History," and Maria Rosa Menocal, *The Ornament of the World: How Muslims, Jews and Christians Created a Culture of Tolerance in Medieval Spain* (Boston: Little, Brown, 2002).

26. Sami Zubaida, "Cosmopolitanism and the Middle East," in *Cosmopolitanism, Identity, and Authenticity in the Middle East*, ed. Roel Meijer (Great Britain: Curzon, 1999), p. 19; Averroës, "The Book of the Decisive Treatise, Determining the Connection Between the Law and Wisdom," in *Decisive Treatise and Epistle Dedicatory*, p. 2; Gallois, "Andalusi Cosmopolitanism in World History," pp. 68–74; Hassan M. Fattah, "Islamic Pilgrims Bring Cosmopolitan Air to Unlikely City," *New York Times*, January 20, 2005, p. A4; Levtzion and Weigert, "The Muslim Holy Cities and Foci of Islamic Revivalism in the Eighteenth Century"; Bianchi, *Guests of God: Pilgrimage and Politics in the Islamic World*; and Reichmuth, "The Interplay of Local Developments and Transnational Relations in the Islamic World," pp. 21ff. Rosenthal points out the popularity of Diogenes in particular at the time, as well the "disproportionate amount of space" devoted to the Epicureans, Sceptics, and Cynics in the introductions to Arabic translations of Aristotle. Rosenthal, *Greek Philosophy in the Arab World: A Collection of Essays* (Great Britain: Variorium, 1990), 3:473, n. 1. For an extensive treat-

ment of this subject, see Dimitri Gutas, "Sayings by Diogenes Preserved in Arabic," in his *Greek Philosophers in the Arabic Tradition* (Great Britain: Ashgate Variorum, 2000), pp. 475–518. There is a burgeoning literature on "digital Islam"; see, for example, Karim H. Karim, "Muslim Encounters with New Media: Towards and Inter-Civilizational Discourse on Globality?" pp. 36–60, and Peter G. Mandaville, "Reimagining the *Ummah*? Information Technology and the Changing Boundaries of Political Islam," pp. 61–90, both in *Islam Encountering Globalization*, ed. Ali Mohammadi (New York: RoutledgeCurzon, 2002). See also Gary Bunt, *Islam in the Digital Age: E-Jihad, Online Fatwas, and Cyber Islamic Environments* (London: Pluto Press, 2003), Bunt's "Defining Islamic Interconnectivity," pp. 235–51, and Jon W. Anderson, "Wiring Up: The Internet Difference for Muslim Networks," pp. 252–63, both in *Muslim Networks*; and Yitzhak Shichor, "Virtual Transnationalism: Uygur Communities in Europe and the Quest for Eastern Turkestan Independence," in *Muslim Networks and Transnational Communities in and across Europe*, pp. 281–311.

27. Here I rely on the understanding of genealogy as articulated by Foucault and Nietzsche. See, for example, Foucault, "Nietzsche, Genealogy, History," in *Language, Counter-memory, Practice*, ed. Donald F. Bouchard (Ithaca: Cornell University Press, 1977).

28. See, for example, Michael Hardt and Antonio Negri, *Empire* (Cambridge, MA: Harvard University Press, 2000).

29. Lapidus, "Hierarchies and Networks," pp. 34, 40.

30. Hodgson, *The Venture of Islam*, 2:349.

31. Bamyeh, pp. 220–22. Richard Bulliet similarly suggests that a "standard indicator of the strength and prosperity of an Islamic state is the remark that the routes were so secure that travelers could move wherever they wished without molestation. . . . unhindered travel appears to have been a goal of medieval Islamic government." "Travel and Transport, Islamic," in *Dictionary of the Middle Ages*, vol. 12, p. 147.

32. Lapidus, "Hierarchies and Networks," pp. 40–41.

33. David Gilmartin, for example, argues that this gap between state power and a moral community "defined by networks and cutting across political systems and political boundaries" became more rather than less marked with the advance of European colonialism and the rise of the nation-state, but in complex and distinctive ways. Gilmartin, "A Networked Civilization?" in *Muslim Networks: From Hajj to Hiphop*, p. 54. In a similar vein, Paul Lubeck delineates a correlation between globalization and the strength of transnational Islamic movements. Lubeck, "Antinomies of Islamic Movements under Globalization," *Center for Global International and Regional Studies Working Paper Series*, WP#99-1, University of California at Santa Cruz, 1999. Recent research on Muslim transnationalism in Europe is particularly revealing in this regard. See, for example, the special issue on "Islam, Transnationalism, and the Public Sphere in Western Europe," *Journal of Ethnic and Migration Studies* 30, no. 5 (2004).

34. Pollack, "Cosmopolitanism and Vernacular in History." See also Robert John Holton, "Cosmopolitanism or cosmopolitanisms? The Universal Races Congress of 1911," *Global Networks* 2, no. 2 (2002): pp.153–70.

35. Pollack, "Cosmopolitan and Vernacular in History," pp. 595, 596.

36. As Peter van der Veer points out, nineteenth-century European cosmopolitanism was "always complemented by a Christian cosmopolitanism of both the Catholic and Protestant kind. . . . Liberal cosmopolitanism and Evangelical cosmopolitanism developed side by side in the colonial era." "Transnational Religion," p. 15.

37. Mehta, "Cosmopolitanism and the Circle of Reason," p. 632.

38. For arguments that do imply such relinquishment, and strenuous claims to the contrary, see Martha Nussbaum's argument for cosmopolitanism and responses initially published in the *Boston Review* 19, no. 5 (October/November 1994), subsequently published as *For Love of Country: Debating the Limits of Patriotism*, ed. Joshua Cohen (Boston: Beacon Press, 1996). For a measured adjudication between two positions often portrayed as antithetical, see Jeremy Waldron, "Minority Cultures and the Cosmopolitan Alternative," in *The Rights of Minority Cultures*, ed. Will Kymlicka (Oxford: Oxford University Press, 1995), pp. 93–119.

39. See, for example, Amy Waldman, "Seething Unease Shaped British Bombers' Newfound Zeal," *The New York Times*, July 31, 2005, and Elaine Sciolino, "Europe Meets the New Face of Terrorism," *The New York Times*, August 1, 2005.

40. Voll, "Islam as a Special World-System," p. 217; the term "Islamicate Culture," is Hodgson's, see *Venture of Islam*, pp. 349–50.

41. Robinson, "Ottomans-Safavids-Mughals."

42. Hodgson, *The Venture of Islam*, vol. 2, p. 336.

43. The invocation of "Muslim networks" as a medium, method, and metaphor for the articulation and transformation of a cosmopolitan imaginary is explicitly developed by Cooke and Lawrence in *Muslim Networks: From Hajj to Hiphop*, but also crucial in this connection is *Muslim Networks and Transnational Communities in and Across Europe*, ed. Stefano Allievi and Jørgen S. Nielsen (Leiden: Brill, 2003) and Mandaville's *Transnational Muslim Politics*.

44. Bamyeh, *The Ends of Globalization*, p. 103.

45. Gary Bunt, "Defining Islamic Interconnectivity," *Muslim Networks: From Hajj to Hiphop*; Masud in "The Obligation to Migrate: The Doctrine of *hijra* in Islamic Law," *Muslim Travellers*, pp. 42–43; Pnina Werbner, "Global Pathways: Working Class Cosmopolitans and the Creation of Transnational Ethnic Worlds," *Social Anthropology* 7, no. 1 (1999): 17–35; Peter Mandaville, "Sufis and Salafis: The Political Discourse of Transnational Islam," in *Remaking Muslim Politics: Pluralism, Contestation, and Democratization*, ed Robert W. Hefner (Princeton, NJ: Princeton University Press, 2005).

46. Khalidi, "Islamic Views of the West in the Middle Ages," pp. 35–36.

47. Hashmi, "The Qur'an and Tolerance," p. 81.

48. Khalidi, "Islamic Views of the West in the Middle Ages," p. 35.

49. Robinson, "Ottomans-Safavids-Mughals," p. 173.

50. Ibid., pp. 172, 163.

51. Ibid., p. 172.

52. Gergen, "Narrative Structures in Social Explanation," p. 96.

53. Hisham Sharabi, *Arab Intellectuals and the West: The Formative Years, 1875–1914* (Baltimore, MD: Johns Hopkins Press, 1970), p. 27.

54. Qutb, *Amrika min al-dakhil bi minzar Sayyid Qutb.*

55. Zubaida, "Cosmopolitanism and the Middle East," p. 21.

56. Ibid., pp. 15–16.

57. Waldron, "Minority Cultures and the Cosmopolitan Alternative," p.102.

58. Fahmi Huwaydi, "Didd kawkalat al-ʿalam!"[Against Coca Cola-ization of the World!], *Al-Ahram*, October 10, 1995, p. 11.

59. Pollack, "Cosmopolitanism and Vernacular in History," p. 622. Among others, Ahmed Moussalli and scholars engaged in the Islamization of Knowledge Project have been advancing this kind of negotiation between engagement and authenticity. *Cosmopolitanism, Identity, and Authenticity in the Middle East*, p. 8.

60. Mehta, "Cosmopolitanism and the Circle of Reason," pp. 631, 632.

61. The reference to a "human condition" as opposed to "human nature" draws on Hannah Arendt's argument that humans beings are distinguished by the conditions of language, natality, and mortality and crucially, awareness of such conditions. Arendt, *Human Condition.*

62. Tariq Ramadan, *To Be a European Muslim: A Study of Islamic Sources in the European Context* (Leicester: The Islamic Foundation, 1999), pp. 149–50, emphasis in the original; Sadiki, *The Arab Search for Democracy*, p. 362.

63. As Fred Dallmayr argues drawing on Aristotle, even in instances where norms are widely shared, political questions about power, interpretation, and authority can become more rather than less insistent. Under such conditions, Dallmayr writes, "it is insufficient—on moral and practical grounds—to throw a mantle of universal rules over humankind without paying simultaneous attention to public debate and the role of political will formation." "Cosmopolitanism, Moral and Political," *Political Theory* 31, no. 3 (June 2003): p. 434. On the absence of politics from certain strands of the new cosmopolitanism, see J. Peter Euben, *Platonic Noise* (Princeton, NJ: Princeton University Press, 2003), pp. 112–40.

64. For a discussion of the complex epistemological standing of experience, see Joan W. Scott, "Experience," in *Feminists Theorize the Political*, ed. Judith Butler and Joan W. Scott (New York: Routledge, 1992).

65. Aristotle, *Metaphysics*, trans. Hippocrates G. Apostle (Bloomington: Indiana University Press, 1966), 980a25.

66. Heraclitus in *Ancilla to the Pre-Socratic Philosophers*, pp. 31, 101a.; *Histories* I:8.

67. Sulayman al-Tabarani, *Al-Muʿjam al-Awsat* (Amman, Jordan: Dar al-Fikr, 1999), vol. 1, p.17, no.25. Another version appears in ʿAli ibn Balaban, *Al-Ihsan fi Taqrib Sahih Ibn Hibban* (Beirut: Muʾassasat al-Risala, 1991), vol.14, p.96, no. 6213. I am grateful to Wael Hallaq for these references.

68. Maimonides, "Letter on Astrology," trans. Ralph Lerner, p. 186, and Ibn Falaquera, "Epistle of the Debate," trans. Steven Harvey, pp. 193–94, both in Lerner's *Maimonides' Empire of Light: Popular Enlightenment in an Age of Belief* (Chicago: The University of Chicago Press, 2000); Ibn Khaldûn, *Muqaddimah*, vol. 2, p. 346.

69. Quoted by Elliot R. Wolfson, *Through a Speculum that Shines: Vision and Imagination in Medieval Jewish Mysticism* (Princeton, NJ: Princeton University Press, 1994), p. 46, 5.

70. Tavakoli-Targhi, "Imagining Western Women," pp. 74, 79.

71. It is unsurprising that the Persian characters register European women, to whom they have limited exposure and even less understanding, as indices of civilizational essences along the lines, for example, of Tahtawi's view of Frenchwomen or Tocqueville's construction of Native and African-American women. Montesquieu, however, had extensive exposure to such women, just as Ibn Battuta was quite intimate with many of the women of the *Rihla*. Why the author has carefully drawn non-European characters with such limited knowledge of Frenchwomen may reflect his imaginative reconstruction of how foreigners might behave, his own limited understanding, his projection of such limits onto his Persian characters, or all three.

72. Mahfouz, *Rihlat Ibn Fattūma*; R. el-Enany, "Najīb Mahfūz in Search of the Ideal State: A Critique of his *Rihlat Ibn Fattūma*," in *Golden Roads*, p. 161.

73. El-Enany, "Najīb Mahfūz in Search of the Ideal State," p. 161.

74. Mahfouz, *Rihlat Ibn Fattuma*, p. 10.

75. Ibid., p. 24, 139, 151.

76. Ibid, pp. 30, 86. Reading the novel's ending as a "failure," as Wen-chin Ouyang does, thus misses much of the point. Ouyang, "The Dialectic of Past and Present in *Rihlat Ibn Fattūma* by Najīb Mahfūz," *Edebiyat* 14, no. 1/2 (2003): p. 87.

77. Lear, *Open Minded: Working Out the Logic of the Soul* (Cambridge: Harvard University Press, 1998), pp. 50–51.

78. Euben, *The Tragedy of Political Theory*, p. 124.

79. Ibid., p. 113.

80. Wolin, *Politics and Vision*, p. 19.

81. Shaked, "Quests and Visionary Journeys in Sasanian Iran," *Transformations of the Inner Self in Ancient Religions*, ed. Jan Assmann and Guy G. Stroumsa (Leiden: Brill, 1999), p. 77.

82. Wolin, "Political Theory as a Vocation," p. 1077.

83. Descartes, *Discourse on Method*, part I.

84. Kwame Anthony Appiah, *The Ethics of Identity* (Princeton, NJ: Princeton University Press, 2005), p. 242.

85. Metha, "Cosmpolitanism and the Circle of Reason," p. 628.

86. Paul Ricoeur, *History and Truth* (Evanston, IL: Northwestern University Press, 1965), p. 278, emphasis in the original.

87. "It is through wonder that men now begin and originally began to philosophize; wondering in the first place at obvious perplexities, and then by gradual progression raising questions about greater matters too ... (thus the myth-lover is in a sense a philosopher, since myths are composed of wonders)," Aristotle's *Metaphysics* (982b9–10). And "wonder is the feeling of a philosopher, and philosophy begins in wonder," Plato's *Theaetetus* 155d; Lear, *Open Minded*, p. 51.

88. Appadurai, *Modernity at Large*, p. 9.

89. Zerilli, "Doing without Knowing," p. 449; Wolin, *Tocqueville Between Two Worlds*, pp. 35–36.

GLOSSARY OF ARABIC AND GREEK TERMS

ʿAbbasids — The early Islamic dynasty based in Baghdad (750–1258).

adab — Cultural habits, customs, and norms of conduct; literature or the tradition of *belles-lettres*.

ʿadl — Justice.

ahl al-rihla — People who have traveled.

ʿajaʾib (pl.) — Wonders, marvels, curiosities, oddities, miracles.

ʿAli — Cousin and son-in-law of the Prophet Muhammad, ʿAli was the fourth Caliph, and was assassinated in 40 A.H./661 ce. Revered by both Sunnis and Shiʿa, ʿAli is of particular significance to the Shiʿa, who regard him as their first Imam.

ʿalim (pl. *ʿulama*) — Religious scholar, one who is knowledgeable.

ʿata — Gift, present, alms.

ayat (sing. *aya*) — Signs, as in divine marvels and miracles; verses of the Qurʾan.

baraka — Blessings, holiness, charismatic and saintly power.

Berber — A common term (derogatory in origin) used to refer to Imazighen, the original non-Arab Tamazight-speaking inhabitants of northwest Africa.

bidʿa — Innovation, novelty; also heresy.

al-bidan/al-abyad — White people/a white person.

balad (pl. *bilad*) — Country, land.

bilad al-Nasara — Lands of the Christians.

bilad al-Rum — Lands of the (Christian) Byzantines, as distinguished from the Latin Christians who inhabit *bilad al-Ifranj*.

bilad al-Sudan — Lands of black people.

dar al-Harb — House/Abode of War.

dar al-Islam — House/Abode of Islam.

din — Religion, faith.

dunya — This world, worldly existence, earthly or temporal matters.

fiqh — Islamic jurisprudence.

fitna — Civil strife, temptation, disorder, chaos, sedition, dissension.

hadith/ahadith — The report(s) of the words and deeds of the Prophet collected and recorded in the centuries following Muhammad's death.

hadiyya — Gift, often connoting that which those of lower social status give to those of elevated social status, at times with an expectation of reciprocity.

Hanafi — One of the four main schools of Sunni Islamic law, named after Abu Hanifa (d. 767), or an adherent of this school.

Hanbali — One of the four main schools of Sunni Islamic law, named after Ahmad b. Hanbal (d. 855), or an adherent of this school.

hiba — Gift, often used to designate a gift of God to humans or from an elite to someone of lower social status.

hajj — Pilgrimage to Mecca.

hijra — The migration of the Prophet and the early community of Muslims from Mecca to Medina that inaugurates the Islamic calendar.

hubb al-watan — Love of homeland, love of country.

hurriya — Freedom.

al-Ifranj — Literally, "the Franks," refers to Latin Christians, or European inhabitants of Charlemagne's empire, as distinguished from Byzantine Christian inhabitants of *bilad al-Rum*.

ijaza — Authorization, license; formal permission to transmit a *hadith*, a text or religious knowledge more generally.

ijtihad — Literally "exerting oneself"; independent reasoning, judgment or interpretation, particularly the effort to derive religious guidance from the sacred texts in matters not already explicitly regulated in Islamic law.

ikhtilaf — Disagreement, differences of opinion, particularly although not exclusively among scholars of Islamic law.

ᶜilm — Knowledge.

iltizam — In the Ottoman Empire, an agrarian system of tax farming that, under certain conditions, strengthened local centers of power and wealth; Muhammad ᶜAli abolished the *iltizam* in his drive to establish a centralized bureaucracy in Egypt.

imam — Religious guide, prayer leader; for the Shiᶜa, their divinely designated leader.

insaf — Equity.

isnad — Chain of authorities crucial to the transmission of a tradition, and the integrity of which helps to determine the reliability of any particular *hadith*.

ᶜiyan — Witnessing direct observation, seeing with one's own eyes.

jihad — Literally to struggle or to strive, often used synonymously (if inaccurately) with holy war.

kafara (also *kuffar*, both plural) — Infidels, unbelievers.

kaffara — Expiation, penance, atonement.

madhhab — School of Islamic law.

Maghrib — Literally "the place of the setting sun"; the west, more specifically the region of Northwest Africa.

Maliki — One of the four main schools of Sunni Islamic law, named after Malik b. Anas (d. 795) or an adherent of this school. The school particularly prevalent in the Maghrib.

Mamluk — A military slave; also a regime established by emancipated Mamluks; the Turco-Circassian rulers of Egypt from 1250–1517.

Marinids — Ruling dynasty of Morocco from the thirteenth to fifteenth centuries.

Mashriq — Literally "place of sunrise"; the (Islamic) East.

mizan — Balance, measure, comparison.

mujahidin — Those who struggle for *jihad*.

mutakallim — Muslim theologian.

nahda — Rebirth, renaissance, revival.

nomos (pl. *nomoi*) — Custom, law.

Oikoumene — The inhabited as opposed to the uninhabited world; initially, this referred to the Hellenic as opposed to the barbarian world, but it later came to denote a wider understanding of "the whole."

qadi — Muslim judge.

al-Qaʿida — Literally "the base," the loosely linked and elusive network of *jihadists* affiliated with Osama bin Laden.

qasida — A specific kind of Arabic poem.

rafidi — Literally "turncoat, renegade, fanatic," at times used by Sunnis to disparage Shiʿa.

rihla — Journey, travel; a book of travels; a genre of Arabic travel literature.

rihla hijaziyya — Journey to the Hijaz, in what is now Saudi Arabia.

rihla sifariyya — A journey for primarily diplomatic purposes.

Shafiʿi — One of the four main schools of Sunni Islamic law, named after Muhammad b. Idris al-Shafiʿi (d. 820), or an adherent of this school.

shahada (verb *shahida*) — To witness, experience first-hand, certify, and confirm; martyrdom.

shaikh — Respected elder; learned religious person; a Sufi master.

Shariʿa — Islamic law, all the exhortations and prohibitions derived from the Qurʾan and the normative example provided by the life of the Prophet Muhammad.

Shiʿa (sing. *Shiʿi*) — Literally "partisans of ʿAli," the Shiʿa are members of the community of Muslims that broke with the Sunnis early in Islamic history over the legitimate successor to the Prophet Muhammad.

Sufi — A Muslim mystic.

Sunna — The tradition of the Prophet as reported in the collected reports (*hadith*) of Muhammad's words and conduct.

Sunni — Those who follow the Sunna of the Prophet, the Sunnis prevailed in the early conflict with the *Shiʿa* over the successor to Muhammad.

talab al-ᶜilm — Search for knowledge.

tamaddun — To become urbanized, civilized.

tamassur — To become sedentary, urbanized.

taqlid — Imitation, adoption; following the precedent of promulgated legal rulings of a *madhhab*.

tariqa (pl. *turuq*) — Sufi order, religious brotherhood.

theôria (pl. *theôriai*) — Etymological precursor to the English "theory," the practice of journeying abroad particularly for the sake of observing/acquiring knowledge about other people, places, institutions, religious practices, and festivals.

theôros (pl. *theôroi*) — A spectator, a state delegate to a festival in another city, one who travels to consult an oracle, one engaged in a *theôria*.

thauma (pl. *thaumata*) — Marvel, curiosity, something miraculous.

umma — Muslim community, derived from the Arabic root meaning mother, source, origin, foundation; membership is determined not by national citizenship or geography but by religious belief.

wali — Ruler, governor, benefactor.

watan — Homeland, country.

ziyara — Visits to shrines, particularly of revered Sufis.

BIBLIOGRAPHY

Abdel-Malek, Anouar. *Idéologie et Renaissance National: l'Egypte Moderne*. Paris: Editions Anthropos, 1969.

Abou El Fadl, Khaled. *And God Knows the Soldiers: The Authoritative and the Authoritarian in Islamic Discourses*. Lanham, MD: University Press of America, 2001.

———. *Speaking in God's Name: Islamic Law, Authority, and Women*. Oxford: OneWorld, 2001.

abu-Lughod, Ibrahim. *Arab Rediscovery of Europe*. Princeton, NJ: Princeton University Press, 1963.

abu-Lughod, Janet L. *Before European Hegemony: The World System A.D. 1250–1350*. New York: Oxford University Press, 1989.

Adams, Percy G. *Travelers and Travel Liars: 1660–1800*. Berkeley: University of California Press, 1962.

———. *Travel Literature and the Evolution of the Novel*. Lexington: University Press of Kentucky, 1983.

Adonis (ʿAli Ahmad Saʿid). "Beyond the East/West: Towards a Culture of the Future." Lecture delivered at Dartmouth College, May 9, 2001.

Ahmed, Jamal Mohammed. *The Intellectual Origins of Egyptian Nationalism*. New York: Oxford University Press, 1960.

Ahmed, Leila. *A Border Passage: From Cairo to America—A Woman's Journey*. New York: Penguin, 1999.

Akhavi, Shahrough. "Sunni Modernist Theories of Social Contract in Contemporary Egypt." *International Journal of Middle East Studies* 35, no. 1 (2003): 23–49.

Ali, Ahmed, trans. *Al-Qurʾan*. Princeton, NJ: Princeton University Press, 1984.

Ali, Said Ismail. "Rifaʿa al-Tahtawi." *Perspectives: revue trimestrielle d'éducation compare* 24, no. 3/4 (1994): 649–76.

Allen, Roger. *The Arabic Novel: An Historical and Critical Introduction*. Syracuse, NY: Syracuse University Press, 1982.

Allievi, Stefano, and Jørgen S. Nielsen, eds. *Muslim Networks and Transnational Communities in and Across Europe*. Leiden: Brill, 2003.

Allouche, Adel. "A Study of Ibn Battuta's Account of His 726/1326 Journey through Syria and Arabia." *Journal of Semitic Studies* 35, no. 2 (autumn 1990): 283–99.

Alloula, Malek. *The Colonial Harem*. Translated by Myrna and Wlad Godzich. Minneapolis: University of Minnesota Press, 1986.

Altman, Israel. "The Political Thought of Rifaʿah Rafiʿ al-Tahtawi: A Nineteenth-Century Egyptian Reformer." Ph.D. Diss., University of California at Los Angeles, 1976.

Amrouche, Fadhma A. M. *My Life Story: the Autobiography of a Berber Woman*. Translated by Dorothy S. Blair. New Brunswick, NJ: Rutgers University Press, 1989.

Anderson, Benedict. "Exodus." *Critical Inquiry* 20, no. 2 (winter 1994): 314–27.

————. *Imagined Communities*. London: Verso, 1992.

Anderson, Jon W. "Wiring Up: The Internet Difference for Muslim Networks." In *Muslim Networks: From Hajj to Hiphop*. Edited by Miriam Cooke and Bruce B. Lawrence. Chapel Hill: University of North Carolina Press, 2005.

Appadurai, Arjun. "Disjuncture and Difference in the Global Cultural Economy." *Public Culture* 2, no. 2 (1990): 1–24.

————. *Modernity at Large: Cultural Dimensions of Globalization*. Minneapolis: University of Minnesota Press, 1996.

Appiah, Kwame Anthony. *The Ethics of Identity*. Princeton, NJ: Princeton University Press, 2005.

Arendt, Hannah. *The Human Condition*. Chicago: University of Chicago Press, 1958.

Aristotle, *Metaphysics*. Translated by Hippocrates G. Apostle. Bloomington: Indiana University Press, 1966.

————. *The Politics of Aristotle*. Translated by Ernest Barker. New York: Oxford University Press, 1995.

Arkoun, Mohammad. *Rethinking Islam: Common Questions, Uncommon Answers*. Translated by Robert D. Lee. Boulder, CO: Westview Press, 1994.

Asad, Talal. *Genealogies of Religion*. Baltimore: Johns Hopkins University Press, 1993.

————. "The Idea of an Anthropology of Islam." Center for Contemporary Arab Studies. Georgetown University, 1986.

Asbridge, Thomas. *The First Crusade: A New History*. Great Britain: The Free Press, 2004.

al-ʿAsqalani, Ibn Hajar. *Durar al-Kamina fi Aʿyan al-miʾah al-thaminah*. 4 vols. Hyderabad, al-Dakan, al-Hind: Matbaʿat Majlis Daʾirat al-Maʿarif al-ʿUthmaniyya, 1929.

Atlas, James. "Leo-Cons, A Classicist's Legacy: New Empire Builders." *New York Times*, May 4, 2003, section 4, p.1.

al-ʿAttar, Hasan. *Hashiyat Abi al-Saʿadat Hasan al-ʿAttar ʿala Sharh al-tahdhib li-ʿUbayd Allah ibn Fadl al-Khabisi*. Cairo: Matbaʿat Bulaq, 1879.

Augustine. *The Confessions of St. Augustine*. Translated by Rex Warner. New York: New American Library, 1963.

Averroës. *Decisive Treatise and Epistle Dedicatory*. Translated by Charles E. Butterworth. Utah: Brigham Young University Press, 2001.

Avery, Catherine B., ed. *The New Century Handbook of Classical Geography*. New York: Appleton-Century-Crofts, 1972.

ʿAwad, Louis. *al-Muʾaththirat al-Ajnabiyya fi al-Adab al-ʿArabi al-Hadith*. 2 vols. Cairo: Jamiʿat al-Duwal al-ʿArabiyya, Maʿhad al-Dirasat al-ʿArabiyya al-ʿAliah, 1962.

————. *Rihlat al-Sharq wa al-Gharb*. Cairo: Dar al-Maʿarif, 1972.

————. *Tarikh al-Fikr al-Misri al-Hadith: min al-hamla al-Faransiyya ila ʿasr Ismaʿil*. Cairo: Maktabat Madbouli, 1987.

ʿAziz, Khayri. *Udaba ʿala Tariq al-Nidal al-Siyasi: Rifaʿa al-Tahtawi, Salamah Musa, ʿAbbas al-ʿAqqad, Muhammad Mandur*. Cairo: al-Hayʾa al-Misriyya al-ʿAmmah li-l-Taʾlif wa al-Nashr, 1970.

al-Azmeh, Aziz. *Islams and Modernities*. London: Verso, 1996.

Bacon, Francis. *New Atlantis and the Great Instauration*. Edited by Jerry Weinberger. Arlington Heights, IL: Harlan Davidson, 1989.

Badawi, Ahmad Ahmad. *Rifaʿa Rafiʿ al-Tahtawi*. Cairo: Lajnat al-Bayan al-ʿArabi, 1959.

Badron, Margot, and Miriam Cooke, eds. *Opening the Gates: A Century of Arab Feminist Writing*. Bloomington: Indiana University Press, 1990.

Balibar, Etienne. "The Borders of Europe." In *Cosmopolitics: Thinking and Feeling Beyond the Nation*. Edited by Pheng Cheah and Bruce Robbins. Minneapolis: University of Minnesota Press, 1998.

Bamyeh, Mohammed A. *The Ends of Globalization*. Minneapolis: University of Minnesota Press, 2000.

———. "Global Order and the Historical Structures of *Dar al-Islam*." In *Rethinking Globalism*. Edited by Manfred Steger. Lanham, MD: Rowan and Littlefield, 2004.

Bayat, Asef. "The Use and Abuse of 'Muslim Societies.'" *International Institute for the Study of Islam in the Modern World Newsletter* 13 (December 2003): p. 5.

Beckingham, Charles. "In Search of Ibn Battuta." *Royal Society for Asian Affairs* 8 (1977): 263–77.

Behdad, Ali. *Belated Travelers: Orientalism in the Age of Colonial Dissolution*. Durham, NC: Duke University Press, 1994.

Benjamin, Walter. "The Task of the Translator." In *Illuminations*. Edited by Hannah Arendt. New York: Schocken, 1988.

Berlin, Isaiah. *Against the Current: Essays in the History of Ideas*. London: Hogarth Press, 1979.

Berman, Marshall. *The Politics of Authenticity: Radical Individualism and the Emergence of Modern Society*. New York: Atheneum, 1970.

al-Beruni. *Alberuni's India*. Edited by Edward C. Sachau. London: Trübner, 1881.

———. *Kitab al-Biruni fi tahqiq ma li-l-Hind min maqulah maqbulah fi al-ʿaql aw mardhulah*. Edited by Eduard Sachau. Hyderabad, India: Matbaʿat Majlis Daʾirat al-Maʿarif al-ʿUthmaniyya, 1958.

Betts, Christopher J. *Montesquieu: Lettres persanes*. London: Grant and Cutler, 1994.

Bianchi, Robert R. *Guests of God: Pilgrimage and Politics in the Islamic World*. Oxford: Oxford University Press, 2004.

Bill, Clarence P. "Notes on the Greek Θεωρός and Θεωρία." *Transactions and Proceedings of the American Philological Association* 32 (1901): 196–97.

Birkett, Dea. *Spinsters Abroad: Victorian Lady Explorers*. Oxford: Basil Blackwell, 1989.

Blake, Susan L. "A Woman's Trek: What Difference Does Gender Make?" In *Western Women and Imperialism: Complicity and Resistance*. Edited by Nupur Chaudhuri and Margaret Strobel. Bloomington: Indiana University Press, 1992.

Blanks, David, ed. *Images of the Other: Europe and the Muslim World before 1700*. Egypt: American University in Cairo Press, 1996.

Blecher, Ian. "How Cult Internet Character Mr. Perestroika Divided N.Y.U.'s Political Science Department." *New York Observer*, January 7, 2002, p. 3.

Bloch, Ernst. *The Principle of Hope*. Translated by Neville Plaice, Stephen Plaice, and Paul Knight. Cambridge, MA: MIT Press, 1986.

Bloch, Ruth H. "American Feminine Ideals in Transition: The Rise of the Moral Mother, 1785–1815." *Feminist Studies* 4, no. 2 (June 1978): 101–26.

Blunt, Alison. *Travel, Gender, and Imperialism: Mary Kingsley and West Africa*. New York: Guilford Press, 1994.

Borm, Jan. "Defining Travel: On the Travel Book, Travel Writing, and Terminology." In *Perspectives on Travel Writing*. Edited by Glenn Hooper and Tim Youngs. Great Britain: Ashgate, 2004.

Bosworth, C. Edmund. Review of Ross E. Dunn's *The Adventures of Ibn Battuta: A Muslim Traveller of the 14th Century. Journal of Islamic Studies* 4 (1993): 109–10.

Bourqia, Rahma. "Don et théâtralité: Réflexion sur le rituel du don (Hadiyya) offert au sultan au XIXe siècle." *Hesperis* 31 (1993): 61–75.

Bousquet, G. H. "Ibn Battuta et les institutions musulmanes," *Studia Islamica* 24 (1966): 81–106.

Boyer, Marjorie Nice. "Travel and Transport, Western European." In *Dictionary of the Middle Ages*. Vol. 12. Edited by Joseph R. Strayer. New York: Charles Scribner's Sons, 1989.

Breckenridge, Carol A., Sheldon Pollack, Homi K. Bhabha, and Dipesh Chakrabarty, eds. *Cosmopolitanism*. Durham, NC: Duke University Press, 2002.

Brotton, Jerry. *Trading Territories: Mapping the Early Modern World*. New York: Cornell University Press, 1998.

Browne, Daniel P., and Neal H. Schultz. "A Visit with Ibn Battuta: Prince of Travelers." *Social Science Record* 30, no. 2 (fall 1993): 29–31.

Bryson, Norman. *Vision and Painting: The Logic of the Gaze*. New Haven: Yale University Press, 1983.

Buckley, Terry. *Aspects of Greek History, 750–332 BC*. New York: Routledge, 1996.

Bulliet, Richard. "Travel and Transport, Islamic." In *Dictionary of the Middle Ages*. Vol. 12. Edited by Joseph R. Strayer. New York: Charles Scribner's Sons, 1989.

Bunt, Gary. "Defining Islamic Interconnectivity." In *Muslim Networks: From Hajj to Hiphop*. Edited by Miriam Cooke and Bruce B. Lawrence. Chapel Hill: University of North Carolina Press, 2005.

———. *Islam in the Digital Age: E-Jihad, Online Fatwas, and Cyber Islamic Environments*. London: Pluto Press, 2003.

Callaway, Helen. *Gender, Culture, and Empire: European Women in Colonial Nigeria*. Urbana: University of Illinois Press, 1987.

Campbell, Jane. "Multiracialism and Politics in Zanzibar." *Political Science Quarterly* 77, no. 1 (March 1962): 72–87.

Campo, Juan Eduardo. "The Mecca Pilgrimage in the Formation of Islam in Modern Egypt." In *Sacred Places and Profane Spaces: Essay in the Geographics of Judaism, Christianity, and Islam*. Edited by Jamie S. Scott and Paul Simpson-Housley. New York: Greenwood Press, 1991.

Caner, Daniel. *Wandering, Begging Monks: Spiritual Authority and the Promotion of Monasticism in Late Antiquity*. Berkeley: University of California Press, 2002.

Chakrabarty, Dipesh. *Provincializing Europe: Postcolonial Thought and Historical Difference*. Princeton, NJ: Princeton University Press, 2000.

Chardin, Jean. *Voyages de Monsieur le Chevalier Chardin en Perse et autres lieux de l'Orient*. Amsterdam: Chez Jean Louis de Lorne, 1711.

Chaudhuri, Nupur, and Margaret Strobel. *Western Women and Imperialism: Resistance and Complicity*. Bloomington: Indiana University Press, 1992.

Chejne, Anwar G. "Travel Books in Modern Arabic Literature." *Muslim World* 52, no. 3 (1962): 207–15.

Chelhod, Joseph. "Ibn Battuta, Ethnologue." *Revue de l'Occident Musulman et de la Méditerranée* 25 (1978): 5–24.

Chew, Samuel. *The Crescent and the Rose*. New York: Oxford University Press, 1937.

Cicero. *De Legibus*. Translated by Clinton Walker Keyes. London: William Heinemann, 1928.

Clifford, James. "Diasporas." *Cultural Anthropology* 9, no. 3 (1994): 302–38.

———. "Notes on Travel and Theory." *Inscriptions* 5 (1989): 177–86.

———. *Routes: Travel and Translation in the Late Twentieth Century*. Cambridge, MA: Harvard University Press, 1997.

———. "Traveling Cultures." In *Cultural Studies*. Edited by Lawrence Grossberg, Cary Nelson, and Paula A. Treichler. New York: Routledge, 1992.

Clifford, James, and Vivek Dhareshwar, eds. *Traveling Theories, Traveling Theorists*. Santa Cruz: Group for the Critical Study of Colonial Discourse and the Center for Cultural Studies, 1989.

Cohen, David. *Law, Sexuality, and Society: The Enforcement of Morals in Classical Athens*. Cambridge: Cambridge University Press, 1991.

Cohn, Jonathan. "When Did Political Science Forget about Politics? Irrational Exuberance." *The New Republic*, October 25, 1999, 25–31.

Cole, Juan R. *Colonialism and Revolution in the Middle East: Social and Cultural Origins of Egypt's ʿUrabi Movement*. Princeton, NJ: Princeton University Press, 1993.

———. "Rifaʿa al-Tahtawi and the Revival of Practical Philosophy." *Muslim World* 70 (1980): 29–46.

Coleman, Simon, and John Elsner. *Pilgrimage Past and Present in the World Religions*. Cambridge, MA: Harvard University Press, 1995.

Connolly, William. "Democracy and Territoriality." In *The Ethos of Pluralization*. Minneapolis: University of Minnesota Press, 1995.

———. *Why I Am Not a Secularist*. Minneapolis: University of Minnesota Press, 1999.

Conte, Gian Biago. *Genres and Readers*. Translated by Glenn W. Most. Baltimore: Johns Hopkins University Press, 1994.

Cooke, Miriam, and Bruce B. Lawrence, eds. *Muslim Networks: From Hajj to Hiphop*. Chapel Hill: University of North Carolina Press, 2005.

Cornell, Vincent J. *Realm of the Saint: Power and Authority in Moroccan Sufism*. Austin: University of Texas Press, 1998.

Cott, Nancy. *The Bonds of Womanhood: "Woman's Sphere" in New England, 1780–1835*. New Haven: Yale University Press, 1977.

Crabbs, Jack A., Jr. *The Writing of History in Nineteenth-Century Egypt: A Study in National Transformation*. Cairo: The American University in Cairo Press, 1984.

Curtin, Philip D. *Cross-Cultural Trade in World History*. Cambridge: Cambridge University Press, 1984.

Curtis, Adam. "The Power of Nightmares: Part 1—Baby It's Cold Outside." *British Broadcasting Corporation*. First broadcast October 20, 2004.

Curtis, Barry, and Claire Pajaczkowska. "'Getting There': Travel, Time, and Narrative." In *Travellers' Tales: Narratives of Home and Displacement*. Edited by George Robertson, Melinda Mash, Lisa Tickner, Jon Bird, Barry Curtis, and Tim Putnam. London: Routledge, 1994.

da Costa, Suneeta Peres. "On Homesickness: Narratives of Longing and Loss in the Writings of Jamaica Kincaid." *Postcolonial Studies: Culture, Politics, Economy* 2, no. 1 (1999): 75–89.

Dallal, Jenine Abboushi. "The Perils of Occidentalism: How Arab Novelists Are Driven to Write for Western Readers." *The Times Literary Supplement*, April 24, 1998, 4960:9.

Dallmayr, Fred R. *Alternative Visions: Paths in the Global Village*. Lanham, MD: Rowman and Littlefield, 1998.

———. "Cosmopolitanism, Moral and Political," *Political Theory* 31, no. 3 (June 2003): 421–42.

———, ed. *Border Crossings: Toward a Comparative Political Theory*. Lanham, MD: Lexington Books, 1999.

Dallrymple, William. "The Truth about Muslims." *The New York Review of Books* 51, no. 17 (November 4, 2004), 31–34.

Davidson, Donald. "On the Very Idea of a Conceptual Scheme." In *Inquiries into Truth and Interpretation*. Oxford: Clarendon Press, 1984.

de Certeau, Michel. *The Writing of History*. Translated by Tom Conley. New York: Columbia University Press, 1988.

Delanty, Gerard. "Habermas and Occidental Rationalism: The Politics of Identity, Social Learning, and the Cultural Limits of Moral Universalism." *Sociological Theory* 15, no. 1 (March 1997): 30–59.

Deleuze, Gilles. "Nomad Thought." In *The New Nietzsche: Contemporary Styles of Interpretation*. Edited by David B. Allison. New York: Dell, 1977.

Denzin, Norman K. *Interpretive Anthropology: Ethnographic Practices for the 21st Century*. Thousand Oaks, CA: Sage, 1997.

Descartes, René. *Discourse on Method for Reasoning Well and for Seeking Truth in the Sciences* (1637). Translated by Ian C. Johnston. Nanaimo, B.C.: Prideaux Street Publications, 2003.

de Tournefort, Joseph Pitton. *Relation d'un voyage fait par ordre du Roy*. Lyon: Anisson et Posuel, 1717.

Diderot, Denis. *Histoire philosophique et politique des etablissemens et du commerce des Européens dans les deux Indes*. Geneva, 1781.

Diouf, Mamadou. "The Senegalese Murid Trade Diaspora and the Making of a Vernacular Cosmopolitanism." *Public Culture* 12, no. 3 (2000): 679–702.

Dirks, Nicholas B., ed. *Colonialism and Culture*. Ann Arbor: University of Michigan Press, 1992.

Dodds, Muriel. "The Persian Background of the *Lettres persanes*." *Durham University Journal* 29 (1935): 77–88.

Dougherty, Carol. *The Raft of Odysseus: The Ethnographic Imagination of Homer's Odyssey*. New York: Oxford University Press, 2001.

Drescher, Seymour. *Tocqueville and England*. Cambridge, MA: Harvard University Press, 1964.

———. "Tocqueville's Two Democracies." *Journal of the History of Ideas* 25, no. 2 (April–June 1964): 201–16.

Dunn, Ross E. *The Adventures of Ibn Battuta*. Berkeley: University of California Press, 1986.

———. "International Migrations of Literate Muslims in the Later Middle Period: The Case of Ibn Battuta." *Golden Roads: Migration, Pilgrimage, and Travel in Mediaeval and Modern Islam*. Edited by Ian Richard Netton. Great Britain: Curzon Press, 1993.

Edib, Halidé Adivar. *Memoirs of Halidé Edib*. New Jersey: Gorgias Press, 2004.

Eickelman, Dale. "The Art of Memory: Islamic Education and its Social Reproduction." *Comparative Studies in Society and History* 20 (1978): 485–516.

Eickelman, Dale F., and James Piscatori, eds. *Muslim Travellers: Pilgrimage, Migration, and the Religious Imagination*. Berkeley: University of California Press, 1990.

Eisenstein, Zillah. *Against Empire: Feminisms, Racism, and 'the' West*. London: Zed, 2004.

Ekrem, Selma. *Unveiled: The Autobiography of a Turkish Girl*. New York: Ives Washburn, 1930.

Elad, Amikan. "The Description of the Travels of Ibn Battuta in Palestine: Is it Original?" *Journal of the Royal Asiatic Society of Great Britain and Ireland*, 2 (1987): 256–72.

Elias, Norbert. "The Retreat of Sociologists into the Present." In *Modern German Sociology*. Edited by Volker Meja, Dieter Misgeld, and Nico Stehr. New York: Columbia University Press, 1987.

el-Enany, R. "Najīb Mahfūz in Search of the Ideal State: A Critique of his Rihlat Ibn Fattūma." In *Golden Roads: Migration, Pilgrimage, and Travel in Mediaeval and Modern Islam*. Edited by Ian Richard Netton. United Kingdom: Curzon Press, 1993.

Encyclopedia of Islam. CD-ROM Edition, version 1.0. Leiden: Koninklijke Brill NV, 1999.

Euben, J. Peter. *Corrupting Youth: Political Education, Democratic Culture, and Political Theory*. Princeton, NJ: Princeton University Press, 1997.

———. "Creatures of a Day: Thought and Action in Thucydides." In *Political Theory and Praxis*. Edited by Terence Ball. Minneapolis: University of Minnesota Press, 1977.

———. "Philosophy and Politics in Plato's *Crito*." *Political Theory* 6, no. 2 (May 1978): 149–72.

Euben, J. Peter. *Platonic Noise*. Princeton, NJ: Princeton University Press, 2003.
————. *The Tragedy of Political Theory: The Road Not Taken*. Princeton, NJ: Princeton University Press, 1990.
Euben, Roxanne L. *Enemy in the Mirror: Islamic Fundamentalism and the Limits of Modern Rationalism*. Princeton, NJ: Princeton University Press, 1999.
————. "The New Manichaeans." *Theory and Event* 5, no. 4 (2002).
Evans, J.A.S. "Father of History or Father of Lies: The Reputation of Herodotus." *The Classical Journal* 64, no. 1 (October 1968): 11–17.
Fair, Laura. "Dressing Up: Clothing, Class, and Gender in Post-Abolition Zanzibar." *The Journal of African History* 39, no. 1 (1998): 63–94.
al-Farabi. *Alfarabi, The Political Writings: "Selected Aphorisms" and Other Texts*. Translated by Charles E. Butterworth. Ithaca: Cornell University Press, 2001.
Farmaian, Sattareh Farman. *Daughter of Persia: A Woman's Journey from Her Father's Harem through the Islamic Revolution*. New York: Anchor, 1993.
Farquhar, George. *The Beaux Strategem*. Lincoln: University of Nebraska Press, 1977.
Fattah, Hala. "Representations of Self and the Other in Two Iraqi Travelogues of the Ottoman Period." *International Journal of Middle East Studies* 30, no. 1 (February 1998): 51–76.
Fattah, Hassan M. "Islamic Pilgrims Bring Cosmopolitan Air to Unlikely City." *New York Times*, January 20, 2005, A4.
Featherstone, Michael, ed., *Global Culture: Nationalism, Globalization, and Modernity*. London: Sage, 1990.
Fénelon. *Telemachus*. Edited by Patrick Riley. Cambridge: Cambridge University Press, 1994.
Ferrand, Gabriel. *Relations de voyages et textes géographiques Arabes, Persans et Turks relatifs a l'Extrême-Orient du VIII au XVIII siècles*. 2 vols. Paris: Ernest Leroux, 1913–14.
Fischer, David Hackett. "Freedom's Not Just another Word." *New York Times*, February 7, 2005, p. 21.
Fletcher, Richard. *The Cross and the Crescent: Christianity and Islam from Muhammad to the Reformation*. New York: Viking, 2004.
Fornara, Charles W. *Herodotus: An Interpretative Essay*. Oxford: Clarendon Press, 1971.
Foucault, Michel. *Discipline and Punish: The Birth of the Prison*. Translated by Alan Sheridan. New York: Pantheon, 1977.
————. "Nietzsche, Genealogy, History," in *Language, Counter-memory, Practice*. Edited by Donald F. Bouchard. Ithaca: Cornell University Press, 1977.
Franey, Laura. "Ethnographic Collecting and Travel: Blurring Boundaries, Forming a Discipline." *Victorian Literature and Culture* 29, no. 1 (2001): 219–39.
Frederick, Bonnie. "Fatal Journeys, Fatal Legends: The Journey of the Captive Woman in Argentina and Uruguay." In *Women and the Journey: The Female Travel Experience*. Edited by Bonnie Frederick and Susan H. McLeod. Pullman: Washington State University Press, 1993.
Fussell, Paul. *Abroad: British Literary Traveling between the Wars*. New York: Oxford University Press, 1980.

Gabrieli, Francesco. *Arab Historians of the Crusades*. Translated by E. J. Costello. New York: Dorset Press, 1957.

Gallois, William. "Andalusi Cosmopolitanism in World History." In *Cultural Contacts in Building a Universal Civilisation: Islamic Contributions*. Edited by Ekmeleddin Ihsanoğlu. Istanbul: Research Center for Islamic History, Art, and Culture, 2005.

Gaventa, John. *Power and Powerlessness: Quiescence and Rebellion in an Appalachian Valley*. Urbana: University of Illinois Press, 1980.

Gearhart, Suzanne. *The Open Boundary of History and Fiction: A Critical Approach to the French Enlightenment*. Princeton, NJ: Princeton University Press, 1984.

Gellens, Sam. "The Search for Knowledge in Medieval Muslim Societies: A Comparative Approach." In *Muslim Travellers: Pilgrimage, Migration, and the Religious Imagination*. Edited by Dale F. Eickelman and James Piscatori. Berkeley: University of California Press, 1990.

Gellner, Ernest. *Nations and Nationalism*. Oxford: Blackwell, 1983.

Gergen, Mary M. "Narrative Structures in Social Explanation." In *Analysing Everyday Explanation*. Edited by Charles Antaki. London: Sage, 1988.

al-Ghashi, Mustapha. "Al-Rihla Al-Maghribiyya wa al-Sharq al-ʿUthmani, Muhawala fi bina al-sura." Ph.D. Diss., University Muhammad V, Faculty of Arts, Rabat, Morocco, 2003.

Ghatan, H. E. Yedidiah. *The Invaluable Pearl: The Unique Status of Women in Judaism*. New York: Bloch, 1986.

Ghose, Indira. *Women Travellers in Colonial India: The Power of the Female Gaze*. Delhi: Oxford University Press, 1998.

Ghurayyib, Jurj. *Adab al-Rihla: Tarikhuhu wa-aʿlamuhu al-Masʿudi, Ibn Battuta, al-Rayhani*. Beirut: Dar al-Thiqafah, 1966.

Gibb, H.A.R. *Ibn Battuta: Travels in Asia and Africa, 1325–54*. London: Routledge and Kegan Paul, 1957.

Gibbon, Edward. *The Decline and Fall of the Roman Empire*. New York: Harcourt, Brace, 1960.

Gilbert, Sandra, and Susan Gubar. *The Madwoman in the Attic: The Woman Writer and the Nineteenth-Century Literary Imagination*. New Haven: Yale University Press, 1979.

Gillespie, Michael Allen. "Liberal Education and the Idea of the West." In *America, The West, and Liberal Education*. Edited by Ralph C. Hancock. Lanham, MD: Rowman and Littlefield, 1999.

Gilligan, Carol. *In a Different Voice*. Cambridge, MA: Harvard University Press, 1993.

Gilman, Charlotte Perkins. *The Home: Its Work and Influence*. New York: Charlton, 1910.

Gilmartin, David. "A Networked Civilization?" In *Muslim Networks: From Hajj to Hiphop*. Edited by Miriam Cooke and Bruce B. Lawrence. Chapel Hill: University of North Carolina Press, 2005.

Gilroy, Paul. *The Black Atlantic: Modernity and Double Consciousness*. New York: Verso, 1993.

Ginzburg, Carlo. "High and Low: The Theme of Forbidden Knowledge in the Sixteenth and Seventeenth Centuries." *Past and Present* 73 (November 1976): 28–41.

Godlewska, Anne, and Neil Smith, eds. *Geography and Empire*. Oxford: Blackwell, 1994.

Goldhill, Simon. "Refracting Classical Vision: Changing Cultures of Viewing." In *Vision in Context: Historical and Contemporary Perspectives on Sight*. Edited by Teresa Brennan and Martin Jay. New York: Routledge, 1996.

Goldziher, Ignaz. *Muslim Studies*. 2 vols. Translated by C. R. Barber and S. M. Stern. London: George Allen and Unwin, 1971.

Gooding-Williams, Robert. "Race, Multiculturalism, and Democracy." *Constellations* 5, no. 1 (1998): 18–41.

Goodman, Dena. *Criticism in Action: Enlightenment Experiments in Political Writing*. Ithaca: Cornell University Press, 1989.

Graburn, Nelson H. H. "Tourism: The Sacred Journey" In *Hosts and Guests: The Anthropology of Tourism*. Edited by Valene Smith. Philadelphia: University of Pennsylvania Press, 1977.

Gray, John. "Memoirs of an Arabian Princess." *Tanganyika Notes and Records* 37 (1954): 49–70.

Gray, Vivienne. "Herodotus and the Rhetoric of Otherness." *American Journal of Philology* 116 (1995): 185–211.

Green, F. C. "Montesquieu the Novelist and Some Imitations of the 'Lettres Persanes.'" *The Modern Language Review* 20 (1925): 32–42.

Greenstein, Susan. "Ladies Bountiful." *Women's Review of Books* 9, no. 12 (September 1992): p. 20.

Grene, David. Review of *The Mirror of Herodotus*. *The Journal of Religion* 70 (January 1990): 136.

Grewal, Inderpal. *Home and Harem: Nation, Gender, Empire, and the Cultures of Travel*. Durham, NC: Duke University Press, 1996.

Griffith, Glyne A. "Travel Narrative as Cultural Critique: V. S. Naipaul's Travelling Theory." *Journal of Commonwealth Literature* 29, no. 2 (1993): 87–92.

Grosrichard, Alain. *The Sultan's Court: European Fantasies of the East*. Translated by Liz Heron. London: Verso, 1998.

Grossberg, Lawrence. "Wandering Audiences, Nomadic Critics." *Bringing it All Back Home: Essays on Cultural Studies*. Durham, NC: Duke University Press, 1997.

Gunning, Isabelle R. "Arrogant Perception, World-Travelling, and Multicultural Feminism: The Case of Female Genital Surgeries." *Columbia Human Rights Law Review* 23 (1991–92): 189–248.

Gunny, Ahmad. "Montesquieu's View of Islam in the *Lettres persanes*." In *Studies on Voltaire and the Eighteenth Century*. Edited by Haydn Mason. Oxford: Cheney and Sons, 1978.

Gutas, Dimitri. *Greek Philosophers in the Arabic Tradition*. Great Britain: Ashgate Variorum, 2000.

Habermas, Jürgen. "Remarks on Legitimation through Human Rights," *Philosophy and Social Criticism* 24, nos. 2–3 (1998): 157–71.

Haddawy, Husain, trans. *The Arabian Nights*. New York: W. W. Norton, 1990.

Haidar, Musbah. *Arabesque*. London: Sphere, 1968.

Haig, M. R. "Ibn Battuta in Sindh." *Journal of the Royal Asiatic Society of Great Britain and Ireland* 19 (1887): 393–412.

Hall, Edith. *Inventing the Barbarian: Greek Self-Definition through Tragedy.* Oxford: Clarendon Press, 1989.

Hamalian, Leo, ed. *Ladies on the Loose: Women Travellers of the 18th and 19th Centuries*. New York: Dodd, Mead, 1981.

Hamdan, Jamal. *Shakhsiyyat Misr dirasa fi ʿabqariyyat al-makan*. Cairo: Maktabat al-Nahda al-Misriyya, 1970.

Hamdun, Said, and Noël King, eds and trans. *Ibn Battuta in Black Africa*. Princeton, NJ: Markus Wiener, 1994.

Hamed, Raouf Abbas. *The Japanese and Egyptian Enlightenment: A Comparative Study of Fukuwaza Yukichi and Rifaʿah al-Tahtawi*. Tokyo: Institute for the Study of Languages and Cultures of Asia and Africa, 1990.

Hammam, Mohammed, ed. *Al-Rihla bayna al-Sharq wa al-Gharb*. Rabat, Morocco: Kulliyyat al-Adab wa al-ʿUlum al-Insaniyya bi al-Rabat, 2003.

Hammoudi, Abdellah. *Master and Disciple: The Cultural Foundations of Moroccan Authoritarianism*. Chicago: University of Chicago Press, 1997.

Hanoum, Zeyneb. *A Turkish Woman's European Impressions*. New Jersey: Gorgias Press, 2004.

Hansen, Klaus J. "Tocqueville: Frenchman for all Seasons?" *Canadian Journal of History* 38 (August 2003): 295–305.

Harari, Josué V. *Scenarios of the Imaginary: Theorizing the French Enlightenment*. Ithaca: Cornell University Press, 1987.

Haraway, Donna. *Simians, Cyborgs, and Women: The Reinvention of Nature*. New York: Routledge, 1991.

al-Harawi, ʿAli ibn Abi Bakr. *A Lonely Wayfarer's Guide to Pilgrimage: ʿAli ibn Abi Bakr al-Harawi's Kitab al-Isharat ila Maʿrifat al-Ziyarat*. Translated by Josef W. Meri. Princeton, NJ: Darwin Press, 2004.

Hardt, Michael, and Antonio Negri. *Empire*. Cambridge, MA: Harvard University Press, 2000.

Harris, Hugh. "The Greek Origins of the Idea of Cosmopolitanism." *The International Journal of Ethics* 38 (1927): 1–10.

Hartley, J. P. *The Go-Between*. New York: Knopf, 1954.

Hartog, François. *Memories of Odysseus: Frontier Tales of Ancient Greece*. Translated by Janet Lloyd. Chicago: University of Chicago Press, 2001.

———. *The Mirror of Herodotus: The Representation of the Other in the Writing of History*. Translated by Janet Lloyd. Berkeley: University of California Press, 1988.

Hashemi, Nader. "Islam, Democracy, and Alexis de Tocqueville." *Queen's Quarterly* 110, no. 1 (spring 2003): 21–29.

Hashmi, Sohail H. "The Qurʾan and Tolerance: An Interpretive Essay on Verse 5:48." *Journal of Human Rights* 2, no. 1(March 2003): 81–103.

Hatem, Mervat. "Through Each Other's Eyes: The Impact on the Colonial Encounter of the Images of Egyptian, Levantine-Egyptian, and European Women, 1862–1920." In *Western Women and Imperialism: Complicity and Resis-

tance. Edited by Nupur Chaudhuri and Margaret Strobel. Bloomington: Indiana University Press, 1992.

Hegel. *The Phenomenology of Mind.* Translated by J. B. Hallie. London: George Allen and Unwin, 1961.

Heidegger, Martin. *Hölderlin's Hymn "The Ister."* Translated by William McNeill and Julia Davis. Bloomington: Indiana University Press, 1996.

Helms, Mary. *Ulysses Sail: An Ethnographic Odyssey of Power, Knowledge, and Geographical Distance.* Princeton, NJ: Princeton University Press, 1988.

Heraclitus. In *Ancilla to the Pre-Socratic Philosophers.* Translated by Kathleen Freeman. Cambridge, MA: Harvard University Press, 1978.

Herodotus. *The Histories.* Translated by George Rawlinson. New York: Everyman's Library, 1997.

Hersh, Seymour. "Selective Intelligence." *The New Yorker.* 79.11 (May 12, 2003): p. 44.

Heyworth-Dunne, J. *Introduction to the History of Education in Modern Egypt.* London: Luzac, 1938.

———. "Rifāʿah Badawī Rāfiʿ al-Tahtāwī: The Egyptian Revivalist." *Bulletin of the School of Oriental and African Studies* 9 (1937–39): 961–67.

———. "Rifāʿah Badawī Rāfiʿ al-Tahtāwī: The Egyptian Revivalist." *Bulletin of the School of Oriental and African Studies* 10 (1940–42): 399–415.

al-Hijazi, Mahmud Fahmi. *Usul al-Fikr al-ʿArabi al-hadith ʿinda al-Tahtawi, maʿa al-nass al-kamil li-kitabihi "Takhlis al-Ibriz."* Cairo: al-Hayʾa al-Misriyya al-ʿAmma li-l-Kitab, 1974.

Hocquard, Emmanuel. "Faire quelque chose avec ça."*Ma Haie.* Paris: P.O.L., 2001.

Hodgson, Marshall G. S. "Hemispheric Inter-regional History as an Approach to World History." *Journal of World History* 1 (1954): 715–23.

———. "The Unity of Later Islamic History." *Journal of World History* 5 (1960): 879–914.

———. *The Venture of Islam: Conscience and History in a World Civilization.* 3 vols. Chicago: University of Chicago Press, 1974.

Holland, Patrick, and Graham Huggan. *Tourists with Typewriters: Critical Reflections on Contemporary Travel Writing.* Ann Arbor: University of Michigan Press, 2002.

Holton, Robert John. "Cosmopolitanism or Cosmopolitanisms? The Universal Races Congress of 1911." *Global Networks* 2, no. 2 (2002): 153–70.

Honig, Bonnie. *Democracy and the Foreigner.* Princeton, NJ: Princeton University Press, 2001.

hooks, bell. *Talking Back: thinking feminist, thinking black.* Boston, MA: South End Press, 1989.

Hopkins, A. G. *An Economic History of West Africa.* New York: Columbia University Press, 1973.

Hore, Annie B. *To Lake Tanganyika in a Bath Chair.* London: Sampson Low, Marston, Searle, and Rivington, 1886.

Hourani, Albert. *Arabic Thought in the Liberal Age: 1798–1939.* Cambridge: Cambridge University Press, 1983.

Howard, Donald. R. *Writers and Pilgrims: Medieval Pilgrimage Narratives and their Posterity.* Berkeley: University of California Press, 1980.

Hrbek, Ivan. "The Chronology of Ibn Battuta's Travels." *Archiv Orientálni* 30 (1962): 409–86.

Hulliung, Mark. *Citizens and Citoyens: Republicans and Liberals in America and France.* Cambridge, MA: Harvard University Press, 2002.

Hundert, E. J. "Sexual Politics and the Allegory of Identity in Montesquieu's *Persian Letters.*" *The Eighteenth Century* 31, no. 2 (1990): 101–15.

Hunter, G. K. "Elizabethans and Foreigners." In *Shakespeare in His Own Age.* Edited by Allardyce Nicoll. Cambridge: Cambridge University Press, 1965.

Huntington, Samuel. "The Clash of Civilizations?" *Foreign Affairs* 72 (summer 1993): 22–49.

———. *The Clash of Civilizations and the Remaking of World Order.* New York: Simon and Schuster, 1996.

Hunwick, John. "Ahmad Bābā and the Moroccan Invasion of the Sudan (1591)." *Journal of the Historical Society of Nigeria* 2, no. 3 (December 1962): 311–28.

———. "Islamic Law and Polemic over Race and Slavery in North and West Africa (16th–19th century)." In *Slavery in the Islamic Middle East.* Edited by Shaun E. Marmon. Princeton, NJ: Markus Wiener, 1999.

Husain, Agha Mahdi. "Ibn Battuta and his Rehla in New Light." *Sind University Research Journal* 6 (1967): 25–32.

———. "Ibn Battuta: His Life and Work." *Indo-Iranica* 7 (1954): 6–13.

———. "Studies in the *Tuhfatunnuzzar* of Ibn Battuta and Ibn Juzayy." *Journal of the Asiatic Society of Bangladesh* 23 (1978): 18–49.

Husayn, Husni Mahmud. *Adab al-Rihla ʿinda al-ʿArab.* Cairo: al-Hayʾa al-Misriyya al-ʿAmma li-l-Kitab, 1976.

al-Husry, Khaldun S. *Three Reformers: A Study in Modern Arab and Political Thought.* Beirut: Khayats, 1966.

Huwaydi, Fahmi. "Didd kawkalat al-ʿalam! [Against 'Coca Cola-ization' of the World!]." *Al-Ahram,* October 10, 1995, p. 11.

Ibish, Yusuf. "Ibn ʿArabi's Theory of Journeying." In *Traditional Modes of Contemplation and Action.* Edited by Y. Ibish and P. L. Wilson. Tehran, Iran: Imperial Iranian Academy of Philosophy, 1977.

ibn Balaban, ʿAli. *Al-Ihsan fi Taqrib Sahih Ibn Hibban.* 18 vols. Beirut: Muʾassasat al-Risala, 1991.

Ibn Battuta. *The Rehla of Ibn Battuta (India, Maldive Islands, and Ceylon).* Translated by Mahdi Husain. Baroda: Oriental Institute, 1976.

———. *Rihlat Ibn Battuta.* Beirut: Dar Sadir, 1964.

———. *The Travels of Ibn Battuta.* 4 vols. Translated by H.A.R. Gibb and Charles F. Beckingham. London: Munshiram Manoharlal, 1999.

———. *Voyages d'Ibn Batoutah.* 3 vols. Translated by C. Defrémery and B. R. Sanguinetti. Paris: Imprimerie Nationale, 1949.

Ibn Jubayr. *Rihlat Ibn Jubayr.* Edited by William Wright. Leiden: Brill, 1907.

———. *The Travels of Ibn Jubayr.* Translated by Roland Broadhurst. India: Goodword, 2001.

Ibn Khaldûn. *The Muqaddimah: An Introduction to History.* Translated by Franz Rosenthal. New York: Pantheon, 1958.

Ibn Majah, Muhammad Ibn Yazid al-Qazwini. *Sunan.* Cairo: ʾIsa al-Babi al-Halabi, 1972.

Immerwahr, Henry R. *Form and Thought in Herodotus.* Cleveland, OH: Press of Western Reserve University, 1966.

"Islam, Transnationalism, and the Public Sphere in Western Europe." Special issue of the *Journal of Ethnic and Migration Studies* 30, no. 5 (2004).

al-Jahiz. *Rasaʾil al-Jahiz.* 2 vols. Edited by ʿAbd al-Salam Muhammad Harun. Cairo: Maktabat al-Khanji, 1964.

Janicsek, Stephen. "Ibn Battuta's Journey to Bulghar: Is it a Fabrication?" *Journal of the Royal Asiatic Society of Great Britain and Ireland* (October 1929): 791–800

JanMohamed, Abdul R. "Worldliness-without-World," Homelessness-as-Home: Toward a Definition of the Specular Border Intellectual." In *Edward Said: A Critical Reader.* Edited by Michael Sprinker. Oxford: Blackwell, 1992.

Jannsens, Herman F. *Ibn Batoutah: Le Voyageu de l'Islam.* Brussels: Office de Publicité, 1948.

Jardin, André. *Tocqueville: A Biography.* Translated by Lydia Davis with Robert Hemenway. New York: Farrar Straus Giroux, 1989.

Jay, Martin. *Downcast Eyes: The Denigration of Vision in Twentieth-Century French Thought.* Berkeley: University of California Press, 1994.

———. "Vision in Context: Reflections and Refractions." In *Vision in Context: Historical and Contemporary Perspectives on Sight.* Edited by Teresa Brennan and Martin Jay. New York: Routledge, 1996.

al-Jirahi, Ismaʿil ibn Muhammad al-ʿAjluni. *Kashf al-Khafa wa Muzil al-Ilbas.* 2 vols. Beirut: Muʾassasat al-Risala, 1979.

Just, Roger. *Women in Athenian Law and Life.* New York: Routledge, 1989.

Kabbani, Rana. *Imperial Fictions: Europe's Myths of the Orient.* London: HarperCollins, 1986.

Kalberg, Stephen. "Max Weber's Types of Rationality: Cornerstones for the Analysis of Rationalization Processes in History." *American Journal of Sociology* 85 (March 1980): 1145–79.

Kaplan, Caren. *Questions of Travel: Postmodern Discourses of Displacement.* Durham, NC: Duke University Press, 1996.

Karim, Karim H. "Muslim Encounters with New Media: Towards an Inter-Civilizational Discourse on Globality?" In *Islam Encountering Globalization.* Edited by Ali Mohammadi. New York: RoutledgeCurzon, 2002.

Kaye, Mary Margaret. *Trade Wind.* New York: Bantam, 1981.

Kechechian, Joseph A., and R. Hrair Dekmejian. *The Just Prince: A Manual of Leadership.* London: Saqi, 2003.

Kelly, Christopher. "Civil and Uncivil Religions: Tocqueville on Hinduism and Islam." *History of European Ideas* 20, no. 4–6 (1995): 845–50.

Kempis, Thomas à. *Imitation of Christ.* Edited by Ernest Rhys. London: J. M. Dent and Sons, 1910.

Ker, James. "Solon's Theôria and the End of the City." *Classical Antiquity* 19, no. 2 (October 2000): 304–29.

Khadduri, Majid. *War and Peace in the Law of Islam*. Baltimore: Johns Hopkins University Press, 1955.

Khalidi, Tarif. "Islamic Views of the West in the Middle Ages." *Studies in Inter-religious Dialogue* 5 (1995): 31–42.

Khan, Abdel Majed. "The Historicity of Ibn Batuta re: Shamsuddin Firuz Shah, the so-called Balbani King of Bengal." *The Indian Historical Quarterly* 18 (March 1942): 65–70.

Khan, M. A. Muqtedar. "The Quran Recognizes Jews and Christians as the Spiritual Equals of Muslims." http://www.ijtihad.org/.

Khatami, Mohammad. Interview with Christiane Amanpour. CNN, January 7, 1998.

King, Noël Q. "Egeria, Fa Hsien and Ibn Battuta: Search for Identity through Pilgrimage?" *Identity Issues and World Religions*. Edited by Victor C. Hayes. Australia: Wakefield Press, 1986.

———. "Reading between the Lines of Ibn Battuta for the History of Religion in Black Africa." *Milla wa-Milla* 19 (1979): 26–33.

Kleingeld, Pauline. "Six Varieties of Cosmopolitanism in Late-Eighteenth-Century Germany." *The Journal of the History of Ideas* 60, no. 3 (1999): 505–24.

Kolodny, Annette. *The Lay of the Land: Metaphor and History in American Life and Letters*. Chapel Hill, NC: University of North Carolina Press, 1975.

Kra, Pauline. "The Invisible Chain of the *Lettres Persanes*." *Studies in Voltaire and the 18th Century* 23 (1963): 9–55.

Kroller, Eva-Marie. "First Impressions: Rhetorical Strategies in Travel Writing by Victorian Women." *Ariel* 21 (1990): 87–99.

Kruk, Remke. "Ibn Battuta: Travel, Family Life, and Chronology—How Seriously Do We Take a Father?" *Al-Qantara* 16 (1995): 369–84.

Kymlicka, Will. *Multicultural Citizenship: A Liberal Theory of Minority Rights*. Oxford: Clarendon Press, 1995.

Lamberti, Jean-Claude. *Tocqueville and the Two Democracies*. Translated by Arthur Goldhammer. Cambridge, MA: Harvard University Press, 1989.

Landau, Jacob. "Muhammad Thabit, a Modern Arab Traveler." *The Journal of Arabic Literature* 1 (1970): 70–74.

Lane, Edward. *The Manners and Customs of the Modern Egyptians*. London: Everyman's Library, 1966.

Lapidus, Ira M. "Hierarchies and Networks: A Comparison of Chinese and Islamic Societies." In *Conflict and Control in Late Imperial China*. Edited by Frederic Wakeman, Jr., and Carolyn Grant. Berkeley: University of California Press, 1975.

———. "Islamic Revival and Modernity: The Contemporary Movements and the Historical Paradigms." *Journal of the Economic and Social History of the Orient* 40, no. 4 (1997): 444–60.

Laufer, Roger. *Style rococo, style des "lumières."* Paris: J. Corti, 1963.

Lavelle, B. M. Review of *The Mirror of Herodotus*. *The Classical World* 84 (March–April 1991): 313.

Lear, Jonathan. *Open Minded: Working Out the Logic of the Soul*. Cambridge, MA: Harvard University Press, 1998.

Leask, Nigel. *Curiosity and the Aesthetics of Travel Writing, 1770–1840*. Oxford: Oxford University Press, 2004.

Le Bouvier, Gilles. *Le Livre de la Description des Pays*. Edited by E. T. Hamy. Paris: E. Leroux, 1908.

Lee, Samuel. *The Travels of Ibn Batuta*. London: Oriental Translation Committee, 1829.

Leed, Eric. *The Mind of the Traveler: From Gilgamesh to Global Tourism*. New York: Basic Books, 1991.

Lenker, Michael Karl. "The Importance of the Rihla for the Islamization of Spain." Ph.D. Diss., University of Pennsylvania, 1982.

Leppihalme, Ritva. *Culture Bumps: An Empirical Approach to the Translation of Allusions*. Clevedon, Great Britain: Multilingual Matters, 1997.

Lerner, Ralph. *Maimonides' Empire of Light: Popular Enlightenment in an Age of Belief*. Chicago: University of Chicago Press, 2000.

Leslie, Margaret. "In Defense of Anachronism," *Political Studies* 18, no. 4 (1970): 433–47.

Levi-Strauss, Claude. *Tristes Tropiques*. New York: Penguin, 1992.

Levtzion, Nehemia, and Gideon Weigert. "The Muslim Holy Cities and Foci of Islamic Revivalism in the Eighteenth Century." In *Sacred Space: Shrine, City, Land*. Edited by Benjamin Z. Kedar and R. J. Zwi Werblowsky. New York: New York University Press, 1998.

Lewis, Bernard. *From Babel to Dragomans: Interpreting the Middle East*. Oxford: Oxford University Press, 2004.

———. *The Muslim Discovery of Europe*. New York: W. W. Norton, 1982.

———. *Race and Color in Islam*. New York: Harper and Row, 1971.

———. *Race and Slavery in the Middle East: An Historical Enquiry*. New York: Oxford University Press, 1990.

Lewis, Reina. "Harem Literature and Women's Travel." *International Institute for the Study of Islam in the Modern World Review* 16 (autumn 2005): 48–49.

———. *Rethinking Orientalism: Women, Travel, and the Ottoman Harem*. New Brunswick, NJ: Rutgers University Press, 2004.

Liebersohn, Harry. "Discovering Indigenous Nobility: Tocqueville, Chasmisso, and Romantic Travel Writing." *The American Historical Review* 99, no. 3 (June 1994): 746–66.

Lilla, Mark. "The Closing of the Straussian Mind." *New York Review of Books* 51, no. 17, November 4, 2004, 55–59.

Little, Donald P. "Did Ibn Taymiyya Have a Screw Loose?" *Studia Islamica* 41 (1975): 93–111.

Livingston, John W. "Western Science and Educational Reform in the Thought of Shaykh Rifaʿa al-Tahtawi." *International Journal of Middle East Studies* 28 (1996): 543–64.

Loti, Pierre. *Japan: Madame Chrysanthemum*. Translated by Laura Ensor. London: KPI, 1985.

Louca, Anouar. "Présentation: Le Voyage d'un orpailleur." In Tahtawi's *L'Or de Paris: Relation de Voyage, 1826–1831*. Edited and translated by Anouar Louca. Paris: Sindbad, 1988.

Lubeck, Paul. "Antinomies of Islamic Movements under Globalization." Center for Global International and Regional Studies Working Paper Series WP#99–1. University of California at Santa Cruz, 1999.

Lugones, María. "Playfulness, 'World'-Travelling, and Loving Perception." In *Making Face, Making Soul: Haciendo Caras*. Edited by Gloria Anzaldúa. San Francisco: Aunt Lute Foundation, 1990.

Lugones, María, and Elizabeth V. Spelman. "Have We Got a Theory for You! Feminist Theory, Cultural Imperialism, and the Demand for 'the Woman's Voice.'" *Women's Studies International Forum* 6, no. 6 (1983): 573–81.

Maalouf, Amin. *The Crusades through Arab Eyes*. New York: Schocken, 1987.

MacCannell, Dean. *The Tourist: A New Theory of the Leisure Class*. New York: Schocken, 1989.

Machiavelli, Niccolo. *The Prince and Discourses*. Translated by Luigi Ricci. New York: Random House, 1950.

Mackworth, Cecily. *The Destiny of Isabelle Eberhardt*. New York: Ecco Press, 1975.

Mahbubani, Kishore. "The West and the Rest." *The National Interest* 23 (summer 1992): 3–13.

Mahfouz, Naguib. *Rihlat Ibn Fattuma*. Cairo: Maktabat Misr, 1983.

Majdi, al-Sayyid Salih. *Hilyat al-Zaman bi-Manaqib Khadim al-Watan: Sirat Rifaʿa Rafiʿ al-Tahtawi*. Edited by Jamal al-Din al-Shayyal. Cairo: Maktabat Mustafa al-Babi al-Halabi, 1958.

Makdisi, George. "Ibn Taimiya: A Sufi of the Qadiriya Order." *American Journal of Arabic Studies* 1 (1973): 118–29.

Malti-Douglas, Fedwa. *Woman's Body, Woman's Word: Gender and Discourse in Arabo-Islamic Writing*. Princeton, NJ: Princeton University Press, 1991.

Mandaville, Peter G. "Reimagining the *Ummah*? Information Technology and the Changing Boundaries of Political Islam." In *Islam Encountering Globalization*. Edited by Ali Mohammadi. New York: RoutledgeCurzon, 2002.

———. "Sufis and Salafis: The Political Discourse of Transnational Islam." In *Remaking Muslim Politics: Pluralism, Contestation, and Democratization*. Edited by Robert W. Hefner. Princeton, NJ: Princeton University Press, 2005.

———. *Transnational Muslim Politics: Reimagining the Umma*. London: Routledge, 2001.

Mann, Charles C. *1491: New Revelations of the Americas before Columbus*. New York: Knopf, 2005.

———. "The Founding Sachems." *New York Times*, July 4, 2005, A17.

al-Manuni, Muhammad. *Al-Masadir al-ʿArabiyya li-Tarikh al-Maghrib*. 3 vols. Rabat, Morocco: al-Mamlaka al-Maghribiyya, Jamiʿat Muhammad al-Khamis, Kulliyat al-Adab wa al-ʿUlum al-Insaniyya, 1983.

al-Marayati, Laila, and Semeen Issa. "Muslim Women: An Identity Reduced to a Burka." *Los Angeles Times*, January 20, 2002, M1.

Marincola, John. "Herodotean Narrative and the Narrator's Presence." *Arethusa* 20, no. 1/2 (spring/fall 1987):121–37.

Marlow, Louise. "Kings, Prophets, and the ʿUlama in Medieval Islamic Advice Literature." *Studia Islamica* 81 (1995): 101–20.

Marsot, Afaf Lutfi al-Sayyid. *A Short History of Modern Egypt.* Cambridge: Cambridge University Press, 1985.

Martin, Catherine Gimelli. "Orientalism and the Ethnographer: Said, Herodotus, and the Discourse of Alterity." *Criticism* 32, no. 4 (fall 1990): 511–29.

Marx, Karl. *Capital.* New York: Modern Library, 1936.

Masud, Muhammad Khalid. "The Obligation to Migrate: the Doctrine of *hijra* in Islamic Law." In *Muslim Travellers: Pilgrimage, Migration, and the Religious Imagination.* Edited by Dale F. Eickelman and James Piscatori. Berkeley: University of California Press, 1990.

Matar, Nabil. "Confronting Decline in Early Modern Arabic Thought." *Journal of Early Modern History,* 9, no. 1–2 (2005): 51–78.

———. "Early Modern Europe through Islamic Eyes." Unpublished manuscript.

———. *In the Lands of the Christians: Arabic Travel Writing in the Seventeenth Century.* New York: Routledge, 2003.

———. *Turks, Moors, and Englishmen in the Age of Discovery.* New York: Columbia University Press, 1999.

Mattock, J. N. "Ibn Battuta's Use of Ibn Jubayr's *Rihla.*" *Proceedings of the Ninth Congress of the Union Européene des Arabisants et Islamisants.* Edited by Rudolph Peters. Leiden: Brill, 1981.

———. "The Travel Writings of Ibn Jubair and Ibn Batuta." *Glasgow University Oriental Society* 21, no. 165–66 (1965–66): pp. 35–46.

Mauss, Marcel. *The Gift: The Form and Reason for Exchange in Archaic Societies.* Translated by W. D. Halls. London: Routledge, 1990.

al-Mawardi, Abu al-Hasan ʿAli b. Muhammad b. Habib. *Adab al-Dunya wa al-Din.* Edited by Mustafa al-Saqqa. Egypt: Mustafa al-Babi al-Halabi, 1973.

Mawdudi, Abu al-Ala. *Purdah and the Status of Woman in Islam.* Translated by al-Ashʿarif. Lahore, Pakistan: Islamic Publications, 1991.

McCarthy, Thomas A. *The Critical Theory of Jürgen Habermas.* Cambridge, MA: MIT Press, 1991.

McDonald, Lucille. *The Arab Marco Polo: Ibn Battuta.* New York: Thomas Nelson, 1975.

McDonnell, Mary Byrne. "Patterns of Muslim Pilgrimage from Malaysia: 1885–1985." In *Muslim Travellers: Pilgrimage, Migration, and the Religious Imagination.* Edited by Dale F. Eickelman and James Piscatori. Berkeley: University of California Press, 1990.

McKenzie, Kevin. "The Psychology of Time-Travel: Ambivalent Identity in Stories of Cross-Cultural Contact." *Narrative Inquiry* 9, no. 2 (1999): 391–426.

McNeill, William H. *The Rise of the West: A History of the Human Community.* Chicago: Chicago University Press, 1963.

Meek, James. "Unveiled: The Secret Life of Women: The Female Victims of the Taliban's Brutal Five-year Regime Yearn for Greater Choice and Freedom." *The London Guardian,* November 16, 2001, 3.

Mehta, Pratap. "Cosmopolitanism and the Circle of Reason." *Political Theory* 28, no. 5 (October 2000): 619–39.

Mehta, Uday Singh. *Liberalism and Empire: A Study in Nineteenth-Century British Liberal Thought.* Chicago: Chicago University Press, 1999.

Melman, Billie. Review of Sayyida Salme/Emily Reute, *An Arabian Princess Between Two Worlds*. *The International Journal of Middle East Studies* 26, no. 3 (1994): 525–27.

———. *Women's Orient: English Women and the Middle East, 1718–1918*. Ann Arbor: University of Michigan Press, 1992.

Melville, Stephen. "Division of the Gaze, or, Remarks on the Color and Tenor of Contemporary 'Theory.' " In *Vision in Context: Historical and Contemporary Perspectives on Sight*. Edited by Teresa Brennan and Martin Jay. New York: Routledge, 1996.

Menocal, Maria Rosa. *The Ornament of the World: How Muslims, Jews, and Christians Created a Culture of Tolerance in Medieval Spain*. Boston: Little, Brown, 2002.

Menouni, Muhammad, and M'hammad Benaboud. "A Moroccan Account of Constantinople." In *Les provinces arabes à l'époque ottomane: études*. Edited by A Tememi. Zagwan: Centre d'études et de recherches ottomanes et morisco-andalouses, 1987.

Metcalf, Barbara D. "The Pilgrimage Remembered: South Asian Accounts of the *Hajj*." In *Muslim Travellers: Pilgrimage, Migration, and the Religious Imagination*. Edited by Dale F. Eickelman and James Piscatori. Berkeley: University of California Press, 1990.

Miled, Emma Ben. "Vie de Femmes a Travers La Rihla d'Ibn Battutah." *Revue tunisienne de sciences sociales: publication du Centre d'âetudes et de recherches âeconomiques et sociales* 104/105 (1991): 109–62.

Mill, James. *The History of British India* , 3rd ed. London: Baldwin, Cradock and Joy, 1826.

Mill, John Stuart. Review of *Democracy in America*. *The Edinburgh Review* 145 (October 1840):1–47.

Miller, D. W. "Storming the Palace in Political Science." *The Chronicle of Higher Education*, September 21, 2001, 16.

Miller, Susan Gilson. *Disorienting Encounters: Travels of a Moroccan Scholar in France in 1845–46*. Berkeley: University of California Press, 1991.

Mills, Sara. *Discourses of Difference: An Analysis of Women's Travel Writing and Colonialism*. New York: Routledge, 1991

Miquel, André. *La géographie humaine du monde musulman jusqu'au milieu du 11ᵉ siècle*. 2 vols. Paris: La Haye, Mouton, 1967.

———. "L'Islam d'Ibn Battuta." *Bulletin d'âetudes orientales* 30 (1978): 75–83.

Mitchell, Timothy. *Colonising Egypt*. Berkeley: University of California Press, 1991.

Momigliano, Arnaldo. *Studies in Historiography*. New York: Harper and Row, 1966.

Montaigne, Michel de. *Complete Works: Essays, Travel Journal, Letters*. Translated by Donald M. Frame. Stanford, CA: Stanford University Press, 1957.

———. *The Diary of Montaigne's Journey to Italy in 1580 and 1581*. Translated by E. J. Trechmann. New York: Harcourt, Brace, 1929.

———. *The Essays of Michel de Montaigne*. Translated by Charles Cotton. London: G. Bell, 1913.

Montesquieu. *Lettres Persanes*. Paris: Gallimard, 1973.

Montesquieu. *The Persian Letters*. Translated by C. J. Betts. New York: Penguin, 1973.

———. *The Persian Letters*. Translated by George R. Healy. Indianapolis: Hackett, 1999.

———. *The Spirit of the Laws*. Translated and edited by Anne M. Cohler, Basia Carolyn Miller, and Harold Samuel Stone. Cambridge: Cambridge University Press, 1989.

Moore, R. I. "First Froth." *Times Literary Supplement*, October 1, 2004, 26.

Moosa, Ebrahim. *Ghazālī and the Poetics of Imagination*. Chapel Hill: University of North Carolina Press, 2005.

Moosa, Matti. *The Origins of Modern Arabic Fiction*. Boulder, CO: Lynne Rienner, 1997.

More, Thomas. *Utopia*. Translated by David Wooten. Indianapolis: Hackett, 1999.

Moreson, John. *Information for Pilgrims unto the Holy Land*. Edited by E. Gordon Duff. London: Lawrence and Bullen, 1893.

Morgan, D. O. "Ibn Battuta and the Mongols." *Royal Asiatic Society of Great Britain and Ireland* 11, no. 1 (2001): 1–11.

Morgan, Susan. *Place Matters*. New Brunswick, NJ: Rutgers University Press, 1996.

Morris, Mary. *Maiden Voyages: Writings of Women Travelers*. New York: Vintage, 1993.

el-Moudden, Abderrahmane. *Al-Badawi al-Maghribiyya qabla al-istiʿmar: qabaʾil inawan wa al-Makhzan bayna al-qarn al-sadis ʿashar wa al-tasi ʿashar*. Rabat, Morocco: Jamiʿat Muhammad al-Khamis, Kuliyyat al-Adab wa al-ʿUlum al-Insaniyya bi al-Rabat, 1995.

———. "The Ambivalence of *Rihla*: Community Integration and Self-Definition in Moroccan Travel Accounts, 1300–1800." In *Muslim Travellers: Pilgrimage, Migration, and the Religious Imagination*. Edited by Dale F. Eickelman and James Piscatori. Berkeley: University of California Press, 1990.

———. "Le voyage dans le monde arabo-musulman: échange et modernité." Colloques et seminaries no. 108. Rabat, Morocco: Publications de la Faculté des Lettres et des Sciences Humaines, 2003: 57–71.

Muhammad, Akbar. "The Image of Africans in Arabic Literature: Some Unpublished Manuscripts." *Slaves and Slavery in Muslim Africa*. Vol. 1. Edited by John Ralph Willis. Totowa, NJ: Frank Cass, 1985.

Mulvey, Laura. *Visual and Other Pleasures*. Bloomington: Indiana University Press, 1989.

Muʾnis, Husain. *Ibn Battuta wa-Rihlatuhu: Tahqiq wa-dirasa wa-tahlil*. Cairo: Dar al-Maʿarif, 1980.

———. "Rahhalat al-Islam Ibn Battuta." *Al-Tarikh wa al-Mustaqbal* 3, no. 1 (1989): 141–48.

Murray, Oswyn. "Herodotus and Oral History." *Achaemenid History* 2 (1987): 93–115.

Myres, John. "Herodotus and Anthropology." In *Anthropology and the Classics*. Edited by Arthur J. Evans, Andrew Lang, Gilbert Murray, F. B. Jevons, J. L. Myres, and W. Warde Fowler. Oxford: Clarendon Press, 1908.

————. "Herodotus and his Critics." In *Herodotus: Father of History*. Oxford: Clarendon Press, 1953.

Naddaf, Sandra. "Mirrored Images: Rifaʿah al-Tahtawi and the West." *Alif: Journal of Comparative Poetics* 6 (spring 1986): 73–83.

Netton, Ian Richard. "Arabia and the Pilgrim Paradigm of Ibn Battūta: A Braudelian Approach." In *Arabia and the Gulf: From Traditional Society to Modern States*. Edited by Ian Richard Netton. Totowa, NJ: Barnes and Noble Books, 1986.

————. "Basic Structures and Signs of Alienation in the *Rihla* of Ibn Jubayr." *Golden Roads: Migration, Pilgrimage, and Travel in Mediaeval and Modern Islam*. Edited by Ian Richard Netton. Great Britain: Curzon Press, 1993.

————. "Myth, Miracle, and Magic in the *Rihla* of Ibn Battuta." *Journal of Semitic Studies* 29, no. 1 (1984): 131–40.

————. *Seek Knowledge: Thought and Travel in the House of Islam*. Great Britain: Curzon Press, 1996.

————. "Tourist *Adab* and Cairene Architecture: The Medieval Paradigm of Ibn Jubayr and Ibn Battutah." In *The Literary Heritage of Classical Islam: Arabic and Islamic Studies in Honor of James A. Bellamy*. Edited by Mustansir Mir and Jarl E. Fossum. Princeton, NJ: Darwin Press, 1993.

Netton, Ian Richard, ed. *Golden Roads: Migration, Pilgrimage, and Travel in Mediaeval and Modern Islam*. Great Britain: Curzon Press, 1993.

Newman, Daniel. *An Imam in Paris: Al-Tahtawi's Visit to France (1826–1831)*. London: Saqi Press, 2004.

Nietzsche, Friedrich. *Human All-Too-Human*. Translated by Paul V. Cohn. New York: Macmillan, 1924.

————. *Thus Spake Zarathustra*. Translated by Thomas Common. Buffalo, NY: Prometheus, 1993.

Nightingale, Andrea Wilson. *Genres in Dialogue: Plato and the Construct of Philosophy*. Cambridge: Cambridge University Press, 1995.

————. *Spectacles of Truth in Classical Greek Philosophy: Theoria in its Cultural Context*. Cambridge: Cambridge University Press, 2004.

Niranjana, Tejaswini. *Siting Translation: History, Post-Structuralism, and the Colonial Context*. Berkeley: University of California Press, 1992.

al-Nisaburi, Muslim Ibn al-Hajjaj al-Qushayri. *Sahih Muslim bi Sharh al-Nawawi*. Edited by ʿIsam al-Sababiti, Hazim Muhammad, and ʿImad ʿAmir. 11 vols. Cairo: Dar al-Hadith, 1994.

Nisbet, Robert. "Many Tocquevilles." *American Scholar* 46(winter 1976–77): 59–75.

Norris, H. T. "Ibn Battuta's Journey in the North-Eastern Balkans." *Journal of Islamic Studies* 5, no. 2 (1994): 209–20.

————. "Ibn Battuta on Muslims and Christians in the Crimean Peninsula." *Iran and the Caucasus* 8, no. 1 (2004): 7–14.

Norton, Anne. *Leo Strauss and the Politics of American Empire*. New Haven: Yale University Press, 2004.

al-Nuʿman, Qadi. *The Pillars of Islam: Laws Pertaining to Human Intercourse/ Daʿaʾim al-Islam of al-Qadi al-Nuʿman*. 2 vols. Translated by Asaf A. A. Fyzee. New Delhi: Oxford University Press, 2002.

Nussbaum, Martha. *For Love of Country: Debating the Limits of Patriotism*. Edited by Joshua Cohen. Boston: Beacon Press, 1996.

Nussbaum, Martha, et al. "Patriotism or Cosmopolitanism? *Boston Review* 19, no. 5 (October/November 1994): 3–7.

Orany, Ezzat. " 'Nation,' 'Patrie,' 'Citoyen,' chez Rifāʿa al-Tahtāwi et Khayr-al-Dīn Al-Tounsi." *Mélanges de l'Institut Dominicain d'Etudes Orientales du Caire* 156 (1983): 169–90.

Ouyang, Wen-chin. "The Dialectic of Past and Present in *Rihlat Ibn Fattūma* by Najīb Mahfūz." *Edebiyat* 14, no. 1–2 (2003): 81–107.

Pagden, Anthony. "The Effacement of Difference: Colonialism and the Origins of Nationalism in Diderot and Herder." In *After Colonialism: Imperial Histories and Postcolonial Displacements*. Edited by Gyan Prakash. Princeton, NJ: Princeton University Press, 1995.

Parel, Anthony, and Ronald C. Keith, eds. *Comparative Political Philosophy: Studies under the Upas Tree*. New Delhi: Sage, 1992.

Pavlenko, Aneta. "Language Learning Memoirs as a Gendered Genre." *Applied Linguistics* 22, no. 2 (2001): 213–40.

Pease, Donald E. "After the Tocqueville Revival; or, the Return of the Political: The Tocqueville Revival and the 'Resurgence of Islam.' " *Boundary* 2, 26:3 (1999): 87–114.

Perceval, A. Caussin de. "Relation d'un voyage en France, par le cheikh Réfaa." *Nouveau Journal Asiatique*, Tome XI, Vol. 11 (Paris, 1833): 222–51.

Perkins, William. *The Workes of that Famous and Worthy Minister of Christ, In the Universitie of Cambridge, M. W. Perkins*. London: John Haviland, 1631.

Perlstein, Rick. "Getting Real: Homo Economicus Goes to the Lab." *Lingua Franca* 7 (April/May 1997): 59–65.

Pessen, Edward. *Jacksonian America: Society, Personality, and Politics*. Illinois: Dorsey Press, 1969.

Pickthall, Mohammed Marmaduke, trans. *The Glorious Qurʾan*. New York: Tahrike Tarsile Qurʾan, 2000.

Pierson, George Wilson. *Tocqueville and Beaumont in America*. New York: Oxford University Press, 1938.

Pieterse, Jan Nederveen. "Globalization as Hybridization." In *Global Modernities*. Edited by Mike Featherstone, Scott Lash, and Roland Robertson. London: Sage, 1995.

Plato. *Plato: The Collected Dialogues*. Edited by Edith Hamilton and Huntington Cairns. Princeton, NJ: Princeton University Press, 1987.

Plutarch. *De Malignitate Herodoti*. Translated by Anthony Bowen. Warminster, England: Aris and Phillips, 1992.

"The Politics of Travel." Special issue of *The Nation*. October 6, 1997.

Pollack, Sheldon. "Cosmopolitanism and Vernacular in History." *Public Culture* 12, no. 3 (2000): 591–625.

Pollard, Lisa. "The Habits and Customs of Modernity: Egyptians in Europe and the Geography of Nineteenth-Century Nationalism." *Arab Studies Journal* 7–8 (fall 1999–spring 2000): 52–74.

Poole, Stanley Lane. *Life of Edward William Lane*. London: Williams and Norgate, 1877.

Popper, Karl. *The Open Society and Its Enemies*. 2 vols. London: Routledge and Kegan Paul, 1957.

Powell, Eve M. Troutt. *A Different Shade of Colonialism: Egypt, Great Britain, and the Mastery of the Sudan*. Berkeley: University of California Press, 2003.

———. "From Odyssey to Empire: Mapping Sudan through Egyptian Literature in the Mid-19th Century." *International Journal of Middle East Studies* 31 (1999): 401–27.

Pratt, Mary Louise. *Imperial Eyes: Travel Writing and Transculturation*. London: Routledge, 1992.

Pucci, Susan. "Orientalism and Representations of Exteriority in Montesquieu's *Lettres Persanes*." *The Eighteenth Century* 26 (1985): 263–79.

Qadduri, ʿAbd al-Majid. *Sufaraʾ Maghariba fi Urubba, 1610–1922: fi al-waʿy bi altafawut*. Rabat, Morocco: al-Mamlaka al-Maghribiyya, Jamiʿat Muhammad al-Khamis, Kulliyyat al-Adab wa al-ʿUlum al-Insaniyya bi al-Rabat, 1995.

Qutb, Sayyid. *Amrika min al-dakhil bi minzar Sayyid Qutb*. Edited by Salah ʿAbd al-Fattah al-Khalidi. Jeddah: Dar al-Manara, 1986.

Rabinow, Paul. *Reflections on Fieldwork in Morocco*. Berkeley: University of California Press, 1977.

Radway, Janice. "Reception Study: Ethnography and the Problems of Dispersed Audiences and Nomadic Subjects." *Cultural Studies* 2, no. 3 (1988): 359–76.

Rafael, Vincente L. *Contracting Colonialism: Translation and Christian Conversion in Tagalog Society under Early Spanish Rule*. Ithaca: Cornell University Press, 1988.

al-Rafiʿi, ʿAbd al-Rahman. *ʿAsr Muhammad ʿAli*. Cairo: Maktabat al-Nahda al-Misriyya, 1951.

———. *Tarikh al-Haraka al-Qawmiyya wa-Tatawwur Nizam al-Hukm fi Misr*. 2 vols. Cairo: Dar al-Maʿarif, 1981.

Ramadan, Tariq. *To Be a European Muslim: A Study of Islamic Sources in the European Context*. Leicester: Islamic Foundation, 1999.

Rawlinson, H. G. "The Traveller of Islam." *Islamic Culture* 5 (1931): 29–37.

Redfield, James. "Herodotus the Tourist." *Classical Philology* 80 (1985): 97–118.

Reichmuth, Stefan. "The Interplay of Local Developments and Transnational Relations in the Islamic World: Perceptions and Perspectives." In *Inter-Regional and Inter-Ethnic Relations*. Vol. 2. *Muslim Culture in Russia and Central Asia from the Eighteenth to the Early Twentieth Centuries*. Edited by Anke von Kügelgen, Michael Kemper, and Allen J. Frank. Berlin: Klaus Schwarz, 1998.

———. "Murtadā al-Zabīdī (1732–91) and the Africans: Islamic Discourse and Scholarly Networks in the Late Eighteenth Century." In *The Transmission of Learning in Islamic Africa*. Edited by Scott R. Reese. Leiden: Brill, 2004.

Renan, Ernest. *L'Islamisme et la Science: Conférence faite à la Sorbonne le 20 mars 1883*. Paris: Calmann Lévy, 1883.

Ricaut, Sir Paul. *Histoire de l'État présent de l'Empire ottoman*. Translated by M. Briot. Amsterdam: Chez A. Wolfgank, 1670.

Richter, Melvin. *Essays in Theory and History: An Approach to the Social Sciences.* Cambridge, MA: Harvard University Press, 1970.

———. "Montesquieu's Theory and Practice of the Comparative Method." *History of the Human Sciences* 15, no. 29 (2002): 21–33.

———."Tocqueville on Algeria." *The Review of Politics* 25 (1963): 362–98.

———. "Tocqueville and Guizot on Democracy: From a Type of Society to a Political Regime." *History of European Ideas* 30 (2004): 61–82.

Ricoeur, Paul. *The Conflict of Interpretations: Essays in Hermeneutics.* Edited by Don Ihde. Evanston, IL: Northwestern University Press, 1974.

———. "Existence et hermeneutique." In *Le Conflit des Interprétations: Essais d'herméneutique.* Paris: Éditions Du Seuil, 1969.

———. *History and Truth.* Translated by Charles A. Kelbley. Evanston, IL: Northwestern University Press, 1965.

Rispler, Vardit. "Toward a New Understanding of the Term *bid'a.*" *Der Islam* 68 (1991): 320–28.

Rivlin, Helen Anne B. *The Agricultural Policy of Muhammad ʿAli in Egypt.* Cambridge, MA: Harvard University Press, 1961.

Robbins, Bruce. "Comparative Cosmopolitanisms." *Social Text* 31/32 (1992): 169–86.

———. "The East Is a Career: Edward Said and the Logics of Professionalism." In *Edward Said: A Critical Reader.* Edited by Michael Sprinker. Oxford: Blackwell, 1992.

———. "Introduction, Part I: Actually Existing Cosmopolitanism." *Cosmopolitics: Thinking and Feeling Beyond the Nation.* Edited by Pheng Cheah and Bruce Robbins. Minneapolis: University of Minnesota Press, 1998

Roberson, Susan L., ed. *Defining Travel: Diverse Visions.* Jackson: University Press of Mississippi, 2001.

Robertson, George, Melinda Mash, Lisa Tickner, Jon Bird, Barry Curtis, and Tim Putnam, eds. *Travellers' Tales: Narratives of Home and Displacement.* London: Routledge, 1994.

Robertson, Roland. "Mapping the Global Condition: Globalization as the Central Concept." In *Global Culture: Nationalism, Globalization, and Modernity.* Edited by Mike Featherstone. London: Sage, 1990.

Robinson, Frances. "Ottomans-Safavids-Mughals: Shared Knowledge and Connective Systems." *Journal of Islamic Studies* 8 (1997): 151–84.

Romero, Patricia W., ed. *Women's Voices on Africa: A Century of Travel Writings.* Princeton, NJ: Markus Wiener, 1992.

Rorty, Richard. *Contingency, Irony, and Solidarity.* Cambridge: Cambridge University Press, 1989.

———. *Philosophy and the Mirror of Nature.* Princeton, NJ: Princeton University Press, 1979.

Rorty, Richard, and Gianni Vattimo. *The Future of Religion.* Edited by Santiago Zabala. New York: Columbia University Press, 2005.

Rosenthal, Franz. "Gifts and Bribes: The Muslim View." *Proceedings of the American Philosophical Society* 108, no. 2 (April 1964): 135–44.

———. *Greek Philosophy in the Arab World: A Collection of Essays.* Great Britain: Variorium, 1990.

————. *Knowledge Triumphant: The Concept of Knowledge in Medieval Islam.* Leiden: Brill, 1970.

————. "On the Semitic Root s/š-p-r and Arabic *Safar*, 'Travel.'" *Jerusalem Studies in Arabic and Islam* 24 (2000): 4–21.

————. "The Stranger in Medieval Islam." *Arabica* 44 (1997): 35–75.

————. *The Technique and Approach of Muslim Scholarship.* Rome: Pontificium Institutum Biblicum, 1947.

Rudolph, Suzanne Hoeber, and James Piscatori, eds. *Transnational Religion and Fading States.* Boulder, CO: Westview Press, 1997.

Runciman, Steven. *A History of the Crusades.* 3 vols. Cambridge: Cambridge University Press, 1954.

Russell, Mrs. Charles E. B. *General Rigby, Zanzibar, and the Slave Trade, with Journals, Dispatches, Etc.* London: George Allen and Unwin, 1935.

Rutherford, Ian. "*Theoria* and *Darśan*: Pilgrimage and Vision in Greece and India." *Classical Quarterly* 50, no. 1 (2000): 133–46.

————. "Theoric Crisis: The Dangers of Pilgrimage in Greek Religion and Society." *Studi e materiali di storia delle religioni* 61 (1995): 275–92.

Sabry, Muhammad. *Genèse de l'esprit national.* Paris: Vrin, 1924.

Sadiki, Larbi. *The Arab Search for Democracy: Discourses and Counter-Discourses.* New York: Columbia University Press, 2004.

Said, Edward. "Edward Said: The Voice of a Palestinian Exile." *Third Text* 3–4, (spring–summer 1998): 39–50.

————. "The Mind of Winter: Reflections on Life in Exile." *Harper's* 269 (September 1984), 49–55.

————. *Orientalism.* New York: Pantheon, 1978.

————. "Orientalism Reconsidered." In *Orientalism: A Reader.* Edited by A. L. Macfie. New York: New York University Press, 2000.

————. "Traveling Theory." *The World, The Text, and the Critic.* Cambridge, MA: Harvard University Press, 1983.

————. "Traveling Theory Reconsidered." In *Reflections on Exile and Other Essays.* Cambridge, MA: Harvard University Press, 2000.

Sainte-Beuve, C. A. "Montesquieu." In *Portraits of the Eighteenth Century: Historic and Literary.* Translated by Katharine P. Wormeley. New York: Frederick Ungar, 1964.

Salkever, Stephen, and Michael Nylan. "Comparative Political Philosophy and Liberal Education: Looking for Friends in History." *Political Science and Politics* 26 (June 1994): 238–47.

Salme, Sayyida [Emily Reute]. *An Arabian Princess between Two Worlds.* Edited by E. Van Donzel. Leiden: Brill, 1993.

Sancisi-Weerdenburg, Heleen. "Exit Atossa: Images of Women in Greek Historiography on Persia." *Images of Women in Antiquity.* Edited by Averil Cameron and Amélie Kuhrt. Detroit: Wayne State University Press, 1983.

Sandars, N. K., trans. *The Epic of Gilgamesh.* New York: Penguin, 1972.

Sassen, Saskia. *Globalization and its Discontents.* New York: New Press, 1998.

Sawaie, Muhammed. "Rifaʿa Rafiʿ al-Tahtawi and his Contribution to the Lexical Development of Modern Literary Arabic." *The International Journal of Middle East Studies* 32 (2000): 395–410.

Sayyid Ahmad, Ahmad. *Rifaʿa Rafiʿ al-Tahtawi fi al-Sudan*. Cairo: Lajnat al-Taʾlif wa al-Tarjama wa al-Nashr, 1973.

Sayyid, Bobby. *A Fundamental Fear: Eurocentrism and the Emergence of Islamism*. London: Zed, 1997.

Schaub, Diana J. *Erotic Liberalism: Women and Revolution in Montesquieu's Persian Letters*. London: Rowman and Littlefield, 1995.

Schleifer, James T. *The Making of Tocqueville's* Democracy in America. Chapel Hill: University of North Carolina Press, 1980.

Schneppen, Heinz. "Sayyida Salme/Emily Reute: Between Zanzibar and German, Between Islam and Christianity." National Museums of Tanzania, Occasional Paper No. 12. Dar es Salaam, 1999.

Sciolino, Elaine. "Europe Meets the New Face of Terrorism." *The New York Times*, August 1, 2005, 1.

Scott, Joan W. "Experience." In *Feminists Theorize the Political*. Edited by Judith Butler and Joan W. Scott. New York: Routledge, 1992.

Shackleton, Robert. *Montesquieu: A Critical Biography*. Oxford: Oxford University Press, 1961.

Shaked, Shaul. "Quests and Visionary Journeys in Sasanian Iran." In *Transformations of the Inner Self in Ancient Religions*. Edited by Jan Assmann and Guy G. Stroumsa. Leiden: Brill, 1999.

Shapiro, Susan O. "Herodotus and Solon." *Classical Antiquity* 15, no. 2 (October 1996): 348–64.

Sharabi, Hisham. *Arab Intellectuals and the West: The Formative Years, 1875–1914*. Baltimore: Johns Hopkins University Press, 1970.

al-Shayyal, Jamal al-Din. *Tarikh al-tarjama wa al-haraka al-thaqafiyya fi ʿasr Muhammad ʿAli*. Cairo: Dar al-Fikr al-ʿArabi, 1951.

Sheriff, A.M.H. "The Slave Mode of Production along the East African Coast, 1810–1873." In *Slaves and Slavery in Muslim Africa*. Vol. 2. Edited by John Ralph Willis. London: Frank Cass, 1985.

Shichor, Yitzhak. "Virtual Transnationalism: Uygur Communities in Europe and the Quest for Eastern Turkestan Independence." In *Muslim Networks and Transnational Communities in and Across Europe*. Edited by Stefano Allievi and Jørgen S. Nielsen. Leiden: Brill, 2003.

Shklar, Judith N. *Montesquieu*. Oxford: Oxford University Press, 1987.

Silvera, Alain. "The First Egyptian Student Mission to France under Muhammad ʿAli." *Middle Eastern Studies* 16, no. 20 (1980): 1–22.

Singh, Umesh Kumar. "Ibn Battutah's Rehlah." *The Quarterly Review of Historical Studies* 18, no. 3 (1978–79): 192–96.

Smith, Anthony. *The Ethnic Origins of Nations*. Oxford: Basil Blackwell, 1988.

Smith, Sidonie. *Moving Lives: 20th-Century Women's Travel Writing*. Minneapolis: University of Minnesota Press, 2001.

Spahn, Raymon Jürgen. "German Accounts of Early-Nineteenth-Century Life in Illinois." *Papers on Language and Literature* 14 (fall 1978): 473–88.

Spivak, Gayatri Chakravorty. *Outside in the Teaching Machine*. New York: Routledge, 1993.

Stambler, Susanna. "Herodotus." In *Ancient Writers: Greece and Rome*. Edited by T. James Luce. New York: Charles Scribner's Sons, 1982.

Stark, Werner. *Montesquieu: Pioneer of the Sociology of Knowledge*. Toronto: University of Toronto Press, 1961.

Starobinski, Jean. *Blessings in Disguise; or, The Morality of Evil*. Translated by Arthur Goldhammer. Cambridge, MA: Harvard University Press, 1993.

Stoler, Ann. "Rethinking Colonial Categories: Communities and the Boundaries of Rule." *Comparative Studies in Society and History* 31, no. 1 (January 1989): 134–61.

Stowasser, Barbara Freyer. "Religious Ideology, Women, and the Family: The Islamic Paradigm." In *The Islamic Impulse*. Edited by Barbara Freyer Stowasser. Washington D.C.: Center for Contemporary Arab Studies, 1987.

Sublet, Jacqueline. "Les Frontières chez Ibn Batuta." In *La signification du Bas Moyen Age dans l'histoire et la culture du monde musulman: actes du 8me Congrès de l'Union Européenne des Arabisants et Islamisants*. Aix-en-Provence: Edisud, 1978: 305–8.

Subrahmanyam, Sanjay. "Connected Histories: Notes towards a Reconfiguration of Early Modern Eurasia," *Modern Asian Studies* 31, no. 3 (July 1997): 735–62.

Suchard, Tzadok Schmeul. *Make Your Marriage Work*. New York: Suchard, 1981.

Suleri, Sara. *Meatless Days*. Chicago: University of Chicago Press, 1987.

al-Suyuti, Jamal al-Din. *Jamiᶜ al-ahadith li-l-Jamiᶜ al-saghir wa-zawaʾidihi wa al-Jamiᶜ al-Kabir*. Damascus: Matbaᶜat Muhammad Hashim al-Kutubi, 1979–81.

Swaine, Lucas. "The Secret Chain: Justice and Self-Interest in Montesquieu's *Persian Letters*." *History of Political Thought* 22, no. 1 (spring 2001): 84–105.

al-Tabarani, Sulayman. *Al-Muᶜjam al-Awsat*. 7 vols. Amman, Jordan: Dar al-Fikr, 1999.

al-Tahtawi, Rifaᶜa Rafiᶜ. *Al-Aᶜmal al-Kamila li-Rifaᶜa Rafiᶜ al-Tahtawi*. 3 vols. Edited by Muhammad ʿImarah. Beirut: Al-Muʾassasa al-ᶜArabiyya li-l-Dirasat wa al-Nashr, 1973.

———. *Kitab al-Murshid al-Amin li-l-Banat wa al-Banin*. Egypt: Matbaᶜat al-Madaris al-Malakiyya, 1872.

———. *Manahij al-Albab al-Misriyya fi Mabahij al-Adab al-ᶜAsriyya*. Cairo: Matbaᶜat Shirkat al-Rajaʾib, 1912.

———. *Mawaqiᶜ al-Aflak fi waqaʾiᶜ Tilimak*. Beirut: al-Matbaᶜa al-Suriya, 1867.

———. *Takhlis al-Ibriz ila Talkhis Bariz; aw al-Diwan al-nafis bi-iwan Baris*. Egypt: Dar al-Taqaddum, 1905.

Tapper, Nancy. "*Ziyarat*: Gender, Movement, and Exchange in a Turkish Community." In *Muslim Travellers: Pilgrimage, Migration, and the Religious Imagination*. Edited by Dale F. Eickelman and James Piscatori. Berkeley: University of California Press, 1990.

Tauber, Ezriel. *To Become One: The Torah Outlook on Marriage*. Monsey, NY: Shalheves, 1990.

Tavakoli-Targhi, Mohamad. "Imagining Western Women: Occidentalism and Euro-Centrism." *Radical America* 24, no. 3 (1993): 73–87.

———. "Modernity, Heterotopia, and Homeless Texts." *Comparative Studies of South Asia, Africa, and the Middle East* 18, no. 2 (1998): 2–13.

———. "The Persian Gaze and the Women of the Occident." *South Asia Bulletin* 11, nos. 1–2 (1991): 21–31.

Tavakoli-Targhi, Mohamad. *Refashioning Iran: Orientalism, Occidentalism, and Historiography.* New York: Palgrave, 2001.

Tavernier, Jean-Baptiste. *Les six voyages de Jean-Baptiste Tavernier . . . en Turquie, en Perse, et aux Indes.* Paris, 1679.

Taylor, Charles. "Gadamer on the Human Sciences." In *The Cambridge Companion to Gadamer.* Edited by Robert J. Dostal. Cambridge: Cambridge University Press, 2002.

————. *Modern Social Imaginaries.* Durham, NC: Duke University Press, 2004.

Thubron, Colin. "Both Seer and Seen." *The Times Literary Supplement.* July 30, 1999, 12–13.

Thucydides. *The Peloponnesian War.* Translated by Steven Lattimore. Indianapolis: Hackett, 1998.

al-Tirmidhi, Muhammad. *Sunan al-Tirmidhi wa-huwa al-Jamiʿ al-Sahih.* 5 vols. al-Medina al-Munawwara: al-Maktaba al-Salafiyya, 1965.

Tocqueville, Alexis de. *Democracy in America.* Translated by George Lawrence. New York: Anchor, 1969.

————. *Democracy in America.* Translated by Harvey C. Mansfield and Delba Winthrop. Chicago: University of Chicago Press, 2000.

————. *Du système pénitentiaire aux Etats-Unis et de son application en France.* Paris, 1832.

————. *Journey to America.* Edited by J. P. Mayer. London: Faber and Faber, 1959.

————. *Journeys to England and Ireland.* Translated by George Lawrence and J. P. Mayer. New Brunswick, NJ: Transaction Books, 1988.

————. *L'Ancien Régime et la Révolution.* Paris: Michel, Lévy Frères, 1856.

————. *Memoir, Letters, and Remains.* 2 vols. Translated by the Translator of *Napoleon's Correspondence with King Joseph.* London: Macmillan, 1861.

————. *Selected Letters on Politics and Society.* Translated by Roger Boesche and James Toupin. Berkeley: University of California Press, 1985.

————. *Writings on Empire and Slavery.* Translated by Jennifer Pitts. Baltimore: Johns Hopkins University Press, 2001.

Tolmacheva, Marina A. "Ibn Battuta on Women's Travel in the Dar al-Islam." In *Women and the Journey: The Female Travel Experience.* Edited by Bonnie Frederick and Susan H. McLeod. Pullman: Washington State University Press, 1993.

Tsing, Anna Lowenhaupt. "Transitions as Translations." In *Transitions, Environments, Translations: Feminisms in International Politics.* Edited by Joan W. Scott, Cora Kaplan, and Debra Keates. London: Routledge, 1988.

Turner, Victor. *Dramas, Fields, and Metaphors: Symbolic Action in Human Society.* Ithaca: Cornell University Press, 1974.

Tyerman, Christopher. *Fighting for Christendom: Holy War and the Crusades.* Oxford: Oxford University Press, 2004.

Urvoy, Dominique. "Effets Pervers du Hajj, d'après le Cas d'al-Andalus." In *Golden Roads: Migration, Pilgrimage, and Travel in Mediaeval and Modern Islam.* Edited by Ian Richard Netton. Great Britain: Curzon Press, 1993.

Van Den Abbeele, Georges. *Travel as Metaphor: From Montaigne to Rousseau.* Minneapolis: University of Minnesota Press, 1992.

van der Veer, Peter. "Transnational Religion." Working Paper 01–06h, July 2001. The Center for Migration and Development, Princeton University.

van Donzel, E. "Sayyida Salme, Rudolph und die deutsche Kolonialpolitik." *Die Welt des Islams* 27 (1987): 13–22.

Vasseleu, Cathryn. "Illuminating Passion: Irigaray's Transfiguration of Night." In *Vision in Context: Historical and Contemporary Perspectives on Sight.* Edited by Teresa Brennan and Martin Jay. New York: Routledge, 1996.

Vatikiotis, P. J. *The Modern History of Egypt.* London: Weidenfeld and Nicolson, 1969.

Venuti, Lawrence, ed. *Rethinking Translation: Discourse, Subjectivity, Ideology.* New York: Routledge, 1992.

Virilio, Paul. *The Information Bomb.* New York: Verso, 2000.

Voll, John. "Islam as a Special World-System." *Journal of World History* 5, no. 2 (1994): 213–26.

Wahid, Mirza M. "Khusrau and Ibn Battuta: A Comparative Study." In *Professor Muhammad Shafiʿ Presentation Volume.* Edited by S. M. Abdullah. Lahore, Pakistan: The Majlis-e-Armughān-e-ʿIlmi, 1955.

Wahidah, Subhi. *Fi Usul al-Masʾala al-Misriyya.* Cairo: Maktabat al-Anglu al-Misriyya, 1950.

Waines, David. *An Introduction to Islam.* Cambridge: Cambridge University Press, 1998.

Wajcman, Judy. *Feminism Confronts Technology.* University Park: Pennsylvania State University Press, 1991.

Waldman, Amy. "Seething Unease Shaped British Bombers' Newfound Zeal." *The New York Times,* July 31, 2005, 1.

Waldron, Jeremy. "Minority Cultures and the Cosmopolitan Alternative." In *The Rights of Minority Cultures.* Edited by Will Kymlicka. Oxford: Oxford University Press, 1995.

Walzer, Michael. *Interpretation and Social Criticism.* Cambridge, MA: Harvard University Press, 1987.

Wansbrough, John. "Africa and the Arab Geographers." In *Language and History in Africa.* Edited by David Dalby. New York: Africana, 1970.

Waters, K. H. *Herodotus the Historian.* Oklahoma: University of Oklahoma Press, 1985.

Weber, Max. *The Sociology of Religion.* Translated by Ephraim Fischoff. Boston: Beacon Press, 1964.

Weinstein, Michael M. "Students Seek Some Reality amid the Math Economics." *The New York Times,* September 18, 1999, B9, B11.

Welch, Cheryl. *De Tocqueville.* Oxford: Oxford University Press, 2001.

Welter, Barbara. "The Cult of True Womanhood: 1820–1860." *American Quarterly* 18, no. 2, part 1 (summer 1966): 151–74.

Werbner, Pnina. "Global Pathways. Working Class Cosmopolitans and the Creation of Transnational Ethnic Worlds." *Social Anthropology* 7, no. 1 (1999): 17–35.

Wesley, Marilyn C. *Secret Journeys: The Trope of Women's Travel in American Literature*. Albany: State University of New York Press, 1999.

West, M. L. *The East Face of Helicon: West Asiatic Elements in Greek Poetry and Myth*. New York: Oxford University Press, 1997.

Westermarck, Edward. *Ritual and Belief in Morocco*. London: Macmillan, 1926.

————. *Wit and Wisdom in Morocco: A Study of Native Proverbs*. London: George Routledge and Sons, 1930.

Wha, Min Byung. "*Baraka*, as Motif and Motive, in the *Rihla* of Ibn Battuta." Ph.D. Diss., University of Utah, 1991.

White-Parks, Annette. "Journey to the Golden Mountain: Chinese Immigrant Women." In *Women and the Journey: the Female Travel Experience*. Edited by Bonnie Frederick and Susan H. McLeod. Pullman: Washington State University Press, 1993.

Wills, Gary. "Did Tocqueville 'Get' America?" *The New York Review of Books*, April 29, 2004, 52–56.

Wittgenstein, Ludwig. *Culture and Value*. Translated by Peter Winch. Chicago: University of Chicago Press, 1980.

————. *On Certainty*. Translated by Denis Paul and G.E.M. Anscombe. New York: J&J Harper Editions, 1969.

Wolff, Janet. "On the Road Again: Metaphors of Travel in Cultural Criticism." *Cultural Studies* 7 (1993): 224–39.

Wolfson, Elliot R. *Through a Speculum that Shines: Vision and Imagination in Medieval Jewish Mysticism*. Princeton, NJ: Princeton University Press, 1994.

Wolin, Sheldon. "Political Theory as a Vocation." *The American Political Science Review* 63, no. 4 (December 1969):1062–82.

————. *Politics and Vision: Continuity and Innovation in Western Political Thought*. Boston: Little, Brown, 1960.

————. *Politics and Vision: Expanded Edition*. Princeton, NJ: Princeton University Press, 2004.

————. *Tocqueville between Two Worlds: The Making of a Political and Theoretical Life*. Princeton, NJ: Princeton University Press, 2001.

Worley, Linda Kraus. "Through Others' Eyes: Narratives of German Women Travelling in Nineteenth Century America." *Yearbook of German-American Studies* 21 (1986): 39–50.

Wülfing, Wulf. "On Travel Literature by Women in the Nineteenth Century: Malwida von Meysenbug." In *German Women in the Eighteenth and Nineteenth Centuries: A Social and Literary History*. Edited by Ruth-Ellen B. Joeres and Mary Jo Maynes. Bloomington: Indiana University Press, 1986.

Yamamoto, Tatsuro. "On Tawālisī Described by Ibn Batūta." *Memoirs of the Research Department of the Toyo Bunko*. Tokyo: The Toyo Bunko, 1936.

Yared, Nazik Saba. *Arab Travellers and Western Civilization*. Translated by Sumayya Damluji Shahbandar. London: Saqi, 1996.

Young, David. "Montesquieu's View of Despotism and His Use of Travel Literature." *The Review of Politics* 40, no. 3 (July 1978): 392–405.

Youngs, Tim. "Buttons and Souls: Some Thoughts on Commodities and Identity in Women's Travel Writing." *Studies in Travel Writing: Papers from the*

Essex Symposium on 'Writing Travels.' Nottingham, UK: Nottingham Trent University, 1997, 117–40.

———. "Where Are We Going? Cross-Border Approaches to Travel Writing." In *Perspectives on Travel Writing*. Edited by Glenn Hooper and Tim Youngs. UK: Ashgate, 2004.

Yule, Henry. *Cathay and the Way Thither*. London: Hakluyt Society, 1913–16.

Zacher, Christian K. *Curiosity and Pilgrimage: The Literature of Discovery in Fourteenth-Century England*. Baltimore: Johns Hopkins University Press, 1976.

Zaman, Muhammad Qasim. "The Scope and Limits of Islamic Cosmopolitanism and the 'Discursive Language' of the 'Ulama." In *Muslim Networks: From Hajj to Hiphop*. Edited by Miriam Cooke and Bruce B. Lawrence. Chapel Hill: University of North Carolina Press, 2005.

Zerilli, Linda. "Doing without Knowing: Feminism's Politics of the Ordinary." *Political Theory* 26, no. 4 (August 1998): 435–58.

Zolandek, Leon. "Al-Tahtawi and Political Freedom." *Muslim World* 54 (1964): 90–97.

Zubaida, Sami. "Cosmopolitanism and the Middle East." In *Cosmopolitanism, Identity, and Authenticity in the Middle East*. Edited by Roel Meijer. Great Britain: Curzon, 1999.

Zunz, Olivier. "Holy Theory." *Reviews in American History* 30, no. 4 (2002): 564–70.

Zunz, Olivier, and Alan S. Kahan, eds. *The Tocqueville Reader: A Life in Letters and Politics*. Oxford: Blackwell, 2002.

Index